DONALD McGAVRAN

— HIS EARLY LIFE AND MINISTRY —

Dr. McGavran, the founder and "Father of the Church Growth Movement," was on the one side applauded and cherished and on the other, misunderstood and attacked for his ahead-of-time missiological theories. In this well researched and articulated historical document, Dr. Middleton takes us to the origins and early part of the story of McGavran, which facilitates the serious enthusiast to fully understand this great missionary statesman. It also inspires them to greater dedication to the Lord and his Great Commission. I desire that this book will help expunge the misunderstood side of McGavran and to help young scholars rethink their views about the man and his mission.

Since the author, Dr. Middleton, also served as a missionary to India and knew Dr. McGavran personally (as his student and his colleague), this biography becomes so much more authentic—an eyewitness account! By reading this book you will certainly grasp what God can do through a life fully committed to God and to God's cause, not compromising his conviction to the changing trend of this world. McGavran stayed true to his calling, followed his Master's plan, and did God's will. The prayers of McGavran inspire us to understand his deep spirituality and strong biblical theology. Middleton writes, "They are more than a devotional expression of McGavran's spiritual conversations with God . . . they declared his theological convictions."

This book is an invaluable tool for experienced and beginning missionaries. It is a service to the church universal and a stimulant to the hearts and minds that seek to obey the Great Commission of our Lord Jesus.

Rev. Dr. N. Jawahar Gnaniah
East West Community Church
Anaheim, California

Significant movements that have shaped the modern mission movement must be understood and evaluated in light of their context. Vern Middleton has done an amazing work in documenting significant events that shaped the life of Dr. McGavran: his context, the assignments, the difficulties, the growing convictions, the fruitful practices, the field research, and the educational structures (Church Growth Institute; Fuller School of World Mission) that birthed the Church Growth Movement of the twentieth century. It is personal, detailed, and a significant backdrop to understanding Dr. McGavran's seminal perspectives in *Bridges of God* and *How Churches Grow*. These perspectives surely seeded the Unreached People's Movement, Saturation Church Planting, and Church Planting Movements of all kinds in our own day. This book will stimulate and motivate you to action with a still unfinished task.

Bruce Graham
training division director
U.S. Center for World Mission

During his lifetime, Donald McGavran (1897–1990) was acclaimed by many as the most influential American missiologist of the second half of the twentieth century. How quickly the collective memory fades. In the early years of the twenty-first century, McGavran is no longer a household name among more recent missiologists. This book appears at a crucial time. A carefully researched work utilizing the primary source materials found in several archives in two continents makes for an authoritative study. But there is more: extensive interviews conducted by the author during the closing years of McGavran's life brings the narration alive. Vern Middleton came to know McGavran intimately—his private and family life as well as his public life and the background of the issues engaged. Middleton writes as a critical yet devoted follower of his guru. The formation of the man McGavran and his missional protest are brought to life in this scholarly account.

This book will be appreciated by McGavran's former students, associates, and all those whose lives he touched, but also as a significant document and record of McGavran's contribution to mission theology and the development of missiology in North America as well as in India. For further studies of world evangelization in the twentieth century, the genesis of the church growth movement, its related issues and personalities—an essential source.

Roger E. Hedlund, PhD
director emeritus, Mylapore Institute for Indigenous Studies, Chennai, India
chief editor of the forthcoming Oxford Encyclopedia of South Asian Christianity

The good news of Jesus Christ, the only hope for a humanity gone astray from the path of truth revealed in Jesus Christ, drove Donald Anderson McGavran to remain faithful to the gospel and at the same time finds ways and means to be contextually relevant in the great land of India. The book by Vern Middleton invites every serious student of the Word to learn and engage in mission.

Richard Howell
general secretary
Evangelical Fellowship of India and Asia Evangelical Alliance

Fascinating! This is truly a fascinating book on the life of one of the greatest missiologists of the twentieth century. This is not some dry biography. It is well-written and draws from a wealth of unpublished primary source material. Middleton pulls back the curtains of time, revealing the influences on the man, his missiology, and his mission. Here is a glimpse of the father of the Church Growth Movement that few have seen!

J. D. Payne
associate professor of Church Planting and Evangelism
The Southern Baptist Theological Seminary

This book outlines the development of an average missionary into a world-changing missiologist, not omitting the pains and setbacks along the way. McGavran ran ahead of his time with new insights into how churches grow, and God worked in him the humility necessary to present such a message to the mission world. As children of our times, we can only be inspired by this record of the life of Donald McGavran, hoping God will likewise mercifully use us for his kingdom purposes.

H. L. Richard
research scholar presently focusing on issues in South Asian religion and society

A great deal of Donald A. McGavran's insight can be traced to the unique advantage he had of growing up in India as a third-generation missionary. There before McGavran's eyes were not only the expectable ethnic and linguistic divisions of the sub-continent, he also encountered the world's most rigidly stratified system of social classes. No wonder he has been accused of reading into a situation social differences that did not exist. In some such cases he has merely pointed out differences people wished to ignore.

Ralph Winter, September 2001
founder, U.S. Center for World Mission

DONALD McGAVRAN

— HIS EARLY LIFE AND MINISTRY —

An Apostolic Vision for Reaching the Nations

a biography

by

VERN MIDDLETON

WILLIAM CAREY
LIBRARY

Donald McGavran, His Early Life and Ministry: An Apostolic Vision for Reaching the Nations

Copyright © 2011 by Vern Middleton

Published by William Carey Library
1605 E. Elizabeth Street
Pasadena, CA 91104 | www.missionbooks.org

Melissa Hicks, copyeditor
Jennifer Lee, reference assistant
Hugh Pindur, graphic designer
Rose Lee-Norman, indexer

William Carey Library is a ministry of the
U.S. Center for World Mission
Pasadena, CA | www.uscwm.org

Printed in the United States of America

15 14 13 12 11   5 4 3 2 1 BP800

Library of Congress Cataloging-in-Publication Data

Middleton, Vern.
  Donald McGavran, his early life and ministry : an apostolic vision for reaching the nations / by Vern Middleton.
    p. cm.
  Based on the author's dissertation.
  Includes bibliographical references and index.
  ISBN 978-0-87808-469-2
  1. McGavran, Donald A. (Donald Anderson), 1897-1990. I. Title.
  BV2072.2.M44M53 2011
  266'.663092--dc22
  [B]
                    2010048248

DEDICATION

To Helen, the love of my life of fifty-one years. She has persevered with me as details of McGavran's life were being assembled. Her patience, assistance, and encouragement have been without limits. Helen served as a bridge into the hearts of Don and Mary McGavran. She adopted them as her parents, making the bond between our families strong.

DONALD McGAVRAN'S
Vision Statement

Rapid growth of the church must be seen again, as in apostolic times, to be pleasing to God. He wants ripe fields reaped to the last sheaf. The Savior—not secular hunger for numbers—constrains obedient Christians to harvest. Nongrowth, always ascribed to "the difficulty of the field," must now be seen as often due to remediable causes and ended.

CONTENTS

MAP

Various regions where McGavran ministered in India.

FOREWORD

"Prabhu Jesu Masih ke Jai" (Praise to the Lord Jesus) is a phrase that rings in my mind as I recall those open-army-surplus jeep journeys out into the villages surrounding Takhatpur with my father, Donald Anderson McGavran. It was his greeting to the villagers as we arrived and his blessing as we left after meeting with the headman of the village and with the members of the house church in that village.

Our home was open to any and all as farmers, herdsmen, and tiny village-dwellers came into our larger village for the bazaar or because of some problem that they needed help in solving. Dad and Mother were problem solvers or miracle workers in my eyes as well as in the eyes of those they helped. They met with Dad in his office but then were invited to stay for a meal with us.

Dr. Middleton was one of Dad's students at the Institute of Church Growth and the School of World Mission at Fuller Seminary in Pasadena. I would hear about Dr. Middleton's visits to Mother and Dad's home to interview them for his dissertation. He stood high in their estimation and, as time passed, warmly in their hearts. Dr. Middleton was one of the first people to visit after Dad died. His relationship with my parents, especially to my father was that of a *chalah* (a disciple), and I am sure that Dad and Mother regarded him as one of their "sons."

This book is a good descriptor of my father. It gives factual information about his dedication to and performance in the work of saving souls, of following the Great Commission. Dad was a determined servant of the Lord Jesus Christ. He expected much of himself and of those with whom he worked and of those in his family. But undergirding all of that was his love, first of his Lord, then of his family and those with whom and for whom he labored.

I am the sixth child of Donald and Mary McGavran. I lived with my parents but was unaware of much of what went on in their professional lives. So, reading about the progression of the development of the concept of church growth is both concretely educational and a confirmation of those times in my life when Dad's research and study involved much travel and time away from Mother and me. Some situations that I remember take on new meaning as I read this book and see how they influenced Dad's church growth concepts. I am pleased that this book includes information about how closely my mother worked with my father. She often reminded us in her later years that she made the decision to go to the mission field before she met Dad. They both spent their lives in service to the Kingdom whether in village India, in collegiate education, or at Fuller Theological Seminary. They lived life fully and blessed those who knew them.

May this book be a blessing to those who seek to know my father, Donald Anderson McGavran, "The Father of the Church Growth Movement." May it help you to understand his concepts of accountability in knowing how and where churches grow. May it teach you his views of allocating limited resources to places where church growth can and will happen, in the fields that still await the harvest, whether here in the United States or in some far off corner of the world.

Patricia Faith McGavran Sheafor
Crystal Lake, Frankfort, Michigan

PREFACE

There was no more opportune time to begin the biography of Donald A. McGavran than in 1983. At the age of eighty-six, he was alive, alert, and possessed an extraordinarly keen discernment into many issues. The primary archives were still readily accessible. Several of his contemporaries were still alive to be interviewed.

As a missiologist, his ideas and principles have impacted the world. He ranks among the most outstanding missionary statesmen of the twentieth century. He was known and beloved in many countries for his profound insights on what makes the church grow. However, few had the privilege of knowing McGavran the man. He was rather private in his personal life. Not many have had a glimpse into the personal and historical events that converged to create such a missiologist.

This biography has evolved from a long-term relationship with Donald McGavran and with India. The two are inseparable. Our area of ministry in India was in close proximiity to that of McGavran's. Though the family had left the Chattisgarh district, I was able to visit the Satnami field where the McGavrans had served for seventeen years.

We traced their steps into Landour, Mussoorie where, though in a different era, our children, like theirs, studied at Woodstock School. We understood their pain of family separation.

He was my guru and taught me well. Through research on this remarkable missionary, I recognized the greatness of a man whose principles revolutionized the missionary movement in the late twentieth century.

His vision arose from a spiritual passion and daily walk with his Lord and Savior, Jesus Christ. My prayer for this research is that God will use it to stir our hearts towards that same passion that God may use for God's kingdom purposes.

Although biographical glimpses of McGavran's life have been written, none to date focus on the man. Regarding the writing of this biography, Tippett, a colleague of McGavran's, expressed:

> I knew him only by his ideas and reputation and I am certainly not the person to write his biography. For the last decade I have worked with him as a teaching colleague, but in our researches we have gone our own ways. I have learned very little of his private life. When his biography is written the person responsible should be one who knows India well because India still conditions his thinking and behavior in spite of his world vision.

As a biographer I fit the above description. I served eleven years in India. My first-term assignment was to a region less than seventy miles from Harda, the place where McGavran spent his first term. In fact, the Baptist Mission to which I belonged negotiated the transfer of comity arrangements for Harda. Between 1970 and 1976 I had the privilege of teaming up with McGavran for seminars in various parts of India and Bangladesh. On several occasions I was able to visit the Chattisgarh area and see firsthand the nature of the Satnami people among whom McGavran labored for seventeen years. I also followed the missionary pattern of taking my family to Landour, Mussoorie and I, like McGavran, frequently left them in the cool of that hill station while I returned to the heat of the plains for ministry.

THE SETTING

India had a decided effect on the maturation and development of McGavran's spiritual quest. The statement, "The child is father to the man," is an appropriate description of the way India has conditioned his thinking, his values, his priorities, and his spirituality. For this reason, the biography has taken excursions into India's ethos to discover a deeper significance behind the events. I deemed this background material as essential for an understanding of church growth concepts which, when taken out of India, sometimes appear radically different from their original intent.

A creative tension was maintained throughout this historical biography. There was the temptation to focus on the historical background at the expense of the subject. On the other hand, it would have been a distortion to describe McGavran's life without the historical scenery of the mass movements among the Untouchables, the National Council of Churches in India, the independence movement led by Gandhi, the political intrigue formulated around Ambedkar's decision, and the colonial spinoffs reflected in missionary institutions.

Another struggle was the danger of becoming preoccupied with the germinal development of ideas which later blossomed into full-grown church growth principles. These ideas are only a part of the man. Abstract concepts do not reflect his true versatility. Nor do they capture his activity in many cooperative efforts, his skill as a linguist, his challenge to prevailing social conditions, his task as a mission administrator, his vigorous evangelistic programs, his research skills, his influence as a Christian educator, his marksmanship as a hunter, his role as a father and a husband, and his innovative architectural designs and building techniques.

Chapters five and six focus on the internationalization of church growth ideas. McGavran moved from the remote village of Takhatpur, India to center stage in missiological developments. Geneva, London, New York, and Indianapolis were some cities of his battleground from 1954 to 1965.

SOURCES

This manuscript was developed out of primary source material. Archival research and interviews have played a major role as far as information resource was concerned. Secondary sources have been referred to but seldom used, except for the historical background sections. Archives utilized were:

1. McGavran Archives housed at the U.S. Center for World Missions, Pasadena, California. They were moved to Wheaton, Illinois in 1988.
2. Disciples of Christ Historical Society, South Nashville.
3. Mr. H. Hamilton, Leonard Theological College, Jabalpur, M.P. India. The usefulness of the primary documents housed in India was limited due to a lack of xerox machines.
4. National Council of Churches of India, Nagpur, India. Copies of the Sahayak Patrika are housed at this center.
5. The Pacific Graduate School of Religion, Berkeley, California has in its archival resources copies of the *United Church Review*. These contain the editorials McGavran made between 1941 and 1947.
6. United Church of Canada Archives, Victoria College, University of Toronto. These archives contain correspondence over the people movement among the Bhils. There is much useful correspondence between Dr. Russell who was secretary of the Mid-India Council of Churches, and various members during the era 1933 to 1938.

ENGLISH SPELLING

The spelling utilized in this book is based on that established by the American Heritage Dictionary. The quotations from letters written from 1897–1954 retain the spelling of England.

McGavran was highly influenced by English patterns in colonial India. Words such as programme, labour, favour, etc. remain as they were spelled in that era. Names such as Jabalpur, Pune, remain as Jubbalpore and Poona in the quotes. Locations given in the text are according to the provincial names and divisions of India since 1960. Some Indian words were treated as a foreign language expression, even though they are part of the English language. The rarity of their usage in North America merited this treatment.

ABBREVIATIONS

CMS	The Church Missionary Society (a division of the Anglican Church)
DFM	Division of Foreign Missions (a section of the World Council of Churches)
DWME	Division of World Mission and Evangelism (a subsection of the World Council of Churches)
ICG	Institute of Church Growth
IMC	International Missionary Council
IRM	*International Review of Mission*
NCC	National Council of Churches
NCCE	Northwest Christian College
NCCI	National Council of Churches in India, Nagpur, Maharashtra
NV	Disciples of Christ Historical Society, Nashville, Tennessee
PSR	Pacific School of Religion, Berkeley, California
SIM	Sudan Interior Mission
SVM	Student Volunteer Movement
SWM	School of World Mission at Fuller Seminary
UCCP	United Church of Christ of the Philippines
UCMS	United Christian Missionary Service
UCR	*United Church Review*
USCWM	U.S. Center for World Mission
WCC	World Council of Churches

CHAPTER ONE

DONALD McGAVRAN'S FORMATIVE YEARS

1897–1923

BIRTH

Donald Anderson McGavran was born in Damoh, India on December 15, 1897, to John and Helen McGavran. He was born forty years after what the British designated as "the notorious mutiny of 1857." India was wracked by tragic death and pestilence. Bombay was in the desperate throes of the bubonic plague and the devastation of a small pox epidemic. In the city alone, 50,383 people died that year from these infectious diseases.[1] Meanwhile, Central India was facing widespread famine. In some districts the famine claimed so many lives that bodies cluttered the roads; vultures fed on the bodies by day and hyenas by night. Primarily because of the famine, John and Helen McGavran moved to the town of Damoh, eighty miles north of Jabalpur. Their keen desire was to alleviate suffering and attend to the needs of over four hundred orphaned boys because their hearts were wrenched by the rampant suffering and moved mightily by Christian compassion.

Damoh: Birthplace of Donald McGavran. House built by John McGavran.

The British Raj was at its zenith during the period of McGavran's birth. The British system of organization and administration had established India as the pride of her empire. The subcontinent was the crown jewel of the many British colonies. Some questioned

---

1   Elizabeth G. K. Hewat, *Christ and Western India* (Surat: Mission Press, 1950), 309–11.

whether India was more of a "white man's burden" than a bright-gleaming gem.[2] The white man had carved out a caste niche for himself in India. Indians hailed him as *Sahib*. White skin was a badge of honorary status to Indians regardless if one was a citizen of England, the United States, or any Northern European nation. Among the expatriate population of India, however, those of British origin regarded themselves as a cut above the rest.

Donald McGavran's ancestral roots were from the British Raj. (For a fuller description of his family origins see Appendix A at the end of book.) His father was of Scotch-Irish origin on his paternal side, while his mother was born in England. She never lost the poise and queenly bearing learned in her land of birth. There is no doubt that McGavran had a profound respect for and loyalty to the British in spite of his American citizenship.

John proved to be an able architect and builder. "He supervised the construction of buildings looking after the minutest details of gathering materials from their natural state."[3] This skill and ability was evidently passed on to his son, Donald. Numerous institutions such as hospitals and orphan homes, as well as a substantial bridge, were designed and constructed during Donald's time in India.

It is significant that John McGavran was sensitive to social and caste structures in India. In order to remove barriers that kept people from coming to Christ, he established eight distinct Sunday schools among different castes in the region around Damoh.

Like his son Donald, he was not content with institutionalized missions. Upon return after furlough in 1900, he became a touring evangelistic missionary with a staff of several Indian evangelists. Donald McGavran recalls their "Gypsy-like" lifestyle:

> The family would load all they needed for a month's stay on an ox cart and drive out to some village, put up tents in the shade of some tree and stay for a week or two, walking to 15 or 20 villages in the neighborhood. The floor of the tent was dry grass with a mat over it. We children enjoyed each new location, finding new trees to climb, and new grounds to play in. At night there was a big camp fire, around which villagers would gather to hear the gospel and see lantern slides. We children enjoyed these too.[4]

Donald McGavran recalls that his father was a highly disciplined man. He was also a man of deep principle and integrity. In later years, when he was professor at the College of Missions, he was offered coal at a reduced rate for his personal use by the agent who sold coal to the college. In order to avoid the very appearance of evil, John McGavran ordered his coal from a different agent. Again, this same quality was strongly manifested in the life and actions of his son Donald.

---

2   Vincent A. Smith, *The Oxford History of India* (Delhi: Oxford University Press, 1981), 683.
3   A. L. Fishburn, *They Went to India: Biographies of Missionaries of the Disciples of Christ* (Indianapolis: Missionary Education Department, 1946), 46.
4   Donald McGavran, interview by Vern Middleton, Dec. 20, 1984.

The McGavran family (around 1918).
Front row (left to right): John McGavran's sister, John, and Helen (Anderson) McGavran.
Back row (left to right): Edward, Grace, Joyce, and Don (John's children).

In an article written in celebration of John McGavran's fortieth year of missionary service, Donald McGavran saluted him with the title, "John Grafton McGavran-Scholar, Crusader and Saint." Yet such was the humility of the man, that even in the article, Donald McGavran writes of what will happen when he reads it. "He will write me saying, semi-humorously . . . that he hopes my other literary efforts are more reliable than this—and he will mean it."[5]

Donald McGavran does not recall having a close relationship with his father, yet he retains a profound respect and appreciation for all his father meant to him. He says, "My father was good and kind. We always had family prayers at breakfast. We did not have any play together, although we must have played checkers."[6]

THE INDIAN SETTING DURING DONALD McGAVRAN'S CHILDHOOD

We who live in the twenty-first century will find it difficult to understand or relate to the India of 1897 to 1910. British colonial rule was firmly entrenched. There was little sense of Indian nationalism apart from the occasional reformer, who sparked renewed interest in Hinduism. The policies by which India was governed originated in London, where Indian opinion was of little consequence.[7]

From 1870 to 1898, forty thousand miles of railway track were laid and seventy thousand miles of metalled roads (roads with a gravel surface) stretched out across India.

---

5   Donald McGavran, "John Grafton McGavran-Scholar, Crusader and Saint," *World Call* 13, no. 3 (March 1931), 14.

6   Donald McGavran, interview by Vern Middleton, Dec. 20, 1984.

7   Smith, *Oxford History of India*, 684.

More than an incredible engineering feat for providing transportation, this rapidly became the nerve system which enabled the conglomerate of many different languages, races, cultures, and kingdoms to be welded into one nation. The railway system catapulted India into the industrial age. Unfortunately, it also caused deep social trauma, as whole castes of people were dislocated from their traditional trades. The building of the railroad through Central India opened up the previously inaccessible region to Christian missions and most of the agencies located their headquarters in railway towns which they used as centers for reaching more remote areas.[8]

The British benefit to India was far more extensive than material development and communication networks. Before nationalism transformed the spirit of reason to the point of hatred, Indians often acknowledged their debt of gratitude. For example Mr. Naoriji, the first president of the Congress movement, had the following to say in his presidential address:

> We are thoroughly sensible of the numberless blessings conferred upon us, of which the very existence of the Congress is proof in a nutshell. Were it not for the blessings of British rule I could not have come here today, as I have done without the least hesitation and the least fear that my children might be robbed and killed in my absence . . . But there remain even greater blessings for which we have to be grateful. It is to the British rule that we owe the education we possess.[9]

Nevertheless, there was a deep psychological gulf between the British rulers and the Indian people. For the most part, missionaries managed to bridge that difference between their more affluent lifestyle and their transparent lives. India came to trust and appreciate the integrity and justice of the British government. The British administrators established a cantonment area (a ghetto-like region for the administration buildings of the Raj) adjacent to each town. All too frequently the missionary compounds, institutions, and even the churches were located within the cantonment. This was necessitated by the difficulty missionaries were having in purchasing land because often the only place they could obtain land was from the government. This fact identified Christianity more firmly as a Western religion.

CHILDHOOD

Donald McGavran's childhood was rich and varied. He played with the orphan boys, and an Indian lady, called an *ayah*, cared for him while his mother had other duties, so he became bilingual in English and Hindi.

---

8   Ibid., 709–11. See also Sir John A. R. Marriot, *The English in India: A Problem of Politics* (Oxford: Clarendon Press, 1932), 303–304.
9   Stephen Neil, *Colonialism and Christian Missionaries* (New York: McGraw Hill, 1966), 103.

During the hot season from April through June, Helen McGavran would take her children to the cooler mountain air of Landour, Mussoorie, a Himalayan hill station located eight hundred miles north of their Central India mission. John would join them for a few weeks later in the season, in a pattern which a majority of missionary families practised.

Except for a few months of semiformal schooling held in a home near their house in Landour, the major portion of their education consisted of unsupervised reading. McGavran described their situation, "There was nothing else to do, so we picked up all kinds of books and at first laboriously and later effortlessly read through them. We thus accumulated a lot of information and an excellent ability to read. Upon entering public school he found that although he was weak in arithmetic, he was well advanced in reading, history and writing."[10]

This era of McGavran's life ended when the family departed for the US furlough in 1910. Their return journey took them via Edinburgh where John McGavran attended the Mission Convention which became the parent of the International Missionary Council. Because of its recommendation that missionary training schools be established, the Conference was to play a crucial part in determining the ministry of John McGavran from 1912 to 1922.

RESETTLEMENT IN THE USA

Upon arrival in the United States the family settled in Ann Arbour, Michigan for one year while John McGavran completed an MA degree. The children (Grace 14, Donald 13, Edward 9, and Joyce 6) found it was a time of deep cultural adjustment. Since almost all their schooling had been home studies, their worldview was very much that of village India.

Donald (about six years old) and Grace (about seven years old).

In the summer of 1911 John McGavran was called to pastor a church in Tulsa, Oklahoma. During that year Donald McGavran made a commitment to Jesus Christ and was baptised. He also joined the Scout troop which met in the church and enjoyed the

---

10   Donald McGavran, interview by Vern Middleton, Dec. 20, 1984.

hikes and basketball games.[11] Eighteen months later the family relocated to Indianapolis, where Don's father became professor of Indian studies at the new College of Missions.

During the summer after high school graduation, Donald McGavran worked in a print shop as a printer's devil receiving ten cents an hour. He described the experience: "Learning to set type and to distribute it to fifty or more little boxes on a large tray . . . but learning printing was valuable when I became manager of the mission print shop in Jabalpur, India."[12]

BUTLER COLLEGE: FALL 1915–17

Donald and his sister, Grace, enrolled together in Butler College in the fall of 1915. McGavran interrupted his student life at Butler to join the army in April 1917, returning in January 1919. McGavran was elected captain of the debate team. He led his team to victory even though they debated against teams from colleges of considerable size and influence. He was able to graduate in 1920 because of credit received for his work in the French language and his military experience.

Donald McGavran.

McGavran's Military Service

McGavran always possessed an aggressive, bold spirit. The First World War had been raging during his final year of high school and his first two years of college. As a young man McGavran was impatient with his country for its lack of involvement in the war. He wrote, "During 1916 I considered seriously going to Canada and enlisting in a Canadian

---

11   Donald McGavran, "Biographical Sketch" (unpublished MS, Middleton Archives, Vancouver, B.C., 1982), chapter six.
12   Ibid.

regiment. It seemed to me that no self-respecting American could stand by and watch freedom being destroyed and the Kaiser become the ruler of the world."[13]

When the United States finally declared war against Germany, McGavran set aside his schooling and enlisted in the Indiana Cavalry. Fearing he would be rejected because of his slight stature, he temporarily increased his weight by eating bananas and drinking water and was then accepted.

By July of 1917, he was transferred to the 139th Field Artillery located at Camp Hattiesburg, Mississippi. His aspirations for battle were frustrated as month after month of training dragged by. He found army life rather lonely because, as he wrote:

> All my fellow soldiers except one man were river rats from Louisville, Kentucky—a rough lot. They were continually going off to whore houses. A fair number of them contracted gonorrhea and syphilis and thought nothing of it. They were a profane lot.[14]

McGavran utilized his time to study French. His self-discipline and his linguistic skills enabled him to gain fluency in a relatively short period. During this phase he frequently wrote in French to his mother.

In September 1918, the 139th Field Artillery unit sailed for France. Before their departure, John McGavran, who seldomly displayed affection for his children, came all the way from Indianapolis to New York to see him off. As a young soldier heading for battle, Donald McGavran did not fully appreciate this gesture. Later as he looked back, he realized the depth of love expressed in this fatherly, affectionate gesture. His father was seeing his firstborn son heading for war and he realized there was a strong likelihood that he would never see him again here on earth.[15]

---

13   Donald A. McGavran and Burton L. Goddard, eds., *The Encyclopedia of Modern Christian Missions* (Camden, New Jersey: Thomas Nelson & Sons, 1967), 653. Beginning in 1910 and continuing until 1927, this unique school was among the first anywhere to provide a complete curriculum conforming to recommendations of the 1910 Edinburgh Conference. In 1928 this institution became a part of the Kennedy School of Missions of the Hartford Seminary Foundation, Hartford, Connecticut but withdrew in 1941. It then became the College of Missions Foundation at Yale University Divinity School. In 1956 it was reactivated for intense summer training of missionary candidates and volunteers at Crystal Lake, Michigan. Donald McGavran taught courses annually at the College of Missions at Crystal Lake, from 1956–62. In 1961 the library of the College of Missions was given to the Institute of Church Growth at Eugene, Oregon. That library was transferred to Fuller Theological Seminary in 1965. It is currently part of the David Hubbard (formerly the McAlister) Library. Thus in two respects, the library and the missions mandate, there is continuity between the current School of Intercultural Studies (formerly the School of World Missions) at Fuller and the College of Missions.

14   Ibid., 653.

15   Donald McGavran, interview by Vern Middleton, Dec. 20, 1984.

Donald McGavran in his army uniform.

On the high seas near Ireland, a German submarine attacked their ship. They narrowly escaped being torpedoed. After a brief stopover in England, they sailed to Le Havre, France. When they reached Paris, they transferred to a freight train at the railway station. Here again McGavran demonstrated some of his leadership skills and foresight:

> On reaching my box car I noted that there was no food in it. As we had marched through the station, I had seen a huge pile of long French loaves of bread. I suggested to my comrades that we run back, load up with as many loaves as we could carry, and bring them back. Two others joined me, and we picked up maybe sixty loaves. While we were yet a few box cars from our own, the train started. We broke into a run and made it to our car, where our comrades helped us and the sixty loaves—to get in. Those loaves were the only food we had for two days. They also served as pillows at night.[16]

On November 10, their train reached its destination. The unit reequipped with motorized six-inch guns, marched north thirty miles, and was just getting within range to do battle when Armistice was declared. At the time McGavran found this disappointing, but in his later years he perceived the events as God's protection over his life.

---

16 McGavran, "Biographical Sketch," chapter six.

McGavran was discharged on January 19, 1919 and returned to college. The military training McGavran received had a marked impact on his patterns of thinking in later years and his church growth strategies drew insight and direction from his military experience.

McGavran's Final Year at Butler

September 1919 found McGavran back at Butler as a more mature man because of the time spent in the army. However, the greatest change was produced by a spiritual experience at a YMCA camp in the summer of 1919 where John R. Mott was one of the speakers. There he committed himself to a life of missionary servanthood. He writes of this experience:

> Till then, while being a reasonably good Christian, I had determined that my life work would be in some field other than the ministry. My family has done enough for the Lord, I said, I shall make money. I looked to law, geology or forestry as fields of work which were attractive to me. At Lake Geneva, day after day we were challenged to complete surrender to Christ. Let Him decide everything. Everything included making money and my life work. For several days I resisted, but finally I yielded and said simply, Very well, Lord. It is clear to me; either I give up all claim to being a Christian, or I go all the way. Since that is the situation I choose to go all the way. From then on I was sure that if God called me to the ministry, or the mission field, I would go.[17]

As a direct outgrowth of this spiritual encounter, McGavran along with two close friends, kept a weekly prayer pact in which they engaged in Bible study and systematic prayer for the mission fields of the world. The two friends were David Rioch and Lyman Hoover who, like McGavran, had been deeply touched by the power of the Holy Spirit during the YMCA retreat. David felt called to work among the Muslims in northwest China. Lyman was called to China, and Donald felt called to return to India, the land of his birth. Both Lyman and Donald spent their lives in their respective fields of service. It was always a sorrow in McGavran's heart that David lost his faith while at medical school. Some of the letters written by McGavran to David Rioch in later years reveal McGavran's earnest desire to see his friend restored to fellowship with the Lord Jesus Christ.

McGavran was elected as the president of the senior class. Through this office he had a forum for meaningful activity and input into the student affairs. Butler College adopted some of his ideas which became part of the ongoing traditions.

---

17   Ibid.

Donald at Butler College.

During the first semester of his final year he met Mary Elizabeth Howard. In a recent interview, she described the overwhelming impression he made upon her when she saw him in military uniform at the back of a church. Together they attended the 1920 quadrennial Student Volunteer Convention at Des Moines, Iowa led by Robert E. Speer, John R. Mott, and Robert Wilder. The Convention was a high point in SVM. G. Sherwood Eddy brought two addresses which emphasized social reform and there was considerable behind-the-scenes debate among the executive committee as to the amount of program time given to social problems. However for Mary and Don the spiritual impact of the sessions touched their lives as they both dedicated themselves to missionary service. Noting this and her many wonderful qualities, Donald did not delay in courting. Repeatedly in their letters they referred to the common bond they shared from Des Moines. They became engaged in the spring of 1920, and then separated two years while he completed his seminary training at Yale. Their marriage finally took place on August 29, 1922.

MARY ELIZABETH HOWARD

Mary Howard was raised in Muncie, Indiana, the youngest child of Isaiah and Sarah Howard. She attended the Jackson Street Christian Church where she frequently was a soloist. Her gift of music was a valuable asset during her years of service in India.

The Howards dedicated their youngest child to the Lord for missionary service. Mary feels that act of faith on their part is the primary reason why she became a missionary. They also actively exposed her to missionaries, and many were invited to their home.

Upon graduation from high school Mary went to Butler College. The Jackson Street Church provided a scholarship which paid part of her tuition. The remaining portion was met though the sacrificial support of her parents and her brother, Walter.

Mary received her AB degree in June 1922 and then married Donald McGavran three months later. They attended the College of Missions together in 1922–23.

The wedding of Donald McGavran and Mary Elizabeth Howard on August 29, 1922.

SEMINARY TRAINING AT YALE: 1920–22

Don McGavran entered Yale in the fall of 1920, after a summer of working in a factory that manufactured Prest-O-Lite batteries. He had to raise funds for his boarding and tuition fees. He wrote:

> My financial situation is just this; I am on my own resources. That is I am not receiving money from home, except birthday gifts and so forth. I am preaching for a church which gives me ten [dollars] a week. That together with what I earn elsewhere and also with a work scholarship that I expect to get from Yale will see me through the year. However it will just barely do so and would not allow me to purchase books . . . nor would it permit me to buy clothes.[18]

McGavran found the courses at Yale intellectually stimulating. Dr. Kenneth Scott Latourette, the famous historian of missions, was on sabbatical most of the time he was there. After consultation with missionaries, President Paul of the Disciples of Christ and Dr. Fleming of New York, McGavran majored in religious education.

The professor of Christian education was Dr. Weigle, who later became influential across the US, especially in the National Council of Churches. He highly impressed McGavran's thinking.

---

18   Donald McGavran, letter from Litchfield, Connecticut to Stephen J. Corey, Indianapolis, Indiana, (obtained from the Disciples of Christ Archives in Nashville, Tennessee), July 5, 1921.

My work under Weigle . . . is proving interesting and . . . profitable. It deals exclusively with the way in which a lesson ought to be taught; the preparation of the lesson; the preparation of the pupil, etc. getting the idea across, getting the real meaning out of the Scripture passage.[19]

McGavran did well in his classes at Yale, winning prizes in homiletics and graduating with a BD cum laude. Unfortunately, some of the faculty stressed the higher criticism of Scripture. However, McGavran was impressed with the more conservative position of the dean of the seminary.

Dean Brown was at his best today in the Minister's message class. He was defending the higher view of Jesus Christ, namely that he is divine, against the lower view, namely that he is a lovely example of what man can attain to and no more. He had keen logic and good brilliant argument, and a rapid fire presentation and not a little wit.[20]

While at Yale he spent his weekends preaching to a small Congregational Church in Milton, located in the northwest corner of Connecticut. His messages were expository in nature and conservative in content. He was troubled when a message seemed to lack conviction. On one occasion he preached from the text John 21:17. He wrote, "I tried to bring out that if we really loved Christ to over flowing we would aim to feed his sheep especially his lost sheep throughout the world."[21] After preaching a message on tithing, which he felt was well received, his own conscience was disturbed indicating a sensitive spiritual walk with Christ.

How earthly this preaching often seems! It disgusts and shames me . . . I know that the laborer is worthy of his hire and all that, nevertheless, the obvious fact that what secures my services is the money which I am paid, makes me wonder how much of a follower I am of Him whom it is recorded that he never took one penny for his preaching. What slaves we are to money. I do not wonder that the Hindu sages recommend renouncing of the world as the only path to God.[22]

In spite of McGavran's leanings however, he did not leave Yale unaffected. The *Christian Century* reported on April 27, 1922, page 539, that "Yale men challenge their leaders." The incident cited was the Danbury Conference of the Disciples of Christ. McGavran was one of the leaders of this student disagreement. In a letter to the editor McGavran expressed

---

19   Donald McGavran, letter from Yale to Mary Howard, (obtained from USCWM archives), Oct. 20, 1921.
20   Ibid.
21   Donald McGavran, letter from Yale to Mary Howard, Oct. 15, 1921.
22   Donald McGavran, letter from Yale to Mary Howard, Oct. 23, 1921.

resentment that their "liberal and truth seeking movement" had been presented to the public in a "slightly distorted manner."[23] The impact of the theological environment of Yale led McGavran to emphasize Christianization and gradualism over evangelism throughout his first term in India.

THE COLLEGE OF MISSIONS: SEPTEMBER 1922–JUNE 1923

Donald graduating from the College of Missions in 1923.

Prior to entrance into the College of Missions, McGavran exchanged considerable correspondence with Mr. Stephen Corey, the mission executive of UCMS. McGavran had wanted to work toward a PhD immediately following his studies at Yale. He asked for a double concession in that he wanted the year at the College of Missions waived and he requested that the Mission provide a scholarship for PhD studies. Corey's reply to the proposal was firm and courteous:

> We appreciate the fact that you have some advantages because of your being born in India, but we still feel that a year at the College of Missions would be very advantageous. We have never granted scholarship funds to those taking their graduate work outside the College of Missions.[24]

Thus the McGavrans enjoyed their first year of married life studying various courses that would prepare them for India. One course was the Hindi language which Donald

---

23   Donald McGavran, letter to *Christian Century*, (obtained from U.S. Center World Mission Archives), May 15, 1922. U.S. Center World Mission hereafter cited as USCWM.

24   Stephen J. Corey, letter to McGavran, (obtained from Disciples of Christ Archives, Nashville), Aug. 25, 1921. Nashville hereafter cited as NV.

had partially forgotten. The Science of Missions, Sanskrit, Introduction to the Study of Religion, and subjects related to the history and social issues of India were also part of their daily routine. Donald enrolled in a guided reading course in which he studied the Hindu Upanishads, some texts of the Vedanta, and writings of nineteenth century Hindu reformers.[25]

After they settled into their studies, along with fifty other aspiring missionaries, they found the interaction and times of prayer together very stimulating.

McGavran taught a course in religious education at the College of Missions while studying at the College. He also pastored a small country church in New Point, Indiana. The income from these sources, as well as a scholarship, enabled the McGavrans to survive the year.

Mary was pregnant for much of the school year and gave birth to Mary Theodora on July 2, 1923. Mary Theodora was the pride and devotion of Donald McGavran. Her death in 1930 was such a cruel blow that only the grace of God enabled the McGavrans to survive. The summer of 1923 was spent preparing for India. A request came for Donald to speak at a series of twelve youth conferences across the United States. Many young people were challenged through his ministry. As a result, a number of these young people made commitments to world missions as Don and Mary had done only a few years previously.

Ordination

During the summer of 1923, Donald and Mary McGavran were both ordained as missionaries by the gospel of the Christian church. The idea of a joint ordination of a husband and wife was a rare event in those days. This denomination was highly influential in the life of McGavran. He was loyal and faithful to its convictions. To some extent, his church connection provides insight into the way he handled theology and his pragmatic stance regarding church growth principles.

Two men were primarily responsible for the early beginnings of the Churches of Christ, also known as the Disciples of Christ. They were Thomas Campbell and his son, Alexander. Thomas came to the US in 1807 and served as a Presbyterian minister for two years. Thomas' conviction on church division and denominationalism was due to creeds and doctrinal statements. He believed that Christian unity would prevail if these were eliminated. The history of this denomination proved otherwise, for in spite of the lack of creedal and theological statements, the Disciples of Christ have managed to divide over a variety of other issues.

Key statements from the early leaders of the restoration movement in the nineteenth century cast light on their hopes.

---

25   Donald M. Wodarz, *Church Growth: The Missiology of Donald Anderson McGavran* (Gregorian University, Rome, 1979), 42.

The results of our movement will finally be the unity of the brotherhood and the universal conversion of mankind . . . Restoration of primitive Christianity is the key to the conversion of the world at the same time that it is the clue to the unity of the Church . . . The Gospel that saves and unites is essentially the fact that Jesus of Nazareth is the Messiah, the Son of God . . . As the pure simple New Testament Church grows it will press on from neighborhood to neighborhood, state to state and nation to nation.[26]

The movement had a vision that one day the dynamic of their reformation cause would result in the universal conversion of mankind. Like most other church organizations in the early nineteenth century, their leaders, preoccupied with correct ecclesiology, neglected taking the gospel to the pagans in other lands. These churches did not launch a mission cause until 1880.

One of the first to raise a voice for missions within the restoration movement was Archibald McLean. He published a series of missionary addresses in 1885. Prior to that, missions was not a topic of concern at the annual conventions. McGavran recalls hearing the preaching of McLean on several occasions and remembers the "wave of sincere, pure, deeply Christian missionary passion" which he brought to the churches.[27] McLean, who was both the president of Bethany College and the secretary of the Foreign Christian Missionary society of the Disciples of Christ, was also the one used to inspire the early pioneers of the Disciples Mission, John McGavran and G. L. Wharton, to go to India.

In many respects, the Church Growth Movement and concerns reflect some of the ongoing struggles within the Disciples of Christ. Church growth thinking is noncreedal. The movement's publications strive to recapture the evangelistic dynamic which has been nearly lost in the Disciples of Christ and some other church bodies.

---

26   Dr. West quotes within a précis given at the Commission on Theology of Missions at the Christian Theological Seminary Residence Hall, Indianapolis, (obtained from Middleton Archives, Vancouver, B.C.), April 4–5, 1960.

27   Donald McGavran, "Disciples and the World Mission," address to the Commission on Theology of Missions, (obtained from USCWM archives), April 4–5, 1960.

CHAPTER TWO

THE FIRST TERM IN INDIA

1923–30

On a crisp autumn day in September 1923, Donald McGavran and his wife Mary and their baby girl, Mary Theodora, set sail for India from the shores of the United States with a planned stopover in London, England. Their ship was delayed for a full six weeks in London. Finally they were on their way and arrived in Bombay, India in November of that same year. With hearts full of anticipation and enthusiasm they embarked on a new life as missionaries in the Service of Jesus Christ.

Mary, Mary Theodora, and Donald in Landour, Mussoorie, U.P.

Once in India, they headed for Jabalpur, a city located in the State of Madhya Pradesh where Don's parents were working with the United Christian Missionary Society, hereafter known as UCMS. John McGavran had resigned his post as professor at the College of Missions in the US and had travelled to India in 1922. John and his wife Helen had taken up residence in Jabalpur where he served as field secretary for UCMS. John also served on the faculty of Leonard Theological College, a school operated by a union of three cooperating missions.[28]

Donald in India with his mother, Helen (around 1923).

Their bungalow was gladly shared with their son, Donald, and his young family while Don and Mary began intensive study in the Hindi language. For Don, Hindi came easily as it was his first language during nine years of childhood, which had been spent as an MK (missionary kid) in India.

By October 1924, Don and Mary completed their second year course in Hindi. They headed off to a small railway town, Harda, to begin their first assignment. The Harda mission station located 125 miles west of Jabalpur, first opened in 1882 and the mission established several large schools there over the years. Don became principal over all the schools while Mary taught in the boy's high school, superintended the girl's school, and involved herself in the local church programs.[29]

THE CHALLENGE TO THE STATUS QUO OF EDUCATIONAL PATTERNS

McGavran soon became aware of the serious weaknesses of the educational methodology which was central to the entire missionary enterprise in India. What he began to see in

---

28   Donald McGavran, interview by Vern Middleton, Dec. 6, 1985.

29   A series of one-page biographical sketches contain information which help to reconstruct the events of this period (obtained from USCWM archives).

his own mission, the 1929 Lindsay Commission of the National Christian Council later discovered throughout all of India. The provision of "grants-in-aid" from the government of India, to mission educational institutions, had literally downgraded the schools to secular institutions. Over a period of almost two decades Don sought to bring educational institutions back into line with their original Christian purpose. Although a young and inexperienced missionary, he began applying certain principles and standards to the educational goals of his mission's institutions, which he later utilized in his church growth methodologies.

Harda (1927).

McGavran's First Book Challenges Christian Apathy

His first publication entitled, *How to Teach Religion in Mission Schools: A Brief Manual of Method*, was an immediate success. The book, published in 1928, went through several reprints. Translations were published in eight different languages. Through its pages, McGavran was taking the bold step of trying to correct missionary educational patterns that had deteriorated and become increasingly unfruitful in terms of spiritual results. In the opening pages of his book, he reestablished the central purpose of the schools run by missionaries. He states:

> We are molding the character of our pupils, we are building in them the personality of our Lord Jesus Christ, that they may live happy and victorious lives . . . [we are] to give a full rounded education based on the Spirit of Christ, educating not only the head but the heart and the soul of the child, in short implanting in the pupil the life of our Lord.[30]

---

30 Donald McGavran, *How to Teach Religion in Mission Schools: A Brief Manual of Method* (Jabalpur, India: Missions Press, 1928), 2.

Although the above statement is evangelical in tone, McGavran, at this point in his missionary career, thought of conversion more as a Christianizing process rather than a spiritual encounter with Christ. This was because the government prohibited the baptism of children under the age of eighteen, and also the missions were experiencing a degree of resistance in their educational programs. McGavran reasoned, "These present students may not become Christian but in the process of time Christian education will bring their children to Christ."[31]

McGavran did indeed see the issues clearly. The secular influences of the government "grants in aid," as well as the inspections by secular administrators had led to prestige and value in academic pursuits but the spiritual aims had fallen by the wayside. Stridently and urgently he called the educators back to the original vision:

> Missionary educationists, headmasters and teachers must continually fight to keep their vision clear. We have a greater purpose and message than any government ever had. We are building Christian men and women. Until missionaries and teachers alike get and maintain this vision we cannot fulfill our high calling.[32]

During his first term he urged the missionary educators to become better stewards of their missionary calling. This became the early stages of the church growth principle of accountability:

> People wonder that the . . . millions of dollars poured into schools have not produced more of a result among Christian and non-Christian pupils. But it is really no matter of wonder for we have permitted ourselves to be dominated by an educational system which has, with all its admitted excellencies, been . . . "godless."[33]

As a Christian educator, McGavran was never content with merely pointing out and challenging the problems. The greater portion of the handbook focuses on step-by-step assistance in lesson preparation and presentation, memorization procedures, and drama, as a means of bringing life to Scripture for the student. The handbook urges the teacher to take a personal interest in each student, and to pray for the salvation of each one on a daily basis. It challenges the teacher to make home visitation an opportunity of witness to the Hindu families.

---

31 Donald McGavran, interview by Vern Middleton, Feb. 8, 1984.
32 McGavran, *How to Teach Religion in Mission Schools*, 2.
33 Ibid., 4.

Mary and Donald McGavran,
with Helen (left), Mary Theodora (center), and Jean (right).

In the 1934 revised edition of the manual, McGavran incorporated many of these principles, which later became part of his church growth methodology. He stressed that educators ought to maximize their efforts for Jesus Christ and he urged them not to be content with the institutional rut and the status quo. He examined various teaching practises and patterns for giving instruction in the Bible and he insisted that all teaching of the Bible begin with a focus on the life situation of the student. He ruthlessly urged the teachers to discard careless patterns of teaching Scripture which had arisen through the years.

McGavran's Concern to Reduce Caste Tensions

Many who have misunderstood the principle of the "homogeneous unit" in church growth methodology, have accused McGavran of perpetuating caste distinctions. Actually nothing could be further from the truth. In his manual he stressed the urgency of reducing communal tensions in India:

> Men and women are divided according to their race, religion, customs, education, wealth and ability into many exclusive groups . . . The school should definitely aim to make communal lines dim within the school, to establish friendly relationships between different castes and classes and to eliminate everything which tends to mark any one group of pupils of high caste, low caste, rich or poor. This form of

Christian expression is greatly needed in India. If any school teaches brotherhood in the classroom but permits an expression of class distinction in the seating arrangements, mess halls and play fields, what is gained.[34]

This was much more than a theoretical ideal. In 1926, while he was principal at the mission high school in Harda, an Untouchable boy from the Balahi caste requested permission to study there. He granted the request and enrolled him as a full-time student. He faced immediate hostile reaction from students and faculty alike. Teachers threatened to resign if the Balahi boy sat in their classrooms. Students threatened a wholesale boycott of classes. However McGavran stood his ground. A few students stayed home for two days but for the most part the school continued as usual.[35]

McGAVRAN'S AND DUFF'S IDEAS REGARDING CASTE

McGavran's attitude to caste in 1926 was similar to that of most missionaries in India. They saw caste as an exploitative social structure established by and for the benefit of the Brahmin caste. They rightly understood caste to be the backbone of Hinduism. Hence caste needed to be destroyed through the Christianizing process of Western education and by creating a casteless church in India. The origin of this attitude was conditioned by Alexander Duff's educational policies established in 1830. He set in motion a spirit of intolerance toward caste. This issue stirred controversy and tension among missionaries in India, especially after 1890. For years they debated the significance of the people movements, and the merits of destroying caste through the educational methodologies developed in the colonial atmosphere in the early 1800's. However, by the end of the nineteenth century, a few voices began to question the traditional missionary approach to caste issues.

J. D. Maynard, Bernard Lucas, and John Nicolas Farquhar brought moderating insights to the issue. Also, by the turn of the twentieth century, Indian Christian theologians began to be heard. All of this raised in question the educational methodology as a means of destroying caste. Duncan Forrester wrote:

By the turn of the century in the more nationalistic climate of opinion it was becoming obvious that the Christian attack on caste was not about to cause the collapse of Hindu society and that Christian communalism was withdrawing more Christians from a general concern for the good of society and involvement

---

34   Donald McGavran, *How to Teach Religion in Mission School: Revised Edition* (Jabalpur, India: Missions Press, 1934), 102.

35   Donald McGavran, interview by Vern Middleton, May 7, 1986.

with the national movement, thus creating a real danger that the church would become an alien minority encapsulated within Hindu society.[36]

A growing polarization in the missionary community began to emerge. Some missionaries recognized the weakness of the educational approach based upon the pietistic individualism which gathered converts one-by-one. However, it was not until J. Waskom Pickett and McGavran began to publish their research, that the full significance of the people movement issue gained any credibility in the general missionary community. Even to this day, however, churches and Indian leaders remain divided over the issue. Those who have grown up in the anti-caste environment of the gathered church with its dependence on missions still insist that the only true church in India is the "conglomerate" type church without caste distinctions in its ranks. What they fail to realize is that to the Hindu onlooker, Christians behave and act in caste-like ways. They commonly eat meat, which to the orthodox Hindu is offensive. Their employment is usually associated directly, or indirectly, with the mission. This characterizes them as a caste by virtue of the nature of their employment. They intermarry, and in India caste purity is maintained through endogamous and exogamous restrictions. All of these are marks of caste behavior.

On the other hand, the vast majority of Christians in India have come to Christ through "people movements." Although they may retain a caste or tribal identity, most often these people are far less caste conscious than the "conglomerate" church, which appears to turn inward and become preoccupied with its own concerns. A high percentage of the indigenous mission agencies have been launched from churches which have come into being through tribal or caste conversion patterns. The Holy Spirit seems to utilize caste and family structures as viable instruments from which the gospel may flow to ever greater numbers of people groups. McGavran began to challenge traditional missionary attitudes about caste and advocate people movements within castes as he pondered these influences.

His first term in India was primarily spent ministering to upper caste Hindus. Only fleeting contact was made with the Shudra and scheduled castes (Harijan). He remained mostly unaware of the significance of the people movements taking place among the lower caste peoples in Andhra Pradesh, Tamil Nadu, and even in the Kandwa District, fifty miles to the west of Harda, where the Methodists were experiencing a significant people movement from the Balahi caste. During his seven-year first term however he developed a grasp of the nature of the caste system, which provided essential understanding for many of the church growth principles he formulated later. In an unpublished paper entitled, "Education, Religion, and the Advancement of India," he devoted six of its forty-nine pages to issues of caste. Some of the highlights of his assessment are paraphrased as follows:

---

36   Duncan B. Forrester, *Caste and Christianity: Attitudes and Policies on Caste of Anglo-Saxon Protestant Missions in India* (London: Curzon Press, 1980), 132.

1. Caste assumes that the individual is to be subordinated to the social group. Caste reinforces the practice of child marriage which in turn sacrifices the development of the wife. The joint family system subordinates the individual to the family. Caste tolerates no meddling with its mores. The individual has no rights apart from the group.

2. The caste system imposes inexorable economic restrictions on the individual. It also destroys initiative to correct social injustices and weakens attempts at social reform.

3. Caste assumes that men are of several species, each with a distinct nature, function and training. Caste permeates every aspect of life and every Hindu community for them. It is a universal belief.

4. Caste is buttressed by Hindu theology and in turn it buttresses the Hindu belief system.

5. Caste implies an aristocratic social group that puts inferior races in their place and makes them content to be there.

6. The only significant society in India is the caste. It is the society of people whose opinions count, who determine who should marry who, and who determine the associations, forms of livelihood, and security.

7. Caste is priority. A caste member will sacrifice the welfare of a school, or a town if it threatens his caste.[37]

McGAVRAN AS DIRECTOR OF RELIGIOUS EDUCATION

In 1928, McGavran accepted a newly created post within his mission, as Director of Religious Education. In this capacity he began to upgrade the standard of Bible teaching and instruction in spiritual matters in all of the schools administered by the Disciples of Christ. He was in charge of the following institutions: 15 primary schools, 5 middle schools, 1 normal school, 2 high schools and 2 industrial schools for a total of 25. This post also required considerable travel on his part since the schools were spread over an area about the size of the state of Oregon.

During his tenure, McGavran initiated a program of institutes to upgrade the skills of Bible teachers. With the publication of his manual, a tool was thus made available for providing uniform course and subject matter. The intent of these institutes was to stress the development of good methodology. McGavran wrote, "Stress has consistently been laid

---

37   Donald McGavran, "Education, Religion and the Advancement of India," (unpublished MS, [obtained from USCWM archives], 1930), 9–14. This paper may have been written during the early months of McGavran's PhD studies.

on better teaching, more pupil participation, the creation of interest, teaching centering around pupil purposes, more careful preparation, more complete consecration."[38]

The McGavran family, 1947–48.
Helen, Donald, Pat (center), and Winifred (right).

Educational Principles Transferable to Church Growth

In June 1929, McGavran delivered a speech at Landour, Mussoorie (a retreat center for missionaries) on the topic, "The Supervisor of Religious Education."[39] He contrasted the difference between the traditional approach to teaching the Bible and the aim to which he aspired:

> [Formerly] religious education chiefly meant . . . the teaching of the Bible, church creed and ecclesiastical rules . . . The present attitude toward the subject is that Christian education involves developing Christian habits, beliefs, attitude, purposes, skills, knowledge and experience through scores of different techniques and in all the varied activities in which persons engage.[40]

He also set forth three functions of the Supervisor's office, appraisal, training, and improvement through research.[41] These three very significant principles form the backbone

---

38   Donald McGavran, *India News Letter* 7, no. 3 (1929): 14.
39   Donald McGavran, "The Supervisor of Religious Education," (unpublished MS, [obtained from USCWM], 1929).
40   McGavran, "The Supervisor of Religious Education," 1.
41   Ibid.

of church growth. God was preparing him to discover and apply these principles to the "educational" task and later also to his understanding of the central missionary task.

The Principle of Appraisal

Under the subtitle of appraisal, McGavran pointed out that often schools try to avoid evaluation. He wrote:

> A critical evaluation of what is being done is usually resented rather than invited. Self criticism or criticism by others is essential to any progress. Supervision is forever laying down the surveyer's chain of possible achievement along the distance actually travelled. Appraisal is no bludgeoning criticism. It is intelligent thorough acquaintance with a situation.[42]

Here is the precursor to McGavran's church growth principle of "Discovering the Why of It." Thirty years later, in the book, *How Churches Grow*, McGavran elaborated the value of checking performance in evangelism and church planting. He wrote:

> In most forms of human endeavour progress is accelerated by constantly checking performance against defined goals. The navigator repeatedly brings the ship back on course. The teacher gives examinations to find how well lessons have been learned. The business firm measures sales in various territories to discover favourable markets, able men and successful selling methods. It would seem natural for those carrying out the Great Commission to check achievements in church growth to find how well they are getting on with making disciples of all nations.[43]

The value of this principle of evaluation is seldom recognized by supporters of missions, though missionaries are often the most unsupervised people in the ministry. Local pastors have deacon boards to correct unproductive patterns, but foreign missionaries 8,000 miles or more from their mission board and supporting constituencies rarely receive the benefit of godly evaluation.

In his lecture, McGavran insisted that the Supervisor of Religious Education needs to keep records, appraise methods, and note outcomes. Clearly some of his later church growth principles arose directly out of his training and discipline as an educator.

---

42   Ibid., 3.
43   Donald McGavran, *How Churches Grow: The New Frontiers of Mission* (London: World Dominion Press, 1959), 144.

The Principle of Training

McGavran also stressed the need for training as an ongoing process. He listed several ways in which it could be implemented, and emphasized that the motivation must arise from the teacher's desire for improvement. He pointed out that training ought to be more than merely imparting knowledge, and that it ought to include "modeling" of the truth. He also stressed that such training aims to improve self confidence in teachers, create a desire for better teaching, and builds a belief that more effective teaching is attainable.

Summer refresher courses gave special training for teachers teaching Bible in the mission schools. McGavran designed these "institutes" or retreats not merely to impart new methods but primarily to inspire greater spiritual growth and vitality in the inner life of the teachers. He utilized speakers from many different missions and designed the retreats on the basis of inter-mission cooperation. These institutes were conducted in various parts of India during the hot season. They were a regular ministry from 1928 to 1947.

The program for the institutes consisted of sessions on "Making the Bible Desired," "The Dramatization of Bible Stories," and "Story Telling Worship,"[44] along with other practical topics. Of particular interest is the way McGavran designed the devotional periods for these sessions. Each was a model of what the teachers ought to do upon return to their classrooms.

Refresher courses held after 1936 focused on evangelism more than on methods. By then McGavran had gained boldness and a new sense of direction so he insisted that every school should be an evangelistic agency. He encouraged Christian teachers and pupils to engage in direct evangelism to approachable castes; such as the Chamars, Satnamis, Balahis, Lal Begis, and Dumars and he also stressed the need for regular visitation to receptive relatives. He encouraged teachers to use Waskom Pickett's book on *Mass Movements in India* as a textbook. Lectures and discussions were held right in the classrooms. Finally, he also stressed the urgency of regular organized prayer meetings in all the mission schools for revival in the church and direction in witnessing and soul winning.[45] This new emphasis was radically different from the focus he had in 1928.

McGavran's training programs for Christian educators became models for his later development of seminars and church growth institutes which he developed later in his life and which became the means for educating missionaries and pastors in evangelism and church planting principles. During the years 1955 to 1960 he worked on research projects in various countries and held numerous church growth seminars. However he soon realized seminars were limited in effectiveness, and that he needed to bring the entire focus on to developing church growth concepts in the minds of career missionaries.

---

44   Donald McGavran, "Education Committee Report," (chaired by McGavran, [obtained from USCWM], Nov. 1929), 5–6.
45   Donald McGavran, circular letter from Jabalpur to members of a Refresher Course, (obtained from USCWM), April 16, 1935.

In a speech on "The Supervision of Religious Education," he told how the Disciples of Christ in India published a bulletin to train and stimulate teachers. It was loaded with news of happenings, reports of exceptionally good teaching along with the name of the teacher, articles on religious education method, and child study.[46]

So he incorporated the same idea into his program, stimulating church growth and thus the *Church Growth Bulletin* was published and in addition he encouraged the publication of bulletins on church growth in many regions of the world. This, combined with the publication of books on the topic of the growth of churches and missions, has been an important strategy in his training technique.

The Principle of Research

He understood the third dimension of his job as that of researcher. He saw this as essential because out of it would come more knowledge and a stimulus to further thinking and reflection and this in turn would help the teacher to know the student better and thus the teaching process would be sharper and flavored with new insights.

He encouraged teachers to check out the fears, temptations, and religious experiences of their students so their lessons might meet specific needs. He also suggested that research was needed and his proposal cited below became the thesis for his PhD dissertation.

> On the evangelistic zeal of the coming generation in the Christian Church, or on the most effective measures for inculcating habits of stewardship in the Christian Church, on the dominant interests of 7th standard Hindu boys or 1st standard Hindu girls.[47]

When the Church Growth Institute developed in 1962, empirical research became an essential aspect of students training. This technique led to numerous published church growth case studies that became handbooks for churches in many countries. Because of this emphasis missionary research agencies developed using the latest technology to keep abreast of the explosion of available information, and to coordinate the direction needed for today's global enterprise.

Quality through Quantification

In 1938, McGavran gave another educational lecture, to missionary educators in Landour, India on the subject of Managing Day Schools More Evangelically. He lamented the lack of dynamic and direction in religious education. Along these lines he said:

---

46   McGavran, "The Supervisor of Religious Education," 17.
47   Ibid., 19.

Religious education, repudiating what it considered the super emotionalism of the Sunday School has placed its primary emphasis on teaching methods, lesson courses, pedagogical materials, leadership training and similar educational features. It has openly disavowed numbers as a measure of success insisting that quality not quantity is the really important thing . . . Now the result of all this has been that the church has substituted a program that was chiefly heart and little head, for one that is chiefly head and little heart.[48]

With that introduction McGavran launched into the heart of the lecture stating: religious education needs a passion, a passion not for materials and methods, but a passion for the lives of men. He stressed that a sound conversion and the presence of the Holy Spirit were necessary in missionary educators. He had a vital concern for the Christian nominalism that existed among the teachers who merely joined the church as a matter of course. He exhorted, "[You] need to have [your] hearts broken at the cross."

McGavran pointed out that evangelism would not automatically happen: we must see to it that our evangelistic efforts are successful. He insisted on consistent and disciplined prayer for the unconverted, weekly time for evangelism, and a follow-up on students who were from receptive castes.

Here is a radical transformation in McGavran's theology as well as his understanding of the educational process and the educator's responsibility. In the 1920s he was concerned primarily with methods, lesson content, and pedagogical material. Evangelism for him in those years was a long process of bringing Christ into the minds of the students through education. By 1938 he was overwhelmed with a vision for the lost and compelled by the power of the Spirit of God to bring Christ to the hearts of the students and parents alike. His ideas on church growth were no longer academic theories, for they arose from his struggles to penetrate caste barriers with the gospel, and his growing passion for evangelism.

THE LIBERAL ETHOS OF THE 1920s REPLACED BY A PASSION FOR EVANGELISM IN THE 1930s

The patterns of Christian education in the 1920s were called into question by the Lindsay Commission launched by the National Christian Council of India in 1929. Its findings were that the Christian colleges have lost their Christian character. They had been content with service, but the evangelistic purpose of the college had been blurred in its cooperation with the University System.[49] Almost simultaneously the National Christian Council launched another study on the Mass Movements (1930–32). Both of these reports focused on

---

48   Donald McGavran, "Managing Day Schools More Evangelically," (unpublished MS of a lecture given at a conference for missionaries at Landour Mussoorie, India, [obtained from USCWM], 1938).
49   Kaj Baago, *A History of the National Council of India: 1914–1964* (Nagpur, India: The National Christian Council, 1965), 52.

evangelism and converged in the life of McGavran as he developed his concepts of church growth. The educational methodology, as developed in India between 1830 and 1930 eventually led to an institutionalized form of missions, but between 1928 and 1933 many missionaries like McGavran began to question and reevaluate this century-old pattern. At precisely the same time the issue of the Mass Movements came into focus through J. Waskom Pickett. These two developments sparked McGavran's zeal and commitment to evangelism and church growth as the first priority of all missionary endeavour.

The Mechanism of Mobility Germinated in a Concrete Situation

After spending two years at Harda (1927), McGavran made a recommendation to his board, which was at best a very mixed blessing. It helped the future work of UCMS in India but proved to be disastrous for the local Christians. He wrote a letter to Mr. Corey, UCMS executive secretary based in the US, strongly recommending the Harda field be closed.

> The reason for this is that Harda is an isolated field and it must either be expanded, with one or two mission stations established fifteen to twenty miles on either side of it or else we must retire from it . . . we must go and locate where the bulk of the mission is . . . the schools here shall be closed down next year, May 1, 1928.[50]

A distance of 125 miles separated the bulk of the Disciples of Christ groups in Harda. Although daily train connections between the two areas existed, the missionaries felt isolated. McGavran wanted the work in Harda terminated due to insufficiency of funds and lack of a long-term commitment to the area by the mission.

Conversions were not a major concern during McGavran's first term in India. Although they, along with six other missionaries, served in Harda from 1924–30, not a single conversion was recorded from outside the church during that time.[51] Christians in Harda affirmed that McGavran considered the town barren, fruitless, and unreceptive. Receptivity would later become an important focus in church growth theory.[52]

The decision to close the schools in Harda was taken in 1930, after a visit to the field by Corey, the UCMS mission secretary. The town reeled under the impact of this decision. At the time of closure over one-third of the town area was made up of mission institutions.

Wealthy high caste people in Harda purchased these prestigious properties. The local Christians were given only a few of the buildings and for years they were bitter over what seemed to them an injustice. The Disciples actually retained comity rights to Harda until

---

50   Donald McGavran, letter from Harda to Stephen J. Corey, St. Louis, Missouri, May 20, 1926.
51   Donald McGavran, *Understanding Church Growth* (Grand Rapids: Eerdmans, 1972), 54.
52   Oral history—the author worked for several years in a region fifty miles south of Harda in the years 1966–70. Invitations to minister in the local church of Harda afforded opportunity for the local Christians to share their feelings and resentments.

1968 when the region was turned over to the Fellowship Baptist Mission of Canada and the Conservative Baptist Mission of the US.

While he made the Harda closure recommendation, McGavran recognized the potential for church growth among the Balahi caste in the area. During this period an unforgettable incident occurred in his life. A dignified Indian knocked on his door and asked for a few minutes of his time, so with some impatience, McGavran admitted this intruder into his home. The Indian was a Brahman by caste and the son of a Malguzar, a headman of a number of collective villages. However the man was a professing Christian and he requested McGavran to join him in preaching to the villagers, assuring him that a caste-wide people movement would result. McGavran liked the idea but was very preoccupied with institutional responsibilities and committee meetings so he asked the man to return at a more convenient time. For sixty years McGavran lived with an uneasy conscience over that lost opportunity—as the man was put off and never returned.[53]

The Struggle over the Strategy of Gradualism

As has been seen throughout his first term, McGavran's focus was on proclamation and presence, and there was little concern for persuading men and women, boys and girls to receive Christ as Lord and Savior of their lives. In a 1925 report he wrote, "Our task is not to conquer heathenism, but to lift up Jesus in the midst of heathenism. The contrast does the rest."[54]

The upper caste people in Harda wanted the benefits of schooling provided by the mission but rejected the Savior proclaimed by the mission. Many of the teachers in the mission schools were high caste men who opposed Christianity. A few months after McGavran took charge of the schools in Harda, he faced a major crisis because the Hindu teachers went on strike in protest over the requirement of prayers and Scripture reading for all students. Their agitation was reinforced by threats from two prominent town leaders who planned to call a public rally of all citizens if prayers and Scripture were not dropped from the curriculum. In the confrontation, McGavran's five-foot-four-inch stature rose to a full ten feet. He described the battle as the zest of contest and the tang of matching wits.[55] He mobilized four teams of Christian teachers to go door-to-door inquiring directly of the students' parents if they indeed opposed the Lord's Prayer and the reading of Psalm 23. The result of the survey was without a single "disagreeing sentiment" and so the strike and public protest were dropped immediately.

Since McGavran's concept of conversion at that time consisted of a form of gradualism, he saw education as the way into the church, which he described as follows:

---

53   McGavran cited this incident in his church growth lectures at Fuller 1965–1975. He also recounted the tale in a number of interviews between 1983 and 1988.

54   Donald McGavran, "A Day's Fighting," *World Call* 7 (June 1925): 43.

55   Ibid., 43.

Our self-supporting, self-governing, self-propagating Indian church is nowadays going to school. The men and women who in the future will form that kind of church are today in our mission schools ... They are the non-Christians who are in our schools for from four to ten years receiving regular instruction in the Bible and subject to those Christian influences which we are able to throw around them.[56]

In September 1925, he said the mission was in a seed-sowing phase. There was no application of persuasion or of pressing home the lordship of Christ. Rather there was the considered hope that the mission's forty years of preparatory work would eventually produce a harvest in a future time.[57]

While he was living and serving in Harda, McGavran was an active participant in the affairs of the community. He was a member of the Sanskrit club which met to read from the Hindu epics and to compose odes in honor of Tulsi Das, the author of the Ramayana. McGavran's linguistic and literary skills showed well here. He was a first-term missionary who not only had the ability to read Sanskrit but also to compose poetry in that ancient spiritual language of India. The poets club awarded him a coveted *samolan*, a silver scroll, for his skill in their sacred literature. This involvement was another expression of "gradualism" and he rationalized his commitment as follows:

We are not working with savages, but with a cultured people who have a language older and more sacred than Latin, a literature in the modern tongue which commands the respect ... of all lovers of poetry, a religious devotion probably equaled by no nation in the world ... All this brings a pride of race, of culture, of literature, of religion which faces the missionary in practically no other county.[58]

Still even in the midst of his poetic activity he believed that Christianity and modern science were *gradually* eroding the credibility of the stories in epic Hindu literature.

There appears to be a relationship between McGavran's early views on educational gradualism and his principle of church growth called "perfecting." Throughout his first term he believed conversion consisted largely of educating the Hindu mind into Christian beliefs and Western scientific understanding. However, between 1930 and 1934, a series of events occurred in his life, which transformed him spiritually, and he reasserted the primacy of conversion as a means of becoming a Christian disciple. With the dynamic of the new focus McGavran still recognized that the cultural worldview of a people had a way of persisting even in the lives of those being transformed by the gospel. Hence in his second and third terms in India, he replaced the principle of "gradualism," which involved a pre-Christian educational process, with the "perfecting," or post-discipling phase of conversion. His

---

56 Donald McGavran, "Sending the Church to School," *World Call* 7 (Feb. 1925): 21–24.
57 Donald McGavran, "Sown Fields," *World Call* 7 (Sept. 1925): 55.
58 Donald McGavran, "Poets meet in Harda," *World Call* 7 (Dec. 1925): 61.

concept of perfecting is a key to understanding his view of casteward people movements. He became convinced that the only way to remove the evils of caste from India was to disciple large numbers of people within the context of their clan, tribe, and caste, followed by consistent teaching of the Word of God, believing this would replace the racist views of caste with Christian brotherhood. His thesis behind gradualism/perfecting was that:

> Gaps in cultures will be truly closed only when the beliefs underlying the present social order in Hindu India have been brought into harmony or replaced by the beliefs which underly Western civilization.[59]

As McGavran's view on gradualism shifted to discipling, followed by "perfecting" or "character building" during the period between 1930 and 1933, his own spiritual life was being renewed. Yet there remained an intermingling of the old gradualism with the regained perception of the primary place of conversion.

In an article written in 1931 entitled, "Character-Building En Masse," McGavran described the worldview transformation they were attempting to produce through the educational institutions. The following is a summation of its concept of perfecting:

> Christian character is a definable thing. A man of Christian character acts habitually in certain predictable ways . . . He is a friend to all . . . He speaks the truth and searches for the truth in all aspects of life. He honors women as persons equally valuable with himself. He acts chastely. He works industriously and honestly . . . He seeks to live well, to live abundantly . . . He lives in close relationship to God in Christ.[60]

In the same article McGavran goes on to describe that such a Christian character can be taught, induced, and implanted, without any reference to the need for the regenerating power of the Holy Spirit in conversion. His view was not unlike that of T. B. Macaulay who was chairman of the Committee of Public Instruction in India between 1812 and 1837. He wrote optimistically a century earlier:

> No Hindu who has received an English education ever remains sincerely attached to his religion . . . It is my firm belief that if our plans of education are followed up, there will not be a single idolater among the respectable classes in Bengal thirty years hence. And this will be affected without any effort to proselytize; without the smallest interference in their religious liberty; merely by the natural operation of knowledge and reflection.[61]

---

59   Donald McGavran, "Education, Religion and the Advancement of India," 7.

60   Donald McGavran, "Character Building En Masse," *World Call* 13 (March, 1931), 28.

61   Arthur Innes Mayhew, *The Education of India; A Study of British Educational Policy in India, 1835–1920, and its Bearing on National Life and Problems in India Today* (London: Faber and Gwyer, 1928), 15.

Macaulay's views were reinforced by other missionary contemporaries. Alexander Duff along with Charles Grant the President of the CMS missionary society of the Anglican Church strongly espoused the idea that India could be educated into the Kingdom of God. It was the view of Alexander Duff and other missionaries who followed in his train that mass conversions would inevitably follow upon the spread of Western education with its scientific method. Duff's educational methodology is summarized in these words:

> Every branch of sound general knowledge which you inculcate, becomes the destroyer of some corresponding part in the Hindu systems. And if branch after branch be communicated, one stone after another will be thrown down from the huge and hideous fabric of Hinduism; and by the time that an extensive range of instruction is completed, the whole will be found to have crumbled into fragments: not a shred will be left behind.[62]

Thus had the entire missionary enterprise in India built its strategy on the educational approach and McGavran was very much part of this philosophy of mission until 1934.

TRAGEDY STRIKES THE McGAVRAN HOME

Early in March of 1930 the McGavran household was bubbling with excitement. Preparations were getting underway for their first furlough. Suitcases and steamer trunks were packed with clothes and the four McGavran children, Mary Theodora, age seven, Jean, age five, Helen, age four, and Malcolm, age one. They were full of questions, for they only knew America from story books and conversations with their parents.

As the departure date loomed, on a Thursday morning Mary Theodora, their firstborn child began to run a temperature. Doctors were consulted at the local government hospital and a doctor from a neighboring mission. They assured that it was nothing serious and that the temperature may be caused by malarial indigestion. Theodora appeared to be improving on Friday, so McGavran boarded a train to attend a committee meeting in Jabalpur. Within hours of his departure, Theodora's condition took a turn for the worse. Saturday morning Mary took her seriously ill little girl to the city of Nagpur, a train journey of over 150 miles. Upon arrival at the Nagpur hospital doctors immediately operated on Mary Theodora, but it was too late. The appendix had burst sometime Friday. The resulting infection, combined with the heat and pain of the journey, hastened the end for her.

Meanwhile, McGavran had received a telegram informing him of Mary's travel plans to Nagpur. He tried to meet her enroute but missed connections and spent several maddening hours waiting for the next train. By the time he caught up with Mary in Nagpur, Mary

---

62   Alexander Duff, "*Our Earliest Protestant Mission to India,*" (May, 1844). See also, Paton William, *Alexander Duff: Pioneer of Missionary Education* (New York: George Doran Co., 1922), chpt. 6.

Theodora was dead. Donald and Mary McGavran held a small funeral for their daughter and returned back to Harda grief stricken and numb.[63]

The anguished sense of guilt and remorse virtually immobilized McGavran for days. Francis Rambo, a lifelong friend, hastened to be with the family. Her description of his condition revealed the extent of the grief he bore. "Don's state is pitiful . . . The shock of reaching Nagpur after Mary had been thru it all alone was too much for him. He blames himself."[64]

Yet even such an ominous and heavy storm cloud has a rainbow in it. Within one week of the crisis McGavran wrote, "We know as we have not known before that there is life beyond the grave. She is with Jesus, whom she loved. We shall see her again."[65] From this point on a very detectable change in the spiritual life of McGavran became evident. Reason gave way to a deep and growing spiritual relationship with Christ. His letters over the months and years that followed show clearly his growing love and commitment to his Lord and Savior.

As a direct result of his renewed relationship with Christ he was concerned with the issue of the excessive institutional preoccupation of the India field. "I personally think that the whole present distribution of mission forces needs to be reconsidered in an attempt to put more of our force into direct persistent evangelism."[66]

A personal letter written in December 1932 to David Rioch, McGavran's prayer partner at Butler, revealed the spiritual pilgrimage he had experienced. He explained that his optimism in the face of the looming economic depression arose from within and was not disturbed by external circumstances.

My optimism comes from a winning back a feel of the spiritual world. Consciousness of that spiritual world with which this phenomenal world is so completely intermingled and which gives meaning and significance to the phenomenal world faded out for some years, not entirely but largely. It is coming back now and with it comes a feeling that life's burdens are easier to bear and the great goals are worth fighting for.[67]

---

63   Donald McGavran, letter from Harda to Dr. Stephen Corey, Indianapolis, March 13, 1930.

64   Frances Rambo, letter from Harda to Mr. and Mrs. Howard, (Mary's parents) at Muncie, Indiana, March 7, 1930.

65   Donald McGavran, letter, (obtained from USCWM), March 13, 1930.

66   Donald McGavran, letter from New York City to Dr. Yocum, Indianapolis, Aug. 30, 1931.

67   Donald McGavran, letter from Jabalpur, India to David Rioch, Dec. 21, 1932. Rioch was a deep, personal friend of Butler days. They had prayed regularly together but Rioch lost his commitment to Christ while studying for psychiatry.

McGAVRAN AS AN APOLOGIST

Toward the end of McGavran's first term in India, he began developing an apologetic approach to the Hindu. Unlike many other contemporary apologists, McGavran created multiple apologetic approaches. He was very much a practitioner and his concepts arose from his day to day ministry, first as an educator to the high castes of Harda, then as an evangelist to the lower castes of Jabalpur, and finally to the Satnamis of Chattisgarh. The terms apologist, apologetic, and apology in this chapter are used in the theological sense as a way of stating and proclaiming the gospel so that it would be understandable and convincing to the Hindu mind.

For McGavran several distinct influences were converging in his life to inspire and direct his thinking, as he sought to communicate Christ to the people of Central India. One strong factor was his background as an educator. His apologetic was highly didactic in nature. He knew that Christian truth had to become part of the thinking process of the educated high castes, and in the illiterate low caste peoples both in the cultured cities of India as well as the remote rural villages before it would be able to root out Hindu traditions and superstitions. A second influence in his apologetic was that he was face-to-face with grassroots Hinduism. Although he read Farquhar, Chenchiah, and Chakkarai and was personally acquainted with E. Stanley Jones, he did not major in philosophic approaches to the Hindu mind. The popular Hinduism which he encountered required a much more direct approach.

From 1923 to 1940 there was a strong growth and development in McGavran's apologetic. During his first term he sought to make Christ known to the upper castes through daily Bible classes and social involvements. Although he had a liberal view of the Bible at that time, he still had a burning desire to utilize every possible means to spread the good news about Jesus Christ.

His Educational Apologetic

While engaged in PhD studies at Columbia University in 1931, McGavran wrote an essay entitled, "Education, Religion and the Advancement of India." This may possibly have been a preparation paper for his dissertation and was his first attempt to systematize his thought and understanding of the fundamentals of Hinduism. The paper clearly stated his comprehensive grasp of Hinduism and the social ramifications of each doctrine. The thesis statement for this paper was, "The gap in cultures will be truly closed only when the beliefs underlying the present social order in Hindu India have been brought into harmony with or replaced by beliefs which underlie Western civilization."[68]

---

68   Donald McGavran, "Education, Religion and the Advancement of India," 7.

In writing for the secular professors at the Columbia University, he described the conversion process in terms that reflected Farquhar's position that Christianity was the "Crown" of Hinduism. His mentor, Professor Flemming, had warned McGavran frequently against allowing his missionary convictions to appear in his essays. Thus he wrote in such a way that the concept could clearly mean conversion but for his secular professors it would be interpreted otherwise.

> The task is not therefore mere destruction of old beliefs, nor yet merely permitting circumstances to destroy them, but rather a rational constructive effort to substitute for or graft onto the old, a new philosophy or religion, a new system of undergirding beliefs.[69]

The paper set forth thirteen beliefs within Hinduism that serve to enslave the people to a worldview that is both idolatrous and full of inertia. His statements may be summarized as follows:

> Of those thirteen beliefs, the first is the belief that the individual is to be subordinated to the social group . . . Caste tolerates no meddling with its mores. The individual must conform . . . Second, the belief that material things are illusory, evil; . . . the physical is constantly minimized . . . Third, the belief that men are of several different species . . . Caste is an aristocratic social grouping which not only puts inferior races in their places but which makes them happy to be there . . . The caste system automatically deprives them of the opportunities to grow into full free personalities . . . Fourth . . . it is the society of people whose opinion counts, in whom resides the authority to permit or forbid marriage, association, livelihood and security . . . Man's supreme loyalty is given to his caste. Morality tends to be be thought of as operative within the caste . . . Fifth . . . it is wrong to kill. Ahimsa parmo dharma . . . The sixth belief is that the old is better than the new. Ceremonial laws and regulations rule supreme . . . The cosmology of the Hindu religion buttresses this belief in that it teaches that the world is growing steadily worse . . . The seventh belief concerns God. God is conceived as an impersonal neuter . . . Thus neither is the Hindu conception of God an ethical force nor a force toward any kind of progress. Eighth, there is running throughout India the helpless note of fatalism . . . which provides an excellent reason for inertia . . . and makes one helplessly content with the present lot. The ninth undergirding belief in Hindu India is that manual labour is degrading or is the function of the low caste . . . It gives substance to a system of values which exalts limited restricted duties, poverty and helpless contentment . . . The tenth belief is that much of life

---

69   Ibid., 8.

is to be explained in terms of . . . potencies of evil spirits resident in things . . . The eleventh underlying belief is that the cow is deity. The twelfth fundamental belief is that there is no common standard of morality for a society . . . Each caste has its mores, its duties, its dharma, concerning all aspects of life and worship. The thirteenth is that the world is growing steadily worse toward dissolution.[70]

McGavran did not fall into the trap which so many other well-meaning Christian apologists fell into. He rightly discerned the true source of India's social problems and did not place all the blame at the feet of the British Raj. Even as a young missionary he saw that the caste system of India had a stranglehold on society. His current detractors need to read his statements on caste to sense the abhorrence he has toward situations that enable one section of society to exploit and enslave others. He prophetically warned India: "Let Hinduism consciously reform her belief about caste, or revolution will result, for the depressed castes are not going to be content to remain uneducated and subordinate."[71]

He insightfully argued with Indians that the issues were not a difference between the East and the West. As he said, the opposition is not really between Occident and Orient but between modern and medieval. During the years when Europe's tribes were being Christianized, nominalism was widespread. Mass conversions of illiterates allowed the pre-Christian tribal culture and worldview to continue largely unchanged and as a result European peoples were very superstitious, morality tended to be that of the clan fatalism was a common belief, society was aristocratically organized.[72]

The final pages of McGavran's paper were an expansion of principles displayed in Acts 17:16–34. Paul preaching on Mars Hill exclaims, "For in Him we live and move and exist, as even some of your own poets have said, 'For we also are His offspring'" (NASB). His apologetic methodology was to seek out passages in the Bhagavad Gita, the Vedas, and the Upanishads, which foreshadowed biblical principles, and utilized them as points of contact to bring about conversion and social reform.

He also suggested that education may graft the new onto the old by using old terms but with new meaning. He cites the doctrine of *ahimsa* as an area where new interpretation can be applied, explaining that ahimsa (which means nonkilling of any living creature to the Hindu) now means for the Christian respect for personality, the worth of life at its highest, respect for womanhood and childhood.[73]

The last twenty pages of his manuscript were devoted to ways in which Christian education in India could be focused to undermine all of the foundational beliefs of Hinduism. In summary, it is clearly evident that throughout McGavran's first term in India

---

70   Ibid., 9–22.
71   Ibid., 30.
72   Ibid., 25.
73   Ibid., 33.

(1923–30) his entire thinking was focused on using educational methods to Christianize the middle and upper castes.

One year after production of the above apologetic, he produced a dissertation entitled, "Education and the Beliefs of Popular Hinduism." This work revealed an increased understanding of the nature of Hinduism, its foundational beliefs, and great sensitivity to the Indian mind but it did not reflect an advance in his apologetic.

The pivotal insight presented in the dissertation was his classification of nineteen major beliefs of popular Hinduism.[74] He arranged these beliefs under four broad categories: those about theism, the cosmos, relating to man, and miscellaneous beliefs. In order to retain objectivity in his research he sent this compilation of Hindu belief systems to a total of eight scholars in Indology for an evaluation. They gave his list strong approval as truly representative of the overall Hindu belief system. Of even more significance, his statement provided nineteen concise Hindu doctrinal statements and actually listed seventy-one sub-beliefs related to the central tenets of faith. (See Appendix B)

As an apologist or better an Indologist, McGavran had a grasp of both philosophical and popular Hinduism. He also understood the dynamics of the religious forces within Hinduism. He saw clearly its syncretistic nature and the implications of monism. Because his knowledge of Sanskrit enabled him to read the primary documents of Hindu literature he recognized the vast range of Hindu concepts.

The Hindu worldview has a cohesive power over the minds of its devotees. McGavran regarded it as a formidable system which required both missionary diligence and dedication in presenting the claims of the gospel. He wrote:

> Hindu India has a civilization of ancient standing . . . It has had common institutions, common convictions . . . common sacred literature! Its social and religious systems possess certain great underlying convictions. These systems are built on a consistent view of life.[75]

His grasp of the social dynamics of the Hindu system of thought was the background that oriented his thinking in the development of church growth principles. He recognized that Hindu philosophic forces of pantheism, polytheism, ancestor worship, and the joint family system were ubiquitous on the Indian subcontinent. Out of this context he wrote a book in 1974 called *The Clash Between Christianity and Cultures.*

---

74   Donald McGavran, *Education and the Beliefs of Popular Hinduism* (Jabalpur: Mission Press, 1935), 13.
75   Ibid., 8.

CONCLUSION

Many significant developments took place in McGavran's life during the nine-year period described in this chapter, covering his first term in India and a two-year study leave. Obviously this laid the foundation for the entire range of church growth principles he developed later. His training as a Christian educator provided a framework for him to formulate tools and principles of measurement for church growth.

Church growth insights appeared in his declaration of Harda as a resistant region. The mission withdrew personnel leaving only one pastor and an evangelist there, so McGavran recommended a transfer to more receptive areas closer to Jabalpur. This was not the only instance of mission mobility initiated by McGavran during his years of service in India. In chapter four the Disciples of Christ's entrance into the state of Orissa will be recounted. Together these two major shifts in location illustrate the way McGavran's ideas germinated out of concrete circumstances.

The town of Harda provided an ideal laboratory for the study of caste dynamics. This microcosm of the sociological structure of India enabled McGavran to grasp the significance of the strictures and structures arising from caste. These insights could not have been gained in a smaller, less sophisticated village where there is a greater degree of homogeneity. *Bridges of God* could not have been written without the knowledge gained from living and working in Harda.

As an Indologist and apologist McGavran formulated ways of presenting the gospel hoping to undermine the Hindu worldview. He saw that Hinduism was more than a religion—it was a total way of life for the average Indian. He perceived that Hinduism is a cultural package and that even after conversion many assumptions and presuppositions of Hindu origin still persist. Hence McGavran took his former idea of "gradualism" and transferred it to "perfecting." In the former it was a pre-Christian conditioning; in the latter it was a post-conversion educating in all things.

The most striking event in this era of McGavran's life was the spiritual turnaround which began with Mary Theodora's death. The renewed relationship he began to enjoy with Christ became the dynamo motivating and empowering him to be a faithful steward of the resources entrusted to him.

CHAPTER THREE

MISSION ADMINISTRATOR

1932–35

The years from 1932–35 were marked by a global recession and a major shift in the religious climate to a more conservative stance. Jabalpur became McGavran's place of residence during these four years. However, his increasing interest in mass (people) movement opportunities which were now ripening in many parts of India expanded his horizons while he served as chairman of the Mass Movement Committee of the Mid-India Council. He also chaired the Christian Education Committee of the National Council of Churches in India and became administrator and chairman of the significant Central India conference on people movements at Chhindwara in April 1935.

From November 1932 to November 1935, McGavran was the executive secretary-treasurer to Indian missions of UCMS, which consisted of seventy missionaries. He kept the account books, corresponded with the UCMS executive in Indianapolis, and visited the various mission stations. Executive committee meetings lasting three days each month required careful preparation and attention. This was a period of crisis for every mission administrator as the full impact of the Great Depression in North America radically began to affect budgets.

Despite his busy schedule, McGavran gave time and energy to the Mid-Indian Christian Council which was a regional ministry of the National Council of Churches. He developed a voluntary Simple Lifestyle Society. He spent one evening each week discipling the sweeper caste Dumar people. He taught Bible at the Mission High School in Jabalpur, conducted Christian education seminars throughout India and travelled to Bombay once each month to transact mission business. Is it any wonder that Mary McGavran complained she was married to "perpetual motion"?

APPOINTMENT AS SECRETARY-TREASURER

His colleagues and the mission executive recognized McGavran's reputation and leadership skills. Stephen J. Corey, the general secretary of the mission wrote the following words of commendation in 1929:

He is one of the most capable and promising missionaries we have on any of our fields. He is in India serving toward the end of his first term, but has made rapid strides in his leadership while on the field. He is now in charge of the educational work of our Mission as superintendent . . . He is outstanding in his ability. He is a fine scholar, and has a very constructive mind. Our India Mission values his services very highly.[76]

Returning to India, after a two-year study leave, McGavran was elected to the post of field secretary-treasurer in November 1932. The family moved from Harda to Jabalpur, a small city and administrative center for the Government of India where many British officials lived. A sizable missionary community of Anglicans, Roman Catholics, Methodists, and Disciples of Christ were located there and the city was situated at a railway junction. A large military base near the city provided residence for many British officers and their families. It was a colonial administrative center and as such was highly Westernized.

McGavran's induction service into his new post as secretary-treasurer was held in conjunction with the Golden Jubilee Convention of the Disciples of Christ, November 17–23, 1932 at which he presented a summary sketch of the accomplishments of the mission in the period 1882–1932.

Since its beginning . . . this mission has brought to India . . . 178 missionaries whose total years of service amount to over 2,500 . . . there are 15 organized churches, 11 of which employ pastors . . . In addition . . . there are 5 congregations which meet regularly for worship . . . There are 23 grant-in-aid schools. Two large hospitals and a flourishing tuberculosis sanitarium, also two other small hospitals and six dispensaries . . . keep in the foreground the healing work of the Church . . . The evangelistic efforts of Church and mission forces concentrate on about 450 villages and distinct wards of cities.[77]

A succinct description of the responsibilities McGavran faced as administrative secretary-treasurer of the mission, indeed.

COLONIALISM AND ITS INFLUENCE AND IMPACT ON McGAVRAN

Because of McGavran's birth and early years growing up in a village of India he had a clear cultural identity with the land and its peoples, but his strong ancestral ties to Britain also made him sensitive to the problems of colonial administration creating complex tension in

---

76 Stephen J. Corey, letter from Indianapolis to Daniel Fleming, Columbia, Nov. 12, 1929.
77 Donald McGavran, *India News Letter* 2, no. 5 (Jan. 1933), 23.

his thinking. As nationalism increased throughout the 1930s, he believed that leadership should be in the hands of the Indians, yet he recognized the value of colonial rule. He realized that independence would not solve India's economic uncertainty and insisted that India's plight would only be solved when her underlying belief system was:

> Brought into harmony with or replaced by the beliefs which underlie Western civilization. Machinery, agricultural progress, industrialization, and the like are significant in themselves. They bring more abundant life. But they alone are not complete. They must be accompanied by or preceded by a change in the basic outlook of the people before modern civilization can begin to be established.[78]

While the above quote tended to equate progress with Christian beliefs, it did recognize the importance of worldview in bringing economic development. This particular viewpoint was reflected in his book, *The Clash Between Christianity and Culture*. Published in 1974, it produced some controversy among anthropologists.

Colonialism Defined

Before we become more deeply engrossed in the influences which colonialism had on McGavran, a definition of the term must be established. Many of the definitions of colonialism come from men influenced by the Marxist theory, which holds that colonialism and capitalism are inseparable entities. In contrast, Johannes Verkuyl and Hendrik Kraemer, Dutch missiologists, regard colonialism as arising for a various reasons. Kraemer defined colonialism as:

> A country is a colonial country where the real dynamic economic activity is in foreign hands, nourished by foreign capital, directed by foreign personnel, inspired by a foreign spirit of enterprise, primarily directed towards foreign interests. A colonial country is therefore a country which lives . . . in a state of helotism; a country of which people and land are, in the last instance, instruments and means for foreign purposes and where foreign decisions determine these peoples destiny.[79]

Verkuyl's definition of colonialism focused more on the economic issue. He wrote:

> The economic interests of the colonizers were given top priority and the economic interests of the colonized peoples were given second-rating at best . . . The economic drainage policy was typical of every imperialist economy. The largest part of the

---

78   Donald McGavran, "Education, Religion and the Advancement of India."
79   Heinrik Kraemer, *World Cultures and World Religions* (Philadelphia: The Westminster Press, 1960), 65.

profits was siphoned off to the investors of capital. No balance was sought between the interests of the colonized land and the interests of the capitalists.[80]

These definitions, descriptive of India's situation in the 1930s, are more appropriate to development in Africa and Indonesia. The British colonial attitude toward India, dominated by economic interest, as it was, also displayed social concern for the general population. In an interview, McGavran described his assessment of Britain's rule in India.

England unified India and gave it a just, fair government. The British were not corrupt and their administration was enormously superior to anything India had ever experienced for centuries. Britain established irrigation systems, courts of law, systems of education, and brought about the suppression of thugery (castes of thieves who lived by robbery).[81]

India, the prized jewel in Britain's empire, was the first colony to be granted sovereignty and independence.

Issues concerning colonialism and nationalism swirled around India throughout the first half of the twentieth century. During the height of the *swaraj* (independence) movement led by the Congress workers, the missionary community remained for the most part loyal to the British government. Those missionaries who identified with the Gandhi led Congress movement, were often labeled as "recreant priests" and Verrier Elwin was accused of being a "traitor."[82]

Missionaries, who were sympathetic to the Indian struggles for independence, were in some cases not permitted reentry into the country if they departed for furlough. Although our contemporary sympathies may lie with the Indians in their struggle for independence, the issues involved more than just the political realm. There was a definite religious element tied to the movement, hence the missionaries could not always endorse Gandhi's aims. The Bishop of Nagpur declared something of his mixed feelings on the issue:

[Mahatma's] aims appear to be the re-establishment of some form of the Vedic Religion and culture in India, when his party has the power. If an Indian Christian desires to be a nationalist and to see India self-governing he has all my sympathy and so long as his activities are constitutional, my support. But your sympathies are with Mahatma Gandhi and the Congress party—i.e., definitely Hindu and opposed to the spread of Christianity.[83]

---

80   Johannes Verkuyl, *Break Down the Wall*, trans. Leis B. Smedes (Grand Rapids: Eerdmans, 1973), 64–65.

81   Donald McGavran, interview by Vern Middleton, April 18, 1984.

82   Elwin Verrier, *Religious and Cultural Aspects of Khadi* (Sarvodaya Prachuralaya, 1964), 89–90.

83   Ibid., 91.

McGavran endorsed the Bishop's position. He judged colonialism to be a vehicle through which the gospel could be disseminated, churches planted, and God's kingdom extended. Nevertheless, he detested the racist overtones and the institutional domination of the British Empire.

Indian Coworkers

Although McGavran's bias was pro-British, numerous factors thoroughly committed him to total identity with India. Due to his fluency in Hindi and his comprehension of the Indian culture, he was sensitive to the Indian mind-set as he established friendships with Indian Christian leaders. These were deeper than his friendships with his fellow missionaries. Hira Lal and George Hamilton Singh were Indian men who were more than equals in his estimation. Hira Lal's grasp of the Satnami culture, (Satnami culture prevails in the State of Chattisgarh) and his status in that community, were invaluable to McGavran in unlocking the cultural door and gaining an entrance for the gospel. McGavran deeply respected Hira Lal. He would reach down, touch Hira Lal's feet, and address him as guru, honoring him according to Indian custom. In 1934, McGavran wrote an article in *World Call* entitled, "Keenness, Initiative, Vision: The Story of G. H. Singh," which described this Indian colleague as leader and administrator within the mission. These were only two of the many Indian men whom McGavran regarded as peers in every respect.

In 1932, in an article titled "In India," he described the working relationship between Indians and the Westerner. "The Indian Church is working side-by-side with the Western Church. A close harmonious relationship in a common task is being worked out."[84] He went on to cite the National Christian Council as being equally Indian and Western in membership.

In 1937, when most missions were sending home promotional material about the exploits of their missionaries, McGavran wrote and published a book entitled, *Founders of the India Church*. The book was in essence, a series of case studies of Indian men instrumental in initiating people movements among their castes and tribes. Pickett outlined the contribution of these leaders in chapter one of his book, *Christian Mass Movements in India*. McGavran expanded this material by gathering information from missionaries working in the areas where these movements took place. He checked for accuracy of the material in records and other sources of history. The author of such a book can hardly be labeled as promoting missionary triumphalism.

---

84   McGavran, "In India," *World Call* 14 (June 1932).

McGavran Advocated an Indian Lifestyle for Missionaries

While on furlough, from 1930 to 1932, McGavran formed an ad hoc committee of UCMS missionaries to spearhead a movement to take a 10 percent reduction in salaries. This committee polled UCMS missionaries in Africa, China, India, Japan, Mexico, and South America. Eighty percent of them agreed that a voluntary cut was a good move in light of the economic depression.[85]

The McGavran family in India with ("Uncle") Chet and ("Aunt") Miriam Terry, missionaries in the UCMS.

Another demonstration of his desire to rise above colonial patterns was highlighted during the depression years of 1932–34. With three major cutbacks in overall support between June and September 1933, totaling a 50 percent drop in receipts, McGavran faced an impossible situation.[86] Being a creative thinker, he immediately began to challenge missionaries to a simpler lifestyle. In 1933, the *International Review of Missions* published his article entitled, "Missionaries and Indigenous Standards of Living." This article grappled with the problem of missionary salaries contrasted to their national peers, and also deals with the problem of missionary wealth. He pointed out that "the arbitrary power, which superior wealth gives, exercises a dwarfing power on personality."[87] However, he also stated that those missionaries who adopt totally indigenous patterns of living, eventually become a burden on fellow missionaries, because their health breaks down.

---

85   Donald McGavran, letters from New York to Corey, Indianapolis, (obtained from NV), Jan. 21, 1932, Jan. 5, 1932, Feb. 21, 1932.

86   Donald McGavran, letter from Jabalpur, to US Christian Churches, (obtained from USCWM), Sept. 1933.

87   Donald McGavran, "Missionaries and Indigenous Standards of Living," *International Review of Mission* 22 (1933), 33–49. International Review of Mission hereafter cited as *IRM*.

McGavran gathered twenty missionary families together to engage in an experiment in Landour, Mussoorie in June 1933. They called themselves the Fellowship for Ventures in Simpler Living. He warned that they could be misunderstood as a protest against customary missionary practise, or an attack on the way other missionaries live.[88] By autumn, the McGavran family had adjusted their lifestyle to where they were living on less than fifty naipaisa per day per person (equivalent to twenty US cents in those days). However, just as he had predicted, missionaries not involved in the program interpreted this lifestyle as an attack on their own way of living, and so the strategy was dropped to keep harmony within the mission. The realization gradually dawned on him that the regimentation needed for such a simple lifestyle required a semi-monastic order where people took vows of poverty. McGavran complained that indifference, inertia, and selfishness acted as counterforces to his concepts.[89] This was not a total defeat though, for some change did take place in the attitudes of his fellow missionaries. McGavran later recalled an incident where he took G. H. Singh to tea with him at one of the missionary bungalows in Jabalpur. The hostess exclaimed as she poured the tea that, Singh is the first Indian to drink tea in our home.[90]

Before he shelved the idea of a simpler lifestyle, he developed a check sheet which assisted in cutting down on expenses, and directed the energies of missionaries toward developing wholesome relationships with the Indian people. Here are a few of his recommendations:

- Live in an Indian town and Indian style house.
- Travel 3rd class (on the train).
- Walk or ride a bike habitually.
- Wear habitually clothes made of *khaddar* (homespun cotton).
- Identification with Indian neighbors.
- Subscribe to a magazine edited by an Indian.
- Entertain Indian friends for pleasure once a week.
- Visit Indian homes.
- Learn an Indian instrument.
- Belong to some Indian Literary Society.
- Learn polite forms and become graceful in their use.
- Make definite improvement in knowledge of vernacular.[91]

The above suggestions make it obvious that McGavran did not entertain a colonial lifestyle. He was always very Indian in his ways and sensitive to their feelings.

---

88 Donald McGavran, "Strategy for Simple Living" (unpublished MS, [obtained from USCWM], June 1933), 7.
89 Donald McGavran, letter from Jabalpur to Wm. Paton, London, (obtained from USCWM), March 9, 1934.
90 Donald McGavran, interview by Vern Middleton, April 18, 1984.
91 McGavran, "Strategy for Simple Living," 9.

Publications on Colonial Issues

McGavran's article, "Paternalism and the Stony Heart," also shows his balance on the issue of colonial attitudes. A by-product of colonialism was paternalism, and McGavran described it as:

> Paternalism meant that the padre . . . stood in the relation of a kindly father to his converts and to the members of the Christian community. He was called "papa." He provided work for the needy. He educated the children of Christians entirely at mission expense. He provided free medicines to all, including Christians . . . He dealt out justice to members of the Christian community, settled quarrels. He arranged marriages. In the case of orphan reared communities, he had been in very fact for 15 years the father and mother to thousands of Christians.[92]

With a growing emphasis on the indigenous church, there was generalized reaction against paternalism. McGavran pointed out that the move away from paternalism was good and necessary, to get the church off the basis of an isolated orphanage community on which the mission planned to spend itself indefinitely . . . and on to the basis of a vital Christian Movement spreading with inherent power throughout the established people of the land.[93] As well, McGavran warned that such a reaction, although good in itself, could swing too far until the missionary became critical and distant, superior, and unapproachable.[94] He described the need to retain the essential ingredient of love.

> The wrong of paternalism lies not in the relationship, but in the way the relationship expresses itself. The trouble is not love, but ignorant love. If in the desire to avoid ignorant indulgent love, we eliminate love itself, we sin, possibly more grievously than did the paternalists.[95]

In a letter to the *Christian Evangelist*, McGavran dealt more pointedly with the issue of colonialism. Apparently, an American minister of the Disciples of Christ dropped in on the mission, enroute home from a conference in Australia. He wrote an editorial on the colonial like lifestyle of the missionaries. McGavran's reply kindly agreed with many of his observations but went on to clarify his mistaken impressions. McGavran defined colonialism as follows:

---

92   McGavran, "Paternalism and the Strong Hearts," *Sahayak Patrika*, 8 (Nov. 11, 1936).
93   Ibid., 8.
94   Ibid., 7.
95   Ibid., 7.

The genuine colonial pattern meant that white men operating a colony and paying themselves out of funds raised in that colony lived on an exaggerated western scale, and paid nationals in the service of the colony on a lesser scale simply because they were not white men . . . You take the tax money of our citizens and pay yourselves ten times what you pay our citizens of equal qualifications. Unequal pay on the basis of nationality was part and parcel of the colonial pattern.[96]

As McGavran went on to clarify the problem of unequal salaries paid to the missionary in contrast with the Indian pastor, he likened the situation to an army in battle. The salary the army receives is the concern of the sending nation, and it is their business what they wish to pay their men as they fight, although other nations may pay their soldiers doing the same task an entirely different rate. In the same way, the missionary is not a colonialist because his funds are sent from churches overseas; the salary he receives is the business of the home church, not that of the people he serves on the foreign field.

TRANSITION IN THE SECOND TERM

McGavran's writings during this second term in India reflect a decidedly stronger spiritual conviction. Three distinct issues converged in his life to produce this transformation of belief and apologetic. First, his involvement with the Mid-India Christian Council led to a more forthright style of evangelism. One has only to read through the publications of the *International Review of Missions* during the 1930s to sense the strong commitment to proclaim the gospel and persuade men to embrace Christ. Secondly the social unrest among the oppressed castes of India greatly increased in intensity throughout this period and so did McGavran's sensitive spirit to the plight of the Untouchable castes (known as *Dalit*s in the twenty-first century). Dalits motivated him to become a vigorous champion of their rights. However, he also realized that social concern was not the only answer, but that they needed to be transformed by the power of the gospel. Thirdly, the most significant factor grew out of his involvement with Pickett as they continued to research the people movement potential in Central India. McGavran drew inspiration and spiritual direction from this time and creative insights blossomed into new a dimension of thinking and resourcefulness in his life. Every waking moment seemed consumed with a passion to see men and women won to Christ and incorporated into the church.

Thus his second term was one of radical transition, as he made a geographical shift from Harda to Jabalpur and then on to Chattisgarh. He left much of his educational ministry and took up administration and evangelism with great passion. The focus of his ministry switched from the classes to the masses, and he became a champion for the rights of the Untouchables. His apologetics changed from Christianizing through a gradual

---

96   McGavran, open letter to the *Christian Evangelist*, (obtained from USCWM), (1952).

transformation of the basic concepts of nations and tribes, to one of direct discipling through multi-individual conversions of groups in the receptive castes. He changed from a ministry which essentially challenged philosophic Hinduism to a thrust which confronted popular animistic concepts at the village level. In 1938 he published an article in the *United Church Review* entitled, "India's Oppressed Classes and Religion." This apologetic for mission to the Untouchables is developed in chapter four.

Active Membership and Involvement in the Mid-Indian Christian Counsel

There are three natural links between McGavran and the International Missionary Council (hereafter known as IMC). The first was that he belonged to the Disciples of Christ churches. Their constitution expressed a perception of themselves as a mediating spiritual agency in the midst of other denominational bodies, a kindred philosophy to the IMC. Secondly, his uncle, Herbert Anderson, served as the India Secretary of the Baptist Missionary Society, and became the first secretary for the National Council of Churches of India (NCCI). He played such a vital part in the movement that it was said, the National Council would soon have ceased to exist without him.[97] McGavran's third major link arose from the focus and interests of the National Christian Council of India, the Evangelistic Forward Movement of the 1930s, as well as the Mass Movement Research they had authorized, were both influential in igniting McGavran's evangelistic fervor. Thus the National Christian Council of India exercised a major influence on McGavran's spiritual pilgrimage.

Anderson and the National Christian Council of India

Herbert Anderson, a charter member of the National Missionary Council of India, was the personality and power which brought the agency into being on February 4, 1914. Anderson served eight years as secretary of this new organization, before retiring from the office due to poor health. A minute of the Council declared in 1922 that because of the thoroughness of his work and the ability, tact, and courtesy with which he discharged the duties of his office, the Council has been firmly established.[98]

Anderson made occasional visits to the McGavrans in Jabalpur and Chattisgarh after his retirement, and McGavran respected him and sought his council on several issues. His uncle's identity with the National Council certainly made McGavran aware of the significance of the movement.

---

97   Baago, *A History of the National Christian Council of India*, 17.
98   Ibid., 18.

The Evangelistic Forward Movement and the Mass Movement Thrusts

The Evangelistic Forward Movement and the Mass Movement campaigns were essentially one and the same. Sherwood Eddy brought the inspiration for the Evangelistic Forward Movement from China. In 1916, the Council voted:

> That this Council is of the opinion that the Evangelistic Forward Movement now taking place in South India is of such importance that it is desirable that this Council shall appoint a committee to act as a central bureau of information, a clearing house of methods and ideas for this movement, and an advisory body to aid the various Missions and Churches in all matters in which they desire help in promoting the movement in their respective areas.[99]

As a result, evangelism became a priority of the missionaries for several years (1916–20). New evangelistic campaigns were launched, innovative methods using films and literature were employed, and conferences on evangelism were held for lay-workers and pastors alike. There was excitement over this emphasis, and missionaries said, "For once the Churches and missions were doing what they were supposed to do."[100]

During the decade of the 1920s, the tide of evangelism sank to a very low level. Two factors contributed to the dampening evangelistic zeal. Some missionaries were becoming uncomfortable with evangelistic methodologies which brought Christianity into confrontation with Hinduism and Gandhi's Congress Movement encouraged a growing nationalistic spirit. Many Indian Christian leaders therefore opted for less direct patterns of evangelism. The second factor was the growing influence of liberal theology, which stressed social service. Baago described the raison d'être of missions in India during the '20s.

> Rather than making converts, the purpose of Christian Mission was now considered to be the permeation of Indian society with Christian ideals. The goal was no longer primarily to organize a Church, but to co-operate in the universal establishment of the Kingdom of God in all human spheres. The principles of the Social Gospel Movement had taken possession of the field.[101]

But with the Great Depression looming on the horizon in the early 1930s, the conservative missionaries regained prominence, but political, religious, economic and social forces in India were in powerful foment. The Independence movement under

---

99   Ibid., 21.
100 Ibid., 40.
101 Ibid., 44.

Gandhi's leadership was creating nationalistic aspirations; communism, as an ideology, became popular in many sectors; and the mass movement phenomena among the Dalits made the general Hindu populace aware of the need for religious reform. The growing industrial power of Britain was creating havoc and severe dislocation among the weaver and pottery castes in India.

This increasing unrest and agitation across India produced a new sense of the worth and dignity of the individual. Leaders within the National Council of Churches viewed all this as the Spirit's work of making a highway for the Evangel.[102]

A retreat on evangelism was convened in Nagpur by the National Council of Churches (hereafter known as NCC), in August 1932. As an outgrowth of that event, the NCC Council resolved that:

> Believing as we do that the promoting of evangelism is the essential work of the Church and seeing in the present grave world situation an urgent call to a fuller expression of Christian life . . . and to bolder and more convincing presentation of the Christian Gospel, we request the officers of the Council to issue a call to the Churches in India to take up the work of evangelism with fresh resolve and a more earnest response to the leading of the Lord.[103]

Providentially, the Forward Thrust in Evangelism regained momentum by 1932 and for ten years remained the central focus of the NCC Publications of the Council. It reflected deep spiritual concern for proclaiming the gospel to the unconverted and a renewing zeal for evangelism. The appointment of Bishop Azariah as chairman and Rev. J. Z. Hodge, as secretary of the NCC—both evangelists at heart who desired more than anything else to see churches planted throughout India—gave added impetus.

Pickett's book, *Christian Mass Movements in India*, published in early 1933, was an additional force in the renewed emphasis on evangelism. The insights and drama of the research therein stimulated the Christian leaders, and liberal voices were subdued in the light of Pickett's research. He wrote:

> There should be no question about the primacy of the spiritual aim . . . Nothing but failure has proceeded from missionary efforts in which the order of Jesus has been reversed. In one area several highly qualified missionaries tried to lift a group of outcastes from social degradation, poverty and illiteracy as a preliminary to their ministering to their spiritual needs.[104]

---

102 J. Z. Hodge, "Evangelism in India," *IRM* 24 (1935), 498.

103 J. Waskom Pickett, *Christian Mass Movement in India* (Lucknow: Lucknow Press, 1933), 346–47.

104 McGavran, letter from New York to Corey, Indianapolis, (obtained from NV), August 30, 1931.

Meanwhile, McGavran's spiritual pilgrimage after daughter Mary Theodora's death led him to a radical new position on evangelism. While on furlough in August 1931, he wrote the following:

> Our mission has . . . no mass movement. We have to date largely concerned ourselves with bringing up a Christian community of orphans. I personally think the present distribution of mission forces needs to be reconsidered in an attempt to put more of our force into direct persistent evangelism. We cannot go on nursing the Christian community and content ourselves with indirect influence on Hinduism.[105]

Mary and Donald McGavran with their children, post-1930.
Jean (left), Malcolm (center), and Helen (right).

When he returned to India in October 1932, he was in step with the prevailing evangelistic spirit. The Forward Movement in Evangelism galvanized the Christians into action. Churches were challenged to establish five-year goals and leaders set aside Sundays to consider the challenge of various dimensions of evangelism. Tracts and literature were prepared, each mission designated counselors on evangelism, and Christ was uplifted corporately and individually.[106]

The response to the Forward Movement was remarkable. McGavran published an assessment in the November 28, 1934 issue of *Sahayak Patrika*. There was an increased emphasis upon the church—ways and means sought to strengthen it. The second article was the "Rising Tide of Evangelism, of Expectancy, of Prayer, and Consecration."[107]

---

105 Hodge, "Evangelism in India," 499–501.
106 Donald McGavran, "Rising Tide of Evangelism," *Sahayak Patrika*, NCCI, (Nov. 28, 1984).
107 Donald McGavran, "Revival in Sterile Areas," *United Church Review* (Sept.–Oct. 1936).

DISCIPLING DUMARS

Like all missionaries in India, the McGavrans employed a sweeper woman to clean their house and wash the floors. He spoke to Janki one day in 1933 about her spiritual condition. He asked, "Why have you people not become Christians?" Her response was, "Sir, we would have become Christians long ago if only someone had urged it."[108] This conversation grieved McGavran, as her employment on the mission compound brought her into daily contact with twenty-five missionaries and no one had ever bothered to share Christ with her.

McGavran seized a newly recognized opportunity. He began to set aside one night per week for concentrated evangelism among the Dumars, employing diverse methods such as dramas, films, and *bhajans* (Indian music). Out of all this he developed a principle of church growth, which was to use a method as long as it held the attention of the people, then discard it when it was no longer effective. After fifteen months of ministry, he had the joy of baptizing four families.[109]

At this point in his missionary career, McGavran was already hopeful of starting a people movement among the Dumars. He delayed the baptisms of Janki and her husband, Mohan, hoping many others would join them. Janki said, "We are ready but we wait until others are also ready." As this evangelizing discipleship pattern developed, McGavran organized new believers into a *prem sabha* (a spiritual love gathering) for regular nurture and worship, with an aim to develop an indigenous church. He therefore incorporated a lot of Dumar culture in the spiritual exercises.[110]

The Dumar movement was not without struggles and embarrassment. At Christmas 1934, McGavran encouraged the Dumars to prepare a pageant. This they did very acceptably, but he had not anticipated their behavior during the changing of scenes. In that context, they resorted to jokes and pantomime from their Hindu days. McGavran put an immediate stop to the raucous goings on.[111]

As believers were added to the small Dumar church, the caste reacted vigorously. The wife of one of the believers was kidnapped, but police intervention soon got her back home.[112] In 1936, when the McGavrans had to consider a move, the future of the Dumar movement was a major concrern. However, the foundations were laid strongly and the church continued to grow. By 1947, McGavran reported over fifty families had believed in Christ and turned from idolatry.

---

108 Donald McGavran, "Preaching the Word in India," *World Call* (Sept. 1947): 16.

109 Donald McGavran, letter from Jabalpur to John and Helen McGavran, (obtained from USCWM), May 19, 1935.

110 Donald McGavran, interview by Vern Middleton, April 13, 1984.

111 Donald McGavran, letter from Jabalpur to the District Superintendant of Police, Jabalpur, (obtained from USCWM), May 1936.

112 Donald McGavran, "India 1934" (unpublished MS, [obtained from USCWM Archives]).

CHRISTIAN MASS MOVEMENTS IN INDIA

Waskom Pickett jolted India's Christian community into new spiritual boldness in 1933, with the publication of *Christian Mass Movement in India* which gave believers in Christ new optimism. The leadership of the NCC led in creating new strategies for gathering the spiritual harvest. This book, combined with the economic depression and increased spiritual awareness brought a new sense of direction. McGavran described some of this in his annual report for 1934:

> The attention of the entire force is being turned to the redemption from sin offered through the sacrifice of Jesus our Lord, to the power of the indwelling Christ and to the gift of the Holy Spirit. Our message is not education . . . our message is not medicine . . . our message is not rural uplift. But our message is Jesus Christ, the power of God unto salvation.[113]

He hailed the book as the most significant missionary publication of the twentieth century.[114] Repeatedly between 1935 and 1938, he referred to and developed ideas from *Christian Mass Movements in India*. The NCC created the Mass Movement Committee for the Mid-India Council of Churches in 1934. Christian leaders consulted Pickett regularly about various problems in potential people movement areas. NCC headquarters was located in Nagpur. McGavran was able to meet Pickett there occasionally and their friendship grew strong.

Chhindwara Retreat

As chairman of the Mass Movement Committee, McGavran organized a conference on people movements at Chhindwara, forty miles north of Nagpur, in April, 1935. Pickett was the keynote speaker, and Rev. G. S. Ingram led the devotional sessions. Out of this conference came the inspiration and decision to conduct a mass movement survey of the Central India region in January–February 1936, implemented by Pickett. Several other important decisions came out of the Chhindwara conference.

1. Evangelists were to be loaned from one mission to receptive areas.
2. Churches were encouraged to cultivate networks with unsaved relatives.
3. Readings and study sessions centered on Pickett's book were arranged for every region.

---

113 Donald McGavran, "Book Review of Christian Mass Movement in India," *World Call* (June 1935): 29.

114 McGavran, letter from Jabalpur, *Bulletin* no. 5 to members of The Mass Movement Council, (obtained from USCWM), May 18, 1935.

4. McGavran was to publish a weekly News Bulletin on Mass Movements. He carried on this enterprise for two years.
5. An organizational committee worked with McGavran to prepare the Pickett research team.
6. There was an urgent call to prayer for a people movement among Central India castes and tribes.
7. Christian leaders were urged to recapture the primacy of soul winning.[115]

PICKETT'S SECOND BOOK

Pickett and McGavran shared many times of discussion of principles relating to church growth, as expressed in the publication of the book, *Christ's Way to India's Heart* in 1938. For five years church growth had dominated the thinking of a growing number of Christian leaders in India. McGavran described its origins in *International Review of Mission* (*IRM*):

> This dominant philosophy grew up incidentally. The mission situation created the philosophy . . . a missionary arrived, preached the Gospel, gathered a band of converts . . . opened a hospital . . . built churches . . . bred better cattle . . . helped to combat child marriage, and to stamp out tuberculosis. This program in some places built great churches and in others it did not. Why? . . . The correct answer now seems to be that fruitful fields have developed underlying conceptions which have greatly aided in the building of a living growing church.[116]

In the same article, he said Pickett was the originator of this approach.

> The philosophy of church growth formulated by Bishop Pickett can be considered only as indicating the lines along which the Church can cooperate intelligently with God in His great task of redemption. As Bishop Azariah writes, "It is our duty to watch the movements of the Spirit lest we frustrate God's work by our unbelief, indifference or mismanagement of potential situations."[117]

McGavran recognized that church growth could be examined from two perspectives: as a philosophy; or as God's action, creating new churches.[118]

Pickett's book contained seven foundational concepts of church growth. McGavran identified them as follows:

---

115 Donald McGavran, review of *Christ's Way to India's Heart*, by J. Waskom Pickett, *IRM* (June 1938), 2. *International Review of Mission* will be hereafter known as *IRM*.
116 Ibid.
117 Ibid.
118 Ibid.

1. That conversion of an individual is definitely less desirable than the conversion of all members of the social unit to which that individual belongs . . .
2. That new converts must be left in their ancestral surroundings, and must expect to earn their living in their former fashion . . .
3. God's plan for the conversion of India is to preach the Gospel to the poor . . .
4. The natural avenue for the spread of religion is through blood relations . . .
5. Spiritual values must be stressed . . . The concepts which the Christian Gospel gives them of themselves . . . are worth incomparably more to them than any direct social or economic service which the Church could render . . .
6. The centrality of the Church as contrasted with mission institutions . . .
7. The doctrine of mobility . . . that as God opens doors, mission and church resources be taken away from sterile areas and poured into the new fields.[119]

These essential ideas kindled the church growth spirit in McGavran and launched him into a crusade which would occupy the remaining years of his life.

McGAVRAN'S WATERSHED YEAR: 1935–36

Surprises and shocks are part of the process of life. Yet there are events that occur in the lives of men which are like a conversion experience, with an impact which can totally reorient one's life. Such was the case from November 1935 to April 1936 for McGavran. Another appropriate title for this section could be, "McGavran, the Reluctant Prophet." Apart from the death of Mary Theodora, this was the most difficult period in McGavran's entire missionary career. Looking back, it is easy to see the guidance of the Lord, but as McGavran experienced the traumatic events which came cascading in upon him, he wondered if God had forsaken him.

The Great Reversal

In November 1935 at the field missionary conference, Mr. W. B. Alexander, who had been field secretary-treasurer between 1928 and 1932, was voted into office again. McGavran was half expecting this decision. However, when it came, it was a considerable blow to his personal self-esteem. Mr. Yocum, the general secretary of the mission, wrote of his surprise at this unexpected turn in events.

> Your announcement that Mr. Alexander had been elected secretary of the Mission and that the letter you wrote, were considerable surprise. From what you say the Mission evidently feels that you should be released from the details of secretaryship

---

119 McGavran, letter from Jabalpur to G. S. Ingram, Agra, India, (obtained from USCWM), April 28, 1935.

that you might give your time and strength in the field where your interests lie and where there seems just now to be so much promise of fruitage . . . It does seem to me that we are needing more evangelism in our education and more education in our evangelism. You have the educational training and background and you also have the evangelistic passion.[120]

(from left to right) Winifred, Malcom, Helen, Jean, Mary, and Donald (around 1935).

For several months McGavran considered resigning from the mission and exploring the possibility of transferring to another. Leonard Theological College in Jabalpur approached him and offered him the position of principal. This theological college was growing in its prestige and influence, and the offer was attractive for it suited McGavran's training. He wavered in indecision.

I was an educational missionary and did not feel evangelism was my gift . . . If my people think so little of my educational experience and expertise as to put me out into village work, I'll leave this mission . . . All my specialization in Hindi and my study of Sanskrit will be wasted.[121]

During those days of indecision and soul-searching, Herbert Anderson paid a visit. When McGavran shared with him the inner turmoil of his soul, Anderson advised against leaving the Disciples of Christ Mission. He pointed out that others who had followed such

---

120 McGavran, letter from Jabalpur to Pastor Herman, Fullerton Church, California, (obtained from USCWM), Sept. 2, 1935.
121 Ibid.

a path were regarded as being somewhat unstable, and by March 1936, McGavran began to accept the situation. Mary reflected this in a letter written to the Howards, her parents.

> I have been convinced that we probably will be given Evangelistic work very soon out in the open spaces where we can do what we feel needs being done. Don has started such a fine work here in Jubbulpore [Jabalpur] among the Dumars, a sweeper caste. I hope Tom Hill will catch the vision of the possibilities and do a fine work too. So sometime during the next month you will hear of us moving to the country. I'm glad! You mustn't think of this move and change as a demotion. Don will be Director of Evangelism for the Mission and now being free from executive duties will be able to do a whole time job of soul searching and saving. It is a challenging position we face.[122]

Although the letter was positive and optimistic, it does contain guarded statements that reveal something of the trauma they were going through as a couple. Mary enjoyed living in Jabalpur and the many conveniences of city life. One member of the McGavran family who looked forward to the move was Malcolm, their six-year-old son. He said, "I'll be glad when we won't have to be here in Jubbulpore for there are too many meetings Mother and Father have to attend."[123]

Reasons Why McGavran Was Not Reelected to Office

It is difficult to understand fully all the reasons for McGavran's replacement by Alexander as field secretary-treasurer. There were many factors involved, outside of McGavran's own situation. He had faced some very awkward issues while administrating the mission through the depression years. The drastic cuts in salaries and field expenses placed him squarely in the cross fire between the missionaries and the board. With a 50 percent loss in income, he was forced to mediate disputes between the missionaries, which arose from monetary restrictions and reallocations. This, of course, did not make him a popular administrator.

In contrast with to promotional presentation he made at the mission's Golden Jubilee meetings in November 1932, he began to see things somewhat differently when he became administrator. The critical economic situation forced him to reexamine the overall ministry of the Disciples of Christ in India, and his later writings reveal something of his feelings during his tenure as field secretary-treasurer. He wrote:

> An entire mission among unresponsive men and women spent fifty years and $3,000,000. At the end of that time it had twelve congregations totaling 2,845

---

122 Mary McGavran, letter from Jabalpur to Isaiah and Sarah Howard, Muncie, Indiana, (obtained from NV), March 27, 1936.

123 Ibid.

communicant members. At the jubilee, a speaker, lifted to heights of enthusiasm by the occasion, ventured the prophecy that the next fifty years would see another dozen congregations established with a total communicant membership he hoped of 5,000.[124]

The mission saw an annual conversion rate from caste Hindus of only five or six persons per year. However, no one seemed overly concerned with this lack of growth; after all, the missionaries were busily engaged in doing many good works. By letters and regular missives McGavran communicated dissatisfaction with the mission's progress. In one particular letter circulated to his fellow missionaries, he challenged each one of them to set aside just six hours per week for evangelism, and with some irony he questioned whether this was an unreasonable request, in view of what they were called by God to do. Apparently by November 1935, many of his colleagues must have been thinking of ways to put this theoretician on evangelism and church growth into a situation where he would experience what they experienced.

He was a trained educator, full of creative ideas, and as an administrator, he did not find office work particularly inspiring. He wrote, "I delegate [office work] mostly to Miss Hanna Fernandez."[125] Alexander, who replaced McGavran, was a skilled administrator who thrived on desk work. McGavran was not content to sit in an office, he always needed to be in the thick of the battle, and he admitted to being overextended with seminars and committee meetings, rather than administrative duties.

Three weeks before the election in November 1935, McGavran circulated a letter to his missionary colleagues. They misinterpreted his intent and considered the letter a solicitation for their vote.

> The Mission Secretary-Treasurer has a double function, looking after the routine duties here and the business administration of the mission; and the giving guidance to the best of his abilities as to ways and means of forwarding the work to the best advantage. The mission will have to decide who can best perform these functions ... Will the total work of the mission be better with Alexander in the office and McGavran in educational work some place; or with McGavran as Secretary and Alexander in evangelistic work. I think there is no question but that Mr. Alexander will do the office work better than I do. On the other hand if the mission group feels that the sort of thing your Secretary has been able to do during these past few years is what you want done, then I think McGavran in the Secretaryship and Alexander elsewhere would be a good strong combination.[126]

---

124 Donald McGavran, *How Churches Grow*, 102.
125 McGavran, letter from Jabalpur to missionary colleagues, (obtained from USCWM), Oct. 26, 1935.
126 Ibid.

Although the mission enjoyed close, family-type relationships, and several were second generation missionaries who had grown up together, issues were misunderstood. The letter created the opposite effect to what McGavran had intended. His constant stress on the mission's lack of producing new converts was like a thorn in the flesh to his fellow missionaries so that the following paragraph probably prejudiced them against him. He wrote:

> I am an educationist who believes in evangelism, and an organizer who wants to do as much for evangelism as he can, and who believes that everyone whether he is particularly suited for proclaiming the message or not, should be out often and frequently, proclaiming the message and trying to win men and women to Jesus Christ. I have led no one to Jesus Christ this past year, despite fairly regular efforts; but God calls on us to do it just the same.[127]

The other missionaries probably saw in this last paragraph a veiled threat that he would use the position of secretary to pressure them and make their lives miserable with his constant urging for church growth and accountability. Not only that, but he had been agitating for a reallocation of funds for much more money and effort to be directed towards evangelism. In a letter to Yocum in May of 1935 McGavran wrote:

> Our last Executive Committee meeting passed a minute asking Mr. Potee and myself to indicate how the existing division of resources between the Educational, Evangelistic, Medical and Administrative departments could be revised; but the motion was passed in an atmosphere of considerable tension. Since any reallocation of resources would give more money to the evangelistic work (which I happen to be heading) my efforts to secure re-allocation are looked on with some suspicion—that man McGavran seems to be pulling for his own work!! And further, the institutional bias of our mission is so strong, that I doubt if a rigidly democratic group such as ours can come through to a wise re-alignment of forces.[128]

In view of these things the missionaries possibly reasoned that it would be wise to put McGavran out of office so that they could get him out of their hair and off their backs. What they did not recognize, was that in so doing they released the tiger from his cage. Now he was free from the encumbrances of office duties, and able to direct all of his energies and creativity to evangelism. What they feared most came to pass, the tiger made off with a lion's share of the resources allocated for evangelism over the next ten years or so.

---

127 Ibid.
128 McGavran, letter from Jabalpur to Yocum, Indianapolis, (obtained from NV), May 26, 1935.

Appointment to the Satnami Area

The mission charged McGavran to take up the mass movement challenge of the Satnami people, which entailed a move of 150 miles south of Jabalpur. He accepted the appointment to be an evangelist in the Mungeli area on condition that two other couples be placed in the Satnami area with them, so that together a major thrust to harvest a people movement could be attempted. The mission agreed and three couples were assigned to the promising area centered around three towns, Takhatpur, Mungeli, and Fosterpur.

For the McGavran family, this was not simply a backward step in terms of prestige, position and power, and in some respects, a plunge into obscurity. Upon reflection, McGavran recently described the move as a heart rending, and heart searching experience.[129] Mungeli was less than forty miles from the proverbial jungles made famous by Rudyard Kipling and over thirty miles from the nearest railway. Had McGavran known at that point in time that he would serve there for seventeen years he probably would never have gone, but he anticipated a mass movement among the Satnamis within two or three years.

The cost of obeying the Lord's calling at this juncture was immense. However, just as Moses served on the backside of the desert for forty years before God could entrust leadership into his hands, so McGavran had to be willing literally to lose his life, as far as earthly ambitions and goals were concerned. In the '30s, missionary doctors and educators enjoyed considerable prestige and importance while ministering to India's classes, but missionary evangelists lived in obscurity laboring among the illiterate masses in rural villages.

The trauma of this change was heightened because this new appointment literally cut McGavran off from using his expertise in education, his apologetic developed for the higher castes, and his considerable linguistic skill in Hindi. He now had to learn and master a totally new language, the Chattisgarhi dialect. For the next five years McGavran kept a very low profile in India.

One other striking contrast occurred at this point. Waskom Pickett who was a great inspiration in McGavran's life and primarily responsible for bringing the mass movement issue before the world missionary community, also changed his venue of service. He left his ministry of assisting missionaries and evangelists as they labored with the people movements and became a Methodist Bishop, and so while Pickett went to Delhi to serve among India's elite, McGavran left his sphere of prominence and humbly went to serve among India's suffering Untouchables. McGavran even made a trip to the city of Nagpur in 1936 to plead in vain with Pickett not to accept the position of being bishop because the mass movements still needed his continued shepherding.

Moving to Mungeli was difficult in many respects, but there was one very positive factor; Donald's father, John McGavran, had been an early pioneer in that station in 1892.

---

129 Donald McGavran, interview by Vern Middleton, Aug. 12, 1982.

His son's profound respect for his father and the nostalgia of the mission's early beginnings may have assisted in the decision. However the strongest factor in his decision was his conviction that the Satnami caste of Chattisgarh were on the verge of massive conversion to Christ. Although this actual "people movement" never happened, due to political factors, McGavran was right in his assessment and he became God's instrument in initiating an unprecedented growth in church planting and evangelism in the mission.

SUMMARY

McGavran's administrative position as executive secretary-treasurer of the UCMS Indian field provided an ideal situation for the development of church growth missiology. He was ushered out of exclusive educational concerns into the mainstream of missionary administration. The budgetary cuts due to the Depression years made him examine the effectiveness of the mission. He was driven to the conclusion that evangelism was a neglected dimension and that it must be central to the very life of the church and the mission.

The publication of *Christian Mass Movements* in India along with a revived emphasis on The Forward Thrust in Evangelism recaptured an evangelical spirit among the missionaries. McGavran's involvement in the Mid-India Council of Churches placed him in the center of a bold new enthusiasm for proclaiming the gospel.

He experienced great spiritual growth in this era. Any latent professionalism of his first term gave way to a new vibrant love for his Lord and Master. Evangelism was no longer a set method, but an attitude of heart.

McGavran's fledgling attempts to create a small people movement among the Dumar caste in Jabalpur was excellent preparation for his Satnami ministry. Several church growth ideas emerged out of that context.

As administrator McGavran began to understand more fully the diverse implications of church-mission issues. Through the years, he drew heavily upon the insights gleaned during this time.

Although not reelected by his fellow missionaries, it was not a rejection of his leadership. His missionary colleagues continued to hold him in high respect, and he was consistently elected to the executive council for the next seventeen years.

CHAPTER FOUR

FROM THEORETICIAN TO PRACTITIONER

1936–54

God arranged numerous and varied circumstances in McGavran's life which fitted him for the Satnami ministry. Studies, planning conferences, and strategy sessions were held for several years prior to his relocation in Chattisgarh. These preparations worked toward the Satnami people movement, which, in 1935 he believed to be just around the corner. Chattisgarh is the region of thirty-six forts. This title was officially given to the new state created from this region in November 2000.

One of the million Satnamis who do not know Jesus Christ.

On September 10, 1934, McGavran was one of a large group of missionaries and Indian pastors who surveyed and assessed the Satnami region to determine receptivity. McGavran wrote optimistically about the event, "Our area in Chattisgarh calls for a mass movement work amongst the Satnamis with definite expectation that someday the entire group of 600,000 will decide for Christ."[130]

---

130   Donald McGavran, circular letters from Jabalpur to US Supporters, (obtained from USCWM), Oct. 13, 1934.

While working on this survey, McGavran met a Satnami by the name of Vishal Das, one of the five leaders of that caste. Although he had a reputation for being somewhat unscrupulous, he declared that he was ready to convert if he could bring fifteen to twenty villages into Christianity with him. McGavran's impressions of his approach were hopeful and yet guarded.

> He sees no hope for the Satnamis in Hinduism. He is sick and tired of the promises of Hindus. He wants revenge for all the oppression his people suffer. There is an impression that he may be flirting with us to gain something from the Hindus, nomination to the Assembly or something like that. Yet there is an earnest streak. He says, "Sahib, I think God kept me from becoming a Christian twelve years ago. I had no influence then. Now I can bring thousands to Him."[131]

McGavran was not so overcome with enthusiasm that he took everything this Satnami leader said at face value. He expressed his reservations to Waskom Pickett: "I am afraid of accepting as a Christian leader one whose heart is still essentially non-Christian and who looks on Christianity as a higher social division into which one might climb by professing His name."[132] Throughout the balance of McGavran's time as field secretary-treasurer his attention was repeatedly directed to the strong potential for a people movement among the Satnami caste.

CENTRAL INDIA SURVEY

The months after not being reelected were exceedingly difficult for McGavran, but he used the time between December 1935 and June 1936 to do many things he normally would never have had time for. During this period he was "waiting for God's guidance in the matter."[133]

Less than two months after the election defeat, while still in the throes of indecision, he had to fulfill a previously scheduled research engagement with Pickett. The busy timetable for this inquiry began January 13, 1936 and terminated on February 18, a period of thirty-eight days.[134] Pickett had to cut short his research time, which left McGavran to survey two whole districts on his own; that of Jagdalpur, Bastar State, and Mandla District, for additional eight days.[135]

---

131 Donald McGavran, letter from Jabalpur to Waskom Pickett, Bombay, India, (obtained from USCWM), Dec. 27, 1934.

132 Ibid.

133 Donald McGavran, letter from Jabalpur to Cy Yocum, Indiana, (obtained from NV), Nov. 20,1935.

134 Waskom Pickett, G. H. Singh, and Donald McGavran, *Christian Mission in Mid-India* (Lucknow: Lucknow Press, 1936), 11.

135 McGavran, "Mass Movement Committee Report," Submitted to the Mid-India Council, (obtained from USCWM), April 1936.

Nevertheless, the weeks he did spend with Pickett were life changing for him. The area researched was the exact region designated as Chattisgarh in November 2000. McGavran wrote of his impressions back in 1936:

> The mass movement survey of Mid-India has been most revealing. This area including our own mission, is full of openings which elsewhere, have led to the development of great mass movements and out of the them great Christian churches. We stand in the midst of unprecedented opportunity . . . There is a revolution in thinking going on in mission circles . . . The Spirit of God is on the march and . . . we have begun to get insight into how large populations are Christianized just as this spiritual revival is gathering force.[136]

While Pickett was working with McGavran in January 1936, they focused on the Bhil tribe in Western Madhya Pradesh, and they gave considerable assistance to the workers of the twelve missions already laboring among the Bhil tribe, who were in the beginning stages of a Bhil people movement to Christ in Rajputana (Rajasthan). During the months following the survey conducted by McGavran and Pickett, over 25,000 Bhils were baptised. A Bhil Evangelization Council was established at McGavran and Pickett's recommendation and a United Bhil-land Church became the ultimate objective.[137]

In 1938, Dr. F. H. Russell of the Canadian United Church Mission wrote:

> Our numbers are growing incessantly. We reported to the Church council in October last, a community of approximately 30,000. Our pastors and others who have been licensed to baptize have had much of their time taken up with the several thousand still waiting for baptism, but in addition to these large numbers have come in. I myself during my tour of the whole district had the privilege of baptizing large groups in dozens of villages. At the end of the Church year in October last we had 25 congregations organized among the Ratlam area Bhils. The organization of about 32 more has been arranged for and this will be seen to as opportunity offers.[138]

McGavran and Pickett wrote a book *Christian Missions in Mid-India*, later renamed *Church Growth and Group Conversion*. It expressed McGavran's earliest church growth ideas. Singh provided editorial comment. Included in the first two printings was a chapter describing the Bhil movement. In it, Pickett states, "We have nowhere at any time seen another mass movement affecting such a large portion of the population, for Bhils form

---

136 Donald McGavran, letter from Jabalpur to Cy Yocum, Indiana, (obtained from NV), June 3, 1936.
137 McGavran, "Mass Movement Committee Report."
138 Dr. Russell, letter from Toronto to A. E. Armstrong, Toronto, June 20, 1938.

95 percent of the rural population in the region to which we refer."[139] This chapter was replaced in the third edition (1956) after Russell retired to Canada in 1938 and the Arya Samaj, a right-wing upper caste Hindu reform movement, induced the Bhil tribe with threats and bribes to denounce their faith in Christ, which brought about wholesale reversions to animistic-Hinduism. This process of reconversion is called *Shuddi*, meaning purification. However, between 1970–2000 the region became receptive again, and rapid church growth took place in southeast Gujarat and northwest Maharashtra.

Proposed Bengal Mass Movement Survey

In June 1936, McGavran was invited to address the All-Bengal Christian Convention on the topic of "Mass Movements in Bengal," an area which included what is now West Bengal, Bangladesh, and Tripura. His responsibility was to challenge the missionaries and Indian Christian leaders and to formulate an overall strategy for a survey.

By 1936, the term "church growth" was already being used as a technical expression which McGavran employed in the document he presented in Bengal. He showed much skill and insight in recommending that the greatest opportunity for discipling men to Christ, in caste-wise movements, was among "the aboriginal tribes."[140] In this report he cited three reasons for tribal receptivity in Bengal.

> First, the aboriginal tribes of India are one group from whom Christian movements are constantly possible. Secondly, these aboriginal tribes have had large numbers of their people become Christians just across the provincial border . . . Thirdly, quite a number of beginning movements have already taken place . . . All indicate that this group of a million people . . . are definitely responsive to the Christian message.[141]

In this document, McGavran also cites animists as being receptive. He recognized the value of web movements among these people because of their strong social cohesiveness. McGavran also recommended that the second area of research focus on the Nomashudra community. (The term "Nomashudra" has been replaced by the term "Dalit.") He attributed their receptivity to the social unrest rampant in their midst, the awareness of the bankruptcy of Hinduism, and the attractiveness of the truth of the Christian faith. He urged that the best way to reach the unconverted Dalits was to rouse the existing Nomashudra churches to evangelize their own people.[142]

---

139 J. Waskom Pickett, "The Bhil Mass Movement," (Jabalpur: Mission Press, 1937), a reprint from the book *Christian Missions in Mid-India* (Lucknow: Lucknow Press, 1936), 13.

140 Donald McGavran, *Mass Movement Opportunities in Bengal* (Calcutta: Navana Printing Works, 1936), a ten-page booklet, MS for a message delivered in June of 1936.

141 Ibid.

142 Ibid., 4.

Several other recommendations were made in the above document, among them, the urgency of concentrating resources on receptive areas. Here again the fundamental concept of church growth, that of mobilizing resources to reap the harvest while it is ripe, was germinating.

McGavran's final statement in this document related to the receptivity of migrant communities in Calcutta. He urged that churches be established among the immigrant populations of Telegus and Sweeper castes who had settled there.[143]

The Tehri-Garhwal Hill Survey

In May 1936, McGavran was invited by the Methodist Mission to conduct a church growth survey of the mountainous district of Tehri-Garhwal, Uttar Pradesh. Since the area in question was near Landour, Mussoorie, where missionary families of northern India customarily retreated for a summer break, he used a portion of his holiday to undertake this research.

He took a train to Satal and Elmora and then, packsack on his back, he trekked some 150 miles westward back to Landour. He spent two weeks climbing mountains, probing the social and spiritual climate of remote villages for signs of receptivity and growth. His assessment was published and presented to the annual missionary convention held at Mussoorie. The outcome of his insights was the launching of a mission to send evangelists into the villages of the area. In a booklet entitled *The Evangelization of Tehri-Garhwal*, McGavran gave the following points in his summary: "That the 18 percent Oppressed Classes population in Tehri State be recognized by all missionaries and Christians visiting in or resident in Landour or Mussoorie as the people who are blood brothers to the great numbers of Untouchables who have become Christians elsewhere in India."[144]

Thus he focused on the importance of web movements to Christ and he also suggested that the people movements among particular castes in the plains of India were a possible sign of receptivity among similar peoples located in the Himalayan mountains. McGavran urged the missionaries to be diligent in their witness to the hill people they employed during their time in Landour. He stressed that each Christian employee could have the potential of returning to his home village and leading an "entire people to Christ."[145]

Another of his recommendations was to hire evangelists on a year-round basis. He insisted that evangelists have the following qualifications: that they be Christians from among the caste of people being reached, that they be men who understood and were prepared to disciple people in the context of their culture, and that they be willing to expend themselves without reserve for the salvation of their people.

---

143 Ibid., 6.
144 Donald McGavran, *The Evangelization of Teri-Garhwal* (Indian Witness,1936), 12
145 Ibid., 14.

As a part of his developing church growth thinking McGavran stated, "The message should be salvation through the cross of Christ, rather than a promise of mission schools and mission aid for those who become Christian. A self-growing church, self-supporting and self-propagating from the beginning should be the aim."[146]

One other significant perception was gleaned in this survey. McGavran noted that a people movement to Christ had occurred among the Dom castes in the district of Pauri that bordered on Garhwal. His strategy was to encourage the Dom Christians to spread the movement among their caste fellows in the adjoining villages of Garhwal.[147]

The Tehri-Garhwal research arose out of the corporate concern of vacationing missionaries in Landour, Mussoorie. His presentation stirred the community to launch the Hill Villages Mission which continued to function until 1980. In the twenty-first century, McGavran's vision for the conversion of peoples in the Tehri-Garhwal area has become a reality. Church-planting movements are taking place throughout the region.

Besides these research projects described above, McGavran was also instrumental in organizing an interdenominational gathering at the Free Methodist Seminary, Yavatmal (later known as Union Biblical Seminary), for discipling the Mahar caste in Maharashtra in 1938. The significance of that meeting must be understood in the light of the Ambedkar movement, which is described later in this chapter.

Through all of this research and activity, he was also getting a broad picture of the spiritual dynamics among many diverse missions of Central and Northern India. These projects were very appropriate and necessary activities for McGavran during the months between his departure from the office as secretary-treasurer and his assignment as missionary evangelist to the Satnami people.

CHURCH GROWTH CRUSADE

John R. Mott inspired Pickett, who in turn motivated McGavran with the following words: "If you are going to do much good in the church in India you must challenge the assumptions on which you find your associates working. If those assumptions are right, find out why and if they are not right prove them wrong and divert thinking and work in other directions."[148] This adage became an essential presupposition in McGavran's thinking, however, while he was secretary-treasurer of the mission, he acted with reserve, even though he saw many areas which desperately needed change.

From November 1935 to June 1936 he launched a crusade to move the mission from institutional inertia to evangelistic initiative. He began by sending several very probing letters to Alexander, the new secretary-treasurer, which were rejected as being

---

146 Ibid..
147 Ibid., 15.
148 Waskom Pickett, letter from Delhi, India to Donald McGavran, Landour, India, (obtained from USCWM), April 12, 1954.

too controversial and unnecessarily contentious. McGavran then took his appeal directly to the top, by writing letters to Cy Yocum, the executive secretary of the mission in the United States.

> Our church after 50 years has an adult membership of 2,500. During the five years ending 1932 our membership increased by 67. [Many] are coming to believe that the principal duty of the mission is to look after the interests of . . . Christians, to educate, medicate, marry, bury and employ . . . the Christian community . . . This policy is revealed in a budget in which 20 percent of the funds go to direct evangelism and 80 percent to institutional, educational and administrative work.[149]

In the same letter McGavran pressed Yocum to set new directions for the mission and to insist that evangelism receive the highest priority. His final appeal to Yocum was for new recruits filled with passion for the salvation of the unsaved. He correctly sensed that the day of opportunity was rapidly passing and he urged Yocum, "to send men and women called of God to preach the gospel and not fiddle around with institutions . . . men who want to convert a nation. Pauls, Patricks, Livingstones, men of brains and stamina and devotion."[150]

He also wrote several stirring articles and the *International Review of Missions* published his piece entitled, "Christ, Christian American, and the World."[151] In essence, his argument was that the religious philosophy of liberals stressed, "Let's clean up our own backyard before we carry the message to the non-Christian world"—faulty thinking at best, in McGavran's estimation. His answer to that charge was to "uplift Christ," people become Christians because of Christ. The response to this article was beyond expectation and reprints were made in England, Australia, and the United States. In 1936 he wrote again to Yocum, challenging him to press for change in the editorial policy of *World Call*, a publication of their churches. He stated that the central assumptions of the editor were that numbers don't count. "We are not scalp hunters . . . an increasing membership in peace, brotherhood, and just societies is the only real good. Who cares for the salvation of souls per se, we care only for salvation which makes men willing to pursue world peace . . . and to resist Imperialism and economic injustice."[152]

Another article he had written entitled "Revival in Sterile Areas" appeared in the Sept.–Oct. 1936 issue of the *United Church Review*, a widely circulated journal produced by the Presbyterians in North India. Apart from the term, "revival," which was used as a synonym for church growth, the contents read like a summary of *Understanding Church Growth*, which he published thirty-six years later. The essential vocabulary of church growth was in his thinking by that early date, and terms such as, "homogeneous unit," "conglomerate,"

149 Donald McGavran, letter from Landour, Mussoorie to Cy Yocum, (obtained from NV), June 1, 1936.
150 Ibid.
151 McGavran, *International Review of Missions* 25 (1936): 116–129.
152 Donald McGavran, letter from Landour to Cy Yocum, (obtained from NV), Sept. 2, 1936.

"quality growth versus quantity growth," and "group movement" instead of the term "mass movement" appear. He described group movements as occurring when "some great caste reconstructs its life, individual and corporate, around Jesus Christ."[153] This statement was a precursor to Alan Tippett's term, "multi-individual decisions" coined in the 1960s.

In that same article, he singled out five rationalizations for defeat, concepts he later described as "fog." These were: "great ingathering is a matter of time . . . mere length of occupation has very little to do with growth." The second was, "Our people are different . . . blaming it on racial characteristics is a common mistake." The third, "The day of caste-wise revivals has gone." The fourth, "Growth, revival and ingathering cannot possibly take place as long as the Christian community is as morally weak and spiritually unsurrendered as it is," and the fifth was, "Revivals start and continue by the will of God."[154]

Finally, he set forth five principles of church growth. One, that God prepares peoples for God's vineyard at certain junctures in history. Two, that the order of conversion is from the masses to the classes. Three, that conversion from the world occurs best within the context of groups and social units. Four, that the convert must become a winner of souls, especially for his own people. Five, that the homogeneous unit principle is the best context for church planting.[155] All of these he later expanded on in his lectures and book publications.

The Move to Mungeli

As mentioned in chapter three when the field executive committee appointed McGavran to the Satnami region as a missionary evangelist in 1936, it appointed two other missionaries to the same region, so there would be a concerted effort to produce a people movement. It was agreed that Edgar Moody and Herman Reynolds and their wives would join the McGavrans and that McGavran could engage in a special $25,000 fund-raising drive for the project.

McGavran's original intent was to launch the Satnami people movement and then move elsewhere in a period of three to four years, and he felt optimistic about the prospect of such an event. He said later, that had he known it would be a seventeen-year posting, he probably would never have gone. The confidence he had that a movement would begin very shortly was expressed in an article written within weeks of his arrival in Mungeli: "It is the belief . . . that there are twenty-thousand Satnamis who in their hearts believe Christianity is for them . . . but are held back by fear . . . It seems probable that when 500 are won over in a typical group movement other thousands will hasten to declare their faith."[156]

Factors contributing to his expectancy were that the Gara caste people movement in neighboring districts could act as a model for the Satnamis, and that the Mahar caste was

---

153 McGavran, "Revival in Sterile Areas," (Sept.–Oct. 1936), 2.
154 Ibid., 3–4.
155 Ibid., 5–6.
156 McGavran, *World Call* (Jan. 1937), 15.

embroiled in political and spiritual agitation led by B. R. Ambedkar, and finally there was a prevailing spiritual conviction that God was preparing the Untouchables throughout India for a massive exodus from the bondage of Hinduism.

CHURCH GROWTH AND THE CASTE ISSUE[157]

Before describing in detail the Ambedkar agitation and the Untouchable caste situation in India in the 1930s, a brief review of historic events leading up to that time is in order. For the high caste Hindu of India, the good news of Jesus Christ is regarded as the bad news about caste. From the beginning of Protestant era of missions, caste has been recognized as the primary barrier to the advance of the gospel and the extension of the Kingdom of God. The missionary educational methodologies developed in India were expressly designed to destroy caste. Pioneer missionaries to India, like William Carey and Alexander Duff, correctly perceived caste to be the fundamental instrument in Satan's arsenal entrapping men and women in bondage to Hinduism.[158]

Early Jesuit missionaries to India in the sixteenth and seventeenth centuries also encountered the barrier of caste. Roberto de Nobili spent many years seeking to build bridges over which the gospel could flow into the castes. His experiments were bold and innovative, and his critics were loud and vociferous. Yet he carried on in the face of opposition from colleagues as well as the Brahman leaders in Madurai. The result of his lifelong ministry along caste lines, was the conversion of several thousand high caste Hindus. Although Francis Xavier pioneered this field, De Nobili laid the foundation for the social structure of the Roman Catholic Church in India.[159]

Possibly due to the influence of de Nobili's bold concepts, Danish Lutheran missionaries of the eighteenth century developed evangelistic methodologies and church structures that were sensitive and tolerant to caste. Richter stated, "They hesitated to grapple seriously with this deeply rooted national institution. Relying on the aid of the Word of God, on exhortation and their own spiritual influence, they contented themselves with an effort to destroy the evil from within."[160] The focus of their ministries was primarily on the humble fisherfolk along the coast of South India.

Nineteenth-century missionaries in India, for the most part, were highly intolerant of caste and assumed that it must be destroyed. They were right when they claimed that if caste could be destroyed, then Hinduism would also cease to exist. Much of the missionary activity and energy was concentrated on ministering to upper caste Hindus between the years 1830 and 1930. Unfortunately, the strategy chosen by the missionaries

157 Vern Middleton, "Breaking Cast Barriers in India," *International Journal of Frontier Missions* 1, no. 4 (1984).

158 Julius Richter, *A History of Missions in India* (Edinburgh and London: Oliphant, Anderson and Ferrier, 1908), 166–173.

159 Vincent Cronier, *A Pearl to India: The Life of Roberto do Nobih* (New York: E. P. Dutton Co., 1959).

160 Richter, *A History of Missions in India*, 166.

failed to produce the expected results, and in turn was indirectly responsible for the rise of Indian nationalism and the revival of Hinduism.

Toward the end of the nineteenth century and at the turn of the twentieth century, "mass [people] movements" among the scheduled castes and the tribals of India began to spread. In many instances these conversions occurred in spite of the missionaries. Controversy and resistance frequently arose in the Indian Christian community over the acceptance of "mass movement" converts into the Christian church. However, the tide continued to roll on, and within a span of three to four decades the Christian Church in India took on a different appearance. The sociological makeup and image of Christianity appeared to upper caste Hindus as a community of Shudras and Untouchables. Today close to 90 percent of the Indian Christian community has originated from the lowest stratas of society.[161]

Caste Defined

Caste has been the object of much research and discussion. In spite of all the attention it receives, it continues to be one of the most misunderstood dimensions of India. Some authorities find it easier to define caste negatively, describing what it is not, rather than what it is. The following is the author's attempt to describe it: It is the communal extension of the joint family system. It produces a worldview centered around customs and ceremonies. It is primarily relational in its focus and creates an environment that is highly resistant to change. Caste is the very heartbeat of Hinduism.

Another definition of caste is given by Taya Zinkin:

Once again the power of the caste system is described in terms of inertia to change and resistance to external forces. Caste holds together the fabric of society; the integrity of the village is built round the framework of caste; caste may not have revelation behind it; but it does have a network of observances covering every action of daily life. A society so governed is a society with an infinity of resistance to outside attacks.[162]

Caste derives its power from three primary factors: the historical development of India, theological conceptions within Hinduism, and sociological dynamics of ritual and custom that reinforce it.[163]

---

161 Frequent articles on "Mass Movements" appeared in *IRM* and other journals. See V. S. Azariah, "Living Forces behind Mass Movements," *IRM* 18, no. 4 (Oct. 1929): 509–517. See also, V. S. Azariah, "The Caste Movement in South India," *IRM* 21, no. 4 (Oct. 1932): 457–467; C. H. Bandy, "The Building of the Church Among Village Communities," *IRM* 8, no. 2 (April 1919): 193–204; Sydney Cave, "A Typical Mass Movement Church—1806–1918," *IRM* 7, no. 4 (Oct. 1918): 470–480; Hodge, "Evangelism in India."

162 Clark D. Moore, and David Eldredge ed., *India, Yesterday and Today* (New York: Bantam Books, 1970), 98.

163 For an extended detailed discussion on this issue, see Paul Hiebert, *Konduru* (Minneapolis: University of Minnesota Press, 1974), 13–100.

Upward Social Mobility

Upward social mobility in India is not the prerogative of the individual. The exception to the rule is found in secularized cities like Bombay, Madras, and Delhi. Castes do try to raise themselves in the hierarchical ranking, by a process called "Sanskritization." A caste will seek to drop those customs and rituals that identify them with a particular rank and conform more closely to the standards of a higher caste. Many attempts fail, but there are some instances where a caste has risen from the ranks of the Shudras to the Kshatriya.

This desire for social status and improvement has been, in some cases, an instrument used by the Holy Spirit, as Untouchable castes have been able to improve their lot by converting to Christ. This social dimension became a focus of political-religious tension during the 1930s.

Conversion and Caste

From the above descriptions, it is obvious that if caste Hindus are to be reached for Christ the transformation must be effected within caste. Contemporary evangelism must be prepared to allow the gospel to flow along these avenues of social distinction within the Indian culture.

The one-by-one method of conversion developed in the West is useless against the impenetrable dikes of the caste system. Chenchiah, an Indian theologian astutely observed that:

> Hinduism is a highly integrated socio-ethical structure forming an indivisible whole. When confronted with such an organization, pickaxe methods have little or no value. The impossibility of reducing Hinduism atom by atom or block by block needs no demonstration. A great religion like Hinduism can only be changed when its mind and soul are changed or when its life impulses are altered.[164]

Chenchiah recognized that the only way the gospel could penetrate the barriers of Hinduism is to permit the message and the dynamic of the Holy Spirit to work within the existing social structure.[165]

Church and Caste

Christian leadership in India vigorously opposed any method that accepted caste, between 1830 and 1930. The leaders believed the church was above such distinctions, and their

---

164 D. A. Thangassamy, *The Theology of Chenchiah* (Bangalore: Christian Institute for the Study of Religion and Society, 1966), 222ff.

165 Ibid., 236.

ideas were reinforced by legislation and government, reflecting secular attitudes that also wanted to eliminate caste. Several reform movements within India sought vigorously to end caste intolerance and exploitation.

The mass movements to Christianity were thwarted by the church leaders, as they felt the pattern was unbiblical and the outcome would result in a compromise with Hinduism. At a meeting of the National Council of Churches in India (1928), this issue was hotly debated. The anti-mass movement people carried the day until John R. Mott cautioned against a hasty decision and offered to find funding to research the problem.[166]

The Pickett proposal, also later endorsed by McGavran, to establish churches within the context of caste social structures, assumed that the very process would undermine the system. It was believed that as the gospel permeated the lives of more and more people the weeds of caste would be rooted out and the doctrines of karma and samsara would be destroyed. This concept was not radically new, a similar proposition had been put forth in 1912 by Elizabeth Hibbert-Ware. Her strategy was to discover elements within the caste system that were exploitive and degrading, and to expose those aspects by contrasting the dignity and self-worth that comes through kingdom teaching.[167]

Bimrao Ramji Ambedkar and the Mahars

The political and social tensions surrounding the Dalits reached a new zenith, on October 13, 1935 in Yeola, Nasik when leaders from these people groups met, "to review the situation in the light of their ten-year old struggle and the coming reforms."[168] Ambedkar startled the nation by announcing that, although he was born a Hindu, he was determined not to die one.[169] A resolution was passed at the conference, which threatened Hinduism and gladdened the hearts of missionaries working with mass movements. The essence of it was that: "The Depressed classes should leave the Hindu fold and join some other religion that gives social and religious equality to them. Choose any religion that gives you equality of status and of treatment."[170]

Ambedkar was a brilliant lawyer, who had earned PhDs from Columbia University and London University. He was a shrewd politician and a man with a desire to see India established as a secular state. After independence he became the minister of law and Prime Minister Nehru appointed him to the task as one of the primary architects of India's constitution. As a young man he returned to India with great hopes which soon faded when he once again encountered the stigma of caste. He was so humiliated that he determined

---

166   Donald McGavran, interview by Vern Middleton, May 20, 1989. See also the account by J. Waskom Pickett, *Christian Mass Movements in India* (Lucknow: Lucknow Publishing House, 1933), 11.

167   Graham Houghton, "Caste and the Protestant Church," *Transformation* 2, no. 2 (April–June 1985): 32–33.

168   D. Keer, *Dr. Ambedkar's Life and Mission* (Bombey: Popular Prakashan, 1962), 251.

169   "Survey-India" (an editorial), *International Review of Missions*, 26 (1937): 33.

170   Quotes from Loganatha (July 4, 1936), and Godfrey E. Phillips, *The Untouchable's Quest* (1936), 8, as cited in T. S. Wilkinson and M. M. Thomas, C. L. S., *Ambedkar and the Neo-Buddhist Movement*, (Madras: CLS, 1972).

to devote his life to the "deliverance" of his people from the yoke of Hinduism.[171] Much of his political drive arose out of the abuse he received from high caste Hindus.

McGavran and E. Stanley Jones, along with several others from the Mass Movement Committee, sent letters to Pickett and J. Z. Hodge, secretary of the NCC, urging that Pickett quietly seek contact with Ambedkar. Pickett's response was, "I would be very eager to go to the Bombay Presidency, if Hodge and Bishop Azariah approve [the] suggestion."[172] Pickett wrote further that Christian leaders in North India "were emphatically in favour of our trying to receive Dr. Ambedkar and his followers immediately without much demand for prebaptismal instruction."[173]

Pickett met with Ambedkar on several occasions and in a letter to McGavran, written on November 27, 1935, Pickett wrote, "I have just returned from Bombay after a most encouraging interview with Ambedkar. I think Ambedkar's goal is Christianity. I have arranged for Stanley Jones and for Bishop Azariah to see him." They became friends and Pickett also sent his publications to Ambedkar. J. T. Seamands reported that, "One day Ambedkar asked Bishop Pickett to baptise him as a Christian but, afraid that it might ruin his political career, he wanted it done in secret. Bishop Pickett refused, and insisted that he should openly confess Christ as Lord and Savior. This, Ambedkar was not willing to do."[174]

Gandhi brought immense political pressure to bear upon Ambedkar to consider conversion to any religion of Indian origin, but not to Christianity. The Untouchable castes retained their momentum in the fight against Hindu caste structures by holding large rallies in various parts of India. One was held in Lucknow, Uttar Pradesh on June 23, 1936. The following day the Lucknow newspaper recaptured the stirring event as follows:

> Curses are heaped upon Hinduism. Impassioned tones denounce Hinduism as "foolishness," "mockery," and "traffic with the devil." Waves of applause swept over the audience as Hinduism is belaboured. Deep-throated cries of hate issue almost involuntarily from many as the ills of the Depressed Classes are . . . described. Arya Samajists are flayed alive to the accompaniment of cheers.

Gandhi and Ambedkar sparred back and forth over the issue of Untouchability for more than twenty-five years. At the Round Table Conference held in London from 1930 to 1931 Ambedkar insisted on separate electorates for the Depressed Classes. Gandhi objected to this legislation on the grounds that it would develop a political wall of separation within the Hindu community, and he fought back by going on a fast. This brought public pressure

---

171   Fred M. Perrill, *Dr. Ambedkar, and the Christian Message* (Lucknow: Lucknow Publishing House: 1971), 6–36, as an address given in London, Missouri.

172   Waskom Pickett, letter from Lucknow to Donald McGavran, Jabalpur, India, (obtained from USCWM), Oct. 30, 1935.

173   Ibid.

174   Waskom Pickett, letter from Lucknow to Donald McGavran, Jabalpur, India, (obtained from USCWM), Nov. 27, 1935.

to bear upon Ambedkar and his supporters to moderate their demands. Ambedkar finally relented on the basis that the number of seats in the legislature reserved for the Depressed Classes be raised from seventy-one to 148. This was known as the Poona Pact.[175]

THE McGAVRAN-GANDHI CONFRONTATION[176]

Political tensions mounted in India, between 1936 and 1938 over a revolt of the Untouchables and Indian leadership grew more intolerant of the missionary entanglement in the mass movement process. Gandhi tried to stem their involvement by meeting with several leaders of the National Council of Churches, including Azariah and Pickett in March 1937. Pickett reported the details to McGavran who was already known as a crusader,[177] prepared to fight for principle no matter the odds against him. This was exactly the case when he heard of Gandhi's threats to the missionary cause.

By July 1938, a storm erupted in India between McGavran and Gandhi. McGavran published three serial articles in the *World Dominion* journal entitled, "The Battle for Brotherhood in India Today." The third article was particularly offensive to Gandhi, for in it McGavran exposed the way Gandhi was engineering opposition to the mass movements. Indian newspapers, such as the *Madras Guardian*, reprinted the substance of the article in their editorial pages. The points Gandhi found offensive were:

> Mr. Gandhi recently came to Nagpur to see . . . Azariah and Pickett in regard to the movements to Christ numbering two hundred thousand per annum from amongst the oppressed classes. "We shall not allow conversions to continue," Mr. Gandhi exclaimed in conclusion of a three hour conference . . . Gandhi said to Bishop Azariah, "You Christians must stop preaching to and making disciples amongst the Depressed Classes. If you do not, we shall make you. We shall appeal to the educated Indian Christians; we shall appeal to your home constituency; and if those fail we shall prohibit by law any change of religion, and we will back up the law by force of the state."[178]

Gandhi brought considerable influence to bear on McGavran and Azariah to have the statements retracted. McGavran found himself in a very embarrassing situation, because

---

175 Quoted in the "The Gathering of the Peoples," A report from *The Bible Society of Scotland*, USCWM (1937). Further descriptions of the political storm that brewed in India over the Depressed Classes are discussed in Donald Eugene Smith, *India as a Secular State* (Princeton: Princeton University Press, 1963) and William Roy Smith, *Nationalism and Reform in India* (New Haven: Yale University Press, 1938).

176 Vern J. Middleton, material in this section was previously published as "Caste Issues in the Mind of McGavran and Gandhi," *Missiology: An International Review* 13, no. 2 (April 1985).

177 Donald McGavran, "John Grafton McGavran, Scholar, Crusader and Saint: An Appreciation by His Son," *World Call* 13 (March 1931).

178 Donald McGavran, "The Battle for Brotherhood in India Today," *World Dominion* (London: July 1938): 261.

he had simply paraphrased what Pickett reported to him, but did not want to identify his source thus causing serious problems for his beloved mentor. In the next issue of *World Dominion*, two brief statements appeared. The first was an editorialized comment of a letter written by McGavran, the second by Azariah:

> We have now received a letter from Dr. McGavran, telling us that Bishop Azariah declares that the alleged statement was not made by Mr. Gandhi. Dr. McGavran says that he, "heard the story from a dozen different sources, did not hear it was confidential, and incorporated the incident" into his article "in all good faith." He adds: "I am happy promptly to tender complete apologies to Mr. Gandhi and Bishop Azariah."[179]

The second quote in the editorial retraction was a portion of a letter which Azariah submitted to the *Madras Guardian* and was repeated in *World Dominion*. "I exceedingly regret that any reference at all should have been made to that interview . . . Gandhiji and I agreed at the very outset that neither he nor we will publish anything that took place in this interview . . . Every statement—without exception—attributed to Gandhiji by Dr. McGavran is wholly and absolutely without truth . . . The whole . . . is a cruel fabrication."[180]

In the light of such a strongly worded letter, McGavran's response was surprising, for rather than protest the issue and divulge his source, he remained silent. In a later interview, McGavran added, "Bishop Pickett must have breathed a sigh of relief at not being brought into the controversy which he created."[181]

The struggle cited above is evaluated by the thorough research of Susan Billington Harber in her book, *In the Shadow of Mahatma*. She has unearthed numerous resources to support Bishop Azariah's position, and the details are recorded in pages 327–32 of her text.

The drama of the Indian nationalistic revival, which found its inspiration and strength in the twentieth century Hindu Renaissance, was led by M. K. Gandhi and the Congress Movement. His genius was his ability to project an image as a spiritual leader and social reformer, while being constantly embroiled in a most intense form of politics. For this reason, McGavran disliked Gandhi but held Jawaharlal Nehru in high regard.

McGavran's first encounter with Gandhi was in Jabalpur on December 7, 1933. Gandhi gave a speech to the Christian community on the topic, "How Can Christians Cooperate in the Uplift of the Untouchables?" The theme may have been the inspiration for McGavran's church growth concept, "redemption and lift." McGavran published the speech and interjected his own evaluation of the message in the *Sahayak Patrika*. Gandhi described the Congress movement as, "a reform from within. It has nothing to do with

---

179 Donald McGavran, *World Dominion*, editorial (Sept. 1938): 392.
180 Ibid.
181 Donald McGavran, interview by Vern Middleton, Oct. 27, 1983.

politics, although there is not a doubt but that it will have tremendous political results. There is not a single thought of politics in my efforts. I want to purify Hindu society."[182]

During Gandhi's time in Jabalpur, McGavran approached him directly and asked, "Would you favour Untouchables becoming Christians, if thereby they would achieve a greater measure of life than was possible to them as long as they remained Untouchables?" Gandhi's response was, "Under no circumstances do I favour their becoming Christian. Let them seek uplift in Hinduism. They are better off without uplift in Hinduism than with uplift in Christianity.[183]

The nub of the matter was the fear within the Congress Movement of losing the votes of the Untouchables if they converted. McGavran clearly discerned this when he wrote:

> The fact which dominates the whole situation in regard to the anti-Untouchability Movement is that Untouchables to date not counted as Hindus are going to vote either in the Hindu voting block, or in a voting block of their own or possibly in a Christian voting block if such is formed. Gandhi says that political gain does not in the least motivate him. But there is no question that it motivates nine hundred and ninety-nine out of every thousand of those interested in anti-Untouchability work.[184]

In an interview with John R. Mott on December 19, 1936, Gandhi expressed something of the deep agony of soul he experienced over the issue of Untouchability:

> So far as I am concerned with the untouchability question, it is one of life and death for Hinduism . . . if untouchability lives Hinduism perishes and even India perishes: but if untouchability is eradicated from the Hindu heart root and branch, then Hinduism has a definite message for the world. What I am aiming at is not every Hindu touching an untouchable, but every touchable Hindu driving untouchability from his heart.[185]

Gandhi's attitude to Christianity and missionaries hardened as Untouchable unrest increased. He insisted that missionaries, engaged in leading the Untouchable communities to Christ, were violating fundamental principles of the equality of all religions. His view of the Harijans, his name for the Untouchables, was that he did not think them capable of comprehending Christian truth. His political reaction to Christianity as a religion, was that it stood as the domain of the "white arrogant conquerors."[186]

---

182 Donald McGavran, "Gandhi in the Central Provinces," (M. K. Gandhi's speech) *Sahayak Patrika*, (Dec. 1933): 2.

183 Donald McGavran, "The Battle for Brotherhood in India Today."

184 McGavran, *Sahayak Patrika.*

185 Mohandas Karamchand Gandhi,*Christian Missions: Their Place in India* (Ahmedabad: Navajivan Press, 1941), 171–72.

186 S. R. Ghose, "Lecture Notes on the Life of Gandhi," (obtained from USCWM), lecture, 1947.

The article, "The Battle for Brotherhood," that catapulted McGavran into the notorious limelight with Gandhi, also described the atrocities Ambedkar experienced at the hands of the high caste Hindus. McGavran likened Ambedkar to Moses leading the people of Israel out of Egypt. McGavran discerned the significance of Ambedkar's prophetic voice for the Untouchables as important, not only because of the potential of adding three million Mahars to the ranks of the Christian Church, but primarily because Ambedkar was bringing a profound and penetrating indictment, "against the entire Hindu system."[187]

In the same article McGavran defined the term "Mass Movement" to be "the coming to Christ of the people of one caste, in family groups of five to fifty at one time, amounting to two or three hundred or two or three thousand in a year."[188]

He took the mask of Christian identity away from Gandhi. Many Western leaders had become enamoured with Gandhi and viewed him as a saint, with some going so far as to consider him a Christian. McGavran's exposé of his true spiritual nature must have angered Gandhi, for it tarnished his image abroad when it was printed:

> Gandhi himself has emphatically denied that he is a Christian . . . Gandhi is a Hindu and we have every right to expect him to act from the Hindu point of view for the preservation of Hindu culture and religion; for the preservation of caste, which is the essence of Hinduism; for the preservation of a system of graded races as opposed to a system of equal opportunities for all, regardless of racial origin . . . He is a good man and a great man, but he has a clear-cut Hindu bias.[189]

McGAVRAN'S VIEWS ON CASTE

While the air was still clearing from the Gandhi-McGavran encounter, an article appeared in the *United Church Review* entitled, "India's Oppressed Classes and Religion." In this article, McGavran explained his understanding of the caste situation in India and why he viewed people movements to Christ as the only way of ensuring justice for the exploited masses. He insisted that the caste distinctions in India were "artificial compartments having little substance in reality."[190] He singled out sin as the major factor that enslaved the Untouchable castes. The sinful lives of the oppressed castes placed them in contempt by the higher castes, but the sin of pride, greed, and lust for power among the upper castes militated against any social progress for the Untouchables.

He regarded the doctrines of karma and samsara as "systems of thought that demand caste."[191] He described these Brahman-inspired doctrines as "manufactured to make the

---

187 McGavran, "Battle for Brotherhood in India Today," 133.
188 Ibid., 259.
189 Ibid., 260.
190 Donald McGavran, "India's Oppressed Classes and Religion," *United Church Review* (1938): 184.
191 Ibid., 185.

Oppressed classes direct all efforts for improvement toward a meticulous observation of the system."[192] McGavran insisted that any superficial reforms, such as lifting the ban on Untouchables entering Hindu temples and legislation making the practise of untouchability illegal were merely sop, and temporary measures. He stressed that the practise of untouchability is woven into the very fabric of Hinduism, and that any future hope for the Untouchable community lay in one direction only—a radical departure from Hinduism and a embracement of the gospel and the equality to be found in Christ.

The article began by coining the term, "Oppressed Classes," with a plea to adopt the Hindi equivalent, *dabi hui jatiyan*, which literally means the jatis or castes which are suppressed. The article then discussed the various terms applied to castes. McGavran emphatically stated, "To speak of low caste and high caste people is sub-Christian . . . and is an affront to the Brotherhood of Man and to the Oneness of God."[193] He vigorously rejected any form of racism or racist expression. Recently, a similar term has been employed, the *dalat*, or the oppressed.

No other article so displayed McGavran's intense anger aimed at the oppressive power of Hinduism which enslaved one hundred million people. His strong bent toward social action dimension was dramatically demonstrated here as a crusader against the evils of caste and a champion of the rights of the "Oppressed Classes." He viewed the people movement conversion pattern as essential for reaching caste-enslaved segments of Hindu society and recognized that the removal of caste stigma and prejudice would take a generation or two to overcome. However, he also believed that when the goal is clear and the theological foundation for brotherhood is firmly taught, conversions along caste lines would eventuate in an egalitarian Christian society.

JOHN R. MOTT AND THE McGAVRAN INCIDENT

The sequel to the story continued because on December 19, 1938, many delegates to the Tambaram conference of the International Missionary Council arrived in India a few weeks early. Among them was John R. Mott, who used the time to meet with Gandhi, a pattern many Christian leaders followed. Early in the interview Mott said, "I must say I was terribly pained to read of the McGavran incident and greatly relieved to know that the misunderstanding has been cleared up."[194] The conversation shifted to the definition of mass movements. Gandhi complained that Protestant missionaries "will never give up what they call the right of mass conversion."[195] Mott responded by drawing attention to McGavran's rejection of the term "mass" and its replacement with "the conversion of groups

---

192 Ibid., 185.
193 Ibid., 183.
194 Gandhi, *Christian Missions*, 186.
195 Ibid., 187.

and families,"[196] and in an anemic attempt to placate Gandhi's anger, Mott made a further comment, saying, "How can groups or families be converted en masse? Conversion is an individual matter, a matter entirely between one and one's God."[197]

Mott knew better than to state conversion as only an individual, or one by one process. He intervened when the NCC of India was ready to reject the mass movements. He sponsored Pickett's research and discussed the implications of the findings at length. He also wrote the foreword to the book *Christian Mass Movements in Central India*.

THE CHRISTIAN MESSAGE IN A NON-CHRISTIAN WORLD

India in the late 1930s was the scene of intense nationalism. In the political maelstrom of the independence movement, led by Gandhi, the Christian message was regarded, "not as being untrue, but as a destroying and denationalizing force."[198]

Indians regarded their homeland as *mataji* (mother) and as an object of worship. The Bhagavad Gita became the popular handbook of the nationalists, while the Bible was viewed with disdain. Gandhi moved his headquarters from Gujarat to the Sevagram, an ashram outside the city of Wardha, 250 miles west of where McGavran was located.

Meanwhile, the increasing number of Untouchables converting to Christianity only added fuel to the forces of nationalism and the Hindu hatred for Christianity. In this context, sensitive Christians began to dilute the message of Christ, hoping to make it more palatable.

Hendrik Kraemer's book, *The Christian Message in a Non-Christian World*, was written to address the above situation which was displayed all over Asia. The months leading up to the Tambaram Conference were times of intense preparation, and Kraemer's book, which circulated several months prior to the conference, provoked reactions on both sides of the issue setting the stage for theological debate. Kraemer rejected ideas of "preparatio evangelica," "natural theology," and "logos spermatikos."[199] These concepts had given rise to Farquar's idea that Christianity was the crown of Hinduism, which was popular with South Indian theologians such as Chenchiah, Chakkarai, and Bishop Appasamy. Kraemer's book provoked much controversy and heated debate, especially among those of more liberal persuasion.

McGavran obtained a copy of Kraemer's book prior to the conference, and the impact it had on his thinking was comparable to that made by Pickett's book, *The Mass Movements in India*. He responded by producing a three-part book review, which was published in

---

196 Ibid.

197 Ibid.

198 Eric Sharpe, *Not To Destroy But To Fulfill: The Contribution of J. N. Farquhar to Protestant Missionary Thought in India Before 1914* (Lund: Gleerup, 1965), 63.

199 Evert Jansen Schoonhove, "Tambovram," *International Review of Missions* 67, no. 267 (July 1978): 311.

the *Sahayak Patrika* with the intent to challenge the sixty India delegates at the Tambaram conference, to master its contents.

Kraemer's forthright style of writing appealed to McGavran. Here was an ally for the many issues he was battling. He was convinced that the book would pierce the prevailing confused thinking, destroy the uncertainty with which the Christian message was being delivered, and galvanize the church of India into action. Theological expressions made by Kraemer became weapons in McGavran's developing "church growth" arsenal. Kraemer's opening chapter, with its focus on the dangers of relativism reinforced McGavran's position of biblical realism and spurred him to state:

> The roots of relativism are shown to lie in a world view where man is taken to be the measure of all things and pseudo absolutes are readily accepted . . . The great non-Christian faiths . . . are religions of relativism, religions in which there are no absolutes . . . The willingness to equate the best in Hinduism to the revelation of the true God is directly due to the fact that the Christian doing the equating has allowed himself to forget the radically revelational nature of his faith.[200]

Liberal theologians in 1938 were labeling such thinking as nothing more than expressions of religious pride and spiritual arrogance. They opposed vigorous Christian evangelism and bold witness. To this McGavran responded, paraphrasing some of Kraemer's ideas: "When Christians proclaim as final ultimate and absolute truth that it has pleased God to reveal Himself completely and finally in Jesus Christ and that all men are called to consider, repent and obey and adore Him; and at the same time . . . purge themselves of any feeling that they possess this superior, nay unique truth. We are witnesses to, not possessors of, truth."[201] Next, McGavran challenged the erroneous assumptions of Farquar and the Indian Christian theologians of South India, relating their approach to Hinduism:

> It is fundamentally a wrong procedure to take isolated doctrines or segments of doctrines and try to compare them with Christian doctrines. Religions . . . are indivisible unities . . . and are man's approach to God not God's approach to man. The apparent similarities are really dissimilarities. Consequently the idea that Christianity is the crown of an already functioning system is utterly untenable . . . Christianity is the crises, the judgment of all religions.[202]

Such ideas as these became fundamental theological presuppositions for McGavran's church growth principles. Kraemer found McGavran to be a source of encouragement

---

200 McGavran, "Book Review of Christian Message in a Non-Christian World," *Sahayak Patrika* (July 1938), 240.

201 Ibid.

202 Ibid.

during and after the heated opposition he received at Tambaram. They continued to correspond through the years and out of the context of this friendship, McGavran asked Kraemer to write the forward to his next book, *How Churches Grow*, which was published in 1959. McGavran's only lament about Kraemer is that he did soften his position in a later book, *Religion and the Christian Faith*.

McGAVRAN: MISSIONARY EVANGELIST

The following quote from Muhammad Babur, the founder of the Mogul Empire, described the essence of McGavran's action in regard to evangelism. "I placed my foot in the stirrup of resolution and my hand on the reins of confidence in God—and marched."[203] Previously in chapter three, I traced the development of the NCC Forward Movement in evangelism. Here in this context we see the impact of that movement in the life of one missionary.

Evangelistic Patterns for Reaching the Satnamis

McGavran found opportunity to develop and practise various methods of evangelism in Chattisgarh. In view of his beliefs that caste relationships flowed along family lines, he memorized the names of the Satnamis who became Christians, and then sought to follow up all family connections. At one point, he memorized the names of over 10,000 relatives of Christians.

During this time McGavran wrote an unpublished paper entitled, "Family Evangelism," in which he described principles he regularly used in evangelizing the Satnamis. In 1938 he wrote, "The Church expands within the family. By family here is meant not merely the father, mother and children but that great group of people who know themselves to be united by life of the caste and the individual. The Christian faith flows along family lines."[204]

McGavran saw the negative aspects of family ties and relationships as well, and knew that such ties can become barriers preventing entrance into the Christian church. He rightly observed that after the Indian community intermarried over a period of forty years, upward social mobility resulting from the liberating power of the gospel totally isolated these families and their churches from any social intercourse with the unconverted.[205]

He was critical of traditional evangelistic procedures that ignored family ties and marriage relationships, and appalled that so few evangelists took time to learn about family connections. The prevailing pattern repeated in village after village was to preach to everyone in general regardless of family ties and caste connections. He insisted "changes

---

203   S. A. A. Rizvi, *The Wonder that Was India, Part II* (1993), 91–97.

204   Donald McGavran, "Family Evangelism" (unpublished MS, [obtained from USCWM Archives], 1938), 1. Published in *World Call* under the title "So He Went and Told His Brothers," (1939).

205   Ibid., 2.

of belief flow along family lines."[206] His studies with Pickett confirmed that the only places in India where the church was growing rapidly was where the gospel was spreading from relative to relative.

Hira Lal As Mentor

The monsoon season (June–September) of 1936 was used to map out an evangelistic strategy for gathering in the expected harvest of Satnami people. His first concern was to gain an entrance into the hundreds of Satnami villages scattered throughout the region and he turned to Hira Lal, an elderly Indian gentleman converted from the Satnami caste, for courage and assistance and indeed, this man became his guru. The relationship between Hira Lal and McGavran was more like father-son than *guru-chela* (master-student).

Hira Lal had a remarkable conversion and a history of a lifetime of service with the Disciples of Christ mission. He had ministered as a preacher, helper, and *kansama* (cook) with John McGavran from 1892–93. Later he became an orderly in the mission hospital at Mungeli, and by watching the doctors perform surgery and minister to the sick, he gradually gained competence and even performed cataract operations, as well as other surgical tasks. The local people loved and respected him and addressed him as Dr. Hira Lal.[207]

Between 1914 and 1916, a caste known as the *Chungia Chamars* (leather workers who use smoke) became very receptive to the gospel. The title was strongly suggestive of their low caste status, but they were desirous of upward social mobility, and saw in Christianity a source of power and potential for freedom. In April 1917, the leaders of the 50,000 Chungi Chamars of the Mungeli region had gathered at a place called Setganga to consider becoming Christian. Hira Lal was the primary spokesman and evangelist for the event. A Hindu police subinspector heard of the proceedings and was conspicuously present at Setganga. He let it be known that should they become Christian, certain unfortunate events would make their lives miserable. Fearing reprisals, the Chungi Chamars decided to postpone the decision for one year. Tragically, events developed within the mission that kept Hira Lal from regathering the people the following year in 1918.[208]

McGavran arrived in the Mungeli area nineteen years after the above incident. He hoped the spark could be rekindled among the Chungia Chamars. Over the years, Hira Lal continued to minister to these people. He provided hospitality and displayed Christian love on a continuous basis and accompanied McGavran on occasion. In this way, McGavran was introduced to the aristocracy of the caste. Once a relationship in a given village was established, McGavran began a systematic pattern of evangelism.[209]

---

206 Ibid., 3.
207 Donald McGavran, interview by Vern Middleton, April 13, 1984.
208 Donald McGavran, interview by Vern Middleton, Aug. 30, 1983.
209 Donald McGavran, interview by Vern Middleton, April 13, 1984.

The Mungeli Workbook As McGavran's Evangelistic Pattern

In 1937 McGavran, along with Edgar Moody and Herman Reynolds, agreed that a systematic guidebook on the presentation of the gospel needed to be developed for the Indian evangelists. They found this necessary because the majority of the evangelists had been raised in mission orphanages and their education was limited. Since neither Moody nor Reynolds stayed long in the Chattisgarh area, the task fell to McGavran who obtained a copy of a handbook developed by Ingram, an Anglican missionary stationed in Agra. McGavran utilized his format, refining and simplifying the program.[210]

The manual was published in Hindi and the title given was *Awashyak Masihi Gyan,* meaning the "Essentials of Christian Knowledge." The format of the manual reflects McGavran's strong educational bias. Although the preaching was directed to the heart, there was also a strong emphasis on knowledge of content. He reasoned that people cannot act until they know something about Christ. The Christian knowledge imparted would form a foundation from which their faith in Christ could be launched.[211]

The Mungeli workbook is only forty-two pages long, but it contains guidelines and material both for evangelizing a caste, as well as discipling a new body of believers who are in the process of becoming a local church. The first page is entitled, *"Mungeli shaetra ki pracharakon ki pustak"* ("Mungeli book for local preachers"). The contents are:

1. The aims of the gospel workers.
2. Bible stories to be used (fourteen Bible stories formed the core).
3. A program or guidelines for common Christian worship.
   a. The Ten Commandments
   b. The Lord's Prayer
   c. Apostles' Creed
4. The Ten Commandments and the ten benefits of being a Christian in Chattisgarh.
5. Important Christian songs (eleven songs composed in Hindi).
6. One hundred Bible verses which are useful.[212]

The book stressed spiritual preparation and the nature of the work being undertaken. Emphasis was placed on prayer and demonstration of the fruit of the Holy Spirit. The evangelists were urged to exercise faith in God as they proclaimed the gospel message. They were exhorted to make the lessons a part of their own spiritual lives so they could impart more than just head knowledge. McGavran stressed that they must display and

---

210 Ibid.
211 Ibid.
212 Donald McGavran, *Awashyak Masihi Gyan* (Jabalpur: Mission Press, 1937).

demonstrate team spirit and deep loyalty to one another and finally, he emphasized that they were to always display holiness of life and be channels of God's blessing to others.

McGavran described the way he utilized the Mungeli workbook, which contained the materials to be proclaimed, preached, and memorized by village Christians. Every evening they assembled for half an hour of instruction and worship. The Lord's Prayer and other Scriptures were repeated in unison. Fourteen Bible stories formed a year's ministry; each was to be studied for approximately one month. At the end of the year every believer in the village had thoroughly memorized the stories. These illiterate believers would then repeat the stories to their relatives and friends. For the Christian villagers, this program was exciting and useful.[213]

Knowing full well the high value placed on corporate unity within the extended families of India, McGavran aimed to make the worship and spiritual fellowship of all new churches a meaningful experience of oneness in Christ. The guidelines in the workbook stressed repeating memorized portions of Scripture until they became part of their thought processes.

Thirty years before the term "contextualization" was used, McGavran had begun to move in that direction. In connection with the Mungeli workbook, he produced a Jesus *Bhagawat* (a religious narration). He adopted the form of storytelling utilized by the Satnami mendicants. However, when he discovered his evangelists embellishing Bible parables, (e.g., they belaboured the sexual exploits of the Prodigal Son) he dropped this form of evangelism, insisting that they teach without local imagery and color.

The Discipling Process

He organized these eight evangelists into teams consisting of three men or more. They would go into a Satnami caste section in a village where several families had become Christians and begin a two-week campaign visiting from house to house during the day and holding meetings every night.

The unconverted were urged to become followers of Christ. The message focused on the social problems of adultery and fornication and other sexual sins that were common among the Satnamis. Therefore, stress was placed on leaving their *ras lila* (sinful past) and becoming followers of the *Sat Nam* (True Name), Jesus Christ. A second serious problem was that their lifestyle made them vulnerable to the moneylenders causing their properties to be stripped away from them. Again, great emphasis was placed on leaving these old patterns of life, to follow God's plan and in this way their land would be spared.[214]

Results were significant. Although the conversion rate did not approach that of a people movement, McGavran reported 1,100 believers and twenty-four churches established

---

213 Donald McGavran, interview by Vern Middleton, May 22, 1984.
214 Ibid.

between 1940 and 1944.[215] This brought heavy demands on his time and on several occasions he had to intervene directly to rescue properties from the *malguzar* (village landlord). McGavran described how a Christian was forcefully evicted from his property and his house torn down because he had not occupied it for some time. Within the week, McGavran had organized a party of men who assembled a prefabricated house of bamboo walls and mud stucco before dawn on the site. Of course the village landlord was furious but, by law, he was unable to touch the Christian's property once he was resident.[216]

More progress could have been made in the advancement of the gospel had it not been for the quality of the Indian evangelists. McGavran reported numerous reversions directly as a result of their sinful lifestyle.[217] The major problem was that these evangelists had been accustomed to the strictures and structures of the Christian community in various centers so when they moved out among the loose-living Satnami community, they had not developed the moral fiber or strength of character to withstand temptation which overwhelmed them.

In March of 1937, a Satnami leader put his trust in Jesus Christ and McGavran was convinced that here at last was a man possessed of the charisma to lead a people movement. But while McGavran was discipling him, the Satnami suddenly fell ill. He was admitted to the Mungeli hospital and within three days he died. The possible cause was poison and so his death struck great fear into the hearts of the Satnami villagers.

McGAVRAN'S APOLOGETIC FOR THE SATNAMIS

Focusing in on the name of this caste, *Satnami* (which means the true name), McGavran presented Jesus Christ as the Truth, the True Name, and the True Way. Hence Jesus was their *Sat Nam*. He wrote a gospel tract centered on that theme.

His first point of contact with the Satnamis, was to show that Ghasi Das (1810–40), their leader and originator of the Satnami religion, prophesied that men would come wearing hats and would bring a book with teachings about Satnam. He stressed that the Jesus he was proclaiming, was that incarnate Satnam proclaimed by Ghasi Das and he showed that the Satnam of Ghasi Das was essentially the Creator-God.

A second point of contact was in regard to their deep poverty. McGavran described Jesus against the backdrop of Philippians 2:5–7: This only begotten Son of the Father, the Satnam was Jesus. His was the greatest sacrifice ever made. He was born in the poor family of a carpenter. When Jesus was born his people were sharing a shed with the cows. He knew what it meant to be poor.[218]

---

215 Donald McGavran, letter from Takhatpur to Cy Yocum, Feb. 8, 1944.
216 Donald McGavran, interview by Vern Middleton, Feb. 23, 1984.
217 Donald McGavran, letter to Cy Yocum, Feb. 8, 1944.
218 Donald McGavran, "Gospel Tract for Satnamis" (unpublished MS, 1938).

A third stage in his apologetic stressed the healing power of Jesus Christ. His healing influence went with him. He healed the body, the mind, and the spirit. He revived the hopeless. The dead he brought back to life. Then quoting John 8:32 he said, Those "who have found the Satnam (truth in Jesus) have been freed from the bonds of sin, oppression, fear, despair and death."[219]

A fourth focus was the doctrine of man. He explained to them that:

The Satnam who created mankind created all men equal. There can be no high nor low before Him. Differences were created and introduced by men who wished to ill treat and gain undue advantage over others. Wherever people have come to know and accept Jesus according to His promise He has freed them and given them liberty. There were people in Chattisgarh and other places who had been slaves socially and spiritually but who now were freed men and women in Jesus Christ.[220]

EXPERIENCES OF POWER ENCOUNTER

Although McGavran made great strides in his spiritual pilgrimage between 1930 and 1940, it was still difficult for him to reconcile rational thought processes with the various types of demonic forces he frequently encountered. Once when he was in the middle of a baptismal service, a Satnami woman broke up the meeting with shrill cries. He described the incident, "I called aloud to the crowd on the bank," saying, "That is not a woman crying. That is Satan, who has gone into that woman and is crying because his victims are being released. Stop crying Satan!" The wailing stopped as if cut off with a pair of shears and the baptism proceeded in a notable calm.[221]

On another occasion, he was on an evangelistic tour which kept him overnight in a Satnami village, where his host was a Hindu. Early the next morning, McGavran was awakened by the wailing cries of the family. Hurrying into the next room he found everyone gathered around the bed of his host, grieving. When he asked what was wrong, they declared that Satan had come during the night and inflicted a mortal sickness on his host. McGavran took his Bible and walked around the bed from one corner to the next, ordering Satan to depart. When he had finished, he announced that the man of the house was delivered. Much to McGavran's surprise, the man was out of bed within the hour and showed no further trace of fever or any other illness.[222]

Pickett discussed with McGavran the issue of miracles and the supernatural. He said that during the research for Christian Mass Movements in India, he encountered more

---

219 Ibid.
220 Ibid.
221 Donald McGavran, "Evangelism in Central India," *World Call* (Feb. 1942): 11.
222 Donald McGavran, interview by Vern Middleton, April 13, 1984.

demonstrations of the Holy Spirit's power than are recorded in the New Testament, but for the sake of the credibility of the book, he felt he should not incorporate them into his text.

McGAVRAN'S ELEVEN ESSENTIAL POINTS ON EVANGELISM

McGavran's convictions concerning evangelism sharpened through his years of experience and his growing personal relationship with Jesus Christ. During his furlough in 1947, he requested permission to present the nine most effective methods of evangelism to the entire mission board in Indianapolis. They are as follows:

The first factor dealt with one's relationship to Jesus Christ as the most important method of evangelism. Each evangelist must possess:

> An overpowering conviction that believing on the Lord Jesus Christ, surrendering to the Lord Jesus Christ, complete dedication to the Lord Jesus Christ makes an eternal difference, and is the most important thing to the evangelist.[223]

Secondly, he insisted that the board require a quarterly report of every missionary reporting on three points:

> How many people have you personally spoken to pressing on them the claims of Christ during the past three months? How many people are you daily praying for, that they may accept Jesus Christ as Lord and Savior? How many people have you personally won to Christ during the past three months? Seeking souls is a must to every missionary of the Gospel.[224]

Third, he insisted that witnessing to relatives is a most effective method in evangelism. He maintained that every method be focused on the importance of relative witnessing to relative. On the basis of familial intimacy he theorized:

> All methods will gain many times in effectiveness if preceded by a hearty kiss from the witness to the women of the family. If the relationship is such that a hearty kiss is normal and proper, the witness will fall on fertile soil. Therefore I lay great stress on Christians maintaining the most friendly relationship possible with their non-Christian relatives.[225]

---

223 McGavran, letter to Higdon, (obtained from NV), Aug. 14, 1947.
224 Ibid., 2.
225 Ibid.

McGavran's fourth point was to discover some social, educational, or political need and link it to the gospel presentation. Dalits in India are aware of their need for justice from oppression and exploitation—hence the need to link liberation with salvation.

> Linking the Christian message with some widespread clearly recognized need . . . The Christian faith gives power to nation building. The widespread clearly recognized need should be agreed upon by all the Christian staff working in a district, so that the witness of all, hammers home two points, salvation and satisfaction.[226]

McGavran's fifth point emphasized the place and importance of literature wherever people were becoming literate. He emphasized that considerable attention should be given to translation of the Bible and the printing and distribution of the same. He stressed the need for quality publishing of Bibles and tracts in the vernacular language of the people.

McGavran's sixth point stressed that people be discipled in a cell group context rather than through street preaching and through blaring loudspeakers that would be more apt to raise opposition than interest in the gospel. "I stress having Christians invite non-Christians to Church services, to home services, to Bible reading clubs, organized frankly by three or four Christians with a view to inviting in some non-Christians."[227]

Turning next to mission hospitals, McGavran declared that the general pattern of preaching to the patients each morning before the doctors and nurses made their rounds, could be replaced or supplemented by a more personal approach. For example, they could invite convalescent patients to the home of the doctor or a staff member for three or four consecutive meetings.[228]

In McGavran's eighth point he recognized radio broadcasting as an essential dimension of evangelism. He considered this tool particularly suitable for the wealthy, as few average Asians owned radios back in 1947.

Another evangelistic strategy was the use of literacy programs combined with easy-to-read Christian materials for newly literate people. However, on March 27, 1961, he engaged in some heated correspondence with Frank Laubach over this method. His contention was that literacy became an end in itself instead of the sharing of the gospel.[229]

McGavran's tenth strategy was a source of friction and considerable tension in the Mission. His idea was to divert funds from static areas to growing areas. He fostered this plan when he took up the work among the Satnamis in the Chattisgarh. His colleagues were displeased with the special allotment of $25,000 granted to him by the mission. McGavran

---

226 Ibid., 3.
227 Ibid.
228 Ibid.
229 Donald McGavran, letters from Eugene to Laubach, Baylor, Texas, (obtained from USCWM), March 27, 1961, April 12, 1961, April 25, 1961.

also applied the principle on a broader scale. He felt that a mission in the midst of a people movement, unable to cope with the numbers of converts flooding to Christ, should seek the aid of sister missions operating nearby. This emphasis arose out of a sad situation that developed in Bhil area. After the McGavran and Pickett survey, one of the most promising people movements developed. The mission in charge of the work was the United Church of Canada. Over 30,000 Bhil tribals were baptised in a span of three or four years. Tragically, the mission never asked for assistance, and the missionary in charge left the field. Many of the new Christians reverted.

McGavran applied this principle, not only to a mission operating within a given country, but to the larger worldwide missionary enterprise. In fact, while on furlough in 1948 he suggested to the mission board that funds be redirected from India to Africa as the latter place manifested great receptivity. Of course such an idea did not make him popular with his missionary colleagues in India.

The final evangelistic emphasis was another point of contention. He said, "There must be money available to the evangelist missionary to meet the essential needs of the new Christian Churches and Christians."[230] Although this principle was contrary to the three-self emphasis of John Nevius and Roland Allen, McGavran argued: "Christians are poisoned, denied agricultural credit, ostracized, their sick and their dead are not touched. The missionary must be to the Christian group what the community was to them before they became Christians."[231]

To summarize his views on evangelism, the single purpose of his missiological perspective was that all must lead to conversion of people and the planting of churches. For him, every arm or aspect of mission must contribute to the task of winning people to Christ, their submission to His Lordship in baptism, and their incorporation into churches.

SOCIAL JUSTICE ISSUES

McGavran's ideas were frequently rejected because they were so innovative and confrontational. He was ahead of his time throughout the decades of his ministry in India. Louis Gottschalk captured the crux of the matter in the following statement, "Only rarely does it happen that a leading personality, a great book, an original idea, a significant action or any other extraordinary product of the human individual creates among his contemporaries less favorable than favorable reaction."[232]

While Protestant missions in Africa and Latin America were still in the pioneering phase, missionaries in Asia were grappling with the increasingly complex issue of social justice. In 1920, William Paton, secretary of the National Council in India, led the mission-

---

230 McGavran, letter to Higdon, (obtained from NV), Aug. 14, 1947, 4.
231 Ibid.
232 Louis Gottschalk, Clyde Kluckhohn, and Robert Cooley Angell, eds. *The Use of Personal Documents in History, Anthropology, and Sociology* (1945), 61–62.

ary vanguard in an emphasize on social service. This endeavour became known as, "The Rural Education and the Rural Reconstruction Programmes."[233]

Some of his recommendations sounded like contemporary contextualization. For example, Christian schools in the Indian villages were encouraged to redesign their curricula radically so they would be "related to and grow out of village life and needs."[234] The YMCA in India appointed K. T. Paul to organize cooperative societies in villages and assist the exploited masses of India to reach for higher standards of living.

Immediately after the 1928 Jerusalem Meeting of the International Missionary Council, Kenyon L. Butterfield was appointed to make a detailed study of issues of social justice in India's villages. In the forward to his report he wrote:

> Heretofore, Christianity has combatted chiefly Hinduism and animism; now it has to deal with an ardent nationalism, a measure of current materialism, perhaps with communism, certainly with industrialism. There must be a reappraisal of the missionary enterprise in terms of the new problems and in the mood of high adventure into uncharted areas of Christian endeavour.[235]

He rightly perceived, even in 1928, that India's cities would exploit and take advantage of rural villagers. He wrote, "Social conflicts are involved as the cities take on new vigor. There is always a tendency to the exploitation of the rural by the urban, and to the neglect of rural interests and problems."[236] Unfortunately Butterfield was not encultured to India and his analysis of the needs of the country was from a Western perspective. Except for two paragraphs, he neglected the most crying issue of India—that of caste enslavement and the consequent injustice it brought to society. He did not realize that in India the rural-urban tension was heightened by the high caste-low caste conflict.

McGavran did hear Butterfield speak on several occasions while he was touring India in 1929. His message was that the application of scientific methods of agriculture and use of fertilizers, pesticides, and hybrid varieties of grain would assist India's farmers. Butterfield's concept of social justice for India was set forth in a plan called, "Rural Reconstruction Units." Baago has observed that this very plan appears to have been incorporated into the Indian government's present day "Community Development Projects."[237]

The missionaries who served in India over the past 200 years have been in the vanguard of grappling with social evils such as child marriage, suttee, infanticide, headhunting, and racial tyranny in the guise of caste. Biblical ethics and Western social standards of the missionaries were the single most powerful force in confronting such evils and in some

---

233 Baago, *A History of the National Council of India*, 45.

234 Ibid., 46.

235 Kenyen L. Butterfield, *The Christian Mission in Rural India* (New York: International Missions Council, 1930), 3.

236 Ibid., 111.

237 Kaj, *A History of the National Council of India*, 47.

cases completely eliminating them. In other cases, missionaries greatly modified the depth of grief and pain which such practises brought upon the common people.

McGAVRAN AS AN ACTIVIST FOR SOCIAL JUSTICE

McGavran was a social activist throughout his entire thirty years of service in India. He demonstrated a strong sense of righteous indignation whenever he came upon people exploiting others. His primary aims were evangelism and church planting, even though he was also highly committed to virtually every aspect of the rural reconstruction program. He fulfilled all the recommendations of Butterfield and even more. He possessed two skills that enabled him to attend to the needs of the Satnami villagers; the most prominent of which was the remarkable way he identified with them. He ate their food, slept in their homes, fought their battles, and risked his life on many occasions to see that justice was done. He was a village missionary, heart and soul, for over seventeen years. Butterfield rightly observed the uniqueness of such a missionary:

> Very few missionaries live in villages. All too few missionaries know intimately the villages or the villager. Nine-tenths of the missionary work in India is done on behalf of one-tenth of the people. This means that the overwhelming emphasis, so far as the immediate activities of the missionary personnel are concerned, is with the people of the towns and cities.[238]

Like Butterfield, McGavran challenged missionaries living in the cities and towns to reconsider the focus of their effort. He was enraged that ninety percent of missionary effort and investment was focused on one-tenth of the Indian population, spiritually resistant high caste Hindus, while receptive Untouchables in the villages were basically neglected. He wanted justice for the oppressed villagers. He understood the villagers and the village milieu better than the vast majority of the urban-oriented missionaries and his writings and his letters reveal profound insight into daily village life. He, like Gandhi, understood that "the future of India will be decided not in her cities but in her villages."[239]

> The village mind is a complex one, indirect and tortuous in some respects, vigorous and ruthless in others. It is a group mind. There are no secrets in the village. The villager lives under rigorous conditions. His wife and her little children, needing to go to some relatives, walk twenty miles. It is no easier for them than it would be for us. The villager sleeps cold. His wife may have one sari, and a little baby. When the baby wets the sari on a cold December night, the mother freezes all

---

238 Butterfield, *The Christian Mission in Rural India*, 43.
239 M. K. Gandhi, Madras Guardian, June 1928.

night long. Before harvest comes in, many a villager, short of food, just puts twice as much water in the gruel to make it go round. Most villagers are thin.[240]

McGavran was thoroughly acquainted with village intercaste rivalries. He understood the dynamics of their coexistence. He described them as follows: "Quarrels take enormous amounts of time, and lead to endless recriminations, abuse, filthy language, nights spent planning revenge, indigestion, loss of sleep, to say nothing of broken heads, burnt houses, torn saris and long-drawn-out law-suits."[241]

The fact that villagers stare death in the face continually was so real to McGavran that he expended himself without reserve to fight for their very existence. He was subjectively involved in their very lives. To him, their suffering was as real as if they were his own children.

Another stark physical lack is loss by disease. The man gets malaria just at the time of sowing. The baby son dies after two weeks of wasting illness with dysentery. The mother has not been able to work in the fields during this time. The father has been harried with anxiety. His nights have been broken. Much time during his days has been given to trips here and there for medicine. During his absences cattle have grazed part of his crop and thieves have taken more.[242]

He could describe this situation because he had not only observed such circumstances in his daily intercourse with the villagers, but also because he suffered the affliction of their diseases with them. On more than one occasion he was brought to the point of death by malaria and other afflictions. However, we should underscore that, he also realized that apart from the transforming power of Christ, all the social action in the world would not change the age-old customs of village life. For most Indians, becoming a Christian would be the longest single step towards social justice they could possibly take.

His long years in India demonstrated unwavering commitment to social action, as he vigorously opposed misplaced objectives. It was his conviction that when social action and social justice replace, or compete, with evangelism and church planting, the missionary cause has been betrayed.

THE GROWING CHURCH FUND

McGavran's promotional letters home produced money even in times of depression and war. This ability endeared him to the Indians, but created tensions with his fellow missionaries, who at times were envious.

---

240 Donald McGavran, "The Economic Liabilities of Village Christians," *National Council of Churches Review* 73, no. 4 (April 1953): 177.

241 Ibid.

242 Ibid.

He developed another important principle in church growth thinking—an urgency of adequate funding for growing churches. He raised serious objections to the principle of equal division of funds.[243] If a mission with ten stations had one that reported ten times as many conversions and baptisms per year than all the other nine put together, he felt a diversion of funds, to assist the cutting edge of church growth, would be appropriate. The Mungeli-Takhatpur region was in this position; it reported ten times as many conversions as all the other stations combined.

He enjoyed an unusually close relationship with Cy Yocum, the Asian Secretary of the United Christian Missionary Society. In 1937, McGavran proposed that a "growing church fund" of $25,000 be established for the great people movement, which he was convinced would occur among the Satnamis shortly. On December 10, 1937 he wrote, "Add to our budget a special annual sum to enable us to develop our few and precious growing points. That to give a margin in which to operate the UCMS (United Christian Missionary Society) put in their specials, at the head of the list, as the thing most desired in the India Mission, the sum of $25,000."[244]

Today, the request for a sum of $25,000 may seem reasonable enough, but in 1937, in the midst of the depression it was like asking for a million dollars. The appeal was based on five factors.

1. This action is in line with the recommendation of the NCC of India which asks mission boards to make available special sums of money to support preacher-teachers of new groups coming into the faith.
2. This action asks for a very moderate sum of money, a total addition to the annual budget of about $700 for 1938–39.
3. This plan was presented in annual convention and passed.
4. Only such a plan will enable us to launch forth on a plan of raising up men for the new church which is certain to arise.
5. This plan makes it possible for us to avoid that impossibly difficult task of reallocation of resources . . . this additional budget for evangelism and church growth is very needed.[245]

It was not until McGavran arrived in the United States for his 1939 furlough year that the plan for the $25,000 was finally launched. With official endorsement, he swung into action. His creative mind and boundless energy were brought to focus on fund-raising. A series of dramatic articles were written describing accounts of family conversions, people movements, power encounter struggles with unconverted relatives, and the development of new leadership. His appeal was earnest, exciting, and evangelistic. He was able to tap

---

243 Donald McGavran, letter from Jabalpur to Cy Yocum, (obtained from NV), Aug. 10, 1934.
244 Donald McGavran, letter from Mungeli-Takhatpur to Cy Yocum, (obtained from NV), Dec. 10, 1937.
245 Ibid.

the resources of the more evangelical churches and individuals whose giving had dropped due to the inroads of liberal influence.

> Here is the greatest opportunity we have experienced. It is one which may rapidly pass. Out of your millions create a fund of $25,000 to be spent for evangelism, to enable a great church to be born. This sum, contributed as above the budget gifts, will be spent exclusively for promoting the growth of the new churches amongst castes turning to Christ. It will undergird a ten-year evangelistic campaign to nurture group movements among approachable castes. We are pledging our lives. Will you pledge your money?[246]

Personal letters were written to individuals and churches who gave to the growing church fund. Each letter described in detail how the monies were actually spent. They listed the families converted, pastors trained, and chapels built. Considerable correspondence was directed to fellow missionaries in India to get them involved in the promotion. Each missionary received a file of promotional materials which had been developed and written by McGavran. Then too, there were many letters to mission headquarters soliciting cooperation in the promotion and development of donors.

He travelled up and down the United States speaking to churches, youth groups, and individuals about this unique investment opportunity with eternal dividends and all of this promotion produced the desired result. By 1943, the fund had reached the $25,000 mark and then some.[247]

September 1940 found the McGavrans back in India for their third term of service. With the money flowing, McGavran pressed his evangelists and pastors to new heights of evangelistic activity. For example, the goals for 1942 were: 1,000 new Christians in the next twelve months, 50 percent literacy (it was then 9 percent) with all readers reading the Bible, 25 percent of the membership witnessing to their faith publicly at least once a week, and every church with an adult night school.[248]

These goals however were never reached despite vast efforts. Gandhi and his Congress movement had begun to implement a plan of special assistance to the Untouchable communities. Scholarships were provided for children, loans for food grains were given and legislature posts were reserved for Untouchable leaders. All of this seriously undermined McGavran's plans and effort to bring the Satnamis to Christ.

The growing church fund was administrated and controlled by a committee of missionaries in India. There were rules and policies by which funds were to be dispersed. Theoretically, funds were available to all mission stations where conversions were taking

---

246 Donald McGavran, "Christianity in India's Life," *World Call* 22 (1940).

247 Donald McGavran, letter from Takhatpur to Fullerton Christian Church, Fullerton, California., July 26, 1943.

248 McGavran, "Training Teachers for a New Christian Movement," *World Call*, (Feb. 1942), 42.

place and where the gospel was flowing from one relative to another along caste lines. In actual fact, very few stations other than Takhatpur and Mungeli received assistance, for they did not qualify. Very few missionaries with the Disciples actually had time for evangelism due to their preoccupation with the institutions already in place on their stations.

Although the guidelines were clear, the other missionaries were increasingly unhappy with the large amounts of money received by McGavran, and as a result considerable tension arose within the mission. Attempts were made to divert some of the funds. In a heart-rending letter to Yocum, McGavran described his turmoil of mind:

> We find our work constantly handicapped, and the growth of the church endangered, the loss of the battle partially provided for because we seem to engender in our fellow missionaries, at least in some of them, that this is our work, that when the mission makes grants toward the work they are doing something for us personally, expanding our ego. Naturally the question arises, "Why should Don get everything?"[249]

The tension never became a personal conflict. McGavran wrote, "It is therefore no personal quarrel. It is simply that I find myself in the midst of good friends, whose ideas of mission work differ radically from mine. I feel my convictions forcing me out of a group of delightful people."[250] This issue seems to have come to a head when McGavran asked the Executive Committee of the India field "to transfer them to some other field of work."[251] Although this was not an attempt to escape. McGavran wanted to be placed in a more neutral situation, from which he could plead for funds for the developing people movement around Takhatpur. He reasoned that from such a vantage point, he could see that funds kept flowing "without a trace of this ugly suspicion which continually puts me in a false light and destroys my ability to plead" for the needed growing church funds.[252]

Tensions were further aggravated when W. B. Alexander, the field secretary for so many years, retired. The India field council voted Mr. Kenneth Potee in as field secretary. McGavran described the situation: "The change of mission secretaries brings into office one who has never given much time to the evangelistic work and is completely out of touch with this effort here. Naturally he looks at things somewhat distantly."[253]

McGavran chafed from the lack of vision and direction of the missionaries in India. His letter to Yocum reflects his impatience:

---

249 Donald McGavran, letter from Takhatpur to Cy Yocum, (obtained from NV), Dec. 5, 1942.
250 Donald McGavran, letter to Cy Yocum, (obtained from NV), Feb. 8, 1944.
251 Donald McGavran, letter to Potee, (obtained from USCWM), March 7, 1943.
252 Donald McGavran, letter to Cy Yocum, (obtained from NV), Dec. 5, 1942.
253 Donald McGavran, letter to CyYocum, (obtained from NV), May 18, 1943.

Most of our missionaries are in sterile areas. Mission work in sterile areas tends to become institutional. Institutional missionaries are seldom seekers of souls. Work ceases to be regarded as carried on with a purpose to Christianize a countryside, and comes to be regarded as a carrying on even if baptisms never occur. Committees tend to revolve around the pulls of various established works, all of them, including the evangelistic works, sterile as an ox. Then to the missionary family knows intimately a great many of the 2,500 Christians who make up our membership. Their interests and their welfare tend to become the supreme concern of the missionary family. It is easy for the mission to think that its reason for existence is to help this minute church to become more literate, more healthy, more wealthy, more godly, whether growth beyond the confines of this little group occurs or not.[254]

FAMINE, WAR REFUGEES, AND SOCIAL JUSTICE

While his energies were being seriously tried by compatriots whose goals were so radically different from his, another challenge arose. From 1940 to 1942, the monsoon rains failed in Central India. After the third crop failure, the local villagers were reduced to abject poverty.

McGavran faced a moral issue. The $25,000 fund was available, yet all the promotional material promised that the dollars given would be utilized for evangelistic purposes. With that kind of money available during a famine, there was a strong temptation to buy "rice Christians" by helping people out of their desperate plight provided they make a commitment to Jesus Christ. McGavran was a principled man, however, and would not stoop to such manipulation of lives. He described the situation as, "There is great hunger and want on every hand. We could baptize hundreds now, if we were to give them perhaps five rupees ($1.25) worth of help. So far, however, we have refused to promise any help to anyone, and have kept the baptismal ceremony for those whom we felt had in them the germ at least of understanding of and loyalty to the Christian faith."[255]

Except for assistance to some Christian families, the growing church fund was never utilized for famine relief. An appeal went out to America for funds for famine relief in 1942 and 1943 and McGavran set up a relief program that did even more than feed empty stomachs. Understanding the village economic structure, he knew that loss of land to the farmer is worse than death itself, so he did everything he could to rescue their lands from foreclosure. He described something of their desperate situation:

There was very great distress. People sold their tools, their oxen, failed to pay their taxes, and the interest and installments on their debts, mortgages began

---

254 Donald McGavran, letter to Cy Yocum, Feb. 3, 1983.
255 Donald McGavran, letter to Cy Yocum, Oct. 1, 1941.

to be foreclosed, farmers could not get seed grain, did not have enough capital to work their fields, labourers migrated in search of work, abandoned wife and children to save their own lives, families cut down amounts to half of normal ration and fell easy prey to sickness, were struck by malaria epidemic of enormous proportions which swept India.[256]

He designed his program to preserve the respect and dignity of the village farmer, restore him to his land, and feed his family until the harvest came in. McGavran created work for these starving, desperate people when there was none to be had. One such project was to have the people gather lime nuggets off the fields. He paid the people by the cubic foot of gathered stone. These stones were later used to build roads or to burn for lime. The project accomplished three things: the farmer and his family earned money enough to buy food, it cleaned the rubble off the fields, and it provided construction material for roads and buildings.[257]

Another project McGavran created for relief was to have a group of farmers dig a large pit, while others were sent out into the fields to gather a weed which ruined much of the land. He paid them by the headload, and these loads were dumped into the pit and made into compost which was later used as fertilizer. Other innovative projects were set up, such as digging wells and road construction. McGavran described the overall effect of these projects, "This sort of famine relief in the Christian community has prevented deaths in scores of homes, preserved the fields of many families from lying fallow or being sold and has given a chance at new life to hundreds."[258]

Just as the famine crises was being laid to rest, an even more ominous threat rolled into Central India. In 1943, the Second World War was at its height. Information leaked out that the Japanese were going to invade India. The British set up a strategy to draw the invading Japanese force into the heart of India and then cut off their supplies and their retreat. The area selected for the final battle was Chattisgarh. The military command ordered the villagers in the Takhatpur region out of their homes, and for a period of several months, fear and chaos reigned among the ousted Satnami villagers. During these months, McGavran worked day and night to console the villagers and provide shelter and food. Of course, all this activity seriously cut into McGavran's goals for getting a people movement started among the Satnamis.

Once normal routine returned, McGavran found himself increasingly involved in issues of social justice. He described one case in which he was entangled:

---

256 Donald McGavran, letter from Takhatpur to Muncie, Eatin, Tabor Christian Churches, Yorktown, (obtained from USCWM), Nov. 26, 1943.

257 Ibid.

258 Ibid., 2.

The landlord was resolved that he would drive out his Christian peasants. One way or another, he would make life miserable for them. He cut down their trees. He gave the most filthy abuse to their women. He threatened court action for offenses which never occurred. He promised to beat up all Christians . . . The campaign of persecution culminated when the petty police official, who it was said had accepted a bribe from the landlord, arrived in the village and for hours on end exerted all his pressure to get the Christians to offer sacrifices to the village gods.[259]

As his reputation among the villagers grew, many approached him to intercede on their behalf for one issue or another. On one occasion, several people came to him with a complaint of unfair police harassment. Often he found himself wondering if the tale of woe was true. To avoid embarrassment and loss of credibility he developed skills in detecting falsehood. In the case of the police abuse of villagers, it took some time for him to get to the bottom of that issue.

One instance occurred when an attractive villager's wife was in the market with her husband and a policeman came up and pinched her breasts making suggestive comments. This infuriated the husband who knocked the man to the ground. The policeman in turn made life absolutely miserable for this family and a court case resulted. McGavran pled their case before the judge and the villager was not given a jail sentence. McGavran spent considerable time championing the rights of the Untouchables.[260]

Such demands and urgent needs were constantly confronting McGavran throughout his seventeen years as a village missionary, yet he never lost sight of his central purpose of evangelism. In his correspondence with supporters in the US he assiduously stressed that activities related to social justice were secondary to the primary task of proclaiming Jesus Christ to the Hindus and establishing churches in the receptive Satnami villages.

SOCIAL JUSTICE AND EVANGELISM

The issue of social justice versus evangelism was never a case of either/or for McGavran. Both had their place, but he insisted that social action must never be substituted for evangelism. He adamantly opposed all attempts to define "mission" so broadly and so hazily that evangelism became anything one does in the name of Christ.

The missionaries who espoused social action as their primary responsibility played into the hands of Mahatma Gandhi. Gandhi presented his ideas of social and economic uplift, and his reinterpretation of evangelism to be "like the fragrance of the rose which

---

259 Donald McGavran, letter from Takhatpur to L. T. Druck, Muncie, Indiana, (obtained from USCWM), July 31, 1943.

260 Donald McGavran, interview by Vern Middleton, April 13, 1984. Note: letters were sent out requesting police reports on the above issues, but no reply was forthcoming. Apparently there were two massive police files on McGavran's involvements in championing the rights of the Untouchable people.

called upon the missionary to cease from preaching and let his message rest on his silent witness of his life and service."[261] For missionaries serving in India, any attempt to broaden definitions of evangelism and stress social action as a primary ministry of the servant of Christ, led them to fall prey to Hindu syncretistic thought. Hindu leaders sought to instill feelings of guilt and a sense of uncertainty in the lives of missionaries so they would stop preaching the gospel. Hindu reasoning found the exclusiveness of the gospel of Jesus Christ unpalatable. They protested that God is unknowable, hence all religions are man's efforts to search for truth. Therefore, they argued, all religions are equally valid. Another accusation against the gospel stated that it is an act of treason and unpatriotic for a man to depart from the faith of his ancestors.

Donald with village Indians. He was highly relational.

Butterfield's definition of evangelism, a by-product of the Jerusalem IMC, was made without any thought of the apologetic issues the missionaries in India faced during the 1930s and 40s.

It is an inclusive evangelism. Every activity must be spiritualized and truly Christianized. Evangelism is far broader than preaching. There is also the evangelism of service . . . The preacher must proclaim an evangel as broad as all the needs of the villager, and as inclusive as the range of impact of the peculiar Christian message upon all aspects of personal and corporate life.[262]

---

261 Hodge, *Salute to India*, 88.
262 Butterfield, *The Christian Mission in Rural India*, 45.

While mission leaders, such as Butterfield, defined evangelism to be everything the missionary did, Gandhi was defining evangelism as proselytization. This two-pronged attack on the credibility of evangelism left some missionaries with pangs of guilt, and in the throes of confusion.

McGavran developed his ideas on the relationship between evangelism and social action in this environment and in the face of strong opposition from his colleagues. Tom Hill ran the mission press and in 1938 McGavran engaged him in lengthy debate on the issue of the purpose and aim of mission.

Hill's thesis was, "Missions have a dual aim: to do good regardless of what comes of it, just because the Christian heart overflows with goodness, and to build the Church."[263] McGavran countered with a three-page letter in which he argued from the life and example of Jesus. The Savior did not go about in a haphazard fashion, merely doing good. Healing was performed that men might believe. His apostles were instructed to turn men from sin to righteousness. Jesus' chief aim was to establish God's Church.

> The kindly deed done by the foreigner with foreign money is good. But there is a limit to the number of cups so available. If one wants to do more good, if one wants philanthropic service to flourish, if one wants not cups of cold water but rivers of water fresh from God's heart, then we must drive wells which will survive our departure. We must build churches.[264]

Apparently, Hill took exception to McGavran's strong insistence that the many institutions of the mission be evaluated in terms of their effectiveness in producing flourishing churches. In that same letter, he remarked that McGavran ought to apply the same criteria to his "evangelistic institutions." Hill, and many other missionaries in the mission, interpreted McGavran's zeal for evangelism and church planting as the root cause for interdepartmental rivalries. McGavran shattered that delusion with the following statement:

> I am not interested in the evangelistic department, nor the educational department, nor any method, or lack of method. I want to see the church grow. I want to see the terrible spiritual hunger on all sides of us assuaged. I want to see them stop nachaoing (dancing) harlots in the name of religion. I want to see them stop worshipping naked images. I want to see this obscene temple at Setganga torn down. I want to see a church in every village and the open Word of God in every home. I don't care what brings this about—educational or evangelistic or medical.

---

263 Tom Hill, letter to Donald McGavran, Aug. 10, 1938.
264 Donald McGavran, letter to Tom Hill, Sept. 16, 1938, 3.

But the means that are not bringing it about anywhere in India are the means that ought to go, and go soon.

Hill's final paragraph had indirectly accused McGavran of proselytizing, seeking shortcuts and trying to produce a people movement in a reprehensible manner. McGavran's response was not to debate the accusations, but rather indicate something of the sadness of his heart. "Is this your honest opinion? If so, it is interesting—and explains a lot which I had not yet understood. It speaks ill for the mission and its future. I am frankly shocked at the underlying implications in your reaction . . . I have seldom seen a better defense for doing nothing and maintaining the status quo."

This interaction was an example of the ongoing debate, controversy, and tension that McGavran constantly faced with most of his missionary colleagues. Many opted for social service, passing out cups of cold water while McGavran was drilling for streams of water that would flow throughout India. From 1932 to 1954 the argument grew in frequency, scope, and intensity.[265]

His convictions on the priority of evangelism were more than an in-house issue where he was clamoring for a lion's share of the mission's resources. This evidenced itself in his articles and in a personal letter to Abbe Livingston Warnshius, secretary of the International Missionary Council. While on furlough in the United States in 1939, McGavran reacted to an article Warnshius had written saying: "Much time and printer's ink could have been saved by saying in advance, 'We are convinced that everything which is being done by a large number of missionaries should be continued, expanded and pushed to the limit. We are for everything.'"[266]

McGavran went on to press the point that all missionary work is important, but needs to be prioritized. He elaborated as follows:

> In the welter of important demanding, urgent tasks, all of which need to be done, there is imperative need of order of precedence, of synthesis. To achieve their recognized ends of Christian Missions, some very important tasks should be deferred, some expedited. Some deserve 10 percent support, others 90 percent support. Furthermore the relative importance of various types of work differs with the stage of development in which the Church finds itself . . . Whether a mission at work in China gives 10 percent of its time to evangelism and 90 percent to rural reconstruction or in reverse proportion is left to the judgment of local missionaries. For all their devotion and intelligence they lack precisely

---

265 McGavran, *UCR*, 12, no. 7 (July 1941): 159; 12, no. 9 (Sept. 1941): 227; 12, no. 12 (Dec. 1941): 312; 13, no. 3 (March 1942): 65, 70; 13, no. 8 (Aug. 1942); 14, no. 4 (April 1943); 14, no. 9 (Aug. 1943); 14, no. 10 (Oct. 1943); 15, no. 3 (March 1944).

266 Donald McGavran, letter from New Palestine to Abbe Livingston, Warnshuis IMC, (obtained from USCWM), Nov. 3, 1939.

that world view and world experience which would enable them to make a right decision. They should determine their procedure in the light of 150 years of modern exploration in the Christianization of nations and in the light of the total world situation. That is exactly what they do not know and cannot know except guidance be provided.[267]

A spinoff from the Warnshius interaction resulted in his writing of an article for the *Christian Evangelist* entitled, "Evangelism and Basic Missionary Policy."[268] In it he stressed that the "gigantic evils" of that day ought not to redirect the church to "shift its emphasis from territory and numbers to quality of life." He summarized by saying, "Evangelism is essential if social evils are to be eradicated. Territory and numbers must be emphasized if we are to achieve a universal quality of life."[269]

Eighteen years later, McGavran had the article, "Have We Lost Our Way In Missions?" published in the March 1958 issue of the *Christian Herald*. It lists five ways in which missionaries become sidetracked from the essential task of evangelism. The first two of these issues bear directly on the problem of social action versus evangelism.

McGavran discerned that, for some, the controversy over social justice pivoted on their doubts regarding the uniqueness of Christianity. Some mission leaders had begun to wallow in the quagmire of Universalism. McGavran stated, "The first deviation is the imagining that, in some vague way, other religions confer salvation and hence, their followers do not need the Savior. Any person who believes this, weakens his own will to propagate the Christian faith, and lowers Christian mission to the same spiritual level as UNICEF."[270]

By substituting good deeds in the place of fervent evangelism, missions also lose their way. McGavran divided good deeds into three categories; "those done among men we would win to Christ, . . . those done among immature younger churches, . . . those done exclusively as service to man." Without question, he felt these activities were valid and needful provided, "they commend the Gospel, nourish a living Church and so long as such welfare work does not leave us exhausted and unable to search for and win ripe populations."[271]

In conclusion, it must be recognized that McGavran's belief in the absolute priority of evangelism led him into significant involvement in social action during his seventeen years in Chattisgarh. However the tension with his fellow missionaries eventually brought McGavran and his wife to the conviction that they must leave the India field.

---

267 Ibid.

268 Donald McGavran, "Evangelism and Basic Missionary Policy," *Christian Evangelist* (Oct. 10, 1940).

269 Ibid..

270 Donald McGavran, letter from Takhatpur to the International Missionary Council, (obtained from USCWM), Dec. 1943.

271 See Appendix D for a full bibliographic outline of these writings. Two archival repositories have material in the US; The Graduate Theological School, Berkeley, California and Union Theological Seminary, New York.

EDITOR: *UNITED CHURCH REVIEW*

McGavran assumed the task of exchange editor of the *United Church Review* (hereafter known as *UCR*) in May 1941. (See Appendix D for a list of these editorials.) He carried this responsibility along with his many other duties through March 1947. His task was: "To peruse the writings of those who are at the present time bearing the brunt of the Christian battle and to bring from the perusal a winnowed basketful to the readers."[272] He was no stranger to the *UCR* readership, as two of his extensive articles had been previously published in the journal in 1936 and 1938.

The assignment provided a window to the world and respite from the isolation of Takhatpur and village evangelism. Through this work, he regained much of his former high profile with the North India missionary community and with Indian Christian leaders.[273]

As an editor, McGavran's usual style of writing gave way to a more personable format. The range of subjects on which he expressed opinion revealed the breadth and depth of his thinking as well as the diversity of his missionary interests and activities. Unlike much of his church growth writing, these articles showed the spiritual and devotional side of McGavran.[274]

Throughout the next six years, he seldom lost an opportunity to insert a few of his church growth ideas into the editorial column. The monthly contribution actually created a paper trail showing the development of his ideas.

The first column contained a section entitled, "Stages of Church Growth." The essence of his idea on this topic was that generalized statements made about the church in India lead to confusion. He cited this as a major weakness with the Tambaram Conference. He pled for responsible accurate descriptions of various aspects of the church. Three stages of mission were categorized: the early species, or missions still in the pioneering phase, the intermediate species of a small community of two or three thousand believers with several institutions, and the Christian movement species, which manifested strong indigenous patterns.[275]

The next edition of *UCR* examined the problem of comity arrangement between missions. He lamented that most missions retained spiritual control over regions far beyond their capacity to evangelize. Responsible missionary work, he stated, will see that neglected fringe areas are occupied. This concern arose from the situation he found near Takhatpur. McGavran urged the executive committee of UCMS India to invite independent missionaries to man these outlying regions, which they did.[276] Unfortunately the "independents," as they

---

272   McGavran, *UCR* 12, no.5 (May 1941): 18.

273   McGavran, *UCR*, 12, no. 6 (June 1941): 140.

274   Donald McGavran, interview by Helen Cornelson, Mennonite Missionary who served thirty years in a district adjacent to the UCMS region, June 9, 1989.

275   Donald McGavran, *UCR* 12, no. 12 (Dec. 1941): 313.

276   Donald McGavran, *UCR* 13, no. 1 (Jan. 1942): 14.

were known, became a problem to sister missions, as they did not always stick to the remote fringe areas. The result was that they moved into the urbanized areas of the primary mission, often recruiting disgruntled church members from the existing Christian community.[277]

World Dominion published an article entitled, "A Great Church," which he reviewed. The material prompted McGavran to develop a tool for measuring the greatness of a church. His idea was as follows: "I love formulas. Why not get out of our vague inexact thinking about the greatness of churches and achieve clarity and thereby progress by reducing the test to a formula—divide the number of new converts in a given year by the existing membership. The quotient will be called either an Index of Greatness or an Index of Deadness."[278]

This concept was pursued further in the very next issue of *UCR* under the title, "A Church Standard." He asked the question:

> Why should there not be a standard of Church life? It would be applicable to all churches. Pastors could measure their churches against it. Church Boards could see where their churches stood in regard to daily worship, giving, witness bearing, and the other elementary essentials of Christian living . . . I believe the Holy Spirit would use such a means to the sanctification of the Church.[279]

Here were the beginning stages of accurate measurement for church growth, through the use of mathematical formulas, graphs, and tables.

The same issue of *UCR* contained a section entitled "The Church—A Problem or a Power." Here, he contrasted two views of the church. He cited the attitudes of the liberal theologians who were critical of the church because she failed to measure up to certain ideal standards and lead society into a future Utopia. In contrast to these, he described the positive approach Kenneth Scott Latourette had in his descriptive accounts of church history. He rejoiced that Latourette saw the church as a power because he measured her against history and the place a given nation or people might have been, apart from the redeeming grace of God.[280]

Many church growth ideas developed in his thinking as he wrestled with the concepts expressed by theological liberals. During the 1940s, they claimed there were two types of evangelism—conversion and penetration. McGavran reacted by calling the dichotomy both "erroneous and pernicious." He categorically stated that both must function:

> . . . the more conversions there are, the more Churches are established, the greater the number of places in which our Lord is worshipped, the more numerous

---

277 Ibid., 15.
278 Donald McGavran, "Two Schools of Evangelism," 70.
279 Donald McGavran, "Growth the Touchstone," *UCR* 14, no. 4 (April 1943): 63.
280 Ibid.

the open Bibles, the more generally known the Christian way of life, the more penetration of social and religious and political thinking there is. The greatest favour which could be done to Hinduism would be the conversion of a hundred million people in India to Christianity. That would purge Hinduism of idolatry and caste as nothing else will.[281]

In 1942–43 the Second World War fed the growing power of Hindu nationalism in India. With the prospect of an independent India, came increased potential for persecution of Christians. Some missionaries reasoned that such a purge of the Christian community would be healthy. In addition, liberalism having gained ground after Tambaram 1938 gave rise to the philosophy that "making Christians is not really the purpose of the Church in India; rather the Church has a friendship mission to Hinduism."[282]

McGavran labeled any ideas that replaced spiritual reproduction and evangelism with anemic, introverted Christian presence, as heresy. He wrote, "All this is a belittling of spiritual reproduction. It is a denying of the Great Commission . . . one of the touchstones of genuine Christianity must be growth."[283]

The International Missionary Council received an open letter from McGavran in December 1943, which he also published in the *UCR*. The essence of the appeal was that IMC must develop a global strategy for missionaries, mission boards, and denominations. He summarized his point of view as follows: "The IMC . . . has as one of its main functions, constant study of opportunity, continual research into effective methods, uninterrupted assaying of the degree and quality of church growth achieved, the laying down on the basis of this information an elastic global strategy."[284] Proddings such as these served to stimulate and encourage the IMC in its task of acting as a clearing house of information, research, and counsel.

Toward the end of the war years, 1944–45, Indian Christian leadership became increasingly outspoken in its criticism of the church in India. This was, partly due to nationalistic feelings, impatient liberalism, and sensitivity to the Hindu point of view, which resulted in a generally low view of the church. McGavran responded with his high view of the church. "We believe that the Church is . . . the strongest organization in the world, the one least swayed by the storms of race and time, the one most in harmony with the eternal will of God."[285]

Here he articulated an essential church growth point of view which holds the church in high esteem. In the same article McGavran explained that this high view of the church arose not out of blind allegiance, but rather from the theological reality that the church

---

281 Donald McGavran, "An Open Letter," *UCR* 14, no.12 (Dec. 1943): 192.
282 Donald McGavran, "Deadlock in the Indian Church," *UCR* 16, no.11 (Nov. 1945): 127.
283 Ibid.
284 McGavran, "The Growing Edge," *UCR* 18, no. 3 (March 1947): 241.
285 George Beazley, ed. *The Christian Church (Disciples of Christ): An Interpretive Examination in the Cultural Context* (St. Louis: Bethany Press, 1973), 238.

has God's guiding presence: "The grace of God is upon the Church. It is multiplying and exerting an influence entirely disproportionate to its size . . . The Church is going forward with God."[286]

The final editorial produced by McGavran as exchange editor of the *UCR* contained a creative church-growth analogy from the medical world. A Satnami farmer was severely burned by a bomb left in his field during army practise exercises. The villagers sought McGavran's help. This errand of mercy gave him opportunity to observe the treatment. He was fascinated by the treatment the doctors gave. He noted that skin grows from the edges to recover the burned area, and medical doctors multiplied the growing edges by means of skin grafts in order to produce overall healing and health. He drew the analogy by stating:

> The Christian Church in India also grows from the edges. There has to be some Church in living contact with a non-Christian mass for growth to take place. No matter how good the Church is, if living contact is not there, there is no growth . . . Skin grows out of skin; church grows out of church. Isolated Churches not in living contact with the non-Christian world, are like skin grafts that do not take.[287]

He pressed the analogy one point further, noting that just as new growth from a skin graft takes place on the leading edges, so it is with churches. Thus, he reasoned that the focus of missions ought to be poured into those churches in close contact with the world. He lamented that mission aid was poured into areas without growth, preventing the church from having living contact with some strata of India's society.

The impression may be that the editorial column was utilized by McGavran for church growth propaganda. But the ideas singled out here are only a fraction of the plethora of subjects on which he wrote. Throughout the years of World War II, his column became a source of encouragement, instruction, healing, and spiritual strength to the church at large in India. McGavran's optimistic interpretation of history, (e.g., "Turning this Present Adversity for Advance"), his confidence in the sovereign purposes of God being worked out in human history, and his witty illustrations provided balance. Missionaries stuck to their posts and labored in the face of insecurity and insurmountable odds. In a way, the monthly editorial served as pastoral counsel to the large missionary community in India.

When McGavran laid down his pen in March of 1947 to take a furlough leave, he did so with nostalgic reluctance.

---

286 Ibid., 243.
287 Pierce Beaver, *Occasional Bulletin*, June 1967.

ISSUES OF CHURCH UNITY

Church unity and intermission cooperation have received considerable attention since Edinburgh 1910, and particularly since the World Council of Churches was formed in 1948. However, in some evangelical circles even the mention of "church unity" throws some church leaders into a defensive position. This is partly due to this century's Christian denominational fusion which has often been promoted by theological liberals. In reaction, evangelicals have tended to associate church union with such nasty things as theological compromise and theological reductionism. Some fundamentalists have even conjured up images of the antichrist ruling a super-church whenever church unity and inter-denominational cooperation are mentioned.

Interdenominational cooperation was foundational for the founders of the Restoration Movement. Alexander Campbell underscored the essential nature of cooperation when he detailed the missionary outreach of the Disciples of Christ.

1. We can do comparatively nothing in distributing the Bible abroad without cooperation.
2. We can do comparatively but little in the great missionary field of the world, either at home or abroad, without cooperation.
3. We can do little or nothing to improve and elevate the Christian ministry without cooperation.[288]

Archibald McLean led the mission's vanguard of the Disciples of Christ from 1882 to 1920, first as secretary and later as president. He observed after one of his world mission tours:

Missions are drawing Christian people closer together. They feel the need of combining that they may present a solid front to the foe. They are closer to one another than at home for their preaching is more scriptural and more simple.[289]

R. Pierce Beaver observed the same pattern during the eighteenth and nineteenth centuries. He described the dynamic toward unity within the worldwide missionary community as follows:

The rising Protestant world mission was characterized by unity across denominational and national boundaries because of a number of factors. The promoters of mission were a minority who had to battle against the inertia,

---

288 Beazley, *The Christian Church*, 238.
289 Ibid., 243.

indifference, or bitter hostility of the majority. They drew together in the common cause. They were all motivated by the same sentiments, namely, glory to God, love and obedience to Christ, and love of souls. They all recognised each other as belonging to valid branches of the one Church of Christ, and, in practice, as having equally valid and effective ministries. They taught a common message, in the main the interpretation of the gospel expressed in the creed of the Evangelical alliance. They recognized that any difference between them was as nothing compared with the colossal difference between Christianity and heathenism.[290]

It was inevitable that intermission cooperation would be very much a part of McGavran's thinking. The writings and thoughts of prominent church men in the Disciples of Christ influenced his early attitudes. He spent his entire life in a missionary milieu where the dynamic which Beaver described was very much at work. In an interview McGavran confirmed this: "To the degree that such cooperation arose from spiritual union, I have always been heartily in its favour. To the extent that it meant structural unity I am not in favour. Neither do I advocate that all denominations join my particular brand of Christianity."[291]

Cooperative Ventures of the Disciples of Christ

From 1960 to 1989 McGavran was a vigorous opponent of the anti-evangelistic trend within the Conciliar Movement. Even so, he continued to endorse extensive cooperation in world evangelization and church growth. McGavran was active in the Mid-India National Christian Council during most of the 1930s and 40s. The mission in which he served was highly aggressive in terms of seeking to further intermission cooperation. In the 1940s and 50s, he wrote and published no less than six articles relating to the theme of unity and cooperation. As exchange editor of the *UCR* from 1941 to 1947, he regularly aroused missionary interest in the prospect of church union. In light of McGavran's conservative stance on church union after 1960, it is somewhat difficult to believe that he championed it between 1940 and 1955.[292]

In 1955, he described the manner in which the India mission of the Disciples sought to work with other denominational groups in the common task. Some of the joint ventures he cited included: the mission press, owned and operated by the Disciples but serving numerous other missions, a tuberculosis sanatorium that was about to be closed in 1933 when McGavran developed the idea of making it a cooperative venture, and the *Manku*

---

290 Beaver, *Occasional Bulletin*, June 1967.

291 Donald McGavran, interview by Vern Middleton, June 8, 1984.

292 Donald McGavran, *UCR* 12, no. 12 (Dec. 1941): 311; 13, no. 1 (Jan. 1942): 14–15; 13, no. 2 (Feb. 1942): 13, no. 3 (March 1942); 13, no. 7 (July 1942); 13, no. 8 (Aug. 1942); 13, no. 11, (Nov. 1942); 14, no. 1 (Jan. 1943); 14, no. 7 (July 1943); 17, no. 8 (Aug. 1946); 14, no. 9 (Sept. 1943); 17, no. 10 (Oct. 1946).

Ghat mela, an annual four-day camp meeting with a focus on spiritual renewal established by John McGavran as a cooperative venture with three other missions.[293]

Like many other Protestant missions working in India, the Disciples cooperated in Vellore Medical School, the All India Nursing Association, the Allahabad Agricultural Institute, the Landour Language School, the Woodstock Elementary and High School for missionary children, and the Leonard Theological College. McGavran also led his mission into a joint venture with the British Baptists, in the evangelization of the Gara people movement in Orissa. This was the most significant cooperative venture the Disciples engaged in, an evangelistic effort to harvest a people movement that blossomed amidst the Gara caste. It was inspired and directed by McGavran, and resulted in significant conversions and churches, which would have otherwise been neglected.

He described the rationale behind their cooperative endeavours. "Yes, believing that we are commanded to love the brethren, . . . and earnestly desiring the welfare of the household of God, we are doing cooperative work on many fronts. The cooperative aspect of our work does not account for 10 percent of our India budget, nor 10 percent of our missionaries' time."[294]

What he described was typical of most missions. Even missions sustained by highly separatistic churches, have tended to suspend their cooperative arrangements when officials came to them from headquarters.

Unity and Missionary Practise

Between 1949 and 1954, as negotiations for church union mergers were in progress, McGavran began having second thoughts on the alleged benefits of structural union and felt that the emphasis should rather be placed on spiritual union. As early as 1943, he warned against union with the Anglican Church, believing the unified body would be dominated by them. I recall a National Christian Council meeting at which three-fourths of the speaking was done by Anglican Bishops. They were everywhere, in the chair, on the floor, heading committees, restating motions, offering amendments, being deferred to. No doubt they were acting quite impartially, or trying to do so.

Although, McGavran was convinced of the necessity of believers baptism and he was prepared to merge with churches that practised paedobaptism. He suggested that the churches permit rebaptism should a believer so desire. At the same time, he insisted that those churches holding strongly to apostolic succession, should concede that churches which sense no need for a validly ordained presbyter, be guaranteed the right to continue having communion services led by unordained laypersons.

---

293 Donald McGavran, "Disciples Cooperate in India," *World Call* 36 (April 1955): 11.
294 Ibid.

McGavran presented the above views at a meeting of the uniting churches, held in Allahabad in 1950. In the paper entitled, "One Baptism," his argument and logic were such that the meeting broke off in confusion. Those who believed strongly in apostolic succession found unacceptable his suggestion that laypeople be permitted to celebrate communion. In addition the paedobaptist denominations were troubled by his plea that rebaptism be permitted. The Disciples of Christ withdrew from negotiations in the years that followed, from 1952 until 1955.

Perry E. Gresham, president of the Disciples of Christ, and a member of the Faith and Order Conference held at Lund, Sweden on August 15–28, 1952, reported the event and findings to his churches in an article entitled, "Response to Lund."[295] He evaluated the developing patterns of church union. McGavran responded from the perspective of India and their own denominational roots. "The position maintained throughout that we Disciples can and do issue a 'call to unity' which is deeper, more inclusive, and more biblical than that heard at Amsterdam and Lund is well taken. Our plea is ahead of most movements to unity, simply because it is more catholic and more in accord with the New Testament."[296]

Another concern expressed in the letter was that those churches involved in the United Church of South India were, "involved in almost total surrender to the Anglican conviction on order and these ministers are most likely to regard the ministry of all churches outside the historic episcopate as partial or irregular."

By 1953 McGavran perceived that the motivation for church union among the Indians was more nationalistic than spiritual:

The pressures—chiefly nationalistic—which are bringing about union in India, are bringing it about at the extreme right. The Disciple-Congregationalist-Baptist point of view has been jettisoned. The drive to achieve a strong Church is ready to sacrifice the minority insights and the contributions of the Restoration Movement. A strong national Church which can meet the missions and western churches is greatly desired in India.[297]

McGavran took strong exception to Bishop Newbigin's use of the term "reunion" in the book, *The Household of God*, for it implied that denominations had splintered off from the Anglicans. He insisted that if the Disciples were to become part of the church union movement then ordination should have only two questions, "Do you believe that Jesus is the Christ, the Son of the Living God" and "Do you accept the Bible as the rule of faith and practice?"[298]

---

295 Perry E. Gresham, "Response to Lund," *World Call* (1952).
296 Ibid.
297 Donald McGavran, letter from Takhatpur to Perry E. Gresham, (obtained from USCWM), Oct. 1953.
298 Lesslie Newbigin, *The Household of God* (New York: Friendship Press, 1953).

After McGavran left the India field in 1954 the United Christian Missionary Society put pressure on the churches of the Disciples to reenter negotiations. Even though McGavran was no longer a resident missionary, the Indian church leadership still consulted with him; this was especially true of the leaders of the churches established in the Satnami region. Their decisions reflected McGavran's conservative theological views. In spite of the many pressures, the Satnami churches, along with a few others, voted to remain independent of the church union movement. However, the vote ended up as 55 percent in favour of church union with 45 percent opposed.

Tragically, the church union movement was destructive to the fellowship of the Disciples of Christ Churches in India. Considerable tension and litigation arose in the years after 1968, as churches battled churches to gain control of properties and to secure whatever they regarded as their legal rights. For several decades, McGavran was deeply distressed over the polarization among churches, that had previously been of one heart and mind.

With the division in 1968, another problem arose for the nonconciliar churches. Although essentially indigenous, they were now cut off from the denomination's strong central leadership and any support from the United Christian Missionary Society. When the uniting churches brought legal proceedings against these churches, in order to gain control of their properties and buildings, they were in a very difficult situation. McGavran raised funds and sacrificially gave from his own salary for several years in order to assist them to retain their autonomy.

McGAVRAN AS LINGUIST

Although linguistics were never one of McGavran's major concerns, he had considerable aptitude in this area. Born in India, and raised to the age of twelve there, he had the advantage of exposure to multiple languages and dialects. Throughout his teenage years, while living in the US, he continued to hear Hindi regularly. His parents taught the language at the Missionary Training College for prospective missionaries going to India.

As missionary recruits to India both Mary and Donald studied Hindi at the College of Missions for the year they attended there. Upon arrival in India, they continued a second year of study in that language. A mastery of Hindi was vital to their future ministry, since the Harda-Jabalpur area was known for the high quality Hindi spoken by the general population. By the end of that year of study, McGavran's ability in Hindi was like that of a native Indian.

Competence in Sanskrit

Throughout much of his first term (1923–30), he also studied Sanskrit, the spiritual language of Hindu India. This language is the foundation for virtually every language and dialect spoken in North India, and provides the rich theological vocabulary of the Hindu religion. Hence, its mastery gave him the ability to read the Hindu scriptures in the original as well as converse with the learned *pandits* (scholars) on the finer points of Hindu theology.

Bible Translation

From 1936 to 1954, the McGavrans communicated primarily in the Chattisgarhi dialect. McGavran mastered Chattisgarhi by 1939. He, in cooperation with other missionaries of the region, translated the four Gospels and the book of Acts into that language, while maintaining a hectic schedule of evangelism. Four Satnami evangelists assisted him in corrections and idiomatic expressions. He undertook this task in the face of much opposition from the Indian Christians, who worked for the mission and who had accepted Christ while living in the mission orphanage. They considered the Chattisgarhi dialect beneath their dignity.

Scholar and Linguist in Hindi

Another phase of McGavran's linguistic career began after the Second World War. A great host of new missionary recruits began to flood into India. The Hindi-Urdu language school administrators in North India, felt the need to develop a more formalized language school textbook and better training procedures. Caldwell Smith, who was in charge of the institute, recruited McGavran to assist in the design and development of this program.

Therefore, in 1947 McGavran journeyed to Etawah, Uttar Pradesh to join Smith in the arduous task of writing the Hindi textbook. This text was latter affectionately dubbed "*Hari Kitab*," meaning "green book" because of the color of the covers. McGavran and Smith spent two months developing lessons, vocabulary, and grammatical teaching patterns for the entire course.

The dedicatory page of the text has the following statement, "Dedicated in Grateful Memory of Mr. J. G. McGavran and Dr. T. F. Cummings whose principles of language study have been followed in this course and whose enthusiasm has inspired it" (Smith, [coordinator] 1951). A further acknowledgement is made by Smith in these words, "Special recognition must be given to Mr. J. G. McGavran whose grammar outline and principles of coordinated study have been used as a basis for the grammar and exercises of this course."[299]

---

299 Caldwell Smith, *Hindi* (Printed in different presses, Etawah U.P., 1951). Landour Language School. Edition: Rev. ed. Imprint: [New Delhi]: North India Institute of Language Study Society.

McGavran had utilized the basic course material developed at the College of Missions by his father back in 1913–22, and the lessons were developed around these materials.

McGavran received special recognition in the forward of this *Hindi Grammar*. The acknowledgement states, "He prepared the present form of the grammar lessons and exercises and has been of great help in planning the whole course."[300] McGavran had revised his father's notes, extensively improving both the idiom and the grammar. His primary contribution was in vocabulary, grammatical principles, organization, and development of exercises for each lesson. In an oral interview Caldwell Smith described McGavran's input:

> He produced all the Hindi exercises for the course. He provided a basic vocabulary of 2,000 most frequently used words. He developed an effective drill whereby each new word introduced was immediately used four or five times to familiarize the student with its usage and establish it in his or her mind. McGavran also developed an effective drill for mastering vocabulary and gender.[301]

McGavran combined expertise in education and aptitude in language learning to assist in the production of a two-year Hindi language school course. Every missionary coming into India to work in the northern Hindi speaking area became enculturated by working through these lessons. From 1948 to 1972, about 250 missionaries each year, from many diverse missions and countries, developed skills to communicate the gospel to India's millions, in this adopted tongue.

McGavran held refresher courses for teachers during the summer in India.

---

300 Ibid., acknowledgment.
301 Donald McGavran, interview by Caldwell Smith, 1984.

Aside from preparation of this course, McGavran was very actively engaged in the ongoing program of the language school. He served on the examination board to ensure quality and expertise in the Hindi spoken by new missionaries. He also served on the administrative board of the school.

The Disciples of Christ mission in Central India appointed him every year to serve on the committees of the language school. The administrative board set policy regarding the language school facilities and the Indian faculty, hired as instructors.

The language school gained an international reputation for its standards of excellence and linguistic expertise demonstrated in its lesson format. The course essentially combined two streams of thought regarding the language learning process. Cumming's section of the text laid stress on memorization, the use of phonetics, and oral lessons. McGavran's concepts centered on exercises based on proper sentence structure and the retention of the vocabulary through repeated use of a word in its context.

The approach taken by McGavran to language learning was similar to his attitudes regarding church growth. He insisted upon accountability and mastery and he disdained slipshod work. He wrote:

It is a strange fact but many new missionaries resent the idea of mastering a language. They intend to study it as they have many other school subjects and get by with an 85 or 90 percent . . . language ability depends in large part on the ability to speak the new language at mastery level . . . Memorize the sentences till they can be said as Indians and partly by speed of enunciation.[302]

MISSION EXECUTIVE ENCOUNTER

During McGavran's third furlough from June 1947 through December 1948, a primary goal was to press home the church growth point of view to UCMS administrators. He did this combined with the usual deputation derby of speaking at endless meetings, visiting supporters, and traveling.

He requested an audience with the mission secretaries in order to read a seven-page paper proposing revision of mission policies. He felt this was a most opportune time as UCMS was launching a bold new venture, attempting to raise one million dollars and send out many new recruits in the wave of post-war optimism. On December 12, 1947, McGavran presented his strategy of "holding Mission Station Approach areas lightly" and concentrated funds in People Movement areas.[303]

The thesis of his address was that: "Instead of developing just those pieces of mission work which . . . have been established and have survived through the years, whether

---

302 Donald McGavran, "Mastery of Indian Languages," *UCR* 17, no. 12 (Dec. 1946): 176–80.
303 Address to Executives of UCMS, (obtained from USCWM), Dec. 12, 1947.

fruitful or not," UCMS "should launch a new policy of seeking out fruitful pieces of work and developing them."[304]

He reviewed the history of the mission in India, pointing out that most of the mission stations had developed wherever a strong-minded missionary placed them. The philosophy motivating most missionaries from 1882–1930 was to establish a work in unoccupied territory. The stations developed along the railway lines. The early missionaries did not ask where people are becoming Christians, but where have they not heard the gospel.[305]

McGavran reviewed the impact of the famines which had swept through Central India between 1890–1900. He explained how each station had shifted its focus from evangelism to orphanages hoping that the orphans would become the future preachers and evangelists of the mission. Churches emerged to train and teach the orphans. The Mission Station expanded their institutions. The work became visible. A great work was being done and the foundations were being firmly laid for a great church.[306]

He lamented that the mission now prided itself in a church built on orphan Christians and officially opposed a church resulting from a caste-wide movement which would bring in what they described as "large numbers of ignorant converts."[307]

Policies regarding funding had shifted. The vigor of the work became the standard according to which support was given, not the results of the work.[308] He pointed out that this pattern was repeated in many of their fields.

In the space of two hours, McGavran delivered his central thesis of church growth to the UCMS executives. He appealed to them to revamp their policies, and he urged that a department of research be established, to provide data to replace decision making based on hunches with decisions based on facts. He concluded with the suggestion that a researcher be appointed.

Meanwhile, an invitation was received from Dean Shelton asking McGavran to join Butler College as a professor. He turned down the opportunity because he and his wife both felt they must return to India "to preserve the only opportunity of Growth"[309] the UCMS had. In a letter informing Yocum of his decision, he shared further his dream. He wanted a position in the mission which would enable him to help channel and direct the energies of the Society for growth of the Church worldwide.[310]

Ten days before his departure from the US, McGavran received word from President McCormick stating that: "UCMS was not planning any change in basic policy."[311] McGavran retorted: "Is not such a misunderstanding tragic . . . What I have been trying to say is that

---

304 Ibid.
305 Ibid.
306 Ibid.
307 Ibid.
308 McGavran, letter from Muncie to Yocum, Jan. 13, 1948.
309 Ibid.
310 Donald McGavran, letter from College of Bible, Lexington, to Cy Yocum, June 28, 1948.
311 H. B. McCormick, letter from Indianapolis to Donald McGavran, Takhatpur, (obtained from NV), Feb. 16, 1949.

the basic policy of the Christian Mission of the Churches has been sadly wrecked by the persistent backing of sterile fields. Our basic policy is to establish self-propagating, self-supporting, self-governing churches, and we are not doing it."[312]

Policy matters at executive level were not laid to rest. McGavran's critique of UCMS mission strategies was not taken lightly. H. B. McCormick took up the debate. He referred to McGavran's appraisal as "very frank . . . objective criticism of the missionary policies of the foreign division." He described survey work already done which "seemed to indicate that wherever there was a full-rounded program permanent and effective progress was made, but wherever one emphasis or another received major consideration the work was much less productive."[313]

McCormick also rejected the idea that a research man could shed any more light on the task than current administrators and missionaries were doing. He concluded by saying, "It is not a question of 'either,' 'or,' it is a question of both winning and teaching."[314]

McGavran clarified his idea of holding Mission Station Approach centers lightly in the next letter. "The pernicious error . . . which I am now trying to point you to is that of determining allocations of men and money on the basis of the size of the existing work, instead of on the basis of the actual and potential growth.[315]

McGavran then shifted the argument from stations to countries: "India and China have . . . big Crusade allotments . . . yet our net increase in India last year was fourteen souls and in China after 65 years we have . . . a thousand . . . At the same time growing points where the church can multiply by geometric progression, continue to be bypassed."[316]

McGavran concluded the letter with the following:

> The first essential is that you and the board accept the principle that the growth of the church on the field is a major factor in deciding allocation of resource. Once UCMS decides to throw large resources into those areas where the Holy Spirit is moving men to repent of their sins and accept the Savior, even if it means reducing work in non-growing areas, the battle will be half won.[317]

The McCormick/McGavran stalemate subsided with a four-page letter in which statement after statement was reexamined and discarded as inaccurate. McCormick attacked "erroneous assumptions"[318] made by McGavran in an article entitled, "A Christian Looks at Japan" in which he said, "Japan offers a unique opportunity for the growth of the

312 Donald McGavran, letter from Takhatpur to H. B. McCormick, (obtained from NV), March 13, 1949.
313 H. B. McCormick, letter from Indianapolis to Donald McGavran, Takhatpur, Feb. 16, 1949.
314 Ibid.
315 Donald McGavran, letter from Takhatpur to H. B. McCormick, (obtained from NV), March 13, 1949.
316 Ibid.
317 Ibid.
318 McCormick, letter to McGavran, (obtained from NV), May 12, 1949.

Christian church. The times are favorable . . . Yet this great hour finds the Disciples strangely immobile."[319]

On his return voyage to India, McGavran saw the receptivity of hearts to the gospel in postwar Japan and the Philippines. He challenged the UCMS administrators to take funds from the India budget for those two countries. Yocum, who had now taken over the correspondence with McGavran, responded that neither of those two fields currently needed the funds. He also defended the administrative policies of UCMS as being far more flexible than McGavran recognized.[320]

McGavran apologized for what the executives interpreted as "an unfriendly barrage of mean criticism. But pressed further, that: 'despite this danger, I must voice the message that I believe God has given me: that Mission resources should be used in very large measure to strengthen and expand Growing Churches.'"[321]

Having said that, he reiterated his major thesis again: "What is needed, Dr, Yocum, is not gradual, painless, unnoticeable adjustment—the oozing of resources from one field to another, while we continue to pour life into unfruitful situations. What we need is boldly to enter open fields and reap, while at the same time we would hold closed fields with a light staff."[322]

Meanwhile both executives were replaced, Yocum in December 1950, and McCormick in 1951. A new executive, Don West, became a church growth disciple and began to apply these principles in evaluating various UCMS fields in Asia.[323] As soon as Dale Fiers was installed as president, a letter from McGavran arrived on his desk. Again he stated: "There is a pernicious error in our UC Missionary Society set up. I have pointed it out to your predecessors in office, and to the Foreign Division and to the Board of Managers . . . The error is this: that allocations of men and money are determined quite largely on the size of the existing work, instead of on the basis of the actual potential growth of the Church."

In the same letter, McGavran went on to explain the purpose of a mission society:

> . . . it does not exist to get Churches to do missionary work whether there is growth or not . . . it does not exist to keep the machinery going. It exists to extend the Church, to multiply salvation, to bring peoples societies, to a saving knowledge of our Lord Jesus Christ. The growth of the churches must be a critical factor in the distribution of resources . . . Only as the Head of the enterprise is well acquainted with the problem can he steer clear of a fair (and innocuous) distribution of funds, and a genial (and ineffective) carrying on of a grand piece of work.[324]

319　Donald McGavran, "A Christian Looks at Japan," *Christian Evangelist* (March 23, 1949).
320　Cy Yocum, letter from Indianapolis to Donald McGavran, Takhatpur, (obtained from NV), June 29, 1949.
321　Donald McGavran, letter from Takhatpur to Cy Yocum, (obtained from NV), July 9, 1949.
322　Donald McGavran, letter from Takhatpur to Cy Yocum, (obtained from NV), July 11, 1949.
323　Ibid.
324　Donald McGavran, letter from Takhatpur to Dale Fiers, (obtained from USCWM), Nov. 3, 1951.

When McGavran again returned to the United States in 1954 he presented to the UCMS executive a seven-page document entitled, "Mobility and the Implementation of Strategy."[325] There were two essential parts to this presentation. First, he analyzed the UCMS mission statement and strategy, making bold suggestions as to phrasing that needed to be replaced, and paragraph insertions that were essential to church growth. Secondly, he provided a detailed outline as to how UCMS could be radically revamped to become a church growth mission. The dialogue did not stop, but carried on with intensity throughout 1954 to 1960.

THE BRIDGES OF GOD

The McGavrans arrived in India for their fourth term in March of 1949.[326] The contrast between the opportunities they had observed in Japan and the Philippines and the sterile unresponsiveness of mid-India stood out in bold contrast. Their Takhatpur field had experienced little growth during their absence. He wrote, "Growth has stopped—no baptism for over a year—but the possibility of growth still remains."[327] For six weeks, McGavran was depressed.

Finally he turned his attention to two primary concerns, which occupied much of his spare time from 1949 to 1954. He wrote a manuscript, which eventually became the publication, *The Bridges of God*. This he knew, would launch him into the public eye of the international missionary community because of its revolutionary proposal. The other project was the determination to fulfill his nine-year dream of leading UCMS into a fertile region among the Gara caste, in Sarguja situated 150 miles southeast of their Satnami field. Meanwhile, he continued to carry on his daily schedule of evangelism among the Satnami villages, caring for fledgling churches, providing oversight to several institutions including a leprosarium, a boys dormitory, a girls dormitory, a hospital, and an agricultural program.

In many respects, writing the manuscript and exploring ways to enter the new field went hand-in-hand. One seemed to reinforce the other. The former was theoretical expression, the latter was practical implementation.

Here, he thought, was the fulfillment of his great dream and strategy: hold lightly to existing sterile mission stations and find a fertile responsive region where UCMS could pour its resources and energies. The Satnami field that McGavran had thought could be fanned into "revival flames" back in 1936 was now recognized as a smoking firebrand. The factors leading to receptivity in the 1930s were no longer there. Some of the churches McGavran had planted between 1937 and 1947 were now experiencing up to 40 percent reversions.[328] Other factors which had contributed to loss by reversion were the profane attitudes of the

---

325 Donald McGavran, "Mobility and the Implementation of Strategy," (unpublished MS, [obtained from USCWM Archives], Aug. 4, 1954).

326 Donald McGavran, letter to Cy Yocum, "S. S. Oregon Mail," Tacoma, Jan., 9, 1949.

327 Donald McGavran, letter to Cy Yocum, April 1, 1949.

328 Donald McGavran, letter to Ken Potee, full section, (obtained from USCWM), Oct. 24, 1950.

Satnami people and mistakes made by McGavran and others who had labored with him.[329] He estimated that only one hundred families were left who were loyal and committed to Christ.

Ken Potee raised some opposition to McGavran's tactics in July of 1950 as he cautioned against further "ingathering" of new believers and exhorted him to consolidate his work.[330] This was greatly discouraging to him since he now regarded his strategy as being contrary to general mission policy.[331] His reply was with critical insight regarding the process of growth in resistant Hindu India.

> We missionaries suffer two handicaps: we come out here with an individualistic understanding of church growth and revival in our minds and hearts which does not apply here. Then we get saturated with a static station way of operation which further stamps in a pattern which because of sociological, and psychological and religious reasons does not and cannot apply to Church growth among adult Hindus.[332]

By October 1951, both the manuscript for the book and the negotiations for the new Sarguja field were well underway. Frequent journeys to arrange for the transfer of the Gara churches and their Christian community of 3,000 took up McGavran's attention. Adrenaline was flowing, and throughout October he hammered out 5,000 words per day. He explained to his sister Grace that it took him a week to flesh out the outline, but once that was in place his ideas began to flow.[333] This was possible, for McGavran was not writing an abstract theoretical book but rather an autobiography of his years in India. Page after page of *Bridges of God* could easily be identified with places, persons, and issues evolving out of his experiences as a missionary.

He described the essence of his ideas for the book to his sister, Grace:

> The book will run to 65,000 and will be, if successful, a book which will greatly influence the strategy of missions. I advocate the massing of resources behind the growing Christward movements of people . . . I see the Mission Stations as beachheads most of which have been contained and walled off by the Prince of the Power of the Air and the Christward movements as breakthroughs.[334]

---

329 Ibid.

330 Ken Potee, letter from Jabalpur to Donald McGavran, Takhatpur, (obtained from USCWM), July 30, 1950.

331 Donald McGavran, letter to Ken Potee, (obtained from USCWM), Aug. 5, 1950.

332 Donald McGavran, letter to Ken Potee, Oct. 24, 1950.

333 Donald McGavran, letter from Takhatpur to Helen McGavran (mother) and Grace McGavran (sister), (obtained from USCWM), Oct. 1951.

334 Ibid.

From late October through much of November 1952 he took his rough manuscript, his typewriter, a cook and food, and headed for the jungles, where he rented a bungalow from the government. In that quiet setting, he would hunt and stalk prey every morning for an hour or so for physical exercise, but the balance of the day, from 7 a.m. to 6 p.m., was spent typing out and revising the manuscript.

With the work finally in an acceptable form, McGavran made twenty copies and distributed them to mission executives, Pickett, Kraemer, and Latourette. All of these returned their comments and criticisms and their responses brought great encouragement. Don West wrote, "That will blast them out of the water."[335] Virgil Sly, a newly appointed UCMS executive, also wrote a positive response. "Very stimulating . . . confident that the book will cause a chain reaction of thinking in the minds of mission administrators across the world."

Pickett stated that the book would prove to be "epochal." However, he cautioned McGavran to rephrase some of the sentences in a "less dogmatic way."[336] Mary McGavran forwarded this letter to Africa where McGavran was engaged in an analysis of church growth on that continent, and Mary penned a brief comment that Pickett was less than enthusiastic.

On the other hand, there were critics. A. L. Warnshius made a point of highlighting McGavran's limited understanding because of his India perspective. He wrote, "Your description . . . is not accurate with regards to missions in China, Japan, Korea and the Philippines and other countries." He concluded with, "My criticism would be that your repeated and continued reference to the 'Mission Station Approach' limits the value of your book."[337]

McGavran asked *World Dominion* if they would publish his upcoming book on missionary strategy, even before it was in manuscript form. He was bold enough to critique Roland Allen's thesis as presented in *St. Paul's Missionary Methods and Ours*. What he said in the letter was incorporated into the text of his book.[338]

Most of the editing was done by his sister, Grace McGavran. A professional writer, she gave extensive assistance and suggested it be called *The Bridges of God*. She also sent out promotional letters to publishers and took care of necessary details.[339]

Much of the international content was incorporated into the text after McGavran had arrived back in the US in June 1954. Enroute home from India, McGavran had spent two days with Sir Kenneth Grubb of World Dominion Press who was ruthless with his red

---

335   Don West, letter from Indianapolis to Donald McGavran, Takhatpur, (obtained from USCWM), April 25, 1952.

336   Pickett, letter from Delhi to Donald McGavran, Landour, April 20, 1959.

337   A. L. Wanshuis, letter from Bronxville, New York to Donald McGavran, New Haven, Connecticut, (obtained from USCWM), Nov. 22, 1954.

338   Donald McGavran, letter from Takhatpur to World Dominion, England, (obtained from USCWM), Aug. 26, 1951.

339   Donald McGavran, interview by Vern Middleton, March 24, 1984. See also extensive correspondence: Grace to Don, (obtained from USCWM), July 3, 1952; Don to Grace, Oct. 27, 1952; Don to Grace, Nov. 14, 1952.

pen and edited out phrases and expressions that did not appeal to his British English. His editorial assistance actually destroyed the flow and cohesiveness of some sections of the text.

But McGavran pursued its publication with drive and determination because he realized its potential impact. He wrote, "In [*The Bridges of God*] I propose a very fundamental change in missionary strategy—a change that will affect 90 percent of all missionary work done in the world today."[340]

Frank Price, librarian of the Missionary Research Library, stated that it was "the most read missionary book in 1956."[341] McGavran gained notoriety because of the book. (See Appendix C for a full thesis statement of the book.)

NEGOTIATIONS FOR THE GARA FIELD

One hundred miles southeast of Takhatpur, the Gara caste, also known as the Gonda people, responded to the gospel in large numbers. They were a weaving caste and three different missions had small people movements among them. In a letter to Pickett, McGavran stated that 12,000 confessed faith in Christ.[342] His interest in these people began back in 1937, when he wrote the book, *Founders of the Indian Church*. He devoted a chapter to a Gara convert named Habil, who led his village to Christ.[343]

The region where the Gara people lived was West Utkal, in the state of Orissa. McGavran proposed a survey of the area be made in October 1949, offering himself to do it. Traveling on a bicycle several hundred miles he researched the state, compiled the information, and submitted a proposal for the evangelization of the region.[344]

Negotiations between the British Baptist Mission and UCMS carried on for two years over a possible joint venture to harvest the Gara people movement. McGavran was certain that with additional personnel and monies, the Gara people movement of 3,000 could rapidly become 30,000.[345]

Much to the surprise of the UCMS executives in the US, the India field council voted to open the new field of West Utkal in cooperation with the British Baptist in 1952. Between 1949 and 1952, several new UCMS families arrived. McGavran had been very instrumental in their recruitment during his furlough, and so of course they cast their vote behind their spiritual mentor. Three of these families volunteered to shift to the new region.

McGavran's assessment of church growth in the region in 1956 reported 104 churches, 4305 communicant members, with believers resident in 259 villages. His graph indicated 300 baptisms a year of new converts from Hinduism in 1953 and 1954 and 400 baptisms

---

340 Donald McGavran, letter to Professor Ingleheart, (obtained from USCWM), Dec. 14, 1953.

341 Donald McGavran, interview by Vern Middleton, May 12, 1984.

342 Donald McGavran, letter to Pickett, Delhi, Oct. 14, 1953.

343 Donald McGavran, *Founders of the Indian Church* (Jabalpur: Mission Press, 1937).

344 Donald McGavran, letter to Mr. B. Scott, BCMS, Oct. 16, 1949.

345 Donald McGavran, letter from NCC Headquarters, Nagpur to Helen McGavran, Vancouver, (obtained from USCWM), March 2, 1951.

per year of converts from the nominal Christian community for the same period.[346] More will be expressed about this venture in chapter five.

THE PEOPLE MOVEMENT THAT NEVER MOVED

Some of McGavran's prewar optimism regarding the Satnami people movement returned in October 1952, when two leaders of that caste were baptised. Madhav manifested leadership potential from the start and spoke of leading a Christward movement into the church.[347] McGavran had him write a tract entitled, "I am not leaving Satnam, I am finding him. Christians are the true Satnamis."[348]

As a strategist, McGavran pressed the work of evangelism, hoping to produce a positive environment for a people movement. His two-point strategy was as follows:

1. Plan for shepherding any groups which come in:
   a. A pastor resident on the spot with the families. Those being baptised providing the house or the rent.
   b. As a rule we take only those where there are five families or more.
   c. That regular nightly meetings be held in addition to Sunday meetings. That we work out a common curriculum of instruction.
   d. That while we require no set period of instruction before baptism ... we aim to develop a catechumenate requiring at least a month of instruction.
   e. That we set up a lay leaders training school of two weeks, for April end ... at which we aim to get a large number of new converts.
2. Plan now for January and February camps for the star teams:
   a. Preparation of supporting literature.
   b. Choice of about ten villages in each area where churches ought to be started.
   c. A team to go ahead and prepare the ground for a week. Then the star team comes in and presses for decision in a three-day meeting ... if it works it will enable ten churches per month to be started.[349]

Part of his hope for a Satnami people movement came as a result of spiritual warfare. One *malguzar* (village headman) shared a vision he had about becoming a Christian and bringing fifty others with him.[350] There was also a woman and her child, who were both miraculously healed by Christians in Takhatpur after the incantations of a Satnami witch doctor failed.[351] Idolatrous practises of spirit taming, goat sacrifice, and demonic dancing

---

346 Donald McGavran, *Church Growth in West Utke* (1956), duplicated copies, study for UCMS, Indiana.
347 Donald McGavran, letter to Ted McGavran (brother), (obtained from USCWM), Oct. 20, 1952.
348 Ibid.
349 Ibid.
350 Donald McGavran, letter to Mr. Cole, Aug. 10, 1952.
351 Donald McGavran, letter to Carlton, Aug. 10, 1952.

were challenged. A large group of Satnamis in a neighboring district bolted from caste because of corruption and stated that they were searching for a way. Added to this was the blessing of the four Gospels in Chattisgarhi coming off the press.

The fifteen-year longing of McGavran's heart for a Satnami people movement seemed such a possibility that he refused to entertain the prospect of other jobs being offered. He expressed this to Potee: "The one thing that would hold me here for the balance of the term would be to make my major task the further extension and consolidation of the small beginning of a People Movement to Christ among the Satnamis."[352]

Takhatpur became a hub of thriving activity from 1950 to 1954. A small army of personnel was mobilized to create, if possible, a Satnami people movement. Those on the mission payroll were "fifteen preachers, eight medical workers, twelve teachers, four Bible women and five rural development workers."[353] A gift of $20,000 from an Illinois farmer underwrote most of the expenses of the latter group. McGavran had them introduce sugar cane, fruit trees, and new varieties of rice to the Satnami farmers.

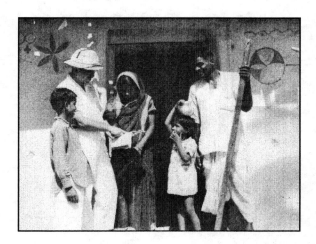

Evangelism—Donald working intimately with families (around 1947).

In January 1954 McGavran, assisted by Yesu Charan, prepared and published a Satnami hymn book. There were a number of choruses in Chattisgarhi, (the local language), composed by McGavran. He recounted an incident of how a chorus came into being. A farmer, sitting atop a loaded oxcart, was singing a very quaint folk tune. As the oxen shuffled by McGavran's home at two miles per hour, the tune was repeated several times. This riveted the lyrics in McGavran's mind. He then composed Christian words for the tune. It became a favourite of the churches.

---

352 Donald McGavran, letter to Potee, (obtained from USCWM), Aug. 1952.
353 Donald McGavran, letter from Takhatpur to Mr. Champie, Jan. 14, 1954.

The hymn book contained mostly hymns designed for antiphonal singing. The preacher sings a line and then the congregation responds. Great hymns of the faith were translated and the Western tune replaced with Indian tunes. More than one hundred and twenty hymns were arranged this way. McGavran's musical ability came from his mother, who, in her time, had also composed Indian hymns.[354] Generally, the hymn book was not accepted by the leadership of the Satnami churches. The Bible School graduates, with Hindi as their mother tongue, felt it demeaning to sing hymns in the vernacular of Chattisgarh.

The extraordinary efforts to begin a Satnami people movement appeared worthwhile. Inquirers were many, but very few followed through to the point of baptism. McGavran prayed and hoped that the "flow" would begin before his departure from India.[355]

McGavran changed the pattern of receiving Satnamis as believers in the final months of 1953. Due to the particular emphasis in preaching, the Satnamis had been coming to Christ because they thought that Christianity was a more powerful religion than theirs. They also regarded Christianity as a place to turn in time of need. McGavran considered this inadequate so he wrote of trying to shift the basis of decision to: "The Christian religion gives us the true God, the only Satnam and His Book and the Church. Needs will come and needs will go . . . but if have the true God our needs will all be met as He thinks best."[356]

McGavran preaching under Banyan tree. This type of evangelism was typical.

This new apologetic approach did not appeal to the Satnamis, and conversions ceased after October 1953.

Throughout this fourth term of service, McGavran's responsibility and scope of ministry were enough for four men. His primary focus was evangelizing the lost and spiritual care of

---

354 Donald McGavran, letter from Takhatpur to Fullerton Church, California, Jan. 10, 1959.
355 Donald McGavran, letter from Takhatpur to Helen McGavran, Vancouver, Washington, Jan. 4, 1954.
356 Ibid.

numerous churchlets. However, he also was superintendent of the Victoria Leprosy Home and the administrator of five other institutions. In addition to these posts, he designed and built a hospital, school, leprosarium, and also a bridge large enough for trucks. Forty years later, these structures are still in use. He was called to analyse the church growth situations in other missions. Several documents exist verifying that activity. He was primarily responsible for arresting a cholera epidemic in the months of July and August 1952. During the monsoon season, a cholera epidemic broke out among the Satnami villages. Thus his preaching schedule included giving several hundred cholera injections in each village.[357]

Is it any wonder that one day when Mary McGavran was asked how she was feeling, her response was, "As well as can be expected, for one attached to perpetual motion." A quote she borrowed from Charlotte Carey (Carey's second wife) who shared a similar fate.[358]

Mary McGavran teaching a student in Hindi.

SUMMARY

The missiological ideas, theories, and principles of church growth that germinated in McGavran's mind between 1923 and 1935 were developed and honed during his Satnami years. As a mission practitioner, he tried to implement various concepts repeatedly only to have them rejected or discarded. His laboratory was a caste that seemed ripe for a people movement, but only yielded nominal results.

The people movement concept with all of its ramifications, became an essential point of view for McGavran. Web relationships, the corporate mind of a social class, multi-individual decision making, and the idea of receptivity within a given group, at a particular historical

---

357 Donald McGavran, letter to Mrs. Darnell, (obtained from USCWM), Aug. 9, 1952.
358 Mary McGavran, letter to Helen McGavran, (obtained from USCWM), Oct. 31, 1951.

juncture all converged in McGavran's thinking. His interaction with social-political issues arising from high level personnel like Ambedkar, Azariah, Gandhi, Mott, and Pickett enabled him to see the dynamics of history in a broader perspective.

Numerous opportunities to conduct field research as a church growth consultant enabled McGavran to develop analytical tools. These were utilized to get an accurate picture of church growth. Throughout this period, he insisted on discarding generalizations. As a scientist, he pressed for hard, cold facts.

He developed strong theological convictions. Kraemer's massive work given at Tambaram, which represented the position of 90 percent of India's rural missionaries, issued a clarion call for a bold declaration of the gospel. Any lingering idea that Hinduism was the "logos spermatikos" or the "preparatio evangelica," were permanently dispelled from McGavran's mind. He may have been influenced by Farquar's idea of Christianity being the crown of Hinduism during his first term when he worked with upper caste Hindus with their sophisticated philosophies. However, most of his second term was focused on the Damars, the Garas, and the Satnamis. All of these castes were Untouchables and their religion was experienced at the popular, highly demonic level.

From 1935 to 1954 he crusaded against the evils of caste. He radically departed from the traditional missionary method of bringing converts into the mission station. He saw the net result of that pattern as essentially creating a Christian caste. He developed Pickett's thesis that caste could only be obliterated when large casteward movements into the Christ kingdom significantly changed the corporate worldview of the Untouchables. He formulated a thesis that discipling had to do with the process of bringing men to commitment to Christ, and becoming responsible members of the church. "Perfecting" was the long-term process of transforming the pagan worldview to a biblical one.

Another concept, which burst into full bloom at this stage of McGavran's life, was the mechanism of mobility. As he interacted, first with the executive committee of the field council and later with the executives of UCMS, he developed concepts of mobilizing resources and personnel to ripened harvest areas. Included in this concept was the need for global research, to provide concrete information for decision making.

The Satnami people were the object of McGavran's spiritual oversight. He translated the Gospels into their vernacular. He published a handbook on worship and a catechism for the forty small churches he established. He developed a Satnami hymnbook to enhance worship. He utilized redemptive analogies to contextualize the gospel for the Satnami people. He championed their rights before the courts. He gave himself without reserve to a people who basically ignored the claims of Christ, or feared to take a stand. Yet, out of those seventeen years of struggle, frustration, and disappointment, a body of knowledge has arisen which has brought blessing, direction, and purpose to countless missionaries throughout the world.

CHAPTER FIVE

CONCEPTS OF CHURCH GROWTH DEVELOPED THROUGH INTERNATIONAL RESEARCH

1954–57

This four-year period in McGavran's life was a very creative period of time. In God's providence, the tapestry of his life had been woven together in a uniquely diversified environment as the world literally became his laboratory to test church growth hypotheses and verify them by research. During this four-year span of time he was catapulted from the obscurity of Takhatpur, India to the prominence of a missionary statesman known from New York to Geneva. His reputation as a diagnostician of the health of local churches spread throughout five continents. Indeed, this was the time when his church growth insights burst the restrictive boundaries of India and were seen to have application to every continent.

Celebrating the McGavrans before going to the US on furlough.
The banner reads, "May happiness and peace be with the McGavrans."

The McGavrans found this phase of their life exhilarating, but filled with a sudden need for adjustments to their new situation. They were deeply enriched by the wide horizons of opportunity and challenge, but at the same time they felt a strong tug of loyalty and commitment to India. Frequently Donald McGavran would allude to *"pyara Hindustan"* (beloved India) in his letters to his wife. Yet, in both of their minds the furlough of 1954 meant the completion of their years in India. He wrote, "As one who has worked here in our Indian mission since the fall of 1923, and feels that he is coming to the end of his useful service . . . My task in the Takhatpur area and . . . my task in the Orissa area seems to be largely done."[359] So the McGavrans severed ties with their India ministry. They sold most of their belongings, even their prized earthly possession, their summer cottage, Council Rock, located at Mussoorie. However, psychologically the break was much harder to make, and for a period of four years, they continually talked of returning.

AFRICAN SURVEY

Although 1954 was scheduled as a furlough year for the McGavrans, Donald arranged to have his family leave India two months after his departure and meet up with him again in London, while he returned by way of Africa. The plan was strategic for his African travel, but it left Mary to attend to the disposal of all their furniture and the accumulation of thirty-one years of household items in two houses. It also made his daughter, Winifred, very unhappy as he missed her graduation from Woodstock School. The UCMS encouraged him to take the trip through Africa because there was some consideration of appointing him as field secretary for the mission operating in the Belgian Congo.[360] He stated, "The purpose of the [trip] was to give me an understanding of Africa that would enable me to edit *The Bridges of God* and make it applicable to the whole world."[361] As described earlier in chapter four, he wrote the manuscript for this book in November of 1952, however the editing process continued throughout 1954.

His plan was to enter Africa at Mombasa and depart from Sierra Leone on the west, joining his family in London. His thinking was as follows:

> I would spend perhaps two days with the secretary of the Christian Council . . . going through the provinces by map and missionary directory, and seeing the degree of occupation by missions, the degree of conversions achieved, the congregations established, and getting the idea of the unfinished task and the degree to which Islam was making inroads. Then I would spend three or four days in visiting typical work—perhaps three days in some mission where there has been great church growth, and a day or so in a mission station where there has been small church growth.[362]

359 Donald McGavran, letter fromTakhatpur to Don West, Indianapolis, Dec. 28, 1953.
360 Donald McGavran, interview by Vern Middleton, Dec. 20, 1984.
361 Ibid.
362 Donald McGavran, letter from India to J. L. Anderson, Nov. 21, 1953.

McGavran was very much aware of the worldwide implications of the principles expressed in *The Bridges of God*, and in his mind the African trip was essential "to supplement and drive home the point of view presented in my book."[363] The drive and the incredible determination with which he pursued his church growth insights came because he fully realized the implications. He wrote, "In [*The Bridges of God*] I propose a very fundamental change in missionary strategy—a change that will affect 90 percent of all missionary work done in the world today."[364]

Even before the trip McGavran was thinking of publishing another book. This would eventually be published under the title *How Churches Grow*. Initially he thought the title should be "The Ribbon of Opportunity," reasoning "that it will be the description of the ribbon extending from Assam to Dakar all across India and Africa about 300 miles wide and as full of Growing People Movements as a dog is of fleas."[365]

Even while still in India, he was dreaming dreams of a church growth institute and School of World Mission. In a letter to Bishop Pickett, who now resided in New Delhi, he wrote:

> There is the possibility that there may be sufficient leading of the Lord, and sufficient opening of doors, so that there may be a kind of Foundation formed in US whereby my activities are directed. If so, there would be a Board of Governors, a controlling committee. Naturally I would hope that this organization, destined to have a profound effect on the course of missionary activities in the years ahead would have the benefit of guidance of one whom I have always regarded as one of my gurus.[366]

McGavran was never arrogant about his ideas, and he always tested his church growth principles by seeking evaluation from others. Almost every one of his manuscripts went through an arduous process of being critiqued by numerous authorities and acquaintances. Also in areas of administration he sought the help of others. For example he wrote to Bishop Whittaker, "I want to ask the privilege of counting on your counsel during the next two years, so that proposals designed to focus attention on Growing Churches and their needs and direct resources to them would be sound from an administrative point of view . . . Eventually I wish to get such guidance committees in all lands where there are growing churches."[367]

---

363   Donald McGavran, letter from Takhatpur to Professor Charles W. Inglehart, Union Theological Seminary, New York, Dec. 14, 1953.
364   Ibid.
365   Donald McGavran, letter from Takhatpur to Hazel Orton, Friendship Press, New York City, Dec. 14, 1953.
366   Donald McGavran, letter from Takhatpur to Waskom Pickett, Delhi, March 21 1954.
367   Donald McGavran, letter fromTakhatpur to Bishop Whittaker, Medak Diocese, and Andra Pradesh, March 1954.

While visiting Kenya, he became very aware that the missionaries were in the midst of many people movements but were unaware of their implications. He lamented that they lived in central stations apart from the villages. Relatively few had a good command of the local languages and rarely did they display any understanding of the village social makeup. He summarized his critique by saying, "Truly, they have fruit only because some people movements have a power which no amount of weakness in the missionaries can stop."[368]

The next leg of his journey was to Uganda. He probed about on his own and was awed by the size of the people movements there. He wrote, "There are over a million Christians here. Many 'Rural Deaneries' with 20 to 300 village churches."[369] In Kampala he encountered strong evidence of the Ugandan revival that took place in the 1930s. He described this as follows: "Those folk pray fervently. I am told they also shake and shiver and shout—but saw none of it."[370] He even preached at their services.

In Ruanda, he observed that the Protestant Church was weak due to "a very strict way of admission" which enabled the Roman Catholics to gain nine-tenths of the Christians.[371] He also observed:

> I am getting a lot of insight into the growth of the Christian Church. Each missionary tends to ride his particular hobby which has part of the truth. If only we could get a wide true methodology. Here in Africa the need is not so much to stress the People Movements—they occur almost without effort—but to develop P.M. into real on-going Churches. Perhaps a careful discussion of this field is my next book.[372]

For the next ten days McGavran travelled extensively throughout Ruanda-Urundi (the contemporary name for Urundi is Burundi). In another of his regular letters to his wife he wrote, "I have been soaking up information about the Christian program in Ruanda-Urundi. Tremendous opportunity and some very bright features, but with the exception of the CMS, rather weak, new or small programs devoted to making quality not quantity. The Protestant program is not anywhere near the opportunity. But within the limits of their means and vision they are doing a good job."[373]

He noted that the Tutsis, who were the ruling tribe, were swept into the Roman Catholic Church while the Hutus, who were the ruled class went into the Anglican Church. In both instances there were definite people movement characteristics.[374] He noted that in

---

368   Donald McGavran, letter from Kenya Mary McGavran, Landour, Mussoorie, U.P., April 29, 1954. All future references to Mary will be to Mary McGavran, unless otherwise noted.

369   Donald McGavran, letter from Kampala, Uganda Mary, Landour, U.P., April 25, 1954.

370   Donald McGavran, letter from Uganda to Mary, Landour, U.P, April 29, 1954.

371   Donald McGavran, letter from Ruanda to Mary, in Landour, U.P., May 2, 1954.

372   Ibid.

373   Donald McGavran, letter from Ruanda-Urundi to Mary, Landour, U.P., May 11, 1954.

374   Donald McGavran, interview by Vern Middleton, Dec. 20, 1984.

almost every country of central Africa there were large people movements progressing. He commented on the situation, "I suppose that all the missionary societies have said that in Africa people are flooding in, but probably no one had written about the fact that peoples become Christian when they can move into the church without renouncing their tribal identity."[375]

At the end of the survey of Urundi he spent a day summarizing his observations. The report, a five-page evaluation, indicated his biases as well as insights. In 1954 his loyalties were strongly within the Conciliar Movement of the World Council of Churches. This was reflected by a reference he made to the evangelical missions as sects. Another point of interest was his constant comparison between India and Africa, but he was beginning to internationalize his missiological insights. He also showed antagonism toward the Roman Catholic Church, using the term "the Romans" throughout the report, but while he prepared the manuscript for *How Churches Grow*, K. S. Latourette chided him for this apparent lack of respect and then the term was dropped. Some of the salient points of his report were as follows:

> All missions make the support of catechists, supervisors and ordained men depend entirely on church offerings . . . The Missions are working consciously toward a United Church though there are few countries in which there is so much right (CMS) and so much left and so little middle of the road . . . Tremendous growth is still possible everywhere . . . The most amateur efforts get abundant results . . . Churches are registering from 10–70 percent per annum in growth . . . As a result of all this, missions are in general scared of growth. They consciously build up a "go slow" attitude. High baptismal standards are enforced . . . As a result of rapid growth and limited resources, there is a good deal of alleged nominal Christianity. Poor shepherding is an undoubted cause of much backsliding.[376]

One of McGavran's major concerns, expressed in this report, was the number of missionaries whose theological background predisposed them to stress individual decisions and a gathered church concept. He noticed scorn towards those whose spiritual experience was different from so-called real Christians and he also noted that these same missionaries who stressed individualistic salvation patterns, laid little, if any, emphasis on church membership.

From Ruanda he made his way to Burundi in the back of a potato truck and then on to Stanleyville in the upper Congo via plane, cycle, and boat. He was astonished at the size of the people movements, and when he compared them with the responses in India, he

---

375 Ibid.
376 Donald McGavran, "Case History: Ruandi-Urundi," (unpublished MS, 1954), 2.

was overwhelmed. He wrote, "Africa is full of tribes trembling on the brink of decision . . . Twenty million Africans have become Christian in the past sixty years. At least eighty million more are going to leave animism in the next forty years . . . Nothing like this exodus has ever been seen before."[377]

Many mission leaders including members of the Africa Committee of the International Missionary Council laughed at his seemingly ridiculous prediction. In an interview later he recalled the sequel to the story.

> I was sure I was right. When I invited David Barrett to come here in 1967, I told him of my prediction. "McGavran," he said, "There won't be 100,000,000. There will be more than that." Barrett sent me the article which was initially published in the *Church Growth Bulletin* and then republished by the *International Review of Missions*. Barrett predicted 357,000,000 Christians in Africa south of the Sahara by the year 2000. At that time he was unknown, and when it was published in Time and other magazines, he became a world figure.[378]

Denominational loyalties to the Disciples of Christ led him to visit six of the Congo mission stations of the Disciples. He renamed the region "Discipleland" in an article published in *World Call*. He spelled out the task before the mission. "First and most urgent, we must expand and take into fellowship of the church all those who can now be won for Christ . . . Second, we must simultaneously create an educated African leadership for our churches, our schools and our laity . . . Third, we must continue to improve the spiritual condition of our sister churches."[379]

In the same article McGavran elaborated his concept of "perfecting."

> We must teach them all things whatsoever our Lord has commanded us. It is not enough to claim a tribe for Christ—to disciple it. It must then be perfected and led to ever fuller Christian commitment. The years must bring a deepening of Christian conviction, Christian habits and customs, Christian organization of the village and the tribe, and Christianization of both the social life and the individual conscience.[380]

From the Belgian Congo McGavran flew to Lagos, Nigeria. His survey of this area led him to develop insights regarding the challenge of Islam. He wrote of the region south of Kano, "the peasants are pagan, but the chiefs, already are Moslem. This is a strategic area

---

377 Donald McGavran, *World Call* 36 (1954): 21.
378 Donald McGavran, interview by Vern Middleton, Dec. 20, 1984.
379 Donald McGavran, "I Visited Congo's Land," *World Call* 37 (Jan. 21, 1955).
380 Ibid.

for missions—but is occupied chiefly by Mission Station Approach Stations—missing a great opportunity."[381]

Prior to this trip across Africa he had little firsthand exposure to "faith missions." In India his associations were primarily with mainline denominational missions and missionaries. As a church growth researcher, he was impressed with the spiritual dynamic and sacrificial spirit manifested by the "fundamentalist faith missions," as he called them. When he arrived at the large Sudan Interior Mission (SIM) station at Kano at midnight he was asked if his mission was part of the World Council of Churches. Not being sure at this point of the implications of the question he replied, "No, I don't think so." His description of SIM was interesting.

> I have been impressed with the quality of the SIM missionaries. They are folk with much devotion and much ability . . . They run their mission in an efficient way. This huge Sudan Interior Mission with all its fine organization and devotion is either doing futile Moslem work—or by over emphasis on the one by one—it helps in fertile territory to create small non-growing mission communities. However in several places it does seem to have broken thru into small ill-understood group movements.[382]

The next stage of research took him to Accra, Gold Coast (Ghana). His time there sparked his church growth thinking with new vitality and vision. His original plan was to travel on to Sierra Leone, and then depart for London, from Dakar, on July 5, 1954, but his plans were changed as a result of the crash of one of the first jet aircraft flying scheduled flights from London to Dakar.

McGavran displayed great ability in gaining an overview and assessment of each country in the brief time at his disposal. One key was his understanding of the social dynamics of societies. In the 1950s, few men had travelled as much as McGavran did. John R. Mott and Robert Speer travelled more extensively, but they were promoters and organizers. They only saw people as nationals, and they failed to discern the processes by which tribes and castes were turning to Christ.

The Gold Coast (Ghana) experience was so significant to McGavran that he made a major study out of the issues. From September 1954 to December 1955, when he was not traveling, he was reading at the Day Missions Library of Yale Divinity School. Much of his reading focused on "West Africa," particularly Gold Coast and Liberia.[383] This research he developed into a church growth case history which all of his students between 1961–75 analyzed and studied as a model. He saw that West Africa was ripe for the Christian message:

---

381 Donald McGavran, letter from Kaduna, Nigeria to Helen and Grace McGavran, Vancouver, Washington, June 4, 1954.

382 Ibid.

383 Donald McGavran, interview by Vern Middleton, Dec. 20, 1984.

Christianity is in a *most* favourable position. All the educated Gold Coastians are Christians. Ninety percent of the schools of all grades are in the hands of the churches and missions. A hundred percent of the students in the University College are Christians. There are churches in practically every village of the Colony and Ashanti self-supporting churches. There is an educated ministry of at least 250 preachers.[384]

In view of the context of this amazing opportunity, McGavran pressed the definition of "perfecting" further. He was convinced that countless thousands were being lost to Islam because the missionaries and the churches were confusing "perfecting" with "discipling."

The Traditional Protestant Approach is to proclaim the Gospel, seek out those who are willing to renounce paganism, idols, fetishes, polygamy, enroll them as inquirers, and after a year or so of training baptise those who pass an examination. These are instructed still further and some become communicants . . . The Mission engages in vigorous Perfecting as a part of the Discipling process. As a result, large sections of each village are left pagans, knowing themselves to be pagans refused by the Church because while they are anxious to become Christians, they do not come up to the standard of knowledge, church attendance, renunciation of beer, tobacco and polygamy, fetishes, Mother Earth ceremonies, etc. The village is split. Frequently the old people give their children to the Church to educate and baptise while they themselves remain pagans.[385]

It disturbed McGavran greatly that Islam had developed the technique of admitting people to that religion along people movement patterns. Islam did not demand Islamic perfection or cultural conformity from the pagans before they were admitted to that religious community.

He was dismayed when he encountered the policy displayed by most missions: "Baptise only the really converted and give them intensive training. We do a very thorough piece of work. No short cuts for us."[386] Great harvest fields were being reaped by Islam because of the failure of Christian missions to develop an effective strategy.

McGavran cited two reasons why a different strategy was not formulated: the failure to adapt North American and European methods to the African situation and the insurmountable barrier of polygamy. He lamented that the missionaries think, "only those who renounce these things can possibly be Christians."[387]

---

384 Donald McGavran, letter from Accra, Gold Coast to Virgil Sly, Indianapolis, June 25, 1954.
385 Ibid.
386 Ibid.
387 Ibid.

While in the Gold Coast McGavran discussed with local missionaries the strategy used by Prophet Harris. In a letter to Virgil Sly, he recounted:

> Prophet Harris, a Liberian, back early in this [twentieth] century went into villages, of the Ivory Coast, preached for a week or so, baptised all the people, threw their idols down, gave them a Bible and went on and the people believing themselves to be Christians waited in some cases ten years for a teacher to be sent to them . . . We must, if we are to claim these peoples for Christ before they become hopelessly entangled in Islam, take them in and then let the Holy Spirit do His work.[388]

While in the Gold Coast he also became acquainted with the writings of J. Spencer Trimingham, as well as the Christian church and Islam in West Africa.[389] As a result of their common views, they struck up correspondence. In one letter McGavran proposed, "You and I, who see the light, are stymied because it is awkward to promote our own point of view and our own books. Therefore what is needed is an organization which will vigorously promote this new light on missionary expansion."[390] This idea germinated and eventually came to fruition as the *Church Growth Bulletin* a few years later.

As McGavran concluded his survey of Africa, he made several summarizing statements. "The central question before the Protestant Churches of Africa is this, 'Do they intend to become small minorities immersed in an Islamic or Catholic milieu, or do they intend to capture whole sections of the countryside for the Protestant Faith?'"[391]

In the same letter he crusaded for fresh commitment to the opportunity in West Africa. "Where are the other millions in Sierra Leone, Ivory Coast, Dahomey, Northern Nigeria, French Equatorial, and South Sudan going? They can be won now—if the strategy is changed to Discipling now and Perfecting as rapidly as possible, and if priority is given to these regions. Otherwise they will merge into Islam."[392]

McGavran departed from Nigeria on July 2, joining his wife and two daughters in London. While in England he spent many hours with Sir Kenneth Grubb of World Dominion Press editing the manuscript *The Bridges of God*.

By mid-August the McGavran family was settled in the UCMS Mission house near the Yale Divinity School Campus. A $2,500 research fellowship as a visiting scholar at Yale gave McGavran the needed time and study to piece together the details of his first international research tour. He wrote:

---

388 Ibid.
389 Donald McGavran, letter from Kaduna, Nigeria to Spencer J. Trimingham, June 7, 1954.
390 Donald McGavran, letter from China Inland Missionary Center, London, to Trimingham, July 15, 1954.
391 Donald McGavran, letter to Virgil Sly, June 25, 1954.
392 Ibid.

This year at New Haven was to be one for study and research—I am a "visiting fellow" of the Divinity School. My travel across Africa needs 6 months further study and inquiry in the library here to make it what it should be . . . I am sure that my contribution to missions at the present lies more in the field of developing methodology and strategy than in missionary addresses.[393]

As his studies progressed McGavran read everything he could find on the work of missions in Taiwan, the Philippines, and West Africa.[394] He corresponded with other researchers. In a letter to Harry R. Boer who had previously submitted his doctoral manuscript to McGavran for comments, he raised a question on the history of conversion in Europe.

What is really required is a careful analysis of what the pure New Testament pattern was, and a historical study to indicate on the basis of fact just how the People Movements of North Europe went on. Were there in fact mass baptisms then? Or was it there also to a much greater extent than is now accepted the baptism of chains of families, each one convinced enough of the Christian faith to be willing to abandon the old gods.[395]

He attempted to clarify some phrasing in Boer's dissertation, and it was later published under the title *Pentecost and Mission*. McGavran expressed the need for more focus on "People" consciousness.

From the point of view of historic accuracy and sociological exactitude the addition of those words, "as a part of a People" are to my way of thinking essential. otherwise readers from the atomistic West, where families do not belong to Peoples, where People consciousness is nil, will say as they read, "Oh yes, it is important to win families for Christ."[396]

McGavran followed up many of his insights on African church growth with vigorous letters of appeal. He perceived the Egon tribe in Nigeria to be highly receptive. He wrote to the Executive Secretary of the mission working in that area:

As I visited Badagri and nearby villages, saw its churches and schools, I was greatly impressed with the fact that you Methodists have in your hand that most precious of all missionary blessings—the valid beginning of a great tribal movement to

---

393 Donald McGavran, letter from New Haven, Connecticut to Spencer Austin, Indianapolis, Sept. 9, 1954.
394 Donald McGavran, interview by Vern Middleton, Dec. 20, 1984.
395 Donald McGavran, letter from New Haven, Connecticut to Harry K. Boer, Sept. 15, 1954.
396 Ibid.

Christ. Cannot the Methodist Mission send out missionaries to claim the whole Egon tribe for Christ till everyone of the 100,000 Egons is a Christian.[397]

He continued to edit the manuscript for *The Bridges of God*. In a letter to Grubb, the editor of World Dominion Press, McGavran wrote, "I have just gone very thoroughly over Chapter III with Professor Paul Shubert, head of the New Testament Department here at Yale Divinity School, and he has been very cordial in his appreciation of it. He says that from the point of view of N.T. scholarship there is nothing in it to which scholars could take exception."[398]

In the same letter he mentioned that he was also looking at the abusive use of statistics which as he put it, "cover up church growth, lull to sleep missionaries, pastors, board secretaries and the public of the sending churches vs. ways which would focus attention on church growth as the main business of missions."[399] His observations were later published under the title, "New Methods For a New Age in Missions" in the *International Review of Missions*.

As research continued his convictions intensified regarding church growth principles. He engaged in correspondence with Dr. G. W. Carpenter, chairman of the African Committee of the International Missionary Council. McGavran proposed an in-depth research on church growth opportunities in Africa. The title of the submission was, "A Study of the Discipling of Africa in This Generation." In McGavran's usual systematic style he wrote the following:

1. The conditions demanding the study.
2. The animistic exodus in Africa leading them to a condition in which tribal movement out of animism to secularism, Islam, Catholicism, or Protestantism.
3. The present African Christian Churches, recently enough converted to be in intimate contact with pagan African Christians—enough to long for their conversion.
4. The dominance of the individualistic processes concepts of evangelism and church growth, in a day when whole peoples (tribes) are being called by God.
5. An aroused but as yet relatively inactive Islam on the northern edge of Animistic Africa, and deeply infiltrated in East and Central Africa.
6. An uneasy political situation throughout the world which threatens disturbed conditions or major changes in control.
7. The tremendous need to coordinate and unify the power of the separated Protestant churches and missions.

---

397 Donald McGavran, letter from New Haven, Connecticut to Basil Clutterbuck, London, Sept. 16, 1954.
398 Donald McGavran, letter from New Haven, Connecticut to Sir Kenneth Grubb, London, Oct. 18, 1954.
399 Ibid.

8. The existence of tremendous and fleeting opportunities for church growth which are vaguely recognized by churches and missions but which evoke no adequate response.
9. The custom of treating Africa as just one more mission field to take its turn at missionary funds and staff along with many other fields.
10 The extent to which Romans are buying up the opportunity with tremendous sending of missionaries.[400]

He listed nine objectives of the study, considering them to be minimal outcomes of the research. These objectives reveal the extent to which his thinking on church growth had matured by 1954.

1. To chart the chief reservoirs of animists.
2. To study the opportunities for great church growth, particularly through claiming whole tribes for Christ.
3. To determine the degree of multiplication now being achieved by the African churches and missions.
4. To describe the methodologies now being used to achieve maximum discipling of tribes.
5. To describe the form which People Movements take in animistic Africa.
6. To study the disposition of church and mission forces relative to opportunities for church growth.
7. To list the forces seriously arrayed against a discipling of the Peoples in this generation.
8. To estimate which areas and which peoples can be won now.
9. To submit plans for a permanent Commission on church growth which would:
   a. focus the attention of Christian leaders on discipling the peoples of Africa;
   b. furnish those at work in the field with information on church growth;
   c. serve as a clearing house for exchanges of information about opportunities for growth and resources available.[401]

McGavran continued to maintain vital links with events in India, especially in the new field of Orissa. Frequently he acted as an interpreter of the events to the executive of the UCMS. He was invited to several board meetings to share his views and ideas, especially on Africa. He also wrote frequently stressing church growth thinking. He wrote to the

---

400 Donald McGavran, letter from New Haven, Connecticut to G. W. Carpenter, Chairman of the African Committee of the IMC, New York, Nov. 20, 1954.

401 Ibid.

president of UCMS, Dale Fiers: "It has been my purpose to illuminate for you from time to time some of the factors which make the conduct of missions a carrying on of missions work. As I do so, the question must continually occur to you, 'Is Don one-sided in all this? Can conditions be as bad as he thinks they are?'"[402]

In the same letter McGavran drew attention to the mission budget as presented in a document entitled, "Capital for Kingdom Building." His concern lay with the Mondombe Station request from the Congo, where the missionary had baptised 4,572 converts in 1953 and seen sustained growth of 30,000 members over a few decades. Yet while other stations were asking for large sums relating to projects and mission station convenience, Mondombe made one simple request which had nothing to do with nurturing the new believers or the mobilization of evangelists to gather in the obvious harvest. This lack of concern for church growth deeply distressed McGavran. He pled for a focus on growth:

> Until the UCMS stresses growth, intends to get growth, requires growth, the mighty machine of missions will succeed, can succeed only in producing more and better mission work carried on regardless as to whether church growth results or not. This is written out of concern that the UC Missionary Society become an organ of the churches which is honestly concerned with the multiplication of churches . . . and acts as if growth . . . of the younger churches was the chief business of missions.[403]

It was remarkable that McGavran received any attention at all from the UCMS mission executive. Its members were highly influenced by the new attitudes emanating from the World Council of Churches. Pessimism was now reflected in the official documents of the Conciliar Movement, some stated: "We are living in the post-Christian age," "We must prepare now to withdraw from our mission fields," and "Missions probably have not many more years of life."[404] McGavran's optimism must have appeared like the rantings of a missionary whose years of service, in the heat of India, had distorted his view of reality.

For the local churches in the US, McGavran's optimistic challenge was good news. They caught his vision and were prepared to give sacrificially to multiply churches and gather in the harvest. Individual churches were prepared to take on the entire support of a missionary couple if they were involved in church planting in the midst of people movements. McGavran wrote after one tour through the churches of California, "There is abundant money for multiplying churches."[405] Other churches wrote, "Could you not

---

402   Donald McGavran, letter while on tour in California to Dale Fiers, President of UCMS, Indianapolis, Dec. 11, 1954.
403   Ibid.
404   Donald McGavran, letter from New Haven, Connecticut to Austin Spencer, Indianapolis, Dec. 31, 1954, 2.
405   Ibid.

come down with a constructive plan for taking advantage of the wonderful Christward Movement in Africa."[406]

STRUGGLES AND DIFFICULTIES IN THIS TRANSITION PERIOD

By November 1954, McGavran was negotiating a staff role with the UCMS. He formulated his own job description as follows:

1. Continue the study of People Movements through (library research) and surveys abroad.
2. Find a People Movement committee under the International Missionary Committee with a branch in England and a quarterly paper.
3. Secure People Movement studies in all courses for new missionaries and nationals at home and abroad. Get the newer theology, methodology and philosophy widely known by the younger generation.
4. Fit into any plans of our folk to fatten up our People Movements. Help raise a half a million for a real Growing Church Fund.
5. Publish a book a year on some phase of People Movements.
6. Teach special courses on Church Growth in Bible Colleges and Seminaries for those interested in younger churches.[407]

Although the position never materialized for him, of the six major concepts in this job description, almost every one of them was fulfilled either through the establishment of the Institute of Church Growth at Eugene, Oregon, or later through the development of the School of World Mission at Fuller Theological Seminary at Pasadena, California.

In 1955 McGavran doggedly stressed to UCMS executives that he wanted to use the next eight years of his life to transform the very nature of the missionary enterprise.

The Bridges of God will be for sale in April, but Virgil, its publication will be merely a shout in the dark, unless there is serious consecutive planned follow-up. Is there some way of using the next eight years of our lives in a serious effort to tip mission practice around the world at least a little bit toward the deliberate reinforcement of people movements to Christ that it be done some way or other, is very clear to me. God is calling me to that task.[408]

---

406 Oswald J. Goulter, letter from Phillips University, Enid to Donald McGavran, Dec. 13, 1954.
407 Donald McGavran, letter from New Haven, Connecticut to Virgil Sly, Indianapolis, Nov. 3, 1954.
408 Donald McGavran, letter from New Haven, Connecticut to Virgil Sly, Indianapolis, Jan. 27, 1955.

He suggested he be appointed as a church growth consultant with a six-year assignment and with a budget allocation. He made a six-point list of the tasks to be performed.

1. Present an annual analysis of church growth and church growth potential for each Disciple Mission.
2. Help raise funds for growing churches of all our missions spotlighting the evangelistic outreach of UCMS.
3. Make studies of church growth for all our mission fields.
4. Become a people movement and church growth specialist for the United Society—someone who knows more about church growth than anyone else in the world.
5. As a missionary of UCMS, as a Disciple render to other churches and boards services in this absolutely central field of church growth.
6. Produce as a missionary of UCMS, a dynamic philosophy and methodology of missions.[409]

As negotiations progressed, McGavran made it clear that church growth must be the heart and core of his future ministry and that he and Mary were to devote the remainder of their active lives to promoting church growth.

Basic to the entire situation are our convictions:

1. That missions have permitted the growth of churches to slip out of the center of the picture and "mission work, done whether or not the churches grow" to become the all-consuming passion;
2. That God gives to us again and again opportunities for church growth, usually in the form of people movements and that these are consistently misunderstood because of our traditional, individualistic methodology, and hence mishandled; and
3. That boards and missions have steadfastly refused to move resources to the aid of growing churches which has resulted in varying degrees of stagnation for the God-given people movements.[410]

The executive committee did not see the issue so clearly. They still wanted McGavran to return to India for another term. The proposal UCMS made at that time was to extend the McGavran furlough one more year. Also to send him to Puerto Rico for a study of church growth there. This he did somewhat reluctantly from October 20–December 20 of 1955. The reasons for his hesitancy were twofold. First, McGavran felt that the Puerto Rican

---

409   Ibid.
410   Donald McGavran, letter from New Haven, Connecticut to Virgil Sly, Indianapolis, June 1, 1955.

church growth situation was so tempered by Pentecostal influences that it would color the facts and brand the Church Growth Movement. Secondly, he felt it was absolutely essential that he to do a survey of various missions in Asia to get a broader picture of principles and patterns of church growth. So McGavran negotiated for a two-year extension of their furlough and the inclusion of the Asian Survey.

In spite of the Puerto Rican proposal from UCMS, McGavran was frustrated. On June 24, 1955, he wrote a letter to missionary colleagues in Takhatpur:

> The society is still asking me to extend our furlough a little and undertake a survey of church growth in Puerto Rico. It is all very vague distressingly so. As you know my chief message for years has been that missions should pour in resources where churches can multiply; and for the first time I am beginning to get through, beginning to be heard, beginning to get action. I have been terribly down-hearted many a time. It looks as if the missionary world had just one ear— and it was deaf. But a lot of little signs are pointing in the right direction. So if the Board comes through clear on this Puerto Rico business I'll have to accept. But my heart tugs for Takhatpur.[411]

This letter revealed McGavran's inner feelings, yet it must be remembered that he could not disclose the new direction the Lord was leading, due to the negative impact such information would have on the ministry at Takhatpur. Therefore, on this very same day, he wrote a strikingly different letter to Virgil Sly, which was a response to a personal interview that took place earlier in the week.

> My understanding of your proposal is that 1) while the present talk is in terms of extending the furlough for a year, we may expect that by this time next year a more permanent arrangement will be worked out; and 2) that there will be both the study in Puerto Rico and that in Thailand, which will enable me to take Formosa and the Philippines on my way.[412]

To McGavran everything seemed very indefinite. By his very nature and training he found it hard to live with an open-ended relationship. Hence he suggested UCMS second him to the International Missionary Council. "If our requests are in any way posing a problem to the Society, I wonder whether a simple way out would be to accede to Dr. Ranson's request and loan us to the IMC for three years. It wants us knowing what we promote, and seems to have a program into which we could fit."[413]

---

411 Donald McGavran, letter from New Haven, Connecticut to Ethel Shreeve and Mary Pollard, Takhatpur, June 24, 1955.
412 Donald McGavran, letter from New Haven, Connecticut to Virgil Sly, Indianapolis, June 27, 1955.
413 Ibid.

In 1954 McGavran's connections were still all oriented toward the mainline denominations. However he was developing a respect for the "fundamentalists," his term for evangelicals. He felt that church growth ideas would offset the polarization created by the theological differences of these two points of view. He predicted the future impact of the Church Growth Movement:

> I covet for the UCMS the interdenominational standing and prestige which championing this move in missionary ends and means will bring. I like to feel also that this stress will help heal the breach between fundamentalists and liberal missions. I want it known that the United Christian Missionary Society is spearheading this evangelistic movement, which is certain to gather momentum whether the UCMS backs it or not.[414]

India Beckons

Meanwhile letters came from India pleading for their return. Those who remained on in Takhatpur sent some very heart-wrenching letters describing the desperate vacuum created by their absence. Then there were also the official invitations both by the Indian Church as well as by the Executive Committee of the field. However the latter seemed a matter of cordiality rather than an urgency. McGavran expressed this in a letter to Ken Potee: "If the Executive's position is, 'We'd be glad to have them back,' of course, but it does not really make much difference. Then you can scarcely blame missionaries if they choose to go where people urgently want them."[415]

Alexander McLeish of World Dominion Press wrote encouraging McGavran to return to India. McGavran responded by describing his new course of direction which was to sell the concept of mobility and the urgency of developing the people movement methodology to mission boards and missions around the world.

The correspondence and cables inviting the McGavrans back to India for their last seven-year term caused tensions and considerable confusion. Although it was clear in McGavran's mind what he wanted to do in the future, neither the UCMS executive nor the India field executive understood it fully. The men of these two committees felt they were being used as an excuse for their nonreturn.

On October 1, 1957 McGavran's letter to Sly revealed his full purpose in being so elusive.

> Mary and I believe that it has been good for the churches around Takhatpur for there to be no definite word now as to our return or non-return. They are still hoping for our return. Every year which passes with the village people hoping that

---

414 Donald McGavran, letter from New Haven, Connecticut to Virgil Sly, Indianapolis, June 1, 1955.
415 Donald McGavran, letter from Indianapolis to Herman and Ken Potee, India, June 5, 1957.

we will return makes the transition to other leaders easier. While waiting for us to return they will come to think of Mr. Samuel and Mr. Paul and others as their own leaders. Furthermore, we believe that it might still be calamitous for a firm announcement that we are not going to return to be made. A clear cut answer will not hurt us but might hurt those beach-head churches.[416]

The whole issue of the McGavrans' return to India was laid to rest on March 15, 1958 and was apparently the first response McGavran made to the Executive Committee of the India field.[417] When he finally said "no" to the possible return to India, the UCMS Executives were upset that he turned down such a cordial invitation. He realized the invitation back to India was principally to carry on missions as usual; planning conferences, settling church problems, running institutions with a little church planting, and evangelism on the side. This McGavran could no longer tolerate; it was highly unlikely he could have returned even had he desired to do so because the aftereffects of the Niyogi Committee of 1954 where the government of Madhya Pradesh conducted an inquiry into missionary activity, which greatly tightened up the entrance of missionaries from the US. McGavran escaped a direct confrontation with that Committee while he was on furlough but the local police in the District of Bhilaspur were very much aware of his being "actively evangelistic." McGavran's reputation as a champion of the Satnamis and because he did not possess the "No Objection to Return Certificate," would have made reentry into India difficult, if not impossible.

While the vision for the development of the Church Growth Movement never dimmed for McGavran, there were many occasions when he talked of retiring to tend a rose garden or farm and forget the whole idea. As early as 1956 while on his Asian research tour he wrote, "We simply must get this incorporation going. Plans, plans, plans and not much hope at present of them materializing. We rest on God's care, even if the future looks a bit uncertain. He has always seen us through, and we can go back to India for a not too bad last term any time we wish, or take a church or do a lot of things."[418]

SHARPENING DEFINITION

Nineteen fifty-five was a period for refining McGavran's insights. Interaction with mission administrators, leaders, and publishers served to sharpen definition and clarity in his church growth concepts.

---

416 Donald McGavran, letter from Enid, Oklahoma, to Virgil Sly, Indianapolis, Sept. 1, 1957.

417 Ken Potee, letter from Jabalpur, India to UCMS Executive, Indianapolis, March 30, 1958.

418 Donald McGavran, letter from Nakum Patharn, Thailand to Mary McGavran, New Haven, Connecticut, Feb. 26, 1956.

People Movement Definition

Grubb of World Dominion Press and a member of the IMC, as well as the Central Committee of the WCC, took a real interest in McGavran. Yet because of his English point of view, he found McGavran's pattern of coining terms highly out of the ordinary. Weekly correspondence with him served to assist McGavran in accuracy of expression. Considerable correspondence arose over the term "People Movement." McGavran wrote:

> The word *"people"* has two meanings, a) persons and b) a single endogamous tribe or caste. I use people in sense b. Thus what I discuss might in India be called a Caste Movement, in Africa a Tribe Movement, in Scotland a Clan Movement. But I needed a universal word, which is *"people."* Hence a *People Movement.* I think you will grant the point in the singular. In the one people . . . there is a people movement to Christ.[419]

The problem over the term was compounded by the fact that Grubb's missionary experience centered in the cities of Latin America. Therefore he possessed little background in tribal and caste corporate expression to assist him in conceptualizing with McGavran.[420] This resulted in a struggle over ideas. McGavran pressed the definition further by refusing to use the term "peoples movements."

> Now let us take a look at the plural. In two hundred tribes in Congo what do we have—People Movements to Christ or Peoples Movements to Christ, Tribe Movements to Christ or Tribes Movements to Christ? Definitely People Movements or Tribe Movements. Please remember that this use of *"people"* is a synonym for caste or clan, is not comparable in any way to the current phrase "a people's government."[421]

Not content with McGavran's reasoning Grubb insisted on the term "peoples movement." At this point in the debate McGavran became rather forceful as to his intent:

> I am afraid I shall have to retain my manuscript from "People Movement." We are establishing a new phraseology and it is important to be accurate. "Peoples Movement" permits the confusion that what we are talking about is the common people as in peoples government. Whereas what we are talking about is not that at

---

419   Donald McGavran, letter from New Haven, Connecticut to Sir Kenneth Grubb, London, Jan. 10, 1955.
420   Donald McGavran, interview by Vern Middleton, June 26, 1986.
421   Donald McGavran, letter from New Haven, Connecticut to Sir Kenneth Grubb, London, Jan. 10, 1955.

all; but is about the "mass movements" it is never rendered "masses movements" nor in the form "group movements" is it ever rendered "groups movements."[422]

In order to clarify the term "people movement" further, McGavran felt it imperative that the old concept, "mass movements" be dropped. He discovered that the latter term carried with it unfortunate implications. He wrote to Pickett requesting that in any republication of materials from the 1930s that "people movements" be used wherever the previous concept occurred. He wrote, "Mass movements throughout the rest of the Christian world have a bad name. Any mishandled people movement is called a mass movement!! Which is part of the problem!"[423] Pickett did not see the validity of McGavran's request and the term was never taken out of Pickett's reprints.

DEFINITION OF THE TERM "GROWTH"

Arising out of a report which was eventually published in the *International Review of Missions* entitled, "Studies in the Life and Growth of Younger Churches," McGavran took issue with the term "growth." He questioned Erik W. Nielson, the author, while the material was still in the manuscript stage. McGavran wrote, "You seem to have defined the 'growth' of the title as meaning, 'the spiritual development of the congregations not including any consideration of their numerical increase.' In this day of possible movements of many whole peoples to Christian faith it would seem an odd procedure."[424]

The next paragraph took McGavran to the heart of the issue and gave rise to a definition regarding biological and conversion church growth.

> For many missions and churches the crucial issues are: a) that a small number of churches have been established which neither have grown, nor are growing, nor are likely to grow in the future: (I use "*grow*" here to mean numerical increase through exterior baptisms. I do not count increase in membership through the birth of children in the Christian community as growth in the missionary sense. By no stretch of the imagination is such increase "discipling the nations"); and b) that these churches are tying up such large amounts of mission resources in evangelism, philanthropy and good mission work which does not multiply the churches, that wide open doors for pentecostal increase are habitually left unentered.[425]

---

422 Donald McGavran, letter from New Haven, Connecticut to Grubb, London, Feb. 12, 1955.
423 Donald McGavran, letter from New Haven, Connecticut to Pickett, New Delhi, India, Feb. 22, 1955.
424 Donald McGavran, letter from New Haven, Connecticut to Erik W. Nielsen, Edinburgh House, London, June 24, 1955.
425 Ibid.

ECCLESIASTICAL IMPLICATIONS OF
PEOPLE MOVEMENTS

There were deep theological implications in the proposals made in the book, *The Bridges of God*, especially as the concepts related to the nature of the local church. McGavran was aware that charges could be laid that accused him of advocating the State Church (People's Church, Volks Kirche) polity. He recognized that there would be those who would say, "*The Bridges of God* . . . proposes a Catholic or State Church solution quite unacceptable to those holding to believer's baptism and quite out of date in today's freedom."[426]

McGavran was not betraying his lifelong convictions for the expediency of people movements. He wrote, "I am one who is a convinced advocate of believer's baptism and comes from a long line of Baptist and Disciple forebears."[427]

He did not explicitly deal with ecclesiastical structures in *The Bridges of God*. However, he was convinced there was enough implicit material that the careful reader would realize his primary concern was with the one-by-one decision-making process. Such a pattern may be necessary in a country with a Christian tradition, but alien to the thinking of those whose culture involves the corporate, social, decision-making process.

CAUSES OF RESISTANCE IDENTIFIED

McGavran also dealt with factors creating resistance to numerical growth. He urged the IMC to set up a study of the reasons why church multiplication was deliberately avoided. He set forth some of the salient causes of resistance.

> Great increase of the churches by conversions suffers in a peculiar way. Where, because of the resistance of the culture involved or any other reason, non growing churches have been established and are the accustomed variety, where ten conversions from the non-Christians in a decade is counted good growth, there a mind set grows up among us missionaries to the effect that "sound spiritual methods prohibit any rapid church growth." To us mission station approach workers interest in rapid church growth appears to be "an unseemly scramble for mere numbers."[428]

Other areas of resistance to growth were identified. Due to the previous patterns of church involvement, most missionaries want an orderly "trickle" of converts into the established churches. McGavran lamented the fact that missionaries in God-given people

---

426 Donald McGavran, letter from New Haven, Connecticut to Kenneth Ritchie Hogg, Jan. 16, 1956.

427 Ibid.

428 Donald McGavran, letter to Nielsen, June 24, 1955. See also McGavran, *Case History*, MS, Ruandi-Urundi (1954), 2.

movement areas often cried out, "Heaven save us from any such rapid increase." They do so because they feel things are out of control when in actual fact the movement is a product of the Holy Spirit's control. He identified the cause of resistance here as being due to an inadequate sociological and theological paradigm. "People move as a social whole. So the church has always been faced with great ingatherings . . . This is substantially the picture today. The sociological and theological understandings of such ingatherings are largely lacking. We are trying to shepherd whole peoples with the tools used for a one by one process."[429]

The final area of resistance he identified was the false perception that if the church becomes spiritually strong then numerical growth will almost automatically occur. McGavran bluntly rejected this notion with the statement, "Evidence does not support that thesis."[430]

During 1955 McGavran identified still another major source of resistance to growth, that of an inadequate understanding of the implications of prevailing cultural patterns in given societies. He was invited to address and sit in on the African Committee of the IMC on several occasions.[431] In this context he encountered many missionary leaders who judged polygamy from their cultural point of view. He perceived this as a major barrier to the conversion of whole tribes in Africa. He shared the insights gained while making his trip across Africa with Grubb. "West Africa Christianity is losing ground fast to the Moslems, often over a simple matter that the Moslems can and do take in polygamists."[432]

McGavran read voraciously on the subject of polygamy. He *discovered* a bold proposal made by the Evangelical Lutheran Church in Liberia. The revised position as presented in 1951 created a 180-degree change of attitude for the mission leadership. He urged Grubb to publish the statement in World Dominion journal since, the whole question of polygamy was a very prominent subject at that time. Grubb responded positively. The article was featured as a news item. The key sentence was, "Where evidence of true faith is shown, parties to an established polygamous marriage may be baptized and confirmed."[433]

MOBILIZING RESOURCES

For over two decades McGavran had repeatedly expressed the concept of transferring resources to fertile fields, while holding sterile areas lightly. UCMS mission treasurer, Spencer Austin, found the concept unacceptable and he reacted by restating administrative policy. "Since $100 out of every $300 will automatically go to Foreign Missions anyway, and since the most urgent needs in Foreign are for putting reinforcements into the areas of greatest growth, the new money will automatically go into such activities."[434] But, McGavran

---

429 Donald McGavran, letter to Nielsen, June 24, 1955.
430 Ibid.
431 Donald McGavran, letter from New Haven, Connecticut to Virgil Sly, Indianapolis, Jan. 8, 1955.
432 Donald McGavran, letter from New Haven, Connecticut to K. Grubb, London, Jan. 18, 1955.
433 Harold Vink, "Thesis on Polygamy," (March 27, 1954), submitted to Kennedy School of Missions.
434 Donald McGavran, letter from New Haven, Connecticut to Spencer Austin, Indianapolis, Jan. 19, 1955.

was insistent that the financial policy of the mission was responsible for curtailing giving and preventing faith pledges. "How resources are gotten to areas of maximum opportunity is really none of my business . . . My job is to keep before you who direct the destinies of our great missionary society the fact that these opportunities exist, that the present machine of missions is largely ignoring them and that starved by lack of resources they are dying."[435]

The treasurer found it difficult to accept McGavran's concepts, so his reaction to McGavran's strategy was negative. He interpreted the principle as yet another of McGavran's many attempts to gain more money for his projects. Austin failed to see that McGavran was arguing from principle and biblical priority, but for Austin this was another "pet project" from another of the missions many missionaries all clamoring for a greater stake in the annual budget.

Realizing the interpretation that could be given to his argument, McGavran attempted to distance himself by stating. "It is no more my work than it is your work."[436] He concluded by absolving himself of spiritual responsibility if the principle was not heeded: "The watchman on the walls of Zion is not shouting, 'My house is being attacked,' he is shouting 'Zion is being stormed.' Having done this my responsibilities are over. The Lord will not require their blood at my hands."[437]

However not content to leave the issue of funding for people movements to the vagaries of mission boards, McGavran sought to establish an umbrella ecumenical agency which would give funding guidelines to mission boards around the world. He made the proposal to Grubb who was chairman of the Churches Commission on International Affairs which was sponsored jointly by the World Council of Churches and the International Missionary Council. McGavran wrote:

> I am struck with the need for the World Church to decide which are the people movements of greatest strategic importance. An ecumenical approach to the extension of Christianity would surely make a careful pronouncement on the matter. Equally important is the need to assign priorities to the various mission works.
>
> 1. No hope of multiplying the churches—least priority.
> 2. Reasonable hope of small increases of the churches—low priority.
> 3. Reasonable hope of leaving widespread sound churches—high priority.
> 4. Reasonable hope of leaving widespread sound churches which have great strategic importance for further multiplication of churches—highest priority.[438]

---

435 Ibid.
436 Ibid.
437 Ibid.
438 Donald McGavran, letter from New Haven, Connecticut to K. Grubb, London, July 7, 1955.

Several weeks later McGavran wrote a similar letter to Dr. Charles Ranson of the IMC. He added several new dimensions to his earlier idea, one of which was to study mission budgets to determine the amounts allocated to evangelism and church growth related activities, versus the amounts given to institutional programs, which have little to do with proclamation and gathering in the lost. He requested an interview with Ranson, which was granted, and as a result McGavran received an invitation to join the staff of the IMC as mentioned earlier.

THE CASE HISTORY METHOD

McGavran utilized the case history approach to missions as a valid form of historiography. He combined three forms of discipline to refine the facts and obtain accuracy. First, he considered on-site research essential and primary to this method. Secondly, he sought out the best in library research, combing archives and other primary source material. Finally, he corroborated his material with authorities on the particular field in question.

As the case history method began to take form within the church growth discipline he discussed the idea with mission historian Latourette. Their correspondence reveals why he considered the case history approach so helpful:

> I find so much mission history is written from the promotional point of view. It lauds whatever was done. It never asks what effect such action had on church growth, nor on whether something else might have won more battles. Using the people movement point of view then as a formula of understanding I would plan to describe perhaps a half dozen missions and their churches, or churches and their assisting missions.[439]

As McGavran's international research progressed he was in regular correspondence with mission personnel around the world. Before his material was ever published he would often distribute the manuscript to as many as ten or twelve different individuals requesting they critique his ideas so as to avoid erroneous statements which might later cause people to label the material as merely, "McGavran's point of view."[440]

Some of the responses given were with a note of sarcasm and somewhat demeaning. A. L. Warnshius wrote an article called, "Group Conversions and Decision Making." Thinking he would be supportive, McGavran submitted *The Bridges of God* manuscript to him for his evaluation. The reply chided McGavran for attempting to internationalize his principles. "The whole book should be limited to a discussion of missions in India letting people in other countries draw their own conclusions regarding the application of what you have

---

439 Donald McGavran, letter from New Haven, Connecticut to Latourette, Yale, Feb. 3, 1955.
440 Donald McGavran, letter from New Haven, Connecticut to Trimingham, Feb. 23, 1955.

written upon their plans and methods."[441] Without directly saying so, Warnshius questioned McGavran's scholarship and his provincial frame of reference. He wrote, "I assume and I am sorry that you do not read Dutch and perhaps not German either or I would refer you to some literature in these languages."[442]

Two months later the role was reversed and McGavran was in the critic's seat as he suggested to Warnshius that his article could be enhanced if certain changes were made in his interpretation of events in the Book of Acts.[443] Yet in spite of the terse tone of these exchanges McGavran included Warnshius' article in the revised edition of *Church Growth and Group Conversion.*

McGavran remained undaunted by criticism and welcomed insights from varied sources. He expressed his appreciation to Grubb for the suggestions others made about his material:

> The professors of mission here are assisting me by reading the early drafts and making suggestions. I plan to submit each reconstruction of history to the field concerned for correction on matters of fact. The history will be reliable, but the interpretation while hailed by many will be challenged by others.[444]

When McGavran submitted his materials to various mission leaders he asked for assistance in six primary ways:

a. Is the people movement approach illuminating as to what really happened?
b. Are there any minor matters which you feel needlessly exacerbate readers?
c. Do you feel like taking issue with the main currents of interpretation and analysis?
d. Are there places where you believe my facts must be wrong?
e. Do you think I carry my point that the people movement point of view is really the Great Commission point of view; Disciple the tribes equals nurture people movements to Christ?
f. Do you think that those who have not read *The Bridges of God* will have enough background to read this kind of history?[445]

By late February 1955 McGavran had produced four case histories which he desired to publish as a single volume entitled *Church Growth and the Discipling of Peoples in All the World.* Again the diversity of these studies indicated the seriousness with which he struggled

---

441 A. L. Warnshuis, letter from Bronxville, New York to Donald McGavran, New Haven, Connecticut, Feb. 21, 1955.

442 Ibid.

443 Donald McGavran, letter from New Haven, Connecticut to Warnshuis, Bronxville, April 15, 1955.

444 Donald McGavran, letter from New Haven, Connecticut to K. Grubb, London, Feb. 20, 1955.

445 Donald McGavran, letter from New Haven, Connecticut to Trimingham, Feb. 23, 1955.

to internationalize his concepts. Their titles were, "Gold Coast Methodism," "Liberian Lutheranism," "Formosan Presbyterianism," and "Filippino Christian-Catholicism." Each of these studies was forty pages. He stated the value of case histories:

> In the development of the church growth school of thought, case studies, mission by mission are essential to real understanding. We need to see how in specific church-mission situations, group conversions and people movements have had definitive bearing on church growth. The widespread failure to take available opportunities of people movement growth needs also to be seen.[446]

October 1956, Dr. Frank Price of the Missionary Research library received several case studies from McGavran. The letter accompanying the submissions contained three statements on the significance of this type of historiography.

He stated that one value of case history approach for church growth is that it reduces subjectivity. A fundamental tenent in McGavran's thinking was that the work of Christ should be open for appraisal and evaluation. However, any evaluation produces defense mechanisms in the leadership of missions or churches being looked at. McGavran pointed out some typical responses: "That is his opinion; but in ours the distribution of effort by churchmen is beautifully calculated to achieve the maximum true benefit of the Church. McGavran overlooks so many things and writes from such a partisan point of view."[447]

McGavran further described how the case history method overcomes any accusation that the evaluation contains unsupported generalizations.

> The case histories, however, give chapter and verse. They document situations. They prove that opportunities for growth in these instances are constantly overlooked. They draw the issue clearly. They give charts showing disastrous losses which were quite unnecessary, and glorious growth which could have been greater. They are not an indictment, but they do constitute an alarming diagnosis . . . of concrete situations . . . They describe goals badly missed, vast sums spent for least return when great returns were to be had, satisfaction with the good which blocked achievement of the best, smooth operation of the machine of missions at the cost of lost churches, or preoccupation with organizational matters so great that the growth of the Church ceased to have any importance for younger Church leaders, missionaries and board officials.[448]

---

446 Donald McGavran, letter from New Haven, Connecticut to K. Grubb, London, Feb. 20, 1955.
447 Donald McGavran, letter from New Haven, Connecticut to Frank Price, Librarian of the Missionary Research Library, New York, Oct. 14, 1956.
448 Ibid.

He concluded that case histories "do not claim to be the complete picture, but they do present a large well authenticated block of evidence on the real state of . . . churches. The wraps are taken off. Promotional presentation is laid aside. There is no attempt to make this inspirational reading."[449]

Chapter two of the unpublished manuscript entitled, "Church Growth in Formosa," focused entirely on the issue of case studies as a valid form of historiography. McGavran sets forth three reasons why some mission histories are unreliable:

a. They are written from the point of view of the Mission. They deal with the coming and going of missionaries, their activities and their dreams, the institutions they founded and built up, and the converts they won. A comparatively small part of the record treats of the growth and development of the churches.

b. Books on missions are almost always a part of the great promotional process which enfolds the entire missionary enterprise. They are written that the enterprise may be seen as a glorious one and donors, past, present and prospective may be satisfied.

c. Books on missions furthermore are commonly impregnated with the individualistic philosophy and methodology.[450]

Later paragraphs in this chapter recognize the bias a church growth writer also brings to mission history. However, unlike conventional historians who do not admit to their presuppositions, the church growth historian, recognizing his bias, strives to "avoid pushing the inferences further than the facts would strictly allow."[451]

McGavran pressed his point regarding the raison d'être of the case study approach when he wrote:

The question is always one of the facts, which reconstruction of history more exactly fits the facts. The only thing which constitutes scholarship in the writing of history is the ability to see and describe what actually happened. In writing the history of church growth in Formosa the only thing which counts is ability to see and describe the development of the congregations. We must see the point of view of the peoples who are becoming Christians. We must try to understand how peoples, tribes and kindred become Christian. The doings of mission, save as they contribute to this end are of secondary value.[452]

---

449 Ibid.
450 Donald McGavran, "Church Growth in Formosa" (unpublished MS, 1955), 12.
451 Ibid., 13.
452 Ibid.

By the fall of 1956 McGavran had assembled another five case histories which he had researched between November 1955 and April 1956. He recognized that though the surveys were international, including, Puerto Rico, the Philippines, Thailand, and India, they were limited to only two churches,—Disciples of Christ and Baptists. While seeking a publisher for these he explained his technique and the value of case histories. "I used five different techniques of investigation, I ask: 'How is the Church growing, how has it grown, and why is it growing, where and why has it stopped growing, what mission procedures help and hinder church growth, and how can we get more church growth.'"[453]

In his promotional statements on the value of this type of writing he said, "Case studies are unvarnished accounts of the growth of Churches, which enable missionaries and their leaders to read without emotional involvement." Further on in the same letter he suggested two other assets for case studies: "They are absolutely factual, and they deal, not in generalizations, but in actual cases."[454]

Since 1955 some historians had deliberately wedded the disciplines of sociology and history together to develop the new discipline of ethnohistory. Thus, in recent decades historians have been more aware of their cultural biases than in the past.

Several years later when the Institute of Church Growth was established, every student was required to write a thesis which amounted to a case history of the development of the church in the mission in which he labored. Many of these case histories have been published, while some never were. Yet they corporately represent a considerable volume of factual information documenting church growth around the world.

INDIAN PUBLISHER UTILIZED

McGavran recognized that mission case histories have limited reader attraction. For this reason he contacted the Lucknow Press in India to act as a publisher for these books. This publisher knew McGavran well, and had worked with him on several previous occasions in publishing church growth research materials. Another advantage in using this Indian publisher was the low cost, since most of the books published by the Lucknow publishing house were subsidized personally by McGavran.

While corresponding with the Lucknow publisher McGavran described his vision for making the Mass Movement research available for missions around the world.

In The Mass Movement Survey of Mid India I am counting on doing some major revision . . . to make the book of greater use to those outside mid-India. You see, in that book, Pickett, Singh and I discuss how it happens that mission work in mid-India did not start people movements to Christ. That subject is of

---

453 Donald McGavran, letter from New Haven, Connecticut to Elfers (Publisher), Sept. 5, 1956.
454 Ibid.

enormous importance to missions all over the world, where they are enmeshed in the Mission Station Approach.[455]

As McGavran addressed the wider world of missions and internationalized his ideas he felt it important to downplay his long years of service in India. For example, when Latourette wrote the foreword to *The Bridges of God*, his original paragraph contained the sentence, "This book arises out of thirty years spent in India."[456] McGavran requested that the sentence be eliminated because he did not want to give his readers opportunity to say, "This concept fits India but does not apply to my situation." Latourette complied.

MECHANISM OF MOBILITY

The summer of 1955 was a time of intense interaction and renewed creativity for McGavran. The people with whom he was in correspondence reads like a "who's who list." As he responded to the various letters each writer almost without exception was channeled into consideration of mobilizing churches and missions for harvest. A proposal was sent to the executive team of UCMS detailing what McGavran entitled as "The Mechanism for Mobility."

The mechanism of mobility has two aspects. First, mobility into the discipling areas. The UCMS determines the size of the circle which one evangelistic missionary can shepherd. Let's assume that the circle size, for the first stage of great growth, is 2,000 members or 4,000 community, ten congregations, 10 teacher-preachers, one circle pastor-in-training. The mechanism of mobility is that the UCMS says, "Whenever one circle has 2,000 members we'll put in another missionary automatically at a further center to disciple another circle." Second, mobility out of a discipled area. It will be expected that no circle will have missionary leadership for more than a few years, say 3–10 years. The missionary's job is to create local leadership and move on. Soon missionaries coming out of discipled circles will provide most of the force required by new opportunities.[457]

The mechanism of mobility contrasted sharply with standard missionary practise. The established pattern was: the missionary arrived, built a house, and won a small church to Christ. He and his successors would live there for the next one hundred years. The idea of

---

455   Donald McGavran, letter from New Haven, Connecticut to Ewart of Lucknow Publishers, India, Feb. 10, 1955.

456   Donald McGavran, letter from New Haven, Connecticut to K. Grubbs, London, Feb. 12, 1955.

457   Donald McGavran, letter from New Haven, Connecticut to UCMS executives (Sly/West/Friers), Indianapolis, Aug. 15, 1955.

moving missionaries from growing segment to growing segment would have revolutionized missions had it been applied.

In keeping with the mobility theme McGavran corresponded with the editor, John C. Scobee, of Le Tourneau's journal *NOW*. He compared his concept of The Mechanism of Mobility with Le Tourneau's electric wheel and the Rubber Tired Trackless Train. He also pointed out that, "It is similar to the methods used by the Apostles. It is firmly based on the Scriptures and abundantly illustrated in Acts."[458]

In another paragraph McGavran compared the mission station approach to the horse and buggy stage; he also used the analogy of trench warfare. He described the creativity of his methodology:

The dynamic biblical methodology should replace it. The dynamic techniques work. But they are so enmeshed in static mission station methodology that they are seldom clearly seen or recognized. All the elements of the electric wheel were present in America in 1910 but enmeshed in other machines, they were not recognized. It took an R. G. Le Tourneau to separate them, put them together, call the thing an electric wheel and manufacture it.[459]

McGavran's concluding paragraph to Scobee presented a threefold proposal. One, that Le Tourneau appoint a committee to thoroughly examine his proposal; two, that a member of the committee be sent with McGavran to Africa and Asia to see the reality of the situation; and three, that an effort be made to begin to put into place ways of implementing McGavran's methodology. This proposal did not fall on deaf ears, for the Le Tourneau Foundation had funded and encouraged the implementation of church growth methodologies in Peru in recent years.

Further insight on his "Mechanism of Mobility" was revealed in a letter to James Dickson of the Presbyterian Church in Canada. McGavran cited two main reasons why missions were mired down in a 150-year old unproductive methodology. "First," he said, "missions are attempting to shepherd tribal movements with tools used for inch by inch progress in the face of resistant non-Christian cultures. The sociological and theological understanding of people movements are largely lacking. Secondly, the resources of missions are spread out and tied down among many mission stations. Egalitarianism reigns."[460]

While corresponding with Dean R. T. Parsons of Hartford Theological Seminary over a research proposal he constructed for the Christian movement in the Gold Coast,

---

458 McGavran, letter from New Haven, Connecticut to John C. Scobee, June 1, 1955.
459 Ibid.
460 Donald McGavran, letter from New Haven, Connecticut to James Dickson, Presbyterian Church of Canada, Toronto, July 21, 1955.

McGavran discussed still other dimensions of the Mechanism of Mobility. His concern with the traditional station approach is that it brought people into identification with the mission, but not the local church. He also criticised the detribalization that takes place through one by one conversions where the Church is seen "in opposition to the tribe, the Christian to the African, the foreign to the indigenous."[461]

Pressing further the theme of Mechanism for Mobility, McGavran wrote to seminary professors of mission to discover if the static approach had its roots in their teaching. He asked, "In connection with the need for directing resources to those people who can now be won to Christ, I am curious to find out the picture of mission work given to the American public by the missionary education movement. What does 'missions' mean to those who write the mission study texts?"[462] The circular letter to the professors was aimed to make them either blush with shame or turn red with anger, when asked:

> I wonder whether during the last thirty years, either intentionally or unintentionally, there has not been a presentation of missions as philanthropy, improvement of the lot of individuals through education and medicine, building of character of a boy here or there, or a man or woman here or there, a rescued person, and usually in the setting of a single mission station or a single church, the difficult slow progress of one by one rescued from the world.[463]

The above material amply illustrates the thoroughness with which McGavran pursued the idea of the Mechanism of Mobility for church growth.

THE SPIRITUAL DIMENSION OF McGAVRAN

Due to the analytical nature and firm disciplines of McGavran's life, his writings and lectures have a heady ring to them, and many seem to lack the spiritual warmth of the heart. However, to characterize his ideas as merely being the product of his head is a gross distortion of a Godward life, set on finding and following the leading of the Holy Spirit.

During June of 1955, at the age of 58, McGavran began experiencing a good deal of pain in his left chest. Over the next several years he lived with a constant awareness that the next moment might be his last. He visited Dr. Millar who solemnly warned him that he had less than five years to live.

The spiritual depth of McGavran grew more evident in this crisis. The fire of his devotion to Christ was expressed as he wrote letters which he thought might be his last.

---

461 Donald McGavran, letter from New Haven, Connecticut to R. T. Parsons, Dean of Hartford Theological Seminary, Hartford, Aug. 3, 1955.

462 Donald McGavran, circular letter from New Haven, Connecticut to Professors Forman and Goerner, Aug. 9, 1955.

463 Ibid.

On June 12, 1955, McGavran wrote a letter of discussion about his health to his son Malcolm, who was a medical doctor. The letter turned out to be one of consolation and spiritual instruction.

> When God wills, I'll be called home, not before; so I am not worrying. I want you all to remember that whether I die in 26 years or 20 days, I try to live so that He will receive me and I have confidence that He will, not because I have achieved but because I have believed as truly as I can. God knows the heart—I am His son. I often say to Mother that my work—as I see it—is now over and the sooner He calls me the better pleased I shall be. Yet who am I to say when to go. It should be, indeed, it will be as my Lord wills.[464]

In 1957, while on a major survey of the Philippines, McGavran wrote his wife describing the living conditions there. He once again alluded to his expectation of being with the Lord. "I have been eating in the hospital mess and the place is always full of nurses and doctors and radio talking fifty to the dozen. I am surprised at myself how I fit in and yell with the best of them; but I do so with an inner understanding that as long as the irons have to be worn, they have to be worn, but that some day I shall be free."[465]

One week later the president of the Philippines died in a plane crash at the airport where McGavran had landed just a few days earlier. This incident prompted him to reflect on the brevity of life.

> It makes me realize how transient life is. Well, I am ready to go any time; and I trust that with all my weaknesses and sins I shall hear "Well done, good and faithful servant" for I have tried and I have worked and I have loved my Lord. Of course, there have been failures. Life is so complicated, and there are so many loyalties, and so many things to do, and just what right is is so often confused, that in doing what appears right we actually do wrong; and sometimes when we do what appears wrong, it turns out to be right. Fortunately we do not depend on our own achievements and accomplishments and goodnesses but rest back on God's goodness and mercy. Nevertheless, I have some things that I still hope to do if God grants me a few more years.[466]

While teaching at the College of Missions and ministering at the Crystal Lake Camp, Frankfort, Michigan in July of 1959, McGavran experienced another slight heart attack. He wrote, "In swimming today I overexerted myself and something happened in my heart. I almost drowned 20 feet from the diving platform . . . At 10 my heart was still beating 100

---

464 Donald McGavran, letter to Malcolm, his son, June 12, 1955.
465 Donald McGavran, letter from Leyte, Philippines to Mary, New Haven, Connecticut, Feb. 25, 1957.
466 Donald McGavran, letter from Mindanao, Philippines to Mary, New Haven, Connecticut, March 17, 1957.

to the minute and dully hurting. I hope that I shall be alright in the morning, but I may not wake up."[467] At this point in the letter he rehearsed his spiritual priorities declaring his spiritual legacy for his family.

> If my call should come tonight, I'll meet you in our Lord's presence when you come on over. Please tell our children and grandchildren that the only thing I feel is really important for each of them is that they personally—each one of them for himself—know Jesus Christ, accept Him as Lord and Savior and give themselves utterly to Him. I am not speaking of conventional church membership or being good, kind, intelligent and courageous. I am speaking of being completely surrendered to Christ and continually searching for His will in intelligent and listening reading of the Bible. Now good night my dear and God's abundant blessing rest on you always. Walk with Him. Lovingly, Donald.[468]

Some years later when McGavran was asked how a man with such a serious heart condition back in the late 1950s had survived to the age of 89 he replied, "A strict diet and God's grace." Being an amateur medic, which was a necessity in his life's work, McGavran became convinced that the problem arose from a buildup of cholesterol so he immediately went on a no-fat diet. He ate breakfast foods for lunch. This regime cleared up the problem and he did not experience any further problem with his heart.[469]

McGavran's devotional life was reflected in the advice he sent to his two youngest daughters, just prior to his departure for the African tour in 1954. He wrote:

> Soak yourselves in the Word of God, that you read daily and thoughtfully of the Gospels and Epistles, that you commit 30 prayers to memory chosen by you and of any good collection because you like them, that you memorize Romans 12:9–21, Colossians 3:1–19, Philippians 2:1–11 and other passages. If you do it every day, you will learn a lot in several years. All this means that you keep bright and shining before you the best possible kind of person—the sort of girl God wants you to be.[470]

The final paragraph to his daughters reflects McGavran's practical application of the gospel. "Strive to be kindly in your judgments of others, true in everything you say, helpful to all, friendly to those in need of friends, and unfailingly pleasant. If you get angry or

---

467   Donald McGavran, letter from Crystal Lake, Frankfurt, Michigan to Mary, Frankfort, Michigan, July 8, 1959.
468   Ibid.
469   Donald McGavran, interview by Vern Middleton, May 16, 1986.
470   Donald McGavran, letter from Bombay to Winifred and Pat, his daughters, Woodstock, Landour, Mussoorie, U.P., India, April 4, 1954.

annoyed just forgive him or her at once and forget the matter. Nothing is worth carrying around remembrance of injuries. That kind of remembrance is a terrific load."[471]

McGavran fully enjoyed his daily walk with Christ. This he expressed to his wife while sharing insights from his devotional time. "It struck me with new force as just sound common sense . . . the narrow way is not a hard way, but so easy, so simple, so joyous, so free of trying to please many masters."[472]

One might think that McGavran's lifestyle would be humanistic. Church growth principles seem so rational that at times the question must arise, "Where is God in all this?" Is this man McGavran motivated by faith in God, or dependent upon the intellectual resources of man? Some insights from his personal life will help to answer these questions. On the eve of his departure from Formosa on January 27, 1956 he wrote:

> Mary Dear, I have had a feeling all this week that our days ahead are going to be happy ones. I can't explain it; except that the Lord is good and He is gracious, abundant in loving kindness and we trust Him and shall trust Him more and more. What comes of sorrow, and it will come, is for our correction and the development of our patience and endurance. Whatever God permits to come or sends we will accept. We are in His hands and if He opens doors we will go in, and if He does not, we'll search for another way. I do hope that you are resting a lot in His love and care, and laying your burdens on Him.[473]

Some suggest that church growth thinking is dominated by the social sciences, and that it excludes the church's dependency upon the sovereign living God. In contrast, McGavran, however attributes the entire Church Growth Movement to the direct work and action of God. In reflection upon the events from 1954 to 1976 he recognized that nothing short of a miracle could have brought together all the ingredients to make the movement worldwide. He made the following statement about the establishment of the School of World Mission at Fuller Theological Seminary.

> This would not likely have happened in 1965 but for God's action in directing President Hubbard a) To start a Graduate School of Mission. b) To write to 200 graduates (BD's) [the equivalent of MDiv today] of Fuller who had gone to mission fields asking, "Any suggestions for the new dean?" c) To hear from 100+ of them, "look up McGavran. He may be saying what we want stressed." d) My PhD gained in 1930–32 and lying unused from then till 1965—33 years, looked good to degree conscious D. H. [David Hubbard] e) NCC Trustees (college at Eugene,

---

471 Ibid.

472 Donald McGavran, letter from La Union, N. Luzon, Philippines to Mary, New Haven, Connecticut, Jan. 24, 1957.

473 Donald McGavran, letter from Formosa to Mary, New Haven, Connecticut, Jan. 26, 1956.

Ore.) refused my offer to stay on at $7,000 a year, [vs. $12,000 a year as dean of the School of Mission] if they would guarantee ICG (Institute of Church Growth) would continue. All these impossible events did happen. Thus the Sovereign Lord—no one else—brought into existence a Church Growth Movement.[474]

McGavran did not limit the hand of God in his life to just the above era. In an interview in 1983, he expressed how providential the provision was for his family to be able to live at the Disciples' Divinity House in New Haven, Connecticut for three years (1954 through 1957). The library resources that were at his disposal were among the best in that day. The location afforded him access to many leading mission administrators, professors, statesmen, and the like. He was relatively free, apart from his world surveys and speaking engagements, to creatively write and reflect. He recognized this as a God-ordained time for consolidating church growth principles.

I simply must spend the year of 1957 till September at least writing. I am simply bubbling over with ideas. The latest one is an extensive classification of younger churches and missions—to work out suitable labels for them all so that we can discuss them intelligently. It is a most necessary task. Let me get all this experience out of my system and into suitable books.[475]

One other dimension of McGavran's life illustrates the way he combined in creative tension, man's responsibility, and God's sovereign rule. He was a man with a definite sense of the call of God upon his life and this call enabled him to persevere through many adverse situations and trials. During a transitional stage of his life, after thirty years of service in India, it was God, he believed, who laid upon him the vision of the Church Growth Movement. His endeavours in this area were not in any way motivated by schemes to build a memorial to himself. In a discussion with his wife over the possibility of their returning to missionary service on the mission field he wrote:

Seeing Edna Gish out here learning a new language, Thai, after years in China makes me wonder whether we too ought fairly definitely to look forward to putting in our last few years in the mission field. Of course, if I could just rid myself of the dream that I had the key to great mission advance and settle down to do a quiet little job in the sphere to which God assigned me (but is it not God who assigns me to this sphere of being a gad fly!)[476]

---

474 Donald McGavran, letter from Eugene to Edward McGavran, New Delhi, Jan. 14, 1972.
475 Donald McGavran, letter from Formosa to Mary, New Haven, Connecticut, Jan. 26, 1956.
476 Donald McGavran, letter from Nakon Pathom, Thailand to Mary, New Haven, Connecticut, Feb. 20, 1956.

Two years after the McGavrans departed from India, a personal letter of encouragement and exhortation was sent to Padre Samuel, pastor of the church in Takhatpur and the ordained supervisor of all the churches in the area. McGavran's spiritual fervor is captured in his intimate expressions to this Indian brother.

> You ask me to regard you as my son, I wish to God that you would regard yourself as my spiritual son and would pitch into the work of serving God's Church and winning God's people. My letter to you might have been written to Tularam Paul, Din Dayal, Dharm and Avadh or a number of others, but dear friend, if my spiritual sons in that area wish to be fully my sons, they must yearn and work for the salvation of the Satnamis. You yourself can do nothing more than . . . keep alive the certainty that this Church has been called out by God to open the door to the entire caste.[477]

Discussing people movements, McGavran recognized these as God's gift to missionaries. One missionary wrote asking, "How can a white missionary set a people movement in motion?" to which McGavran replied:

> He can't. God sets these in motion. But the white missionary can recognize one once it is in motion. He can recognize the first tender start of a people movement. He can sweep away his own preconceived patterns . . . and take every step which God will show him which will make the extension of that first tender start into a powerful indigenous Christward march, led by men right out of the tribe which is turning to Christ.[478]

Finally, McGavran, although very pragmatic in discovering all the ways man can become more effective in the service of the Lord, combined that dimension with one of profound dependence upon God through prayer. In his recommendations for the West Utkal field in Orissa, in 1956 he wrote, "This is the time for great expectations and great prayer. It is no accident that numerous groups are ready to accept the Savior. It is the Lord's doing. He will provide the means to shepherd these seekers. He will be a shield and buckler to those who labour."[479]

---

477 Donald McGavran, letter to Padre Samuel, Takhatpur, India, Feb. 8, 1956.
478 Donald McGavran, letter from New Haven, Connecticut to H. E. McMillan, Elkhart, Indiana, Oct. 3, 1956.
479 Donald McGavran, Orissa Report: West Utkal (1956), 48.

PUERTO RICAN SURVEY:
OCTOBER 20–DECEMBER 20, 1955

The fall and winter of 1955 were largely given over to the preparations and research necessary for his arduous surveys. Except for a few days at home for Christmas 1955 he was travelling from October 20, 1955 to June of 1956. This separation from his wife and family was not easy and he wrote, "I am regretting the long months away from you. A funny old world isn't it? When we get what we want, we find that it has drawbacks!"[480]

Prior to going to Puerto Rico, McGavran prepared a fourteen-page proposal and study guideline. This laid the groundwork for his research. He divided his method of study into three basic divisions: reading, church growth seminar, and questionnaires. McGavran read virtually everything written on the development of missions in Puerto Rico. This again was systematized as he set forth nine major categories for which he needed answers.

McGavran held a three-day church growth seminar for the Concilio Evangelico in Puerto Rico, patterned after the seminars held in India, and this became a standard procedure wherever he researched. Missionaries, pastors, and evangelists from the various missions operating on the island attended. Before they came they were all requested to dig out certain basic facts regarding the growth of their local churches and denomination. This of course, provided unprecedented amounts of information, graphs, and hard facts.

He utilized the same pattern of research that he and Pickett developed in 1936. He trained three helpers to administer the questionnaires and they worked with him in filling in details on each church. The subjects were divided into six major categories:

1. The nature of the newly established churches.
2. The financial aspects of church growth in newly established churches.
3. Leaders' opinions as to reasons for church growth.
4. Causes of loss and decline of congregational members?
5. A comprehensive picture of the new converts.
6. What training in church growth is or should be given to theology?

From the end of October through December 6, McGavran travelled from church to church in Puerto Rico, speaking, praying, assessing, and encouraging the pastors and their congregations. At the conclusion of his stay, he drew up a comprehensive analysis of the situation, as he perceived the facts. First, he wrote up a few brief studies of the growth of various denominations. He used this to illustrate certain principles of church growth. He was particularly impressed with the revival experience which had transformed the Disciples of Christ churches from 1934 to 1936. There was immense church growth during that period, but also there were: "The changed lives, the drink renounced, the homes united, the poor

---

480 Donald McGavran, letter from Chicago to Mary, New Haven, Connecticut, Jan. 16, 1956.

economic conditions gradually changed to solid good living, the children educated, the peace found, the justice done, and the joy received."[481]

His Puerto Rican report contained a section entitled, "Factors Arresting Church Growth." The following is a list of a few of the major negative factors:

1. The mission station approach pattern.
2. The snare of subsidy, regardless of growth.
3. Satisfaction with the existing church.
4. The inside community where the fire burns low (loss of the revival spirit).
5. The blockage of quarrels, poor pastoring, poor buildings.
6. Geared to North American patterns in Puerto Rico.
7. Lack of plans for church growth.
8. Lack of interest in church growth (at all levels of the denomination).
9. Belief that good administration, good churchmanship, good missions is doing what needs doing.
10. Failure to revitalize the lay people for spontaneous evangelism.[482]

The report concluded with a challenge to double the number of Disciples' churches in Puerto Rico in the next decade. McGavran carefully outlined the steps they would need to take to attain it.

McGavran maintained many informal contacts with Pentecostals while in India, but Puerto Rico afforded his first real opportunity to study their patterns of church life and growth. He was impressed:

They are good Christian people. With their own money they have built some nice looking churches. They are intensely biblical. They are earnestly evangelistic . . . But they are Pentecostal!!! This earns them, from a good many of the Old Line Evangelicals like ourselves, a continual and open scorn. These are new Testament people. They worship in churches. They believe the Bible. They give sacrificially for missions. They accept Jesus Christ as Lord and Savior. They manifest the fruits of the Spirit. They call themselves a Church—but because they are somewhat less Pentecostal than the first Church in the days following Pentecost, they are continually treated to a degree of arrogance which we would not think of applying either to Anglicans or to the Romans. We call them not a Church, but "holiness cult groups," "fringe sects," "the lunatic fringe."[483]

---

481 Rough jottings of the Puerto Rican Report, Dec. 7, 1955.
482 Ibid.
483 Donald McGavran, letter from New Haven to Cartwright, Editor of *The Christian Evangelist*, Jan. 7, 1956.

He expressed this after the *Christian Evangelist* published a statement made by a pastor which was rather derogatory toward the Assemblies of God. McGavran's study of this denomination convinced him that such attitudes were unjustified.

McGavran was generally pleased with the way UCMS treated his Puerto Rico report. They mimeographed fifty copies and then called two leaders from the field to receive it. The UCMS administration took his counsel seriously.[484]

ASIAN SURVEY: JANUARY 12–MAY 31, 1956

In order to facilitate entry and acceptance by missionaries in the several countries he was to visit, McGavran obtained letters of introduction; one of which was to General Chiang Kai Shek.[485]

Whirlwind Visit in Japan

In the short thirty-six hours McGavran had in Japan he packed in many meetings and visits. He met with the leaders of the United Church of Christ and spent time with the leadership of the NCC in that country. He had a memorable visit with Toyohiko Kagawa and was also able to spend time with heads of missions which were experiencing rapid growth. He was particularly impressed with the church planting methodology of the Oriental Missionary Society. On the eve of his departure from Japan he wrote:

> I was impressed in Japan first, that church multiplication is abundantly possible, if the right pattern is followed . . . Second, that as in most cases around the world missions have gotten frozen into patterns of work in which it is almost impossible to multiply churches, and indeed, it is almost impossible for national clergy and foreign missionaries to desire to multiply churches.[486]

Taiwan Survey

The visit to Taiwan was in some respects the highlight of McGavran's Asia tour. For the better part of the previous eighteen months, he thoroughly researched the advancement of the gospel in that land. Upon arrival he felt as though he were back among old friends. In his possession was his eighty-five page book, entitled *Church Growth in Formosa*. He shared the manuscript with several missionaries who were generally appreciative of the accuracy of the account. McGavran recounted one such incident:

---

484 Donald McGavran, letter from Chicago to Mary, New Haven, Connecticut, Jan. 13, 1956.
485 Donald McGavran, letter from New Haven, Connecticut to Virgil Sly, Indianapolis, Dec. 22, 1955.
486 Donald McGavran, letter from Formosa to Mary, New Haven, Connecticut, Jan. 23, 1956.

The main part of the evening was spent with George Mackay, a senior retired missionary, whose daughters work here in the Island for the government, and who knew the old days. He kindly read my manuscript and made many helpful suggestions—on the whole his comments fitted in with my understanding of the situation, gained from reading.[487]

As a result of McGavran's visit among a mountain tribal group he became more convinced of the importance of lay leadership. "If all the work is done by the pastor, the laymen get nothing in the way of spiritual exercise. It is better to have a poor job done by the laymen than a good job done by the pastor. Lay leadership is the key to advance."[488]

After seeing the island firsthand McGavran was convinced that Formosa was receptive and ready for the gospel. His assessment was as follows: "The language factor plus the rapid growth of Mandarin churches, plus Christian leaders of the nation, plus the American connection—every one wants to learn English—plus the terrific jolt which Communist China has dealt this island, plus Japan's defeat and ousting, plus the concentration of missionaries here—all combine to make Taiwan a place of unique opportunity."[489] The Taiwan experience, although limited to seven days, was most gratifying. What he saw and experienced ratified many of his church growth ideas which were still in the germination stage.

The Philippine Survey: January 27–February 14, 1956

The delightful people, the idyllic climate, the spiritual receptivity, and the warmth displayed, all created an atmosphere of responsiveness. McGavran was drawn to the Philippines and in several letters to his wife he suggested the possibility of their spending the last seven years before retirement, church planting on those balmy islands.

As he began his survey of the United Church of Christ of the Philippines (UCCP) he was frustrated by the fact that reliable records and statistics were almost nonexistent. The Japanese occupation during World War II and the great shifts of population segments eliminated any meaningful records. Since there was nothing concrete from which to develop his survey, he modified his method of research:

My study in the Philippines lay in asking as many leaders as possible, Filipino and missionary, to tell me what sections of the fields are growing, what makes their churches grow, what makes them stop growing and what mission procedures

---

487 Ibid.
488 Ibid.
489 Ibid.

encourage-discourage church growth? When I found a means of growth which worked for someone, I would ask others whether such a system worked for them.[490]

McGavran visited three sections of the Disciples' area of ministry. His impressions were summarized in the report and the first section concluded with the following comment: "This describes an opportunity for church growth so large, so near, so alluring as fairly to take one's breath away."[491]

The next section of the report was entitled "The Tinguian Opportunity." McGavran singled out this tribe of people as being exceptionally receptive. He pled for the mission to give this tribe priority in evangelism. Almost as an indictment he stated that, "The only reason the 50,000 Tinguians have not received Christ as Lord and Savior is that, we have no sufficiently large plan to disciple this people."[492] He then provided a ten-point description of practical steps needed to gather in the great harvest.

A positive outcome of his time in the Philippines in 1956 was the formation of a friendship with Bishop Enrique Sobrepena. He responded very favorably to McGavran's church growth principles. He felt the sort of thing McGavran did in a small area needed to be done for the entire nation. Consequently he arranged for McGavran and Earl Cressy to return in 1957 to conduct a much wider and detailed survey which resulted in the publication of the book *Multiplying Churches in the Philippines*.[493]

Thailand: February 7–April 24, 1956

The spiritual receptivity of Thailand appeared as hard rock sterility to McGavran. The contrast with the Philippines was like night and day. He described his impressions, "I am very glad to have the experience of Thailand, but this is a very MSA place (Mission Station Approach)—oh very! And with a group of young missionaries without much language. And several ideas as to what is good mission work. Poor Edna [Gish] is getting white haired over it."[494]

He reported to UCMS, "The opportunity for growth is very small. No evangelistic work is being done. The evangelistic budget is used very largely to pay two teachers."[495] McGavran saw the educational philosophy of the Christian leadership as a problem for the missionary enterprise in Thailand. He commented, "The (missionary) group is handicapped. They are absolutely at the mercy of their Thai workers (who) are thoroughly education approach minded though they render some lip service to evangelism."[496]

---

490 Donald McGavran, letter from Nakom Pathom, Thailand to West and Sly, Indianapolis, Feb. 23, 1956.
491 Philippine Report (1956): 9.
492 Ibid.. 15.
493 Donald McGavran, interview by Vern Middleton, Dec. 30, 1984.
494 Donald McGavran, letter from Pathom, Thailand to Mary, New Haven, Connecticut, page 15, Feb. 22, 1956.
495 Donald McGavran, letter from Bangkok to D. West and Virgil Sly, Indianapolis, Feb. 29, 1956.
496 Donald McGavran, letter to Mary, Feb. 22, 1956.

McGavran's assessment of the situation was intensified by the fact that it reminded him of what he experienced in India. The Christian community was a cultural island with no meaningful contact with the larger social makeup. McGavran's observation was, "The community which attends church is the community employed by the mission, and the missionaries, and the boys and girls in the mission school."[497] What concerned McGavran even more was that the youth who became Christians while at the mission school, frequently married non-Christians and in a matter of time totally lost their testimony.

Recommendations for Thailand

McGavran assessed the situation under four categories. First, he considered the ministry in Thailand overly burdened with committees. He said, "For this much Church, all these committees make a top heavy organization."[498] He knew from the administrative procedures he toiled under in India, that a major barrier to church growth can be preoccupation with organization. Secondly, he said they were overinstitutionalized. As so often happens when missions face opposition and a resistant population, they settle into running schools and orphanages. McGavran expressed, "Before they know where church growth is going to occur, they dig in and then are tied by their buildings and property . . . This plan handicaps mobility."[499] Thirdly, he identified an attitude of gradualism. He saw no zeal for the Lord in their spirit, and he declared that they must regain the priority of evangelism: "What is needed is evangelism now, by all missionaries and workers . . . It is not something that can be put off for several years while important preparatory work is being done . . . Ventures in evangelism should start at once."[500] His final comment to UCMS was the application of the mechanism of mobility. He said, "If the purpose of UCMS is to establish churches of Christ here, then the distribution requires revision. Missionary assistance should be placed where church growth is going on."[501]

His final formal report about the Disciples' Mission in Thailand was made in March. He saw five possibilities of church growth. First, 50 percent of the population in Nakon Pathom were Chinese who spoke Swatow. He recommended, "Vigorous, direct, continuous preaching of the Good News among these, using every approach—literature, witness bands, Gospel Teams, visitation evangelism, letters to relatives, drama in the church, protracted meetings and fervent prayer."[502] The Lao Sung tribal group living in neighboring villages, he considered, might become receptive if someone was fluent in their language and visited their villages. Third, he recommended following up on families related to those who were Christian and members of their churches. Fourth, he suggested that the Sam Yek villages

---

497 Donald McGavran, letter from Pathom, Thailand to Mary, Feb. 20, 1956.
498 Donald McGavran, evaluation of the Thailand Report (1956).
499 Ibid.
500 Ibid.
501 Ibid.
502 Donald McGavran, letter from Thailand to Virgil Sly and West, Indianapolis, March 3, 1956.

where Thai rural culture was being revived could become receptive if the thirteen converts there were organized into a church and began to bear an active testimony among their people.

The fifth area of focus was the Karen tribal group on the western edge of Thailand. He felt that the church growth among the Karens in Burma would certainly make these people receptive to the gospel in Thailand, due to tribal networking. McGavran visited Burma enroute to India with the express purpose of soliciting Karen workers from Burma to go to Thailand and assist in starting churches there.

On March 28, just prior to departure, McGavran gave an oral assessment to the entire missionary force. Then he wrote comparing this situation to the one they experienced during their first term in India:

> I hate to hurt people particularly when the judgment has to be one which is highly tentative . . . if this kind of study had been done at Harda during our first term it would have caught us all flat footed . . . I wonder whether those truths, imperfectly apprehended at that time, were the driving force behind my feeling that we should withdraw from Harda. That was a move that should have been completely impossible on sentimental grounds alone. It was our first station in India! But the action was timed exactly right politically and so went through.[503]

The Thailand Report was read to the gathering of the Foreign Division of the UCMS in mid-July. No action was taken until Virgil Sly visited the field later that same year. McGavran was hopeful that some new beginnings would be made. He wrote to John Sams in Thailand: "You are fortunate in being in Thailand when mission policy is really in a fluid state."[504] Yet even with regard to the Karen tribe he prescribed caution: "There is no percentage in engaging in another Tibet, colorful, vigorous, appealing but leaving no Church."[505] Yet he cited several reasons for optimism in the Karen project:

> The important things are: a) the presence of a Talekone Sect whose members are animist; b) its Head who wants an American missionary sent to him—most extraordinary; c) the presence of quite a few refugee Christian Karens of considerable education among these Talekones; d) that our missionaries are enthusiastic about the opening of this new work; and e) the promotional value of a colorful work of this sort which seemingly would issue in considerable assessions to our Church.[506]

---

503 Donald McGavran, letter from Thailand to Mary, New Haven, Connecticut, March 3, 1956.
504 Donald McGavran, letter from New Haven, Connecticut to John Sams, Thailand, July 26, 1956.
505 Ibid.
506 Donald McGavran, letter from New Haven, Connecticut to West, Indianapolis, July 27, 1956.

Two men in Thailand did catch McGavran's vision for the Karens; they were Jesse Esteyes and John Sams. On the basis of their research recommendations combined with McGavran's gleanings from Burma a strategy was formulated. Two elements are of special note; one, that the missionaries assigned to this venture should be strictly a Disciples team. McGavran endorsed this idea with the following comment: "He is advocating that the team which works with the Karens who are emerging into immersionist Christianity in Burma and Thailand should be a solidly Disciple team. It would be a tragedy for Disciples who are believer's baptism folk to be the means of splitting the Karens and indeed of raising the issue at all."[507]

The second comment McGavran made was with regard to an organizational issue. He stressed that this new venture be independent administratively from the missionary enterprise at Nakon Pathom. A people movement situation just does not mix with a mission station approach.

SURVEY WORK SHARPENS McGAVRAN'S THINKING AS A STRATEGIST

Results of hunting at villagers' requests.
McGavran would go to dispatch a leopard who was killing their cattle.

McGavran's ability as a strategist was unmistakably manifested during his 1956 survey of the West Utkal District of Orissa. This ability he gained through a host of diverse situations throughout his life. As a youngster just out of high school, he was a soldier in World War One. Then while in India he would take his family out hunting tigers and he would teach his children to think like a tiger. Also his intense interest in the strategies used in World War II certainly shaped his church growth thinking. When he sent a strategy paper back to Horace Ryburn in Thailand he wrote:

---

507 Ibid.

Moving just any kind of army equipment to a break-through is not sufficient to exploit it. St. Lo. [near beaches of Northern France] did not require trenching machines or infantry. It required tanks, jeeps motorized artillery, and General Patton. The proof of the correct use of the break through is the multiplication of churches by the forces thrown in there.[508]

McGavran hunting gaur (a huge wild buffalo, similar to water buffalo).
The gaur is also called an Indian bison, and it is native to south and Southeast Asia.

Up to this point in time, McGavran had theorized that all that was necessary for a fertile field was to pour in resources of personnel and money. But now he began to see that in addition to resources there must be a strategy and a commitment to it. In a letter to Sly from Orissa he wrote, "Merely reinforcing a potentially fertile field does not necessarily produce church growth. Only reinforcing a field where the staff has worked out a winning combination, and is operating it, and believes in it, will give results commensurate with the reinforcements."[509]

In the same letter McGavran made a recommendation regarding their involvement in the Kond Hills tribal movement to Christ. Before sending any further resources of money and personnel the mission was asked to "give us their plan of expansion and the specific goals in church growth at which they will shoot. Then let us decide if these are adequate."[510]

McGavran's recommendations regarding the Orissa situation were a help to the UCMS. Part of the problem in implementing a church growth strategy for that field was the diversity of nationalities. The situation was of such a sensitive nature that the missionaries dared

---

508 Donald McGavran, letter from Calcutta to Horace Ryburn, Thailand, April 2, 1956.
509 Donald McGavran, letter from Orissa to Virgil Sly, Indianapolis, April 22, 1956.
510 Ibid.

not communicate it to the UCMS Board. The British Baptists saw the church growth ideas as attempts to upset their balance of power and an attempt on the part of the American Disciples to take over the field. Franklin White discussed the problem with McGavran. "I think a lot of their trouble is simply that they do not want us to take the credit for anything, for they are terribly afraid of their position." Franklin further stated, "We simply cannot afford any longer to bide our time in trying to pacify the slow moving, conservative attitude of our [British] colleague."[511]

Several months later, while McGavran was conducting the survey of The United Church of Christ in the Philippines, he was asked to deliver an address to the Missionary Orientation Conference. He chose "Missionary Strategy for Today" as his topic. His opening statement was, "Strategy has to do with essential steps toward the chief goal. It has to do with a grand design. What is it we are undertaking? What is the chief objective? What is the central continuing business that we are at? When we decide that, then we shall know how we can best go forward to mission strategy for today."[512] In that same message McGavran set out the most significant principle of church growth: "The central continuing business of world mission, of every missionary regardless of his task, is the conversion of men and women, and the multiplication of churches."[513]

Although the speaking opportunity was significant, McGavran discerned the attitudes of the listeners. He lamented to Mary, "I did not get very far. The whole drift of today's missionaries in the old line boards is contra to what seems so essential to me. Everyone was quite polite and appreciative, but there was no responding fire. The mission movement of today is in the midst of so many theories, and methods and conceptions that no one knows what the chief end is."[514]

ORISSA SURVEY AND STRATEGY

As described in chapter four, the West Utkal region of Orissa, India was the site of a cooperative venture between the English Baptists and the American Disciples of Christ mission. McGavran initiated this relationship. His contacts came about as a direct result of his interests in church growth and people movements. Hence his visit to this field was not as an objective researcher, but rather as one who possessed strong, vested interests in its ongoing success.

The story began back in 1933 when the Mid-India Christian Council appointed a team of researchers to do a church growth analysis of the missions located in the Central India region. A Baptist missionary from Balangir, Orissa, joined the team and reported how the Lord was blessing the evangelistic efforts of the churches in his region. Seven years later,

---

511 Franklin White, letter from Utkal Orissa to Donald McGavran, New Haven, Connecticut, May 19, 1957.
512 Donald McGavran, address given to the Missionary Orientation Conference, Philippines, Feb. 2, 1957.
513 Ibid.
514 Donald McGavran, letter from the Philippines to Mary, New Haven, Connecticut, Feb. 3, 1957.

in 1940, on his own initiative McGavran visited the Baptist headquarters in Calcutta, as well as the Orissa field to encourage some sort of a cooperative arrangement. It was not until 1949 that the Baptists showed any interest in his overture, when finally they proposed that the Sambalpur District of West Utkal be assigned to the Disciples to evangelize and plant churches. The only requirement made in the proposal was that the Disciples strive to maintain the relationship between the churches.

Three years later at the 1951 convention of the Disciples in India, a committee was appointed consisting of McGavran, Ken Potee, who was the field secretary, and one other to explore the options. When this team visited Orissa, Kenneth Weller, field secretary of the Baptist mission, invited the Disciples to come in and cooperate in the total task, rather than just one district.

At the 1952 convention of the Disciples Mission in India, a two-day battle developed between those who favored the idea of sending missionaries to Orissa to engage in furthering the people movements there and those who wanted to maintain the institutional status quo in the province of Madhya Pradesh. McGavran's recollections of the event were:

> In the providence of God, Don West had been appointed as new secretary and was favorable to the idea. Ken (Potee the field secretary) favored Orissa more as a new promotional departure which would give us a new talking point in the US. Most important Franklin White and Bill Hall both favored it from the point of view that missions are winning men to Christ and multiplying churches. I of course was heartily back of the proposal.[515]

During McGavran's tour in Orissa however, he met Bruce Henry, a missionary from Britain who was in charge of evangelism and church growth. Apparently, McGavran thought Henry did not respond to his suggestions. At any rate he referred to Henry in two of his letters as that "strong-minded man" who insisted that consolidation of the gains made was the healthiest plan for the present. In fact, McGavran was so exercised about this attitude that he recommended canceling the assignments of missionaries who had been seconded to work with the Baptists in the Kond Hills region.[516] McGavran's reaction to Henry destroyed his objectivity.

In 1956 the church union negotiations for the formation of the Church of North India were the major concern of pastors and missionaries. Once again McGavran reacted, and wrote a report recommending that "the only way church union could be feasible with the 'episcopally dominated Churches' would be for the Christian Churches to hastily form a

---

515 Donald McGavran, letter from Drake Divinity School, Des Moines, Iowa, letter to Keith, a UCMS Board Member, Nov. 18, 1958.

516 Donald McGavran, Bhilsapur, India, letter to Sly and West, Indianapolis, May 2, 1956.

church union with the Baptist Churches and then politically they would be strong enough to negotiate from a position of strength."[517]

This report, entitled, "Church Growth in the West Utkal," was a fifty-seven page analysis of the situation. McGavran gave a sociological history of the region, then dealt with the historical factors which led to the Disciples of Christ missionaries becoming involved in the region. He spoke proudly about this union of churches, called simply, "Christian Churches." He also referred to Bible-believing, New Testament Churches numbering well over one million communicant members in India and Burma. The latter part of this chapter contained politically sensitive material which interfered with the broader dealings of UCMS. Therefore, pages two through five were stricken from the report. Yet they reflected McGavran's strong evangelical convictions.

The real meat of his assessment appeared in chapters six and seven. In chapter seven he discussed ten causes as to why growth has been limited. These constitute a classic example of inhibitors to church growth, and can be summarized as follows:

1. The mission had developed an indigenous policy of nonassistance to the churches which resulted in a conscious retreat from evangelism and discipleship. The resulting attitudes produced a spirit of indifference to expansion.
2. Even when a people movement to Christ was evident in 1953–55 the UCMS only provided one additional missionary couple. The mission claimed the reason was lack of funds, yet large sums flowed to institutions.
3. Baptism and church membership were delayed as long as one year, so that adequate instruction could be given. Meanwhile other denominations came along and recruited these new converts.
4. Misplaced priorities resulted in an institutional focus, to the neglect of evangelism and church planting.
5. Caste-like attitudes of arrogance were manifested in the church. Meaningful social relationships with unconverted relatives were forbidden.
6. Assisting missions turned the responsibility for evangelism and expansion over to the local churches, and therefore the resulting missionary model was a nonevangelistic one.
7. Conflicting strategies on how to accomplish the task dissipated the energies of mission personnel and retarded evangelistic growth.
8. Experienced missionary personnel were limited, despite the ripening harvest, because of field responsibilities.
9. Due to the tensions arising from the British versus American origins of the missionaries, policies were adopted to insure a sense of responsibility and

---

517 Donald McGavran, Calcutta, letter to Sly and West, Indianapolis, April 2, 1956.

involvement for the total field. This idea was good in principle as it reduced tensions, but became tremendously costly because of duplication of effort.

10. Preoccupation with building programs at a crucial time of receptivity among the local people meant missing the day of harvest and the opportunity for multiplication of men and women for Christ's kingdom.[518]

McGavran baptizing in a river in Chatisghar.

McGavran ended the report with fifteen dynamic suggestions as to ways the churches could continue to grow and expand. Some of the more significant ones were:

1. Develop a system which will certainly find and disciple all groups now able to be won.

2. Earnest prayer be offered for the winning of 1,500 during 1957 and each succeeding year.

3. Men of managerial status must actually be in the field discipling. The knowledge that the missionary is in his area, endures the same hardships as his men, preaches and teaches, knows the names of a hundred villages and two thousand villagers, and is keenly interested in the establishment of new sound congregations, is of primary importance in the growth of churches.

4. The preparation of a manual for new churches including the minimum essentials for baptism and a course of instruction for the first year following baptism is urgently needed. Essential stories and memory passages such as the Lord's Prayer, ten hymns, and the prayer of thanksgiving for food, should be included.[519]

---

518 Donald McGavran, "Utkal" (unpublished MS, 1956), 37–46.
519 Ibid., 47, 56.

PREPARATION FOR THE BOOK,
HOW CHURCHES GROW

During the months of June through August back in New Haven, McGavran labored on the manuscript of his next book, *How Churches Grow*. Much of the inspiration and motivation for this book arose out of the Asian Survey of 1956. The months of September through December were busy with preparations for the major Philippine Survey of 1957, yet McGavran found time to correspond with publishers and send out copies of his current manuscript to various mission leaders and executives. His general correspondence never betrayed a note of discouragement, however, his personal letters provide some insight as to how he was actually feeling. "My book is making some progress. I am having some difficulty getting anyone whose opinion I value to read the thing at this stage. Everyone is so busy. I need someone to read it de novo from beginning to end and then give me reactions."[520]

As the reviews from his manuscript began coming in, McGavran paid careful attention to the comments and corrected the manuscript, or tightened up his ideas. Some of his reviewers were outstanding writers. McGavran described his feelings about the reviews: "The manuscript is in the hands of Latourette, JC Smith, and England. It has yet to go to Matthews, Price, Goulter and Grace. I must say I await the verdict of these readers with some trepidation. The second book is often a dud. I'd better just plod on and see what happens. I have done my best and I quite realize that some of what I have written needs revision."[521]

While McGavran was in the Philippines in February of 1957 Latourette's critique arrived. Four pages of valuable criticism were provided. He pointed out that, "the breadth of what you well know is entailed in church growth and discipling, but repeatedly have given the impression that you are stressing simply numerical growth."[522]

McGavran developed a deep relationship with Latourette. The intimacy of that friendship was indicated by Latourette's use of "Don" in addressing him. The depth of their relationship is also reflected in Mary's comment in a letter to her husband: "Dr. Latourette is being very solicitous, never failing to cross a room to ask about you, even in a crowded room. Maybe you are on his mind because you got him to thinking."[523]

Church-mission Relationship

While in the process of writing, McGavran was wrestling with issues of immediate concern to missions around the world, and late August of 1956 found him writing a chapter on

---

520 Donald McGavran, letter from New Haven to Helen, his mother, and Grace, his sister, Vancouver, Washington, Nov. 4, 1956.

521 Donald McGavran, letter from Bayaboug, Philippines to Mary, New Haven, Connecticut, Jan. 31, 1957.

522 Latourette, "Critique of McGavran" (unpublished MS, Feb. 15, 1957).

523 Mary McGavran, letter from New Haven to Don McGavran, March 13, 1957.

the subject of church mission relationships, dealing with the difficult issues as it relates to church growth.

Although McGavran himself had been the architect of the constitution for the Disciples' churches in India in 1935–36, he was dissatisfied with the role the mission played in the arrangement. He complained, "What is church and what is mission is thoroughly mixed together. The Executive of the Church in India operates Church and Mission as one unit. Thus under the name 'Church' our mission continues to function."[524] He described this new institution as a "Churchion." He proposed that the mission be autonomous from the Church, pointing out that the mixing of the two deprived the churches of a valuable leadership role. He was concerned that all the pastors simply aspired to serve on the mission's administration council, as it gave them prestige, power and money. McGavran expanded his views on the above issue at an extraordinary strategy session of the Division of World Mission on February 2–4, 1960.

1957 PHILIPPINE SURVEY: JANUARY 8–APRIL 30

January 1957 found McGavran back in the Philippines once more to begin research on the United Church of Christ in that country. This denomination resulted from a merger of Congregational, Presbyterian, the Ilicano Branch of the Disciples of Christ, Evangelical United Brethren, and Independent Methodist Churches. McGavran described the United Church of Christ as being nationwide and having in 1957 a membership of one hundred thousand.

McGavran was to work with Dr. Earle Cressy on the research project with a modest budget for the entire operation of $6,000, which was provided by the cooperating boards.[525] The project was named, "Operation Rapid Growth." The primary purpose was meant to initiate a nationwide evangelistic operation. This did eventually happen nearly thirty years later when Jim Montgomery, developed a strategy called, "Discipling A Whole Nation," identified by the acronym, DAWN.

Cressy was a Baptist who served as a missionary in China and functioned as secretary of the National Christian Council in China for many years.[526] He became a close associate with McGavran for the duration of three months as they worked on the research project. Their findings however were published in two separate volumes, reflecting diverse approaches and reactions to the compilation of data. McGavran's survey when published was titled, *Multiplying Churches in the Philippines*, while Cressy's volume took the title, *Strengthening the Urban Church*.

McGavran's research tended to reflect his tough-minded, incisive methods as he probed beneath the surface of information, while Cressy often accepted reports at their face value.

---

524 Donald McGavran, letter from New Haven to John Mackay, President of Princeton Seminary, May 1957.
525 Herb Works, "The Church Growth Movement to 1965" (unpublished MS, May 1974), 142.
526 Donald McGavran, letter from Manila, Philippines to Mary, New Haven, Connecticut, Jan. 8, 1957.

All of which created some difficulty and frustration which surfaced in a letter McGavran wrote to his wife: "There is a terrific lot of church activity which has little or no significance for church growth. Cressy talks a lot about what he has been told of good ways of doing things but the churches show no growth. He still talks about them with great enthusiasm, and when I put in a mild question (I hope it's mild) as to actual results, he answers that he had not asked about that!!!"[527]

The pace of research was intense, as McGavran rode by bus to most of the churches and areas he was to examine. These were rigorous journeys, but the spectacular scenery helped him endure the discomforts. His only complaint was that his "suitcase is taking a beating in these buses. It will never look the same again."[528] The people who hosted his stay at various places, gave him the red carpet treatment, as Filipinos are prone to do. He wrote, "These are homes of much culture and abundant cuisine!!"[529]

At his request, McGavran asked to see tribal churches, most of which required several hours of arduous hiking to access. McGavran's stamina for a sixty-year old, must have surprised many, although he did describe these areas as "very much a young man's world, with most of the country up and down."[530]

McGavran's primary time and focus was on the United Church of Christ, but he had several positive encounters with missions of more evangelical persuasion, and the contrast was like a breath of fresh air to him. Of the former he wrote, "One [missionary] was evidently quite willing for his church of 159 to continue at about that, with a little work for children contemplated . . . no plan for instructing inquirers and indeed not knowing where five decisions for Christ, made in his church this last year have gone."[531]

He described the evangelicals in different terms: "I dropped in to see some ultra conservative Baptists. They have shifted from the easy going old boards out into hard clear, literal biblicism. They have also shifted onto complete self-support . . . They told me they had grown from 600 to 6,000 in 9 years."[532]

McGavran was particularly impressed with the missionaries of the Overseas Missionary Fellowship. Their spirit of dedication and their servant-like attitudes, combined with their zeal to share the gospel of Jesus Christ struck a responsive chord in his heart. His words to Mary sum up his feelings about them: "If I were younger, I'd try to get you to go OMF with me, in some fruitful territory."[533]

In 1956, while doing research in Thailand, McGavran met a young Filipino nurse who was serving as a missionary there. Here was a Third World missionary serving outside her own country. The significance of this caught McGavran's attention, a full fifteen years

527 Donald McGavran, letter from Philippines to Mary, New Haven, Connecticut, Jan. 30, 1957.
528 Donald McGavran, letter from N. Luzon, Philippines to Mary, New Haven, Connecticut, Jan. 22, 1957.
529 Donald McGavran, letter from N. Luzon, Philippines to Mary, New Haven, Connecticut, Jan. 24, 1957.
530 Donald McGavran, letter from N. Luzon, Philippines to Mary, New Haven, Connecticut, Jan. 8, 1957.
531 Ibid.
532 Donald McGavran, letter from Manila to Mary, New Haven, Connecticut, Feb. 11, 1957.
533 Donald McGavran, letter from Leyte, Philippines to Mary, New Haven, Connecticut, Feb. 25, 1957.

before Peter Wagner sparked his classes at the School of World Mission to research this topic. McGavran made the following comment to his wife, Mary: "She is home now on furlough and having a conference with the board secretary! That is a measure of a new day. It is incidentally one which does the souls of nationals a great deal of good. It is a balm to them and lifts their horizons. We too, they say, have missions and missionary societies and board secretaries and missionaries on furlough and at work."[534]

While surveying the Philippines, Don West wrote to McGavran, requesting that he research the group called "Iglesia Ni Cristo." In the 1956 report of Philippines, McGavran described a little about them in the manuscript on *Church Growth and Mission.* This was one of the issues to which Latourette took exception. He said in his critique, "Are you not too uncritical of the Iglesia Ni Cristo? It certainly has been growing in numbers, but has proper provision been made to have its members observe all things commanded by Christ?"[535] McGavran should have given more heed to these comments than he did at that time.

Near the end of his research in the Philippines, McGavran made an insightful comment to his wife regarding the overall impact the opportunity had afforded.

> This period has been good for me Mary. It has broadened my base a good deal and given me a kind of confidence in the new deal in missions which I had not had before, rounded out my education so to speak. Now if the good Lord only gives me ten more years, and under circumstances where I can use this knowledge in the field where it will count. I'm not sure that teaching in our colleges will do that—for it is a highly specialized knowledge, and what I shall be teaching there is elementary missions. We shall see. The first year will tell the story.[536]

Although McGavran's research was published in the book *Multiplying Churches in the Philippines,* there was a lot of material which he could not publish. For example he stated, "I have avoided mentioning specific fields as particularly ripe because in a widely read report that can invite opposition or competition."[537] However, even in those early years of the Church Growth movement, McGavran's assessment was quite accurate. He sensed that the Philippines as a nation was trembling on the brink of unprecedented openness to the gospel. "Ripeness may occur anywhere. Here there is not the sharp contrast which you find in other lands . . . The choice has to be made between ripe fields and riper fields."[538] Later in the same letter McGavran listed eleven areas which were particularly receptive to the gospel. Then in a very systematic way he dealt with each area, suggesting concrete steps which could be taken to enhance evangelism and church growth.

---

534 Latourette, letter from Yale University, New Haven to Donald McGavran, Philippines, Feb. 15, 1957.
535 Donald McGavran, letter from Davas City, Mindanio to Mary, New Haven, Connecticut, March 5, 1975.
536 Donald McGavran, letter from Leyte, Philippines to Mary, New Haven, Connecticut, Feb. 25, 1957.
537 Donald McGavran, letter from the Philippines to O. G. Fonceca, Secretary of Evangelism, UCCP, Manila, Philippines, March 31, 1957.
538 Ibid.

Concerns About the Roman Catholic Church

In a land such as the Philippines where the Roman Catholic Church held such absolute control on the people and the culture, it was difficult for McGavran not to express his convictions. He wrote, "My study has raised continuously the question of the correct and effective attitude for evangelicals toward the whole Roman Catholic position. True, the question was seldom mentioned to me during my three month stay there. but it underlay everything."[539]

Although McGavran's attitudes toward the Roman Catholic Church were negative and defensive in 1957, he took Latourette's advice and began to examine their strategies and methods. In an article entitled, "The Independent Church in the Philippines" published in the summer of 1958, McGavran explained the source of his concern regarding the Roman Catholic Church. He described the early Catholic missionaries to the Philippines as follows:

> The Spanish missionaries were members of the Spanish religious orders—Franciscans, Augustinians, Recollects, Jesuits and Dominicans—and were sent out by them. For many years they were the only parish priests. Since animated by their faith, they would go to lonely posts and there render able service, they came to be used not only as priests but also as governmental agents. They became the backbone of Spanish colonial administration. Even more than that they became a government within a government. The friars regarded their temporal power as a sacred trust.[540]

He recognized that "some of the friars were men of genuine piety and justice, but as a class their lives belied their profession. Quite openly they had mistresses and concubines, and sons and daughters."[541] A later paragraph gives further historic insight:

> The Roman Church in the Islands was not hated as a church. Some of the leaders of the rebellions were agnostic, but as a rule they did not rebel against the Roman Catholic system—only against Spanish control of it. Luther, Calvin and others saw that essential Christianity was belief in Christ, not in the Roman Church. No Filipino leader prior to 1900 realized this truth. No revolutionary discerned that back of Spanish tyranny lay the authoritarianism which is the Roman Catholic Church.

---

539 Donald McGavran, letter from New Haven to John MacKay, President of Princeton Seminary, May 1957.
540 Donald McGavran, "The Independent Church in the Philippines," *Encounter* 19, no. 3 (1958): 300.
541 Ibid.

The conversion of the Islands had been to a nominal Christian life. Subsequent church efforts made it a point to maintain this nominality. The hierarchy did the thinking. It took good care that the masses did not think for themselves.[542]

McGavran's statements about the Roman Catholic Church in his book and report, *Multiplying Churches in the Philippines*, upset the missionary leadership of the United Church of Christ. In a joint report and evaluation of his manuscript by their Executive Committee the following was stated: "In his interesting chapter entitled 'Recapturing Protestant Certainty' it is quite preachy for a survey. He is certainly expressing a personal opinion which is not generally shared. The basic thought is good but it is not clothed in the right terms for the Philippines."[543]

McGavran expressed alarm that the spirit of ecumenicity which was being exercised among Protestant Churches in North America was being transferred into the Philippines and being applied to include the Roman Catholic Church. Although there was some criticism of McGavran's position on the Roman Catholic Church from the more liberal missionaries of the United Church of Christ, there was also strong support for his insights from the missionaries, bishops, and ministers of the United Church of Christ in the Philippines. As well as that, his position was supported from some churchmen in the US. For example, on June 1, 1957, Dr. John A. Mackay, President of Princeton Seminary, commented on chapter six: "Both the chapter and the entire book would have considerable usefulness for churchmen in Latin America. The Philippines is different of course; but it has in common the Roman Catholic background."[544] Meanwhile, he also received some very pointed criticism from American church and mission personnel. McGavran wrote, "My chapter six 'Recapturing Protestant Christianity' is getting me a reputation for being extremely conservative by some here . . . What a welter of opinions we live in!! and how readily some people label others."[545]

Amongst many activities during the summer of 1957, one was to finalize publication of the manuscript produced from the Philippine survey. Extensive correspondence between McGavran and Norwood Tye, over that manuscript, continued for an entire year and several revisions were required. Problems arose over funding for the publication and a number of letters addressed that issue. Finally, just prior to the publication, the "Iglesia Ni Cristo" sect in the Philippines managed to find some favourable comments about themselves which had been made by McGavran. The unpleasant result was that Ralph Toliver, a missionary serving in the Philippines with the Overseas Missionary Fellowship, wrote a letter of grave concern to McGavran in November of 1957. He cited a quotation made by McGavran.

---

542 Ibid., 301.
543 Norwood Tye to McGavran, A quote from Mitton Vereide, June 7, 1957.
544 John A. MacKay, letter from Princeton Seminary to Donald McGavran, New Haven, Connecticut, Aug. 14, 1957.
545 Donald McGavran, letter to Norwood Tye, Nov. 20, 1957.

It had been printed in the May, 1957 issue of *Pasugo* magazine of Iglesia ni Cristo, on page 36: "I have read the English section (of *Pasugo*) carefully and rejoice in your effective presentation of the truth as revealed in the Bible. It should lead many people to embrace pristine Christianity as handed down by the Lord and recorded in the New Testament."[546]

Toliver pointed out that Iglesia ni Cristo was Unitarian in theology and cultic in its claims. He cited the very next page in *Pasugo* following the quote from McGavran, where the deity of Jesus Christ was "disowned by a series of cynical and sarcastic remarks on John 1:1." Then on page 39 of the same magazine, Mr. Felix Manalo, the founder of the cult was given the title, "angel of the east based on Revelation 7:2." Toliver requested McGavran clarify his position in light of these theological distortions and received this unfortunate response which displayed a measure of theological naïveté on McGavran's part.

> I feel perfectly free to commend Churches and friends without pointing out where I believe them in error. Exactly so, with Iglesia ni Cristo. There are matters on which they are right, I commend them. They are intensely biblical I commend them . . . In regard to the person of our Lord, to the extent that they say he is only a man, they are it seems to me quite wrong. Surely no one is likely to take a kindly word of commendation as a blanket endorsement of their entire position.[547]

Apparently the many theological struggles in India had centered around the contextualization of Christianity for the Hindu mind, and McGavran had never experienced the theological dynamics of a large cult like Iglesia Ni Cristo before, so his desire to endorse church growth made him extremely vulnerable at this point.

SUMMARY

Research dominated McGavran's time from 1954 to 1957. His year of reading at the Day Library enabled him to confirm many observations he had made as well as to explore many new areas.

His periods of travel and research in Africa, Puerto Rico, the 1956 Asian trip which included Japan, Formosa, Philippines, Thailand, and India, and the comprehensive study of the Philippines in 1957 all heightened his international insights and broadened his understanding of church growth application.

The process of publishing *The Bridges of God*, the writing of the manuscript for *How Churches Grow*, the publication of *Multiplying Churches in the Philippines*, and the writing of numerous case histories all assisted in sharpening his definitions and clarifying his concepts.

---

546 Ralph Toliver, letter to Donald McGavran, Nov. 5, 1957.
547 Donald McGavran, letter to Ralph Toliver, Sept. 11, 1958.

Donald in the mid-1950s.

Throughout this period the many articles he published displayed his broadened application of church growth principles. *World Dominion* (March/April 1955) carried the article "Satan and Missions," in which he demonstrated how the rejection of People Movements, as a valid form of conversion, is to fall prey to Satanic deception. In 1955, the *IRM* published his article, "New Methods for a New Age in Mission," in which he contrasted the difference between the mission station approach and the people movement pattern. He characterized the former as centered in individualistic decision making patterns, and transplanting cultural Christianity. The *Christian Evangelist* also carried an article of McGavran's in 1955, entitled, "Preaching Missions in a Whirlwind," in which he attacked two prevailing conjectures; the false presupposition that Christian presence is enough to do the job of evangelism, and the growing tide of syncretistic attitudes toward non-Christian religions.

The fall of 1957 brought another new dimension into McGavran's life, that of peripatetic professor for the universities and seminaries of the Christian churches. Research continued, and with it, a growing audience of disciples.

CHAPTER SIX

PERIPATETIC PROFESSOR OF MISSIONS
1957–60

On July 10, 1956, Dale Fiers and Virgil Sly, executives of the UCMS, offered McGavran a two-year position as peripatetic professor of the College of Missions, effective on July 1, 1957.

> During the summer the UCMS ran a [six week] summer school for missionary candidates at Crystal Lake, northwest, lower Michigan. There were ten or twelve dormitories, in each of which was a candidate family . . . Virgil Sly, Don West and I were the speakers. This College of Missions formerly operated in Indianapolis from 1913 to 1926 and then moved to Hartford and became part of the Kennedy School of Missions. But the College of Missions charter was intact under the state of Indiana, so they said to me, "You are the professor of missions." The summer at the lake was very pleasant. I taught two hours a day.[548]

His job description included responsibility for research for the mission, which meant that McGavran was to visit various mission fields and then "devise means to keep the Foreign Division accurately informed as to the growth and development of the Church on each field."[549]

McGavran wrote his own job description in July 1956. He submitted a "Memorandum of the Information Needed for Effective Missions Today," to the International Missionary Council with copies to the executive of his mission. This brief document became one of the primary guides to his future responsibilities. UCMS slightly modified the title to read, "Memorandum on Employment of Don McGavran by the College of Missions."[550] This appointment was originally intended for only two years, but McGavran did not view it as temporary, because his conviction was that God was leading him into a broader ministry of challenging missions regarding their mandate for church growth. He expressed this clearly in a letter to Don West in August, 1956.

---

548 Donald McGavran, interview by Vern Middleton, Dec. 20, 1984.
549 Donald McGavran, letter to Dale Fiers, July 30, 1956.
550 Virgil Sly, letter to Donald McGavran, Dec. 1, 1956.

Our present feeling about our future is that the most useful use of our next seven years is to keep on focusing the attention of our own people, and the missionary world in every way possible, on the need for emphasizing church growth and specially group conversion as a means to sound and substantial church growth . . . If my labours can bring about a more biblical approach, can swing the mighty currents of mission even a small percent back to the Great Commission, I shall do much more of permanent usefulness . . . than if we go back [to India] to blast our way through the Satnami defenses.[551]

This conviction spurred McGavran on in writing his manuscript *How Churches Grow*, and a letter to Grubb of World Dominion Press ably summarized the purpose and intent in his new book:

Great Commission missions need to focus attention where the Church by whatever means, in whatever organization, during whatever state of felicity or persecution is growing. I shall hit hard this whole inherited complex mechanism which is resolved to do good church work or good missions work, whether the Church grows or not. That was once necessary . . . It is no longer necessary in many situations where the churches are growing and can grow much faster than the present mission set up, handcuffed by outmoded [concepts] and methods, permits.[552]

Although negotiations for his new job carried on throughout 1956, a final letter of acceptance was sent off to Virgil Sly on December 1, 1956, which included a clause making Mary McGavran officially hostess for the annual College of Missions meetings at Crystal Lake. McGavran accepted with pleasure and anticipated years of happy association.[553]

PREPARATION AND PLANS FOR POSITION

As a peripatetic professor he began his preparations with great vigor, seeking information from the colleges and seminaries as to the nature of courses he should teach, with the suggestion of courses he would prefer to teach. He had some reservation about the effectiveness of teaching church growth concepts to undergraduate students. However, he did look forward to the opportunity to meet and develop relationships with colleagues in the various seminaries.[554] McGavran realized that if the direction of missions were to be changed, it had to start with what prospective missionary candidates were taught. Therefore

---

551 Donald McGavran, letter to Don West, Oct. 8, 1956.
552 Donald McGavran, letter to Kenneth Grubb, Aug. 25, 1956.
553 Donald McGavran, letter to Virgil Sly, Dec. 1, 1956.
554 Donald McGavran, letter to Dean S. J. England, May 2, 1957.

the departments of mission in various colleges had to understand church growth. Without putting himself in center stage as the author of the Church Growth movement, he described the new direction as the policy and vision of UCMS.

> Missions today is a very different thing from what it was thirty years ago. The Great Commission is still marching orders; but how the discipling of the nations is to be carried out has changed. The United Missionary Society under Dr. Sly's far sighted leadership is developing a strategy to fit today and, even more, tomorrow. Things are moving rapidly, and my task . . . is to present to our churchmen in training the missionary task as we now envisage it.[555]

He proposed these courses for fall 1957: Christianity Confronts Nations on the March, Missions Tomorrow, and The Church in the Ripening World.[556] McGavran was eager to join the faculty at Phillips University for the fall semester of 1957 as he sensed a deep evangelical commitment from Dean England who was anxious to have him come for an entire year and had promoted his arrival among the students.[557] It was an added bonus for the McGavrans to have their daughter Pat on the campus her sophomore year.

From May to September he worked diligently preparing the courses he was to teach. His thoroughness and attention to detail resulted in several of these courses being published as books. In May he wrote to all professors of mission at the colleges and seminaries of the Churches of Christ, asking for assistance. Though in actuality, he was probing the quality and evaluating the depth of insight on current issues of mission which his colleagues' courses were imparting. His request ran as follows: "I am anxious to obtain from all our professors of missions lists of the courses which they are now teaching with a description of each, and of the bibliographies which they are now using. I want the benefit of as much light from my comrades in the field as possible."[558] This research led to a meeting of the professors of mission in June of 1958, where McGavran reviewed the current status of mission courses with them and challenged them to new levels of teaching.

UCMS granted McGavran $500 for the purchase of books which would accompany him from seminary to seminary. He saw the introduction of these books to various seminaries as a means of building up their resources.[559]

---

555 Ibid.
556 Ibid.
557 Dean England, letter from Phillips University, Enid, Oklahoma to McGavran, Dec. 21, 1956, May 22, 1957, May 24, 1957, May 28, 1957, May 29, 1957.
558 Donald McGavran, circular letter to Professor of Missions, May 21, 1957.
559 Donald McGavran, letter to Virgil Sly, May 25, 1957.

McGAVRAN'S THEOLOGICAL INFLUENCE THROUGH HIS BOOK *HOW CHURCHES GROW*

McGavran had deep theological convictions. His view on the authority of Scripture, the miracles, the Virgin birth, and Christ's vicarious sacrifice was decidedly evangelical. In a letter to Kenneth L. Wilson, then editor of the *Christian Herald*, he stated, "I am a reformed liberal or a liberal conservative. I read both *Christianity Today* and the *Christian Century*. I follow Hendrick Kraemer, and oppose Hocking in the matter of attitude to other religions. While generally in favour of church union and cooperation, I find the arrogant attitude of some cooperative churchmen toward those who differ with them a serious sin."[560]

After Wilson read his manuscript *How Churches Grow*, he became enthused over McGavran's clear-cut biblical position on discipleship. His comments indicate the theological impact the manuscript had on his mind. Wilson wrote:

> This is perhaps one of the most burning challenges that could be presented to our generation . . . Your logic is inescapable . . . Many people have drifted away from "discipling" simply because that was the easier course. As we have seen our missionary zeal dimming, we have rationalized our theology into justification of the social Gospel . . . As you point out, the groups holding the belief that they were right, were saved, were Christians—have been the growing groups. To what extent Christians are prepared to stand on their uniqueness, the rightness of Christianity and the wrongness of every other religion, I do not know. They should observe where their philosophy of un-uniqueness is leading them. Your book will push a good many people into a new evaluation of their personal attitude toward missionary activity.[561]

Wilson requested that the concepts from *How Churches Grow* be condensed into an article, suggesting the title, "Have We Lost Our Way in Missionary Work?" With only slight modification McGavran complied, and the article was published in the *Christian Herald* in March, 1958. The heart of that article was found in the following five points:

> There are many ways of getting lost. Indeed the difficulty is not losing our way but keeping our sense of direction. The first deviation is the imagining that in some vague way other religions confer salvation and hence their followers do not need the Savior. Any person who believes this weakens his own will to propagate the Christian faith. The second deviation substitutes good deeds done to men for the winning of lost men to Christ. The Christian mission becomes charity on the

---

560 Donald McGavran, letter to Kenneth L. Wilson, Editor of Christian Herald, Aug. 12, 1957.
561 Kenneth L. Wilson, letter to Donald McGavran, Sept. 30, 1957.

other side of the world. A third deviation occurs when Churches and missions have become wedded to unproductive ways. An exploratory evangelistic, medical or educational approach started thirty years ago in an attempt to plant churches, carries on indefinitely. The fourth deviation may be labeled "Passion to Perfect." Many churchmen stress "teaching them all things" in place of "make disciples of all nations." A fifth wrong turn—failure to gather and use accurate meaningful reports on membership increase—almost guarantees staying lost.[562]

Whenever McGavran had a few days in one spot he would pursue the editing of the manuscript, "The Church in a Ripening World," which was eventually published in 1959 as *How Churches Grow*. In letters to his various reviewers, he described the book as follows:

I deal with the heart of mission—the deliberate attempt to bring men to Christ and multiply churches to the ends of the earth. I take the Great Commission seriously assuming both that it is the final word of our Lord and that it sums up what the New Testament Church did. This book is not an extension of my writing on people movements. It is broader and deeper than that. It takes for granted that the central continuing business of mission is discipling the nations and extending the Church. It asks, "How are we getting on with the main job?" It discusses factors, which promote and prevent church growth. It is frank, critical and I hope constructive. It sweeps away much encumbrance and lays bare the essentials.[563]

Although Harper and Row, Abingdon, Revell, and MacMillan rejected the manuscript in the fall of 1957, that only made McGavran more determined than ever to find a publisher. In 1958, Westminster Press and the Methodist Publishing House were asked to publish the manuscript and once again letters of refusal were received.[564]

GRADUATE SCHOOL OF THEOLOGY:
PHILLIPS UNIVERSITY

McGavran settled into his teaching role at Phillips University in Enid, Oklahoma at the end of August 1957. He and his wife lived in the home of Dr. Oswald Goulter, the missions professor, who was on sabbatical.

Every Sunday throughout the semester was booked with the presentation of missions to churches within a one-hundred-mile radius of the college. McGavran used this exposure in the local churches to stir up their vision, to raise funds for special projects in India, and for the unified budget.

---

562 Donald McGavran, "Have We Lost Our Way in Missions?" 2–3.
563 Donald McGavran, letter to Dale Fiers, June 14, 1957.
564 Donald McGavran, letter to K. L. Wilson, Oct. 11, 1957.

September through January were also devoted to a backlog of correspondence. McGavran's ability with words shows up in his copious letter writing. He jokingly chided Franklin White: "Don't groan, the daily letter from Don is not going to become a habit."[565] Among the many issues of vital concern to him, even though he had been away from the India field for the better part of four years, was a proposal for church union of several leading denominations to form the Church of North India. He knew that the churches of the Disciples of Christ would go into the union, "not because of conviction, but because of convenience." He predicted that such a merger would offend the "conservative wing" of the Christian churches in the US, and that a considerable number of the churches in India would opt for an independent status once the union took place. What particularly disturbed McGavran was the idea of churches with a congregational form of church polity that practised believer's baptism being handed over "to some episcopally governed pedo-baptist body."[566]

McGavran discussed this Indian church union proposal with the professors at Phillips University. He recognized some of the long-term implications for the Christian churches in the US. He also perceived the difficulty faced by UCMS in cooperating with and supporting churches that would, to all intents and purposes, be Anglican in theology and practise. He warned the result would be considerable confusion and that it would be a serious setback to the churches in India.[567] And indeed ten years later when the Church of North India was formed, it divided the Disciples Churches and created a tumultuous atmosphere of litigation.

Meanwhile, Mary Pollard, their faithful coworker in India, came home on furlough and visited the McGavrans at Phillips University in early November. During her visit they openly explained their new leading and direction, which did not include returning to India.

McGavran continued, however, to exercise a measure of influence and control over developments in the Satnami churches in India. He still raised and directed funds to be used to assist village congregations to buy land and become self sufficient. That kind of concern endeared him to the many Christian villagers around Takhatpur. Some missionaries on the field responded to McGavran's suggestion to buy land saying, "The mission was in the business of selling land not buying it."[568] However McGavran still sent $200 of his personal money for the purchase and improvement of land for the Christian villagers.

McGAVRAN'S VIEWS ON THE INDIGENOUS CHURCH

During the period of 1940–60, the concepts of Roland Allen and John L. Nevius on indigenous church were very popular among most missionaries. McGavran had difficulty with some aspects of the strategy. One reviewer of *How Churches Grow*, Dr. H. Cornell

---

565 Donald McGavran, letter to Franklin White, Sept. 8, 1957.
566 Donald McGavran, letter to Virgil Sly, Sept. 16, 1957.
567 Donald McGavran, letter to F. White, Sept. 22, 1957.
568 Ken Potee, letter from Jabalpur, India to Donald McGavran, Dec. 12, 1957.

Goerner, professor of missions at Southern Baptist Theological Seminary in Louisville, questioned McGavran's position on the philosophy of the indigenous church.

McGavran replied with a five-page letter that foreign funds should be used "if it seemed they would stimulate church growth and make it possible to win the winnable, and the withholding of funds if it seemed they would not serve those ends."[569] Goerner wrote, "Your letter is the finest statement on the basic problem that I have ever read. I can agree with your statement just about 100 percent."[570]

McGavran stated, "The growth of the churches in New Testament times was largely a people movement growth among a very ripe population. The one missionary method is not normative for all the vast variety of populations in various stages of ripeness."[571]

He went on to make some direct comments about Roland Allen's concept of spontaneous expansion:

> We missionaries in India, when we would gather during the summer, have for the last thirty years discussed Allen again and again. Almost all of us felt that Allen stated a new needed principle of mission. Yet we would come regretfully to the conclusion that a) his system simply would not work at all where one by one ingathering against great opposition was going on; and b) that his system would not work too well when people movements among the depressed classes were going on because the resulting Christians needed a large degree of education and help at the beginning to get their churches really going.[572]

McGavran's down-to-earth illustration drove home his point: "Subsidy is like mother's milk. It is always required in the beginning. But the sooner the new churches get onto self support and self control the better. The mother's milk can then be used for other new born babies. And there is great danger that mother's milk be continued far beyond the time it is helpful."[573]

He was frightened by the popularity of the indigenous method for three reasons:

> First, it is closely connected with lack of money. It seems to offer a cheap way to do the job. It watches churches flounder and Christward movements stagnate from the safe stronghold of a correct ideology. But in ripening populations all round the world now is the time for vastly increased missionary expenditure devoted to discipling the peoples. Second, devotion to indigenous methods have often meant spending money like water for education, medicine and agricultural

---

569 Donald McGavran, letter to Cornell Goerner, Sept. 7, 1957.
570 Dr. H. Cornell Goerner, letter to Donald McGavran, Sept. 14, 1957.
571 Donald McGavran, letter to Cornell Goerner, Sept. 7, 1957.
572 Ibid., 2.
573 Ibid., 3.

improvement of Christians and even non-Christians while cutting down efforts for the actual planting of churches. Third, a number of leaders of long established young churches are today very critical of the "sects" as they call them for too free use of foreign money to establish their churches. These old line leaders having their congregations by the hundreds, decry for the "sects," the very system which they used to come to their present membership.[574]

A number of mission executives indicated that his position on this issue was very helpful. Several expressed their struggle in living up to Allen's ideals while attempting to deal with the practical situation at hand. McGavran's position also casts light on the way he utilized financial resources in the Takhatpur region.

By the close of 1957 McGavran was receiving recognition as a church growth consultant, far and near. Daily letters from very diverse missions and denominations arrived at his desk requesting his opinion on some issue or another.

HIGHLIGHTS OF 1958

The McGavrans' nomadic routine of moving from seminary to seminary continued throughout 1958. Two schools where they served during that year were the School of Religion at Butler University and the Divinity School at Drake University. Another important event of 1958 was the Jamaican Survey undertaken from July 10 to August 31. Aside from his regular pattern of teaching, church meetings, correspondence, and research, a new dimension was added in 1958 as he took up a crusade for the rights of Black Christians in America. It must also be remembered that this period from 1957 through 1960 was mainly devoted to his work with institutions and churches connected with his own denomination. These were the pivotal activities.

Butler University: January 27–June 11, 1958

The McGavrans shifted from Phillips University to Butler University to commence teaching in the School of Religion (theological seminary) for six months. Enroute to Butler, McGavran visited Pentecostal friends who had served with him in India. This visit provoked correspondence showing his growing appreciation for Pentecostal type churches.[575]

The Assemblies of God (denomination) have an excellent measure of conversion, an excellent system of training their missionaries and an excellent degree of devolution to national churches. What would happen, I ask myself, if the

---

574 Ibid., 4–5.
575 Donald McGavran, letter to Robert Cummings, Jan. 30, 1958.

Assemblies would set up a plan to measure responsiveness contra resources assigned in all fields of operation? And then, looking to God for guidance and careful not to outrun Him, were to concentrate men and money at places where churches could be multiplied.[576]

McGavran's course descriptions and work load at Butler were similar to his fall schedule at Phillips. Students were interested in his courses and each class numbered about one hundred. McGavran even recruited students for his courses during registration day.[577]

The McGavrans extended themselves to the students, resulting in deep personal friendships. One student wrote, "Your lectures were inspiring." Professor of Missions at Phillips University, Oswald Goulter, wrote: "Everyone expresses delight with the classes you conducted at the seminary; you seem to have given a boost to missionary interest, for I have the largest classes I have ever had in the seminary."[578]

As so often happens to professors, some of his students became more vigorous in their advocacy of the church growth point of view than McGavran himself. A student named "Dick," in the process of research for an assignment, took it upon himself to write Dr. Donald Baker, (Africa field secretary of the Disciples), to chide him on his incorrect methodology. For a time this student managed to produce tension between McGavran and Baker, whose friendship was a longstanding one. In trying to get to the nub of this issue, McGavran identified the problem as not the field strategy, where there was a balance between discipling and perfecting, but rather: "I protest vehemently that it cannot be the will of God for the scores of thousands in our field, yet unwon, to emerge into Roman Catholicism or to become hardened pagans. I protest that for the Christian Churches of America to permit this to happen is a betrayal of trust; that we the Christian churches are failing our Lord at this point."[579]

Don Baker's reply was both balanced and thoughtful: "For emphasis on the stage especially in art and books generally, one overemphasizes in order to make a point. I was trying to correct Dick's over-insistence upon numbers. Don, if we let that one thing dominate our thinking, we would be no better than the RCs who care nothing about the quality, or at least, who put quality second in their thinking, and who emphasize numbers."[580]

Some of the further comments in Baker's letter were very helpful to McGavran in developing an international view of what is involved in perfecting and correcting his predisposition for measuring patterns from his India experience.

---

576 Ibid.
577 Donald McGavran, letter to Dean O. L. Shelton, Butler University, Jan. 12, 1958.
578 Oswald Goulter, letter from Phillips University to Donald McGavran, Feb. 6, 1958.
579 Donald McGavran, letter to Don Baker, Mondombe, Congo, Jan. 14, 1958.
580 Don Baker, letter to Donald McGavran, Feb. 15, 1958.

In connection with the "perfecting" we have borne in upon us the sad thought that we simply do not have anyone in our group who has a cultural background going back for centuries. "So what," we hear someone saying. Well the what is this: we cannot form leaders in the same length of time that they can be formed in other mission fields.[581]

In the end, the differences of opinion were resolved with the result that McGavran made an even greater effort to recruit funds and personnel for the African field, which he knew was very ripe for the gospel.

Emphasis on Wider Issues

As requests for McGavran to speak at various churches and mission conferences began coming in from the Indianapolis region, deliberate focus was placed on the broader issues of church growth and missions. Since most knew him as the author of *Bridges of God*, he was frequently asked to speak on "people movements." His typical response to such requests was: "Mission and church growth is a large and complex subject. The evidence for it requires time to present a discussion of it and cannot be sandwiched into a panel, or compressed into twelve minutes before we close. Unconvincing and hurried presentations do no good to any one."[582]

R. Pierce Beaver invited McGavran to speak to the annual meeting of the Association of Professors of Missions held in Boston on June 16 and he assigned him the topic, "The Role of the Missionary Today." Since this was one of five papers which were bound and sold as a limited edition entitled "Missionary Vocation,"[583] McGavran was somewhat defensive about the material others would be presenting. In a letter to Beaver, "The missionary role will depend in large part on the outcome of papers 1, 2 and 3. (McGavran's was to be paper four) Since my paper cannot be written after we have the benefit of hearing and discussing the other papers, I am inclined to think that what I shall have to do, is present my philosophy of mission and role which is congruent to it."[584]

McGavran wanted to know the views that others would be presenting. Something of the debating spirit of his college days seems to have returned to him. Since Beaver could not give any details on what the other speakers' views would be, he ended up virtually giving him a blank check as to what emphasis he would bring, but he advised him "to treat the burning issue of the missionary's place and work today in view of the combined maturity and adolescent sensitivity of the young churches, nationalistic pressures, the welfare state etc."[585]

581 Ibid.
582 Donald McGavran, letter to Anita Harris, Division of Foreign Missions, NCC, New York, Feb. 17, 1958.
583 Pierce Beaver, letter to McGavran, Feb. 28, 1958, March 17, 1958, March 27, 1958.
584 Donald McGavran, letter to R. Pierce Beaver, March 24, 1958.
585 R. Pierce Beaver, letter to Donald McGavran, May 27, 1958.

A week later McGavran replied, asking Beaver about three matters of concern which arose from reading an article by Beaver entitled, "The Christian World Mission, A Reconsideration." The issues were: a definition of Apostolate, the function of the Holy Spirit in proclamation, and the end of old missions and the beginning of new. A notation was made at the bottom of McGavran's carbon copy. "If he replies 'yes' [to the statements made by McGavran] then he will be open to difficulties. If he qualifies his reply I shall have drawn his teeth in the June 16th meeting."[586]

Pierce Beaver's reply dated May 27, 1958 contains several classic statements on mission:

> The Apostolate is the central function of the Church and consequently of every Christian disciple. It is proclamation of the Saviorhood of Christ (reconciling man to God and man to man in Christ) and of the Lordship of Christ over all of human life. It is by word, by deed, and the demonstration of reconciliation in worship and in fellowship. It consists of two aspects. One we may call evangelism. The other we may call mission or sending. So apostolate is world mission in its totality—the major function of the church between the Ascension and the coming of the Kingdom of God in all its fullness.[587]

McGavran's comments in response to this were, "On the Apostolate he states a good position. This is what the church and local churches everywhere should be doing, and as they do this they will unquestionably carry out mission."[588]

On the second issue, namely the "role of the Holy Spirit as the great missionary of God and the relationship of the missionary Church and its missionary agents to him," some difference of opinion occurred.

Pierce Beaver stated his position rather forcefully:

> I fear the spiritual pride, the ecclesiolatry and the statisicism (sic) which so often result when the missionary gets to thinking that he rather than the Holy Spirit works or effects conversion. The Holy Spirit goes before the missionary and prepares hearts and minds to hear his proclamation of the message. The same Holy Spirit assists the missionary to understand his role, to gain insights, to apply his studies, to devise and experiment with ever more effective policy, strategy and tactics in communicating the Gospel. The Holy Spirit effects conversion, including reconciliation.[589]

---

586 Donald McGavran, letter to R. Pierce Beaver, March 24, 1958.
587 R. Pierce Beaver, letter to Donald McGavran, May 27, 1958.
588 Notes on the edge of a carbon copy of a letter from Donald McGavran, letter to R. Pierce Beaver, April 5, 1958.
589 R. Pierce Beaver, letter to Donald McGavran, April 5, 1958.

McGavran's response to the above statement was: "This doctrine must be modified otherwise we run into neutral proclamation, irresponsible proclamation, and indeed a pseudo proclamation masquerading as Christian and shielding itself from the cross under the doctrine that witness is also through deeds and life and innocuous procedures."[590]

This point of view came out of concern over churches which were becoming more liberal in their theology and used such reasoning to excuse themselves from bold proclamation, effective evangelism, and the multiplication of believers which McGavran espoused. His conviction at that time was that many missions were carrying on good mission work, but there was little if any multiplication of sound Christian churches, hence his concern over Beaver's statement.

The concluding sentences of Beaver's paragraph on the Holy Spirit must have been written as a result of his reading of *Bridges of God* and the interpretation he gave to McGavran's ideas:

> I think that such an understanding keeps the missionary evangelist free from spiritual pride, takes from him the pressure to prove his faithfulness by statistical success, teaches him patience, frees him from the danger of panic, enables him to participate more effectively in communication, safeguards him from the "colonial mind" and enables him to allow the young church to develop its indigenous life.[591]

Further Insights on Mobilizing Resources

Positive reviews and comments continued to pour in as *Bridges of God* was read, digested, and criticised by missionaries and mission leaders around the world. Several denominational leaders reported having purchased a sizable quantity of the book and sending them to all their missionary personnel. One such report came from W. Drew Varney, administrative associate of the American Baptist Foreign Mission Society. He submitted several outstanding reviews from their mission leaders. These were thoroughly studied by McGavran before he responded. Once again, such interaction sharpened his thinking and definition as he wrestled with the issues of "perfecting and discipling," highlights of his reply were:

> I am delighted at the degree of understanding evidenced—and at the degree of difference of opinion. All this is to the good. I have no illusions that I have said the last word on the subject! Differing conditions in differing populations are so great that we need many serious theses on cases of church growth as we feel our way toward methods which really carry out the Great Commission.

---

590   Donald McGavran, letter to R. Pierce Beaver, April 5, 1958.
591   R. Pierce Beaver, letter to Donald McGavran, May 27, 1958.

I am currently reading two little books on Church Growth in Brazil and Korea. We need a hundred such studies each one knowing the others, and carrying forward the search for better ways of discipling the nations. The growth of the Church is susceptible to scientific study.

In the respondees' comments there is a very large degree of agreement on the point that where churches can multiply, there resources be concentrated. To get growth their concentration of resources at the point of growth is needed, not just in the country where growth is going on.

Mere concentration of resources (men and money) will not achieve victorious ingathering of a ripe people. My researches over the last three years have made me vividly conscious of the fact that if into a ripe situation churchmen of one kind of training are sent, they will stop the ingathering. Much much more is needed than mere concentration of any kind of men and money. It will take the right kind of men, careful planning, and skillful administration for church growth.[592]

GERMINAL STAGES OF THE CHURCH GROWTH INSTITUTE

While teaching at the Theological School of Phillips University during autumn of 1957, McGavran had several conversations with Dean England over the possible development of an institute of church growth. McGavran knew his ideas needed an institution which could provide a vehicle for their dissemination. Gouther requested:

> Your suggestion about developing our Seminary Missions Department in such a way as might have ecumenical appeal, especially to those many missionaries who have no particular denominational ties but are allied to the Interdenominational Missionary Council and other Faith Missions. Would you outline the plan in some detail? [593]

Without hesitation he sent an organizational outline of what he felt would be necessary for a School of Church Growth. The following are some of the main points:

I.   This would be a School of Missions. It would grant an MA. Its relationship to the seminary would be close. Organizationally it might be a department or a daughter . . . It would need budget in addition to professors' salaries, library

---

592   Donald McGavran, letter to W. Drew Varney, Feb. 18, 1958.
593   Gouther, letter to Donald McGavran, Feb. 6, 1958.

funds, lectureships, advertisement, secretarial help, scholarship funds, and research enterprises.

II. Would it need missionary apartments? $200,000 in twenty missionary apartments would be very useful. It would guarantee the school.

III. Curriculum:

    a. The school should specialize in courses essential to the central task of missions. These might include: The Indigenous Church, Church Growth, Development of Leadership, Functional Comparative Religion . . . The Dynamics of Younger Churches, the Theology of Missions.

    b. The S of M should offer courses in History of Missions, Descriptive Comparative Religions, and National Cultures.

    c. Courses favoring Latin America and Africa should be stressed.

IV. Staff: Three professors would be excellent. Phillips should keep its eye on Franklin White of Orissa. He combines practical experience, fine mind, good speaking ability and a dynamic biblical point of view. The Seminary should hand pick from among the present missionaries young men of great promise and missionary passion who have had experience and success in planting churches and consider that the most important thing in missions. The School of Missions should have a definite philosophy.[594]

These policies were implemented several years later at the Institute of Church Growth in Eugene, Oregon and still later at the School of World Mission at Fuller Seminary in Pasadena, California. In autumn 1958, he actively began to pursue the idea of a church growth institute. Teaching ministerial candidates had never been overly satisfying for him so in a letter to Professor Cal Guy of Southwestern Baptist Theological Seminary. McGavran inquired about the possibility of an opening for a teaching post, where the students would be missionary candidates.[595]

One month later in correspondence with UCMS regarding a possible return to India, he proposed the concept of a single institution where church growth could be taught. He wrote:

We think, therefore, that the best use to be made of our next six years would be to set us to teaching missionaries and nationals, our own and those of other boards, how churches grow and stop growing, and how to use the sacred resources of the Church that they may grow more. We therefore propose that, instead of sending the Professor of the College of Missions from seminary to seminary to teach ministers in training, you make him available at one center to teach church growth—a very wide and complex subject. Missionaries on furlough, candidates

594 Donald McGavran, letter to Gouther, Feb. 22, 1958.

595 Donald McGavran letter to Cal Guy, Southwestern Baptist Seminary, Fort Worth, Texas, Oct. 31, 1958.

and nationals in church work would come there for counsel, study and research. In short, let us create The College of Missions Institute on Church Growth.[596]

McGavran reasoned that such an institution would make the Disciples leaders in discipling. He described the outcome of such a ministry: "The Institute of Church Growth would not only gather students and candidates. It would gather leaders of many boards and Churches, men who are engaged in church growth, for mutual consultation, study, research and publication. We would render a service to the entire (missionary) movement."[597]

He dispatched another letter eleven days later, and this time he presented three points. First, he wrote that an Institute of Church Growth would fulfill the recommendations of the Willengen Report of the International Missionary Council, which stated:

> We recommend that the International Missionary Council consider the establishment of regional centers for study and research on questions related to "the work of the Christian mission and the growth of the Church" affording opportunity to individuals and groups for study, writing, training and conference, and also undertaking the publication of relevant studies and research.[598]

Second, he reasoned that outstanding missionaries under the UCMS board should not have to go to Southern Baptist Seminaries to upgrade their missiological training. Third, because as a researcher McGavran had been a humble learner, the mission personnel on the various fields had treated him as a peer and not thought of him as a resource person or an instructor. A church growth institute would change all that. The whole approach would be different.[599]

Sly's response to McGavran's visionary proposal was courteous, but cautious. He stated, "I am in no position to make any final comments concerning the proposition you have raised. I am quite confident we cannot move into the area as you have indicated under the present financial arrangement."[600] This was reiterated in June 1959.

In McGavran's next letter he requested the use of the College of Missions building at Crystal Lake from July 6–August 6, 1959 for a summer session on church growth. In order to avoid Sly's usual comments over fiscal restraints, McGavran made it clear that such a session would cost very little.[601]

His search for a way to create an institute continued during the fall months when he taught missions at the Divinity School of Drake University, Des Moines, Iowa. However

---

596 Donald McGavran, letter to Virgil Sly and Palmer, Nov. 15, 1958.
597 Ibid.
598 Willingen Report, Report of Group V Resolutions in Reshaping the Pattern of Missionary Activity, Willingen, Germany, July 1953.
599 Donald McGavran, letter to Virgil Sly and Palmer, Nov. 26, 1958.
600 Virgil Sly, letter to Donald McGavran, Dec. 23, 1958.
601 Donald McGavran, letter to Virgil Sly and Palmer, Nov., Dec. 31, 1958.

the UCMS executives were still convinced that the McGavrans should return to India. The correspondence revealed that during September to December of 1958 the last bridge was finally burned as far as a return to India was concerned.[602]

SEARCH FOR A PUBLISHER OF
HOW CHURCHES GROW

Considerable correspondence throughout 1958 was spent trying to find a publisher for the manuscript *How Churches Grow*, and distribution of other publications on church growth. Several publishers rejected the manuscript, however McGavran did not give up easily, nor did he interpret these refusals as a personal affront. He recognized that further polishing and clarifying of the text was needed, but he believed the real reason for the rejection was a spiritual battle. In a letter to Professor Cal Guy, McGavran wrote:

> Hugh Vernon White's theology of mission (which was also Hocking's theology of Mission) has come to be the orthodox theology of mission in board after board. Indeed, this point of view has captured the leadership of missions in most old line boards. They deny it, but they distribute their budgets in accord with it. I am engaged in a battle with a highly entrenched system which has much good in it.[603]

After Harper's, Scribner's, MacMillan, Abingdon, Westminster, Revell, Bethany, and Methodist (Abingdon) had refused the manuscript, McGavran turned to his trusted friends across the Atlantic, the World Dominion Press. He described the thesis of his manuscript to Grubb and then stated the following: "Opportunities are being lost. Naturally I ask why. This book gives my answers. What makes churches grow? What makes them stop growing?"[604] From that question Grubb eventually derived the final title for the published book.

When he submitted the manuscript of *How Churches Grow* to various publishers, McGavran had also submitted an impressive collection of favourable reviews from such mission notables as Heindrick Kraemer, Cal Guy, Pierce Beaver, and Waskom Pickett. Yet he recognized that the publishers were faced with a very serious problem, because books about churches and the way they grow were not the best sellers. He lamented this in a most revealing comment made to Bishop Waskom Pickett: "It is strange thing, books about foreign cultures, abstruse subjects, human interest stories about missionaries, church union and many other subjects sell well; but writings about the growth of the churches have difficulty getting printed and sold."[605]

---

602 Donald McGavran, letters to Virgil Sly and Palmer, Oct. 28, 1958, Nov. 15, 1958, Nov. 26, 1958, Dec. 28, 1958, and to Clyde Pray, Nov. 2, 1958.
603 Donald McGavran, letter to Professor Cal Guy, March 9, 1958.
604 Donald McGavran, letter to Grubb, April 14, 1958.
605 Donald McGavran, letter to J. Waskin Pickett, March 29, 1958.

When it is realized that McGavran's manuscripts on case histories were receiving an even greater degree of rejection by publishers, it is amazing that he remained so optimistic. Added to his frustrations he had ordered two thousand reprints of the case histories published in 1936, updated under the title *Church Growth and Group Conversion*. Lucknow Publishing House in India reprinted them but due to bureaucratic delays, the Suez Canal crisis, and other minor problems, the books finally arrived in the United States in late 1957. After extensive advertising McGavran found it hard to even give away these books, in spite of his wife Mary's efforts in creating, and distributing flyers describing the book which cost her considerable amount of energy, time, and money. All of these frustrations confirmed McGavran's recognition that he needed to find a means by which church growth thinking could gain a public forum.

Letters between Grubb of World Dominion Press, who was a member of the Central Committee of the World Council of Churches, and McGavran flew back and forth almost weekly as the final acceptance for publication of his book finally fell into place. World Dominion agreed to publish it for the English readership, while Moody Press was prepared to publish it for the American readers.[606] Hendrik Kraemer wrote the foreword for the book.

A most interesting sidelight developed because Grubb had the manuscript sent to a theologian of notable missionary stature, who was obviously English. Grubb would not reveal his name to McGavran, but whoever he was, his diagnosis was brilliant, and his comments candid and refreshing.

In many respects it is a maddening manuscript. At a whole series of points the style and argument is arrogant beyond measure, which is the more exasperating when you cannot help feeling that, again and again, the "evidence" is doctored to fit the case.

My main criticism would be that the book is a sociological study without being recognized as such. He does, here and there, acknowledge that there are imponderables in the situation, but it is not acknowledged nearly enough that he is de facto dealing with the sociological aspects of 'church growth' and that when he is talking theology, he thinks of that within a sociological context.

McGavran is saying something which is by no means unimportant and nevertheless we are told that in certain situations "Gathered Church convictions" produce church growth while in others they block it. This may be perfectly true, but then he ought to try to disentangle the sociological side from the theological side. The book is full of categorical and rather slick statements which frankly makes one mad.

---

606   Donald McGavran, letter to Grubb, March 10, 1959.

On the whole therefore the book should be published. McGavran is so "one-eyed" that he sees a perspective which several of us in our sophistication are tempted to overlook and I therefore believe that we need his voice. If World Dominion Press is prepared to run the risk of publishing a book which can be heavily (and rightly) criticised, I think it may do us all a service by publishing this manuscript. I have read the manuscript. It is stimulating and irritating and for once there is within the field of missiology a book that dares to be outrageously provocative—which is always refreshing.[607]

The penetrating insights of the unknown commentator were accurate. Indeed, some of the major weaknesses and strengths of McGavran's church growth thinking have been identified. McGavran's training and church affiliation all predisposed him to a sociological framework. At the same time his theology, although deep and stable, was never held in such a way as to blind him to the positive dimensions of Christ's Kingdom as manifested in any denomination. Another significant point in his analysis was McGavran's way with words. The reviewer's use of terms like "maddening," "arrogant," and "outrageous" reflect the way McGavran provoked some of his readers into a love-hate relationship. What may have appeared as arrogance to the English reader, really arose from his single-minded conviction that the Church must take the Great Commission seriously.

McGAVRAN AS A SOCIAL ACTIVIST

Some who are acquainted with the Church Growth Movement have serious reservations over the homogeneous unit principle. However in McGavran's thinking that never meant segregated and racist churches. When the McGavrans arrived in Indianapolis on January 27, 1958, they prayerfully sought a church in which to worship. They wrote of their decision:

God led us to think seriously about the matter of inter-racial brotherhood in our churches. We realized that while we talked favorably about integration and had helped pass resolutions we had not joined a Negro Church. We thought a little bit of do would be worth more than a lot of talk. We joined the next Sunday and have had a worshipful stimulating morning service every Sunday since. We have been blessed in fellowship at the (black) Second Christian.[608]

The open letter to the forty-nine white Christian churches in Indianapolis appealed to them both as individuals and as corporate bodies of Christ. McGavran was very forthright in his judgment on the total segregation that existed between the White and two Black churches

---

607 Grubb, letter to McGavran, July 18, 1958.
608 Donald McGavran, open letter to pastors of Christian churches in Indianapolis, June 12, 1958.

of their denomination. He wrote, "This is really a shocking condition. It is not pleasing to God . . . As long as (segregation) remains true, in Indianapolis, all our Brotherhood resolutions in favor of brotherhood are open to the charge of insincerity."[609] It is significant that McGavran used exactly the same appeal to Brotherhood back in 1938, when he had so vigorously reacted to Mahatma Gandhi's attempts to keep the Harijan people within the suppressive Hindu system.

Donald McGavran.

McGavran proposed that "short-term fraternal members" be assigned to integrate with the Black churches and that in turn the White churches invite Black families to come and experience fellowship with them. He suggested that such a year-by-year arrangement would have long-term results, namely: "Out of the adventure into Brotherhood your church will get back two persons each year who have had a wonderful experience in a sister church heretofore unknown to them. As we get to know each other better, we will find that a lot of fears and inhibitions have been baseless. We'll meet a lot of wonderful people. Mutual respect will mount."[610]

---

609   Ibid.
610   Ibid., 2.

Before the McGavrans left Indianapolis, they helped Pastor R. H. Peoples of the Second Christian Church to draft a proposal. The Black church tendered that "it be made a matter for the conscience and action of congregations, boards, and enlightened church school classes,"[611] and not merely an act of the individual within the local church. It also recommended that the relationship be "short term fraternal memberships" rather than permanent membership. The McGavrans twice appealed to sensitive white church leadership in the area to support this venture. The Downey Avenue Christian Church did respond and McGavran encouraged them with a letter in the spring of 1960.

In the fall of 1958 the McGavrans moved on to the Divinity School of Drake University, Des Moines, Iowa. During that same autumn Governor Faubus of Arkansas was rigidly resisting attempts at integration in his state. As a direct response, McGavran organized twenty carloads of students from the Divinity School of Drake University to go down to Little Rock and hold a three-day prayer meeting on the Governor's front lawn. However just before they were to leave Iowa on Nov. 26, 1958, the dean of the university objected to the venture and the protest was called off.[612]

SUMMER OF 1958 AND THE JAMAICAN SURVEY

McGavran's daily regimen during 1958 was hardly that of a sixty-one year old man. Herbert Works cataloged his activities as follows:

He began the summer of 1958 with a meeting of the Association of Professors of Missions at which he presented a paper. (Actually this meeting was preceded by a three-day meeting of the professors of missions of the Christian Churches). After the summer session of the College of Missions, he went to Minnesota to lecture on church growth at St. Olaf's Evangelical Lutheran Missionary Training Summer session. Early in July he lectured at the Missionary Training Conference of the National Council of Churches of Christ at Meadville, Pennsylvania. Only a few days remained for preparation for the Jamaica Survey, July 10–August 31, after which a hurried trip to Des Moines was necessary to begin the Fall Semester at Drake University.[613] It is obvious from the above description that McGavran was not thinking of retirement. His horizons were bursting beyond the borders of his denomination. His reputation as one having a prophetic message for prospective missionaries was growing. The adage, "a prophet is without honor among his own people," was true in his case.

---

611 Donald McGavran, letter to Barton, Sept. 11, 1958.
612 Donald McGavran, interview by Vern Middleton, May 16, 1986.
613 Works, "The Church Growth Movement to 1965," 148.

June 19–20 was spent in the UCMS mission headquarters in Indianapolis, digging up records and insights on the Jamaican field. His preliminary research revealed that Jamaica was one of the mission's more difficult fields. Part of the problem was sporadic support provided and that four attempts had been made to withdraw from that country, over a period of one hundred years.[614] On July 10, McGavran left for Jamaica to conduct the survey, together with his wife, which was a rare privilege for Mary.

Near the conclusion of his research in Jamaica McGavran wrote, "This study, done among an English speaking people, has been able to probe depths my other studies could not reach. We are confident we are getting a true picture of the situation and that the picture is one of considerable interest to Disciples of Christ and indeed to missions in general both in Jamaica and other lands."[615]

Unlike the situation in previous surveys, the missionaries and pastors of Jamaica showed a somewhat cynical attitude to "visitors" who became experts after only a few weeks investigation. This was probably because of the proximity of the island to the US. Sensitive to their reactions and feelings, McGavran expressed that such attitudes, "will militate against any present statement being useful."[616] Because of his sensitivity he made the following recommendation: "This points in the direction of not producing the report now. The best results can be obtained if the Church union Commission and the Seminary Board could therefore invite us back for a six months study and could appoint a Jamaican to collaborate with us."[617]

While serving at Drake Divinity School in the fall of 1958, he carried on correspondence with missionaries and denominational leaders regarding the Jamaican report. The ideas exchanged were developed and expressed in the publication of the report, "Church Growth in Jamaica." In a letter to Rev. John Perry, principal of Union Seminary in Jamaica, McGavran wrote:

> Jamaica in many respects is a preview of missions in many parts of the world and is therefore more important than would at first appear. But the stoppage of church growth in the face of a huge section of the population out of the church needs very careful consideration. Also the problem of illegitimacy as it bears on church growth is simply being shoved into the background and treated as a delicate topic which should not be discussed.[618]

This paragraph summarized several major chapters of the report which was published in 1962. However, he knew that mere surveys would have little impact unless they were

---

614   Donald McGavran, letter to Mrs. Powers, July 2, 1958.
615   Donald McGavran, letter to Mae Yoho Ward, Aug. 22, 1958.
616   Ibid.
617   Ibid.
618   Donald McGavran, letter to Rev. John Perry, Principal of Union Seminary, Jamaica, Oct. 13, 1958.

published, read, and studied. He also recognized that his reports would make a significant impact on mission policy and funding for a particular field. He expressed concern over the ethics of the situation in a letter to Dr. Mae Yoho Ward:

> In a field where there are so many interior obstacles to church growth, am I justified in enthusiastically pointing out what needs to be done to obtain church growth, and thus creating a false impression that we just need to pour in more resources and make a few adjustments and we shall have a growing field. I have been debating whether I should send in a very brief resolution saying: Jamaica is getting plenty of aid now. Watch and see. If it institutes a genuine system of membership accounting on the one hand so that its statistics are reliable, and if it really breaks out of its shell and grows then consider additional aid.[619]

As McGavran developed this report, he was faced with the problem of personnel on the Jamaican field. He wanted to keep his report objective, but there were delicate administrative issues there. The position of "field secretary" was shared with a Jamaican as the front man and a missionary from the US in the background doing administrative details. Nevertheless he felt he could not include a recommendation to change it. He wrote, "I am saying nothing about this problem in my report. Yet it is central to the entire report. Almost all recommendations depend on administration to carry them out. Yet unless we solve this problem I don't have much hope of anything happening."[620]

The critical issue behind this dilemma was that Jamaican pastors and evangelists were receiving a considerable subsidy from the mission without being supervised. The Jamaican leaders did not see supervision as part of their job description, and McGavran doubted if the Jamaican church workers would accept American supervision. What disturbed him was that the subsidy put pastors in a comfortable middle class bracket while 90 percent of the people on the Island were laborers and peasants. Yet the pastors only visited rural chapels once in a month, or in some cases once in two months.

In a letter to Grubb, McGavran summarized the entire second chapter of his report in a brief paragraph:

> You have here a wonderful example of what happens when an entire population of animistic people become nominally Protestants and churches and missions have an unimpeded field for 170 to 200 years. The pre-Christian state, the great movement, 1790–1830 of the colored (Eurafrican caste) to Christ largely in the Methodist Church, the greater movement, 1790–1840, of the slave population to Baptist Faith, and then the hundred years of "consolidation" during which with a

---

619 Donald McGavran, letter to Mae Yoho Ward, Nov. 24, 1958.
620 Ibid.

constant force of a hundred or so missionaries, the communicants in the island rose from 60,000 to 130,000, while the population rose from 440,000 to 1,400,000, and thus the percentage of Christians in the population fell from 15 to 9.[621]

On December 31, 1958, McGavran submitted the first draft of his Jamaican report to the UCMS executive leadership. The manuscript was immediately duplicated and fifteen copies were sent to Mae Yoho Ward who was to go through it with the ministers of their denomination in Jamaica. Any changes they would recommend would be fielded through the Central Committee and forwarded to McGavran for final revision. However, even as he submitted the report there was a note of disappointment, for it was not the intention of UCMS to publish the material.[622] In fact, none of McGavran's research manuscripts were published between 1954 and 1958 except for the Philippine Survey of 1957. At this point McGavran urged UCMS to develop an annual budget of $20,000 for the purpose of research and publication.[623]

DRAKE DIVINITY SCHOOL: SEPTEMBER 1958–
JANUARY 1959

Although McGavran enjoyed the facilities, the challenge of teaching seminary students and the opportunity of meeting new people at Drake, were mentioned in his letters and indicated a growing restlessness. McGavran was not searching for security or tenure in some professorial post. His vision of what was needed to get church growth ideas into the missionary enterprise was rapidly developing. From September 1958 through the fall of 1959, McGavran was driven by a single compulsion to launch an Institute of Church Growth.

He taught four courses at Drake, "The Church in a Ripening World," which was essentially material from his manuscript, later entitled *How Churches Grow*, "Missions Today and Tomorrow," "Christianity Confronts Nations on the March," and "Church Growth Case Studies."[624]

Early in November McGavran received a letter from a professor of missions requesting a list of books on Theory and Practice of Missions. McGavran's answer was both illuminating and penetrating as to the unspiritual trends he was fighting in the fifties.

McGavran began by pointing out that such a list would be largely determined by one's philosophy of mission. Then he hastened to add, "We are in the midst of a tremendous confusion as to what mission essentially theologically is."[625] McGavran quoted from an unfortunate definition on mission which he had recently received: "Missions is that activity

621 Donald McGavran, letter to Grubb, Dec. 1958.
622 Donald McGavran, letter to Virgil Sly, Dec. 31, 1958.
623 Donald McGavran, letter to UCMS, Dec. 10, 1958.
624 Donald McGavran, letter to Becker, March 30, 1958.
625 Donald McGavran, letter to Bill, Nov. 14, 1958.

of the Church which makes Christianity relevant to the modern world and hence its primary task is to discover the place of religion (not Christianity but religion) and mental health, the Church's responsibility in the middle east, moral problems in the use of atomic power, religion and law and the unity of the Church."[626]

Then in the next paragraph he stated his own philosophy of mission and explained that this philosophy would determine the list of books he recommended namely that "the supreme concern of Christian Missions is to proclaim Christ and persuade men to become His disciples and responsible members of His Church."[627] This was always the driving conviction of his life.

He then sent an annotated bibliography to this missions professor which addressed his philosophy of mission. Of first priority were books on the indigenous church by such authors as Hodges, Ritchie, Allen, and Soltau. The second category included a most interesting analysis of Harold Lindsell's books and approach to mission.

Lindsell is good. He is a very kindly logical clear thinker, a thoro-going (sic) conservative. He is a church planter by theology; but is very much addicted to ed-med-ev approach (education, medical, evangelism). This basic rightness on mission however leads him to believe that ed-med-ev is really the best way to plant the Church. He does not recognize at all that often the triune approach is really a way of saying that we do not consider church planting of paramount importance. If it were pointed out to him, he would answer, "It may be for you liberals; but it is not for real true conservative born again Christians."[628]

It is clearly evident that McGavran was really engaged in a battle on two fronts. He believed the liberals had abandoned their vision for the lost and for church planting, while the conservative evangelicals were entrenched in institutional methods which were both static and unproductive.

HIGHLIGHTS OF 1959

Nineteen fifty-nine was a year of destiny for the McGavrans. While carrying on as peripatetic professor of missions, McGavran served at Northwest Christian College in Eugene, Oregon from February 7 to June 30; then in the fall he taught at Bethany College in West Virginia which was home for the McGavrans from September 1959 to June 1960.

After exhaustive correspondence and negotiations with the UCMS executive, the way was finally cleared for McGavran to start a church growth institute. He wrote an acceptance

---

626 Ibid.
627 Ibid.
628 Ibid.

letter to Ross Griffeth, President of Northwest College on August 29, 1959, committing himself to the development of such a school at Eugene.

In late August, almost as a venture of faith, the McGavrans purchased a cutover acreage on the outskirts of Eugene, which became known as their Fox Hollow home.

Northwest Christian College: February–June 1959

The prospect of going to Eugene for the spring semester of 1959 was anticipated with mixed emotions. There was the attraction of being close to Helen and Grace McGavran, Donald's mother and sister, who lived in Vancouver, Washington, as well as Ross Griffeth, the president of the college who was a strong evangelical and missions enthusiast. However, the prospect of teaching only undergraduate students concerned McGavran because so much of his course content was on issues entirely beyond their frame of reference, and also the unsettled nature of their lives was beginning to take its toll on them. McGavran sorrowfully expressed his disappointment to Sly and Palmer of "seeing opportunities to render a significant service to the cause of planting the church around the world,"[629] but feeling frustrated with his utter inability, in his current status, to do anything about it. The life of living constantly in temporary situations was beginning to cause irritations. McGavran described their plight:

> As it is now, shifting from pillar to post, setting up a little shelf of books and a portable typewriter in the back end of my bedroom, having a changing address which monthly loses me a good many letters, and earning my living by teaching college students most of whom will never see the mission field. We might as well be back in India, at a static situation but at least at the front.[630]

They left Des Moines near the end of January and drove to Oregon, and their reception at Northwest Christian College was warm. Griffeth determined to use the McGavrans extensively. By December 1958, all weekends and many evenings were booked for speaking engagements during their time in Eugene. The response from the area churches was so positive that Mary McGavran went in one direction and Don McGavran in another.[631] McGavran tried to reorganize their schedule so that both engagements were in the same direction and transportation would not be a problem.[632]

The teaching load at Northwest was considerably lighter than at previous graduate schools. There was an 8 a.m. class four days a week and a two-hour class every Monday.[633]

---

629 Donald McGavran, letter to Sly and Palmer, March 12, 1959.
630 Donald McGavran, letter to Sly and Palmer, April 6, 1959.
631 Ross Griffith, letters to McGavran, Dec. 10, 1958 and Dec. 15, 1958.
632 Donald McGavran, letter to Griffith, Dec. 29, 1958.
633 Ibid.

But this in no way implies that McGavran was idle. He reported the following activities to UCMS in April 1959. "In addition to doing an acceptable job teaching, we make a study of the Yakima Indian Mission, get a book published on *How Churches Grow*, write articles for the International Review of Missions, and between us, speak more times in churches than many of our missionary colleagues on regular assignment."[634]

Developments Towards a Church Growth Institute in 1959

A letter arrived from Sly which virtually laid to rest any prospect of the McGavran's return to India.[635] However, that same letter proposed further commitments as a peripatetic professor, and McGavran responded, "It has been a wonderful experience. Yet it is far from being the best use of our training, insights and present abilities."[636] The teaching assignments had been tentatively tolerated, as they afforded the opportunity for international surveys and speaking opportunities at various missionary conferences. McGavran followed up by answering five questions which he presumed might be in the minds of UCMS administrators regarding the future of a church growth institute. The questions were: "Where would we get the funds? What are the running expenses? What is the staff of the Institute? Who would the students be? What would the terms be?"[637]

McGavran continued to press the urgency for continued research. In a letter to Grubb, he lamented that agricultural missions easily received and expended $100,000 for clearing a few square miles of jungle, but he was not able to get any funds for the publication of a book on church growth. He then generalized by stating that his problem was symptomatic of a broader issue: "One of the most urgent requirements today in missions is a) much research which takes church growth seriously; b) much writing and publication without year long struggles . . . c) distribution to church men . . . at the frontier (of) genuine communication on the central continuing business of the church-growth."[638]

A few days later McGavran received an encouraging review and response regarding *Bridges of God* from Howard McFarland, who had served with the Christian Missionary Alliance in the Belgian Congo, reporting how a piece of research he conducted could have saved the CMA mission from losing thousands of youth to Catholic schools. Then he asked how he could become a qualified researcher. He was obviously impressed with McGavran's answer, for he became a research fellow at the Institute of Church Growth a few years later. McGavran did quote McFarland's complete letter to Sly and Palmer and added:

---

634 Donald McGavran, letter to Sly and Palmer, April 6, 1959.
635 Virgil Sly, letter to McGavran, Feb. 4, 1959.
636 Donald McGavran, letter to Sly, July 17, 1959.
637 Ibid.
638 Donald McGavran, letter to Grubb, March 3, 1959.

Many others want to know more about how churches grow. If we had The Institute on Church Growth we would have a constant stream of men and women of all races visiting, studying, finishing up their researches, and publishing them. If we had such a place, it would be easy to write McFarland and get him to do . . . a directed piece of research on church growth, which would benefit their work and add to the general knowledge of how churches grow.[639]

At times the correspondence between McGavran and the UCMS executive became a trifle feisty, and he even described the letters on one occasion as "blood on a battle field."[640] He rarely backed down on an argument as his sharp mind honed in on the issue under discussion. So with regard to an Institute of Church Growth, he wrote: "The issue is a good deal bigger than a personal one. Indeed, the real issue is not at all what Don McGavran is going to do. The real issue is how the United Missionary Society can begin to get an adequate amount of quality church growth."[641]

Then after two pages of tightly knit reasoning he concluded:

What I am saying adds up to this. We can spend a million a year; but if we do not train in the planting of churches, we shall not get any further degree of church planting than we are now achieving. Our present degree of church planting is not good missions. But if out of our million a year, we take ten thousand in addition to our salary, we can fructify a great many of our good procedures and send out a generation of missionaries and nationals alive to both correct central intention and stated goal and to effective ways of achieving it.[642]

The above quotes are illuminating because out of the twelve fields where the UCMS was serving only two were producing any substantial growth. Sly responded with a courteous letter dated March 30, making the UCMS administration's position clear—they wanted McGavran to continue on as peripatetic professor until retirement. To which McGavran responded:

The Division gains nothing much by sending us round to all these colleges, putting in time. Any missionary could do the same with about equal effect . . . Why not, therefore, put us, as our present cost to the society, at one place and give us our whole time work, this for which our life and your assignments (research

---

639   Donald McGavran, letter to Sly and Palmer, March 12, 1959.
640   Donald McGavran, letter to Palmer, March 19, 1959.
641   Ibid.
642   Ibid.

overseas) of the last five years have trained us, and which is the work to which we feel God is calling us?[643]

In April 1959, McGavran was not considering the possibility of a church growth institute at Northwest Christian College. He requested permission to write to three seminary administrators, John C. McGaw of Drake Divinity School, Stephen England, dean of the Graduate School of Theology at Phillips University and Beaufort A. Norris, president of Christian Theological Seminary, to propose that the institute be started in one of their graduate divinity schools. The letter was sent to those three administrators and copies were also mailed to Ralph Palmer of UCMS and Ross Griffeth, president of Northwest Christian College. The opening paragraph explicitly stated that this was strictly a personal communication and then continued by answering the question, "Why establish a graduate Institute of Church Growth?" A one-page outline of the essential ingredients for the running of such an institute, came next, with this summarizing paragraph:

Much missionary work is being done all over the world by boards and missions for a small return in the growth of younger Churches. Part of this is due to lack of resources and irresponsiveness of some populations. But very much is due to the fact that church growth has not been stressed and missionaries and churchmen have not been trained in how churches grow in the specific populations to which they go. In all North America there is no educational institution giving training in church growth abroad.[644]

In his letter to McGaw, he concluded his rationale for such an institute with this statement: "There is a rising tide of interest in church growth." This was not just a promotional statement, since there were now many missionaries and mission executives who had become greatly influenced by McGavran's church growth ideas. However, among the conciliar churches (mainline), a definite shift away from this emphasis developed, as their growing theological and spiritual malaise became a major point of contention for McGavran throughout the 1960s.

The response of these seminary administrators to McGavran's proposal for a church growth institute was none too encouraging. McGaw was not overly impressed with the proposal as he found the ideas too illusive.[645] Norris "talked with his missions professor about such an institute, but concluded it should have national sponsorship."[646] Stephen England at Phillips University was the most positive in his response, and a continuous

---

643 Donald McGavran, letter to Sly, April 6, 1959.

644 Donald McGavran, letter to John C. McGaw, Drake, President Briggs, Stephen England, Dean of Graduate School of Theology at Phillips and Beaufort Norus Christian Theological Seminary, April 21, 1959.

645 John McGaw, letter to Donald McGavran, May 19, 1959.

646 Works, "The Church Growth Movement to 1965," 166.

stream of correspondence began between McGavran and England for the next four months. Meanwhile, since McGavran was presently located at Northwest Christian College, (hereafter designated NCCE) Griffeth was also in negotiations with him. In a way, McGavran played the two schools against each other, first reporting to the one and then to the other what the latest offer had been. This was done not with a view to get the best deal but rather to provoke Dean England to action. In McGavran's mind the NCCE situation was not as desirable as Phillips University, since it was only an undergraduate institution, was nonaccredited, was not in the heartland of the US, and the budget would be a serious limiting factor.

Griffeth had the upper hand in these negotiations though because all McGavran's communications with him were on a face-to-face basis, and since he had been president of NCCE for almost twenty years he was able to operate with a measure of freedom knowing his board of trustees would stand behind his decisions. Griffeth wanted McGavran at NCC due to his profound respect for him. In fact, he regarded him as the Apostle Paul of the twentieth century. He had also observed the very positive influence McGavran had on the student body in effectively imparting a vision for missions. This was important since NCCE had the reputation of being a source of many missionary candidates. The college had received a $10,000 bequest which Griffeth was able to utilize to fund the proposed institute. At a convention of the Christian churches in Denver in August, McGavran's youngest daughter, Pat, assured Griffeth that her dad would choose NCCE.[647] This was verified by a letter of tentative acceptance on August 29, 1959.

There were other factors which tipped the scales toward NCCE. One was that Griffeth would give McGavran a free hand as director of the institute, with no other assignments, while England would have considered McGavran primarily a professor of missions and secondarily a director of the institute. In addition both England and President Briggs of Phillips were due for retirement in 1960 and 1961 respectively and their looming departures would leave McGavran with no assurance that his position as director of the Institute would not be cancelled by 1961. He clarified his position in his letter of August 29, regarding Enid versus Eugene: "The calls are about even, with the advantage here of burgeoning land, wonderful climate, property we like, and vacation land all around. Nevertheless, if your call means that starting in the fall of 1960 we shall have the mandate and money to run an institution centering attention on the younger Churches, we shall come to Enid."[648]

His time frame for the start-up of such an institution was realistic. He told England that to build sufficient momentum would take anywhere from two to four years. Therefore his negotiations with both institutions included a four-year financing commitment.

That letter of acceptance meant the termination of employment with the UCMS after thirty-eight years of service with a termination date of January 1, 1961 and commencement of service with NCCE as director of the Institute of Church Growth on the same day.

---

647 Donald McGavran, interview by Vern Middleton, Salem, Oregon, June 12, 1987.
648 Donald McGavran, letter to Dean England, July 22, 1959.

The UCMS agreed to pay McGavran's salary for 1961,[649] even though they considered he was unwise to terminate his employment with them and give up the benefits they provided.[650] His final acceptance letter was rather matter of fact for such an emotional occasion. "I accept the call to join the Faculty of Northwest Christian College as professor of missions and director of the Institute of Church Growth, according to the provisions of salary etc. moving expense, work budget, and approach to foundations and donors described in your letter of June 1959 and today."[651]

Years later correspondence was renewed again between McGavran and Griffeth after an interview made by Middleton with the latter in a rest home in Salem, Oregon in June 1987. McGavran wrote to Griffeth upon hearing the contents of the interview: "Be assured, Ross, that your invitation to me back in the summer of 1959 . . . was an act of God. I was ready to quit. No one was paying attention to what I was saying . . . Then you offered me a firm position on the NCC faculty, a salary of $7,000 a year and three $1,000 scholarships to be given to career missionaries who would come to study church growth."[652]

As McGavran looked back on the events of those formative years in the Church Growth Movement he clearly saw the sovereign hand of the Lord at work:

> What I believe really happened, Ross, was that God the Father Almighty took the issue of church growth out of my hands and yours and led both of us to make decisions according to His will. Certainly He has blessed the church growth movement enormously. The unbelievable has happened. From a tiny little beginning back in January 1961 the church growth movement has now spread to all six continents. Church growth movements . . . are now stimulating . . . hundreds of denominations.[653]

Fox Hollow Property

For several years the McGavrans toyed with the idea of buying a retirement home somewhere near Vancouver, Washington so they could be near his mother. In 1957 they explored property along the Colombia River. Then while serving at NCC in 1959, they began house hunting in earnest because he was feeling some discouragement over resistance to an institute of church growth and the continual rejection of his manuscripts; the search for property was made with a view to retirement and the possibility of providing additional income. Two properties attracted them. One was a farm with a walnut grove just south of Salem, Oregon. A second site was a home in Eugene, with a large rose garden, because rose

---

649 Donald McGavran, acceptance letter to Griffith, Aug. 29, 1959.
650 Donald McGavran, interview by Vern Middleton, Dec. 20, 1984.
651 Donald McGavran, acceptance letter to Griffith, Aug. 29, 1959.
652 Donald McGavran, letter from Pasadena to Griffith, Salem, June 15, 1987.
653 Ibid.

gardens were his hobby. Still struggling with an inner compulsion that God was leading him into a wider ministry, they drove along the old Fox Hollow Road.

> We went for a drive up the hill and saw the sale sign at the driveway . . . We climbed up the hill behind the house and discovered a wonderful view in all directions. I said, "Let's buy this!" Mary looked at the house. It was dilapidated. Twenty-five thousand dollars was more than I could afford. I talked to my sister Grace . . . "take part of it and we take part." The down payment of $5,000 we could manage, and so we pooled our resources and bought it in the summer of 1959.[654]

The Fox Hollow farm of 440 acres with 100 acres of prune orchard became an influential factor in his negotiations over Enid or Eugene, as the place to begin the Institute of Church Growth. McGavran wrote:

> We made a down payment of $5,000 on a piece of property we liked very much. The sizable payment which would make the property ours was to be made on July 22nd—today. When that payment is made, the die for us will be cast in favor of our ending our active service in this delightful climate and this vigorous Christian college . . . On receipt of your letter of July 9th, I attempted to defer payment until August 5th and have succeeded.[655]

That property was a lifetime dream come true for the McGavrans, but it did not stand in the way of their call and obedience to God. He explained in yet another letter to England, "If the Institute of Church Growth at the Graduate Seminary is guaranteed by you . . . we are prepared to forfeit our deposit of $5000 and give up the idea of retiring in the fabulous northwest. We would do it simply on the basis that all our life we have tried to do God's will, and we think that a genuine opportunity to start an effective Institute of Church Growth would be God's call to us."[656]

A payment of ten thousand dollars was due on the property on August 7. One day before the payment was due, Richard Guske, the realtor, had a heart attack. The ensuing confusion gave McGavran more breathing room in his negotiations with England over the possibility of beginning an Institute of Church Growth at Enid.[657] The final down payment was not made until Griffeth confirmed that the Church Growth Institute would be established at NCC in Eugene, thus ruling out Enid.

So in 1961 the McGavrans settled into their Fox Hollow home. They installed a concrete floor, which leveled the house for the first time in years and they also spent the summer

---

654 Donald McGavran, interview by Vern Middleton, Dec. 20, 1984.

655 Ibid.

656 Donald McGavran, letter to England, July 22, 1959.

657 Donald McGavran, letter to England, Aug. 8, 1959.

renailing the siding. They also began a church in their home which grew over the years into a suburban church in Eugene.

The value of that ranch quickly escalated so that when it was sold a decade later, the funds realized were used to endow the Donald McGavran Chair of Church Growth of the School of World Mission at Fuller Theological Seminary in Pasadena.

McGavran Decried the Term "Evangelism"

Ralph Palmer of the UCMS had arranged for McGavran to speak on evangelism at a retreat in July 1959. McGavran wrote, "I shudder at this word 'evangelism.' It has become so departmentalized that it does not carry much meaning . . . Would it be possible for example to use the words 'How the Church Grows' in the place of 'Evangelism' in the programs?"[658]

The next day McGavran wrote to Kraemer regarding the foreword he was writing for *How Churches Grow*. Again the topic of evangelism arose. McGavran's comments in this letter clarified his reasoning behind his dislike for the term "evangelism":

In the older Churches, the word "evangelism" has come to mean the sort of thing Billy Graham does, and for which he is vigorously attacked by the liberal wing of the American churches . . . Your introduction is going to be influential . . . I fear that this word "evangelism" in it may induce an aversion in some before they read a single page. They will be the ones who need the message of the book most![659]

Syncretistic Concerns

Early in 1959 the McGavrans saw the movie, "The Inn of Sixth Happiness," which was Hollywood's screen version of the book *The Small Woman*. McGavran was deeply exercised by Hollywood's misrepresentations of the missionary enterprise. He expressed two concerns. One had to do with the actress and the other; the syncretistic slant given to the content. He protested the unsuitability of Ingrid Bergman playing the part of Gladys Aylward, in view of Bergmans "unsavory marital relationships."[660] The second issue was a subtle statement made in the film implying it was Gladys Aylward's philosophy of conversion. "I do not care whether a person is a Christian or a Buddhist or a Confucianist, if I can help him to respect himself as a person."[661] McGavran urged Charles Ranson of IMC to locate Aylward to see if that was indeed her position, and if not, to assist her in having that statement removed from the film.

---

658 Donald McGavran, letter to Palmer, April 23, 1959.
659 Donald McGavran, letter to H. Kraemer, April 24, 1959.
660 Donald McGavran, letter to Charles Ransom, IMC, Jan. 11, 1959.
661 Ibid.

The prevailing theological mood in the late 1950s was shifting again and McGavran's insight into the subtle dangers of Buddhism and Hinduism arose from the experience of years of ministry in India. He watched with growing concern as liberal theology appeared to be leading America down the garden path of syncretism. In March 1959, he wrote the following in support of Kraemer's apologetic approach to non-Christian religions:

> I rather imagine Kraemer's convictions are going to find an unexpected use in the next thirty years in America. The secular mind here, with its relativistic. agnostic, scientific orientation (particularly in University circles) is a perfect seed bed for Hindu, Buddhist and Bahai movements. I continually run across people who believe that all religions are about equal ways to God, or alternatively are good for you if you believe them and get satisfaction out of them.[662]

Kraemer invited McGavran to "make a condensation of my two books in simple, crystal clear, American vernacular."[663] McGavran's response reveals how he perceived his strengths and weaknesses. "It . . . certainly should be done, but whether I am the one to do it is an entirely different matter. True, I have had a good deal of experience with non-Christian religions. I believe vigorously that yours is the correct position in regard to them . . . But these are scarcely qualifications for writing an American version. I am neither professional theologian nor professional writer."[664]

McGavran never undertook that assignment, but his analysis of the ecumenical trends and the theological compromises of that era is most illuminating. The following perceptive insight was one of the driving forces behind his church growth thinking.

> The American theologian usually has no concept of the vitality of non-Christian faiths and of the degree to which they are riding chariots of modern secular paganism into the citadel of the Christian faith . . . He formulates his statement of theology believing that the main task of Christianity is to be kindly, inclusive and humble in the presence of good men seeking God . . . He shies away from anything which appears even remotely "unecumenical" even to non-Christian religions. He is against the sins of racial and religious arrogance, economic injustice and military dominance. If the non-Christian religion is for justice . . . the American theologian is not likely to be greatly concerned with what they (sic) believe about God, man, sin and salvation.[665]

---

662 Donald McGavran, letter to Margaret Sinclair, Editor, *IRM,* March 6, 1959.
663 H. Kraemer, letter to Donald McGavran, Jan. 30, 1959.
664 Donald McGavran, letter to H. Kraemer, Feb. 17, 1959.
665 Ibid.

In the fall of 1959 while lecturing at Bethany College, he was asked to deliver an address on the subject of syncretism. He entitled this discourse, "What Shall the Christian Say of Other Faiths?" and it was a thoughtful apologetic on the Christian's approach to non-Christian religions in the midst of pluralistic thinking. He stated authoritively that, "It is the responsibility of modern Christians by diligent study of the scriptures, and the grace of God . . . they must continually measure the thought processes of men and the structures of society by Christ's standards. They must continually condemn in Christ's name the bad, false, and ugly."[666]

He also described the prevailing spirit of the late '50s as pluralism, which said, "Leave other religions alone to go their own way. You have plenty to do in rectifying your own religion. Look on the good in other religions and assume that the processes of criticism will arise within them. Rectifying them is not your business."[667]

McGavran recognized the alarming sweep of radical social change which was transforming society all around the world. It distressed him deeply that old mainline churches in America lost their voice and the will to stand against this rising tide of pluralism. McGavran said of them, "They have made the greatest adjustment to the climate of today. They have the fewest defenses against relativism."[668] His spiritual convictions still enabled him to see God's hand at work in a revolutionary way, so he spoke with steadfast optimism: "We live in the midst of 'super-gigantic' revolutions . . . Societies solidified in ancient forms are becoming liquid. Whatever the minor effects of the many revolutions that swirl around us . . . one major effect is that mankind is being redistributed on a huge scale. Old loyalties and allegiances are being broken up and national psychologies, sociologies are being remade wholesale."[669]

The lecture he gave at Bethany that fall may have sounded like the thunderings of John the Baptist. McGavran was speaking to a church, a scholarly community that still possessed the outer trappings of Christian conviction, but the inward vital life of Christ was gone from their actual experience. To them McGavran proclaimed unequivocally: "You cannot believe that all 'religions' are true and pass no judgment on anything 'religious.' This is the twilight of truth. This is the suicide of faith. Any branch of the Church can sign its death warrant by consistent espousal of such fuzzy inclusiveness."[670]

In contrast, McGavran emphatically declared that full responsibility of the church is more than a social gospel: "This is the time to proclaim God's will. He has called us the light of the world. Being the light of the world does not mean merely living by the side of the road and being a friend to man. The Church must proclaim God's rule and judgment. God's rules are clear. His measuring rod is not hidden. The Church must proclaim it."[671]

---

666 Donald McGavran, "What Shall We Say of Other Faiths?" (unpublished MS, 1959), p. 2.
667 Ibid., 3.
668 Ibid.
669 Ibid., 4.
670 Ibid., 9.
671 Ibid., 5.

McGavran preached for a verdict, and his words were censorious:

> Many moderns have deified reason. They have no measuring stick, except the changing shifting standards of what seems right or reasonable today. Having come to disbelieve in revelation . . . they are then willing to accept any formulation of men's beliefs as a manifestation of the culture of those people . . . God opposed such latitudinarian views . . . He taught the children of Israel that there was a difference between revelation and relativism. Only those Israelites survived who accepted revelation . . . The life of the Christian church also has been one long battle between Branches of the church which accepted Jesus Christ and the Bible as the revelation of God and those who reduced them to a subordinate position and left themselves free to follow . . . the god "reason." True Christian Churches however always accepted reason as a servant, insisting of course that in the last analysis Christ would judge reason.[672]

The Yakima Survey

Mrs. Mary Dale invited the McGavrans to come and survey the Yakima Indian field, a project of the UCMS, during their Easter vacation, in March, 1959. Much of their research was spent in the company of Clifton Peightal, director of the Yakima Indian Christian Mission. What McGavran discovered was a reservation where large sections of land were sold off to white folk, leaving the Indians without a means of livelihood. Their pitiful plight was compounded by the fact that all the local jails were full of Indians. As for Christian influence, a large segment of the Indians worshipped in Shaker assemblies but very few were part of the UCMS mission church.

After the actual research was completed, McGavran began to analyse the data and realized that the principles and problems he was wrestling with applied, more or less, to "all the Indian tribes in the Northwest."[673] Deeply troubled by the paternalistic dependence created by the mission, he hopefully asserted that: "There must be some churches and some Indian Christians who manifest the same sturdy independence and inner faith which we saw in the Bible Shakers. There must be some orthodox Indian Christians who know the victory in Christ and value it for its own sake and who share in Christ's passion that all men know and love and obey Him."[674]

Another concern was the way American Indian Christians were segmented into pockets due to denominational activities. He recognized that these small pockets of isolated churches actually militated against each other and prevented the growth and identity of

---

672 Ibid., 10–11.
673 Donald McGavran, letter to Peightal, Yakima, Washington, April 2, 1959.
674 Ibid.

vital, strong, genuine Indian Christians where could they reach "out to share their treasure with others" and be "concerned about other Indians."[675]

A third dimension which disturbed him was the lack of studies of the Indian situation which were church centered. He laid the blame for this failure on the strategy and nature of missions which were serving Indian communities. "So much of 'Indian work' is philanthropic missions and measures its success not in the establishment of the church . . . but in cultural advancement of Indians."[676]

A fourth situation McGavran felt needed to be addressed was their pathetic spiritual state. He wrote: "Their hopelessness, their inner resentments against the whites, their adherence to the old as an escape mechanism, their basking in alleged glories instead of attacking present problems, the tyranny of drink and loose sex relations—all this is an essential part of their problem."[677]

While McGavran was reading widely on the history of missions among the North American Indians, he received a letter from Nielsen, a Disciples of Christ missionary in Northern Rhodesia. McGavran's response to the letter casts light on his views of handling indigenous movements that lean toward the heretical or schismatic. He studied people movements in diverse places, such as the Indian Shakers in the Olympic peninsula of Washington state, the Alice Movement in Rhodesia, the Prophet Harris movement in Liberia, and the Sampson Opon movement among the Ashantis and the Iglesia Ni Christo movement in the Philippines. McGavran rejected the typical attitude and treatment of Western missionaries to these movements as being an error of the first magnitude. He warned:

> If we do not make provision for tribal and caste-wise movements into the Church (discipling the people in Christ's name, at the cultural level where they are now,) we should expect that they will go elsewhere . . .
> It is an error . . . to imagine that we can admit a regulated trickle of individual converts, more or less divorced from powerful tribal currents of thought and feeling into congregations on the western pattern. It is part of the same error to imagine that we can accept as Christian only those who are willing and able at one bound to step into the world of biblical interpretation, theology, hymnology . . . which is normal for western man with a thousand years of Church behind him.[678]

He sought to identify the correct attitude toward indigenous movements which appeared to be heretical. He wrote:

---

675 Ibid.
676 Ibid.
677 Donald McGavran, letter to Peightal, Yakima, Washington, May 21, 1959.
678 Donald McGavran, letter to Nielson, April 17, 1959.

Ability to recognize responsiveness . . . to guide, and assist such movements (without approving everything they do) . . . Indeed, to take such movements, allowing them considerable freedom and enormous appreciation, and contain them within the Church is a wisdom and skill missions desperately needs . . . While it is essential to maintain the identity of biblical Christianity it would seem the part of common sense a) to extend the tolerance we now exercise toward the historic varieties of Church toward those yet to be born; and b) to establish and maintain friendly connection and communication with those which seem to us so unbiblical that we, at least, cannot call them Church.[679]

McGavran's ideas in this area were two decades ahead of many others.

A YEAR AT BETHANY

The McGavrans departed for Bethany College, West Virginia in January 1960. The spiritual climate at Bethany was like a desert compared to NCC at Eugene. McGavran reported that the chapel meetings were a waste of time. Students would attend chapel and study while the service was going on. He described it all as "a pretty secular affair . . . One fraternity of Bethany required those joining to spend a night in a whore house."[680] The school was struggling to survive, and as a result, admitted non-Christian students, who totally changed the environment there.

Returning to Bethany was like going back to their family roots. The place literally pulsated with denominational history and McGavran ancestral history. He referred to the school as the "fountainhead" of the Christian churches. In a letter to his grandson, Andrew, he reveals how significant the place was to him:

I am writing to you from Bethany West Virginia. When you get old enough look this place up on a map and when you get to be a young man come and spend some days here. Here your great great grandfather and great great grandmother met and were married. In these hills and fertile lovely valleys they had their farm. Your great great great grandfather Grafteon helped found Bethany College. He gave a considerable amount of money and a considerable amount of land that young men might have the blessings of a Christian education. He also freed the slaves he had inherited from his father, holding that, while they were valuable property, it was not pleasing to God that men should own men and buy and sell them like cattle.[681]

---

679 Ibid.
680 Donald McGavran, interview by Vern Middleton, Aug. 17, 1986.
681 Donald McGavran to Andrew, his grandson, on his first birthday, Sept. 25, 1959.

While at Bethany McGavran began to see how to apply church growth insights to the North American scene. He described his application of the homogenous unit principle to the US as follows: "There I found that the Presbyterian, Methodist and Baptist churches were in the cities. Out in the mining areas, there were churches of God, Pentecostal churches, Assemblies of God, and Nazarene churches. I began to see that while we don't have tribes and castes in America, we do have segments of society. This was influential in my thinking."[682]

Fallout from the Decision to Start a Church Growth Institute

The first item McGavran had to address was his relationship to UCMS. Although the association as an employee of the mission was to terminate on January 1, 1961, McGavran regarded the resulting new affinity as that of a partnership. For one thing, Sly had assured him over the telephone that UCMS would pay his salary during 1961. Such a severance allowance may appear rather pitiful after thirty-seven years of service, but in 1959 it was standard practise, and in fact, McGavran considered it a very generous act. He wrote: "I value not only the cash assistance, but even more your partnership, thus expressed, in the enterprise."[683]

For the McGavrans, the termination of such a long-standing relationship was no easy matter, and with deep sorrow they came to the parting of ways. McGavran expressed his disappointment in UCMS for not responding to his vision for the Church Growth Institute. "I had so greatly hoped that the Society would fill the great vacuum in missionary training by starting the Institute itself. But what is to be is to be!"[684]

The extent of his frustration and his persistence in pressing on, despite serious setbacks, was captured in a letter written to his daughter, Helen Corneli, which discussed an article by Lewis Mumford on social action issues. McGavran wrote:

> I mistrust Lewis Mumford because . . . of his arrogant vituperative assault on those who differ with him . . . I find myself in Lewis' position—ardently advocating a course of conduct of procedure which is regarded as extreme by a great body of men. Emotionally I would like to use all Mumford's phrases for those who should move but don't, for those who should see my solution but don't; but intellectually as I look at the situation in the cold light of reason . . . Those who differ from me do not have "congealed minds." I have every right to present my position, and I hope to carry the day, but if I do it will be because my peers and my equals and my betters whose judgment I respect . . . have come to believe as I do.[685]

---

682 Donald McGavran, interview by Vern Middleton, Dec. 20, 1984.
683 Donald McGavran, letter from Bethany College to Sly, Sept. 9, 1959.
684 Ibid.
685 Donald McGavran, letter from Bethany to Helen Corneli, his daughter, June 1959.

Only rarely did he reveal his inner frustration with UCMS, and then it was only with long-standing friends who understood and appreciated his point of view. Mary Pollard was such a person—a long-time colleague and friend throughout the years in India.

> The cause into which I am throwing myself, seems so counter to the tide and meets with so little encouragement on the part of notable leaders of missions. As you know my thesis is that the supreme and controlling aim of the Christian mission is to make Christ known to all people and to persuade them to become disciples and responsible members of His Church. To the extent that this drive is helpful to the mission machine, in our own and other Churches and Missions, it is tolerated and even mildly encouraged . . . But for this emphasis I am looked on as a partizan (sic) and unbalanced person, whose stresses, far from being encouraged must constantly be checked and compensated against. This year for example I am sent to teach here at Bethany with my main course Old Testament History!!! It is almost as if the Division said, "Let us keep Don busily engaged in other matters so that he won't be so continually in our hair in regard to church growth. I really have been turned out to grase (sic.)—but am able to get in some good licks here and there . . . Now the Institute of Church Growth at Eugene is a very long shot. Our board could have said "Here is a thirty-five year missionary, and we'll keep him on salary while he teaches 'how churches grow' for the next six years and we'll encourage some seminary to start an Institute of Church Growth and contribute Don's services to it." But not our board. So all the seminaries turned down the idea of starting an Institute. Only NCC, at Eugene (a little known college) took it up. The Division is contributing my services there for one year—then they will have me off their salary roll, and the problem of Don McGavran's employment and emphasis will be solved.[686]

Handling the situation with UCMS was one thing, but dealing with the situation in India was quite another. Even though seven years had elapsed since the McGavrans' departure, those who labored on in Takhatpur had done so with high hopes of their return. This was reflected in the letter to Mary Pollard and Padre Samuel.

> Mary and I want to tell you (as our closest friends and comrades of many and many a year) that Northwest Christian college has called us to establish and maintain, for the years till our retirement at 68, an Institute of Church Growth . . . While we have been doing this peripatetic around . . . we have kept the door open to a possible return to India and to Takhatpur. At one time it looked quite likely. But when this opportunity came to direct the Institute of Church Growth we could not do other than accept it, though doing so closes fairly certainly any

---

686 Donald McGavran, letter from Bethany to Mary Pollard, Takhatpur, Oct. 10, 1959.

chance of coming back to India. We write these words with real sorrow, for our churches there and our friends there are and have been and will be very much on our hearts.[687]

Two days later McGavran wrote to his missionary comrade, Ken Potee, field secretary for the Disciples in India, about some property matters in Takhatpur. Potee had insisted that McGavran's application to return to India go through the National Council of Churches. McGavran interpreted this as an attempt to prevent his return. This cooled their relationship. As a result McGavran's letter reveals another side of his feeling about India: "I really do not feel anymore that Takhatpur is my station or that these affairs are my concern. I did my bit as to the Lord, and it is up to my successors now. I have ceased to carry the burden. He has put me to work in a different part of the same task and I just throw my energies into this part."[688]

With regard to the administrative aspects of the Takhatpur ministry, this was true, but the volume and nature of correspondence indicated that McGavran was still regarded as station superintendent by Takhatpur missionaries and pastors. He still raised monies for field projects. He still evaluated personnel and made recommendations as to their area of usefulness. He still devised ways to work around roadblocks erected by the field secretary at Jabulpur, who according to McGavran had, "no vision about church growth in our Chosen People (Satnamis)—is probably skeptical about it—and will be quite content to take our trainees and set them to all kinds of other ministerial jobs."[689]

Continued Interaction With UCMS Administrators

Through the summer and fall of 1959, McGavran continued vigorous deliberation with the UCMS Executive. A commission on the theology of mission had been established by the Division and McGavran feared it would produce a correct, but anemic, theology of mission which would become "a chain around our ankles."[690] All of the delegates were personal acquaintances of McGavran but he protested that not one of them

was seriously concerned with missions. Bob's main concern is unity. Bill's main concern is a theology to fit America's climate of thought. Reed's main concern is theology in the light of modern American sociology . . . Not a single one of them flames with the purpose that Christ be proclaimed to the end of the earth. Furthermore none of them knows the non-Christian world . . . None of them has cast his life as a grain of wheat into a dark furrow to die that men and women

---

687 Donald McGavran, letter to Pollard and Padre Samuel, Takhatpur, Sept. 15, 1959.
688 Donald McGavran to Ken Potee, Jabalpur, India, Sept. 17, 1959.
689 Donald McGavran, letter to Pollard and Padre Samuel, Nov. 24, 1959.
690 Donald McGavran to Sly, Nov. 7, 1959.

there may come to know Him Whom to know is life eternal. None has identified himself with a non-Christian population and buried his children and shed his blood among them.[691]

McGavran pointed out that the Churches of Christ produced very few theologians and that their liberal leanings generated little, if any, evangelistic or missionary zeal. He suggested the names of several international missiologists and theologians who should be invited to sit on the commission, namely, Lesslie Newbigin, Hendrick Kraemer, or Emil Brunner.

Reflection on the concerns cited provides ample material to reconstruct the context in which the Church Growth Movement took root. His denomination was concerned over church unity. It had been weakened theologically by liberal influences especially among the leadership. There were a few like Don West who spoke out energetically against the lack of passion for evangelism but the Commission members were able to pour cold water over his pleas for an "effective, telling advocacy of evangelism."[692] However the voices of protest were very much a minority, while the advocates of social action were gaining control in virtually every dimension of the denomination.

Correspondence with Kenneth N. Taylor, who was director of Moody Press, indicated the theological significance of McGavran's writings and church growth concerns. The "Fundamentalists" as McGavran then called them, hailed his material with enthusiasm. Taylor used such phrases as, "extremely stimulating," "ahead of its time," and "of great value" in describing the manuscript, *How Churches Grow*. He was ready to publish the manuscript as it was, except for a few minor changes which he felt were vital for "political reasons."[693] The arrangement that McGavran and Taylor were trying to work out was a threefold publication of the book; World Dominion Press for the British and overseas market, Friendship Press for the more liberal group in the US, and Moody Press for the "Fundamentalist" camp. McGavran recognized that his church growth insights applied equally well to all three groups. He wrote:

> The Evangelical heart of American Christianity in its mission work around the world is handicapped and hindered by most of the same concepts customs climates and obstacles, as afflict the Christians of the World Council branches. Gradualism, Equalitarianism, Cultural Overhang, Immobility, Philanthropy instead of church growth, Gathered Church Convictions, Addiction to Ploughing instead of Reaping, Inability to see ripe fields . . . The Evangelical Heart of American Christianity, because of its biblical theology is in a much better position to go ahead if these burdensome concepts . . . are recognized and renounced.[694]

---

691 Ibid.
692 Donald McGavran to Don West, Indianapolis, Sept. 21, 1959.
693 Donald McGavran, letter to Kenneth Taylor, Moody Press, Chicago, March 10, 1959, April 17, 1959.
694 Donald McGavran, letter to Kenneth Taylor, Dec. 19, 1959.

Eventually he settled for having only World Dominion Press and Friendship Press publish *How Churches Grow.*

Letters were sent to UCMS headquarters try to arouse creative ways of taking hold of the burgeoning opportunities that were available to them. One example was a letter McGavran sent outlining a church-planting strategy for reaching the migrating Puerto Rican population that was pouring into the cities of the US.[695] The outcome of his proposal was that instead of multiplying churches among the Puerto Ricans, the UCMS raised $700,000 to establish a service center which resulted in one small church. Meanwhile, the Pentecostals were opening up storefront churches to minister to the spiritual needs of these people. In another letter he directed the UCMS regarding ways the mission could be mobilized to gather in receptive peoples in the Congo;[696] in yet another, he inquired as to the application of his Jamaican Survey;[697] and in still another, seeking materials to bring further insight on the Yakima Indians.[698]

A YEAR OF PREPARATION AND ORGANIZATION FOR THE INSTITUTE: 1960

McGavran continued his peripatetic routine throughout 1960, lecturing at Bethany during the spring, and at the Pacific School of Religion, at Berkeley in the fall. But most of his energy was directed to preparations for the founding of the Institute.

Recruitment of Students for the Church Growth Institute

In December 1959, J. Waskom Pickett recommended that Keith Hamilton study under McGavran at the Institute of Church Growth at Eugene. He was the first student to commit himself and was the only student for the first semester in 1961.

When McGavran read an article Alan Tippett published in the *IRM*, entitled "Probing Missionary Inadequacies at the Popular Level,"[699] he began corresponding with him regarding the possibility of his attending the ICG. He wrote, "Please understand that the Institute of Church Growth is a beginning venture. We do not know how large a response we shall elicit. At our opening session we are going to have just one research fellow—a Methodist superintendent, Keith Hamilton of Bolivia . . . Some Baptists, Lutherans and Brethren are in correspondence . . . but the numbers may be small for years."[700] Also in that same letter concluding sentences present the very heart of the new Institute. McGavran

---

695 Donald McGavran, letter to Dale Fiers, Dec. 1, 1959.
696 Donald McGavran, letter to Robert Nelson, Dec. 1, 1959.
697 Donald McGavran, letter to Mae Yoho Ward, Dec. 10, 1959. and Dec. 19, 1959.
698 Donald McGavran, letter to Russell Carter, White Swan Reservation, Washington, Dec. 1959.
699 Donald McGavran, letter from to Paternoster, Feb. 12, 1960.
700 Donald McGavran, letter to Alan Tippett, Nausori, Fiji, Jan. 2, 1960.

stressed that documentation of sociological factors was critical to growth: "I know of no other institution dedicated entirely to learning all we can about the processes by which it pleases God to multiply His churches and spread them abroad throughout the earth. Here your insights and discoveries about the way in which churches grow would be enlarged, sharpened, and corrected."[701]

In late January he received a query from Rev. R. Baker, a missionary from Nigeria who was serving with the Christian Reformed Board. Baker worked among the TIV tribe and wanted to spend a few weeks researching under McGavran's guidance. In preparation for the few weeks they would have together, Baker was asked to dig out "accurate figures as to church membership"—similar figures for missionary personnel serving on the field: "All the incidental remarks, or actions, or policies bearing on 1) what the mission conceived its task to be, 2) how it made converts, 3) how it had lost converts, 4) flurries of interest . . . 5) ways converts were treated, and 6) evangelistic effectiveness of the younger Churches."[702]

McGavran Utilized as a Consultant to UCMS

An extraordinary meeting of the UCMS Division of World Mission was called February 2–4, 1960. McGavran was invited to present a forty-five minute paper on strategy issues and then act as a consultant during the remaining days, on matters relating to the principles and practises of the mission, especially.[703] His paper entitled, "The Implementation of the Strategy for the India Mission," basically reviewed the four structures that made up the ministry in India, the Mission, the Committee on Evangelism, the Convention of the Churches of Christ, and the Church in India. McGavran described these "as a four ring circus" and recommended that they be "compressed into two: The Church in India and its Executive Committee."[704]

Throughout the strategy statement McGavran's understanding of the Indian mind was clearly highlighted. He wanted structures and committees made up of people without vested interests, but he lamented, "How to obtain a Board which is impartial is a problem."

One of the most significant sections of his strategy paper had to do with the role of younger missionaries in future leadership. He was concerned that missions were sending an increasing numbers of specialists who were helpful to the churches only in a very marginal way. He urged that future missionaries be "meat and potato types,"[705] those who will work actively in church planting and evangelism. He frowned on the idea of sending out young missionaries who were trained in the theologies of Niebuhr and Tillich, to teach in seminaries

701 Ibid.
702 Donald McGavran, letter to R. Baker, Nigeria, Jan. 25, 1960.
703 Donald McGavran, letter to Ross Griffeth, Eugene, Oregon, Jan. 8, 1960.
704 Donald McGavran, "The Implementation of the Strategy for the India Mission" (lecture, Indianapolis, Feb. 2–4, 1960).
705 Ibid., 6.

in Third World countries. He suggested that a missionary should spend a minimum of one term pastoring in the context of the country before assuming teaching responsibilities.

Also, McGavran was alarmed that many of these younger prospective missionary candidates were devoid of a spirit of servanthood. Of one such candidate he wrote: "I was talking with a very fine man who is thinking of missions—but he said, 'Can you keep up the intellectual life on the mission field?'" I simply quoted in answer our blessed Lord's word "Unless a grain of wheat fall into the ground and die it abides alone. We need missionaries who go out to die. If they go out for other reasons they will not make good missionaries and they will not last."[706] He also suggested in the same strategy proposal that UCMS would do well to "devise a plan to use Indians as missionaries."[707]

The Meeting at Wichita

McGavran was invited by George Earle Owen to attend the Second Consultation on Internal Unity at Wichita from February 7–9. This was a denominational meeting designed to reestablish communication between the pacifists and the nonpacifists; and between those espousing different brands of church unity. McGavran found the attitude of both sides hardened and entrenched, and their disposition toward one another "shocking" for a church supposedly committed to "including all who accept the Lordship of Jesus Christ and the Bible as the rule of faith and practice."[708]

McGavran was asked to address the Consultation on the topic of evangelism. However, he was not satisfied with the anemic statement produced by the Evangelism Section. UCMS planned to publish the product of the Consultation. McGavran vigorously protested that the sections were weighted unfairly, "Unity–5 pages, Younger Churches–4 pages, and Evangelism–1."[709] His objections to the "witness" section of the report were summarized in a letter to George Beasley:

a. They hide their passion for evangelism under terrible complexity, a certain ivory towerism and an excessively broad definition of evangelism.

b. There should be a ringing call to evangelism in this somewhere.

c. There should be several paras (sic.) all the way through pointing out that ordinary Christians do, can and should evangelize . . . Evangelism is not correct theology: it is bringing lost sheep into the fold.

d. The hopefulness and responsiveness of vast sections of the world are not reflected in this statement.[710]

---

706 Ibid., 7.
707 Ibid., 8.
708 Donald McGavran, letter to Palmer, Feb. 11, 1960.
709 Donald McGavran, letter to Sly, Feb. 11, 1960.
710 Donald McGavran, letter to George Beasley, Feb. 29, 1960.

Church Growth Institute Preparations

From an evangelical perspective, McGavran considered the NCCE to be ideal. In a letter to Carlton Buck he explained this, "Of all our various colleges, NCCE has easily the best Christian environment. It is really a Christian college. So many of the others are church related—in a rather distant relationship."[711]

Much of the correspondence McGavran carried on in 1960 was directly concerned with the organization and administration of the Church Growth Institute. In a letter written January 14, 1960, he instructed Griffeth to try to postpone the beginning date of the Church Growth Institute until January 1, 1961. Apparently some of the UCMS executives had been suggesting McGavran's departure from the mission should take place in September 1960.[712] A month later, another letter was sent to Griffeth detailing such issues as additional library books for the Institute, which UCMS was willing to contribute from their College of Mission library, setting up of conferences, and hammering out lines of authority and procedures for decision making.

Correspondence with Victor Hayward

Regular correspondence commenced with Victor E. W. Hayward, who was research secretary of the IMC, which later became the Commission on World Mission and Evangelism (CWME) of WCC in 1961. McGavran and Hayward corresponded throughout the 1960s. In 1960 Hayward was preparing for a WCC meeting to be held at Delhi in December 1961. McGavran was hopeful that the IMC could be mobilized into assuming responsibility of mobilizing for church growth research. He proposed seven functions for an IMC Center for Research. Although it is difficult to assess the impact these proposals had upon the development of the CWME research center, some of these concepts were evident when it was organized in 1961.

1. To chart areas in which great church growth . . . was occurring. On great maps notable growth would be entered in red . . .
2. To sense the many different major problems of church growth and stimulate responsible study of these . . .
3. To furnish guidance as to how studies can be done so that results would be valid and comparable . . .
4. To encourage publishing results and build up in each sending land and in each mission land at least one library of factual studies in church growth . . .

---

711 Donald McGavran, letter to Carlton Buck, Jan. 14, 1960.
712 Donald McGavran, letter to Griffeth, Jan. 14, 1960.

5.   To encourage seminaries and colleges to establish institutes of church growth where missionaries could be taught how churches today are growing . . .

6.   To carry on itself key studies at specially crucial or neglected spots . . .

7.   To campaign that half of one percent of income should be devoted by each board to continuous research in church growth about the central continuing task about discipling the nations.[713]

The dynamics of this dialogue will be explored later.

Hayward responded to McGavran's letter in a courteous way but expressed some disagreement with McGavran's thesis: "Many of us could not accept numbers as a satisfactory criterion of the growth of the church . . . We would agree that numbers are one of the criteria by which growth can be estimated . . . to imply that numerical expansion is the heart of the subject would be a dangerous dis-service to the cause we have at heart."[714]

In response, McGavran pointed to issues dealt with in his book which was being published by World Dominion Press, *How Churches Grow*. Then he clarified his reasons for emphasizing numerical growth, "I do hold that for a number of reasons much mission has come to accept no-growth as good mission."[715] He stressed this point because he had observed that missions often neglected growth, due to vested interests. He also noted that liberal churches and missions lost their will to evangelize because of syncretistic theologies and he also noted that in the late fifties the US government was earnestly seeking friendships with other nations, and he had come to believe that this policy was influencing American missionaries in their preference of aid over evangelism. He then explained his emphasis on numbers as a necessity because:

> Under these circumstances, in an attempt to rectify these unfortunate conditions . . . I hold that world mission for some years ahead should pay special attention to growth in numbers. It must rescue itself from becoming aid in perpetuity to stopped little younger Churches . . . The danger is not—believe me—of overstressing numbers. The danger is that actually finding lost sheep . . . will be left out of the picture entirely.[716] McGavran warned that failure to focus on numerical growth in preference to a broader view would eventuate in defending no-growth. He closed the letter by stating, "Until we get Churches growing greatly, keeping up with the population explosion . . . we need one devoted exclusively to finding out about how Churches grow."[717]

---

713   Donald McGavran, letter to Victor Hayward, CWME Research Secretary, London, Jan. 1, 1960.

714   Victor Hayward, letter to Donald McGavran, Feb. 3, 1960.

715   Donald McGavran, letter to Victor Hayward, Feb. 25, 1960.

716   Ibid.

717   Ibid.

Spring Vacation 1960

McGavran valued his time so that even his vacation periods were structured to squeeze as much out of each day as possible. During Easter vacation of 1960, the McGavrans took a six-day swing through the country, visiting various members of their family, which is an indication that in the midst of an intense life based on ideas and principles, McGavran valued and maintained strong family ties and connections.

Summer 1960

Early in June 1960 the McGavrans left Bethany to teach missionary candidates for two weeks at The College of Missions at Crystal Lake. On July 7 they reloaded their 1950 Oldsmobile and trailer and headed west to their Fox Hollow home in Eugene, Oregon, arriving there on July 23.

The summer was spent repairing the house in Eugene, cleaning up the yard, and fixing up the water supply; then they headed back to Berkeley, California so he could complete his last assignment as peripatetic professor of missions.

EXPRESSION OF COMPANIONSHIP

The relationship between McGavran and his wife, Mary, deepened and strengthened throughout the period 1954 to 1960, as they functioned as a team. He drew much support, encouragement, and inspiration from Mary's quick mind. While in Thailand McGavran penned the following words to Mary, his dear wife, in another demonstration of the proverb "that behind every great man there stands an even greater woman":

> Mary Dear, I want you to know how much I appreciate your carrying on the way you do and have through all these years. Specially when I see a good many missionary women of the younger generation who are helpless as puppies, and take their men out of the work, and use up their time and gum up the work, and remember what a courageous and wonderful helpmeet you have been. I am filled with thankfulness to God for you. It would have been impossible to do half of what I have without your cheerful cooperation.[718]

Mary's keen spirit of discernment and sensitivity to others was often a moderating force in McGavran's life. She discerned from his letters that he was absolutely appalled at the pitiful missionary effort he found in Thailand, so she wrote, cautioning him not to

---

718   Donald McGavran, letter from Thailand to Mary, New Haven, Connecticut, Feb. 26, 1960.

write up his survey in such a way that he might destroy the very spirit of the missionary team there.[719]

While McGavran travelled, Mary maintained the home front, looking after her family responsibilities, managing the UCMS guest home, sending manuscripts of books and articles to publishers, writing letters, and even speaking in local churches on a regular basis. Without a spirit of complaint she wrote, "I find I have more time in the office now than when you were home . . . All sorts of things you do when you were home now need my attention."[720] She maintained this workload in spite of having undergone major surgery only eight weeks before.

Mary was an incredible asset to McGavran in yet another way; her winsome disposition and charming personality opened many doors of opportunity for them. McGavran recognized this when he wrote to Mary regarding her service as a hostess at Crystal Lake: "Accepting the position of hostess, you would wow them and charm them, and the contact would be useful to us as a family."[721]

While McGavran was on his Asian tour of 1956, the mission's house on the edge of the Divinity School campus in New Haven was to be demolished. However Mary suggested to Dale Fiers that the mission buy a mansion for sale on a half acre of land, about a block away, which would make the Disciples Mission house secure in the future. Dale Fiers gladly agreed and Mary almost single-handedly negotiated the purchase of the building, managed all the affairs with the mission executive, and fundraised considerably for this home. During the period of September 1957–January 1961, the McGavrans had developed a nomadic lifestyle as they shifted from college to college. This, along with the nagging doubt about whether they should return to India, left them feeling depressed and insecure at times. During one of those times in the summer of 1958 that Don wrote the following to Mary:

> Here at 60—no home, jaunting around in a trailer, greatly respected yes—as an employee, a somewhat troublesome employee! But still no home, and you loading trailers and shifting from house to house. That you accept it with a cheerful gallant spirit and take it in your stride and wait patiently for a turn of the tide or for this driven husband of yours to find haven (or heaven) for all this I am most grateful and humbly thankful. You are a wonderful woman. I never cease to marvel at you.[722]

Although Mary sometimes had reason to feel a trifle exploited and controlled by her husband's vision and mission in life, she was never known to express resentment or become impatient with her lot in life.

---

719 Mary McGavran, letter to Donald McGavran, March 5, 1956.
720 Mary McGavran, letter to Donald McGavran, Jan. 23, 1956.
721 Donald McGavran, letter to Mary, April 2, 1956.
722 Donald McGavran, letter to Mary, June 14, 1958.

QUOTES FROM HELEN McGAVRAN'S LETTERS

In mid-December, 1960, Don and Mary McGavran once more drove back to Eugene. Awaiting them at the Fox Hollow house was a letter from Helen McGavran, Don's mother. She wrote:

> Your letter, received yesterday which tells of the very full program you have for the "two weeks ahead"—is very good news . . . and we can quite understand how you will have time for nothing else and we rejoice with you . . . we suppose that you will not be able to spend a day next week in coming up to see us. And as my contribution to the work for The Kingdom, I give up that pleasure putting all personal feeling into the background, yes happy if I can have a share.[723]

Also Grace McGavran, Donald's sister, who had invested $6,000 of her own money in the Fox Hollow property, added a note to her mother's letter stating: "We'll be thinking of you . . . tramping the acres. Take me along in spirit."[724]

In a note appended to the letter, Helen McGavran enclosed the following anonymous poem, which she had found in a magazine.

> Whether you will or not you are a king.
> For you are one of the time-sifted few
> That leave the world when they are gone,
> Not the same place it was. Mark what you leave.[725]

One year later, Helen penned in her almost weekly letter to Don and Mary, an assessment of Donald McGavran's achievements, from a mother's perspective, for his sixty-fourth birthday.

> A time surely for celebration! For those years certainly have been marvelously full of accomplishment. I have been going over, in my mind, these years, from your babyhood on and to me it seems almost unbelievable that one person could have succeeded in doing all that you have done. You have worked mightily in the forefront of the battle. And to think that you are still leading out, still leading others on, and that you are enabled still to do so, probably for many years ahead. I feel somewhat overwhelmed, and at the same time filled with thankfulness, and

---

723 Helen McGavran, letter from Vancouver, Washington to Donald McGavran, Dec. 22, 1960.
724 Ibid. (Note added to the letter by sister, Grace.)
725 Ibid.

with the highest hopes that you will continue to overcome difficulties even to the gaining of strength and wisdom as you forge on, as I know you will.[726]

SUMMARY

Helen McGavran's assessment seems a fitting summation of this brief section of his life. Indeed, McGavran did attain the status as internationally recognized missionary statesman and the foremost authority on the subject of church growth during the short period between 1957 to 1960. The principles formulated in the context of India now took on worldwide application, and the stage was set for the fulfillment of his dream; the Church Growth Institute.

As a peripatetic professor he organized his ideas around church growth principles. His teaching material drew heavily upon the significant researches he had conducted and the case history series he had written.

During this entire period his conviction grew that a church growth institute had to be established, and he pursued this goal with single-minded determination. Opposition to such an institute arose from those he thought would be the main source of encouragement and revenue. UCMS leadership respected him as an individual but found his principles to be a severe irritant since they conflicted with their general policy and direction.

The publication of his book, *How Churches Grow*, did much to paint a new public image for McGavran. He was no longer viewed as merely the "people movement advocate." Church growth was perceived as a comprehensive system for analyzing the life of the church.

Moving from campus to campus over a period of four years enabled McGavran to sense the spiritual drift in the US. He was troubled by the growing popularity of Universalism and the loss of conviction of the uniqueness of Christ. He was certain that the principles of church growth would generate spiritual dynamic and recapture the missionary spirit of the early decades of the century.

McGavran's step of faith in launching the Institute of Church Growth in the face of many uncertainties demonstrated his burning conviction that God was calling him to a creatively new dimension of ministry.

---

726   Helen McGavran, letter to Donald McGavran, Dec. 12, 1961.

CHAPTER SEVEN

THE WORLDWIDE CHURCH GROWTH MOVEMENT TAKES SHAPE

1961–65

The beginnings of the Institute of Church Growth at Eugene, Oregon produced some profound changes in McGavran's life. The previous seven years, 1954–60, may be characterized as a period of quest, although full of research, new insights, writings, and teaching. As described in the last two chapters, McGavran was driven by the deep conviction that his insights could change the course of mission history. He knew his church growth principles were the key that would give new direction and dynamic to many missionaries and missions around the world. But he needed a forum by which a paradigm shift could be effected.

The move to Fox Hollow farm on the outskirts of Eugene, apart from Council Rock, the summer retreat, filled the McGavrans with a measure of contentment. It was the first place they could call their own, apart from the summer retreat in Landour, India. The overgrown farm reminded them much of the jungles of India. The progressive development of the Institute of Church Growth also brought a degree of satisfaction.

TIES SEVERED WITH UCMS

The first major change for the McGavrans came in 1961. Donald, at the age of sixty-four, with only four years before retirement and thirty-eight years of service behind him, severed ties with UCMS. The decision appeared foolish and irresponsible; it meant loss of a pension and the support and backing of the mission. He was fully convinced that church growth principles would dramatically revitalize missionary ministries. He longed for UCMS to receive the full benefit of the movement, as well as due recognition for the part it had played in the development of the ideas. For that reason he requested that UCMS consider funding the ICG. McGavran's salary was assured by NCCE through 1965. However, he earnestly desired a continued relationship with UCMS.[727]

---

727 Donald McGavran, letter from Eugene, Oregon to Howard Cole, board member of UCMS, Yakima, Washington, (obtained from USCWM archives), March 2, 1961.

The crux of the matter pivoted on two different understandings of the situation. McGavran saw himself as director of an ecumenical institution which was more directly tied to the mission than it was to the college in which it was located. But the UCMS saw the situation differently since it had a policy that it would not contribute faculty to any of the denominational colleges and seminaries. After several appeals, both direct and indirect, the matter was dropped but the wound of separation from UCMS remained for years to follow.

Another decided change in this period of McGavran's life was in the arena of theological camps. His church growth principles were evangelical in zeal and orientation. Meanwhile, the prevailing theological mood in the Conciliar Movement was liberal, with focus being given to issues of church unity and social justice. McGavran found himself being catapulted solidly into the evangelical camp. At the same time his lifelong ties and friendships with those of the Conciliar Movement were being tried and tested. They regarded his ideas as only one small part of the mission program. They tolerated his ideas but felt that his insistent emphasis on church multiplication was somewhat extreme.[728]

FACTORS BEHIND LOCATING THE INSTITUTE OF CHURCH GROWTH AT EUGENE, OREGON

In retrospect, the decision to locate the Institute of Church Growth at Eugene in 1961 was a result of divine providence, but during the planning stages of 1959–60, it certainly did not appear as the most strategic place for the institute.

Ross Griffeth, the president of NCC, was a man of kindred spirit to McGavran. He had boundless energy and an expansive vision. The two shared spiritual and theological convictions. Thus Griffeth recognized the genius of McGavran's ideas. In an interview he described him as "The Apostle Paul of the twentieth century."[729] Griffeth was prepared to back McGavran financially and administratively, using his office as president, the college raised money for ICG. McGavran described Griffeth's involvement with ICG as "a normal extension of his long standing concern for the evangelization of the world and the recruitment and enlisting of missionaries."[730]

Another vital factor for the ICG was its location directly opposite the University of Oregon. Griffeth worked out a reciprocal relationship with the Department of Anthropology in which the University would grant a PhD while honoring the work done in the Institute of Church Growth.[731] The influence of the Department of Anthropology of the University of Oregon, on the formation of the ICG's curriculum was extensive.

---

728 Donald McGavran, interview by Vern Middleton, May 17, 1986.
729 Donald McGavran, interview by Ross Griffeth, June 5, 1987.
730 Donald McGavran, letter to Addison J. Eastman, Missionary Personnel Program, New York, Nov. 22, 1960.
731 Donald McGavran, letter to Waskom Pickett, Glendale, California, March 7, 1961.

PROMOTIONAL BLITZ

Throughout the period from 1960–65, McGavran used correspondence to advertise the Institute. Hardly a letter left his desk without a paragraph or two about it. On the average McGavran wrote ten or twelve letters a day. A majority of these were to mission executives, missionary statesmen, and leaders of major institutions. He urged mission executives to send one or two of their best men for training in church growth. He also corresponded directly with numerous missionaries and invited them personally to come to the ICG. The offer of three $1,000 fellowships per year also made his invitation very attractive. In addition, he gave the venture wide publicity in magazines and news notes.[732]

Included in every letter was a printed advertisement which was entitled, "Response to the Question: Is this just another scheme for training missionaries?" The second section described the essence of the institute.

Does your scheme give concentrated training on what makes churches grow—stop growing? In each specific population to which a missionary goes? . . . The Institute of Church Growth has been assembling such information for years. We are competent in this one field. Case studies in church growth are our specialty. There is plenty we do not know yet, but we claim to know more about church growth than any other institution in the world. And teaching church growth is our sole concern. Narrow? Yes. Crucial? Yes. As narrow and as crucial as "making disciples of all nations."

Unless one takes Hocking's stand that the era of church planting is over, multiplying churches remains a chief end of mission. Not the chief, but a chief end of mission.

Specialized training which takes the increase of members with life and death seriousness becomes essential for some churchmen in each field. If the missionary is broadly trained in everything else, but knows only the American pattern of church growth . . . you send him out seriously handicapped in carrying out the Great Commission. Let us help remove this handicap for a few of your messengers for Christ.[733]

Several mission executives came to see this for themselves. This became a major embarrassment for McGavran in the fall of 1960. He was not even in Eugene. He was teaching at the Pacific School of Religion at Berkeley, California. He was also concerned over the lack of offices and classrooms. He sent an urgent letter to Griffeth requesting him

---

732 Donald McGavran, letter from Crystal Lake to Ross Griffeth, Eugene, Oregon, June 25, 1960.
733 A one-page advertisement produced in 1960, obtained from USCWM archives.

to at least "get a physical set up which will look respectable and be respectable."[734] Some mission leaders had to be headed off.

SLOW BEGINNINGS

Keith Hamilton was the first and only student of the ICG from January to June 1961. Pickett referred him to the ICG in late 1959. He was a Methodist superintendent working in the country of Bolivia. The correspondence with Hamilton was significant since McGavran was honing his own insights on church growth research. In a letter on June 27, 1960, he wrote: "If you are to do a significant research you will need—'To define it. To gather facts and materials on a wide front. To test various hypotheses you now hold or come to hold.'"[735]

McGavran proposed the following outline for the research:

I.   The present situation:
    a.   History of the growth of . . . churches in Bolivia
    b.   Sociological structure of the peoples
    c.   Statistical picture of the present churches
    d.   Thirty-year graph of growth for total Methodists
    e.   The organization as it affects growth
    f.   What factors have led Aymaras to become evangelical?
    g.   Individual and group accession
    h.   The mission philosophy . . . past forty years
    i.   The present pastorate or ministry.
II.   What factors have retarded . . . church growth?
III. What are the most effective ways of training nationals
IV.   Biblical content for a Lay Training Program.[736]

This outline was considerably modified by Hamilton, yet the main ideas were still clearly discernible. It is clear that McGavran greatly influenced a majority of the theses written under his supervision, with a few notable exceptions.

McGavran's letter on September 28 made a thorough critique of Hamilton's questionnaire warning that: "Research bogs down if it gathers too many facts which do not bear on the problem."[737]

This letter was over five pages in length and much of it had to do with principles to guide research in church growth. Later this material was reproduced in pamphlet form. In the midst of the detailed information, McGavran wrote the following:

734 Donald McGavran, letter from Berkeley, California to Griffeth, Eugene, Oregon, Nov. 16, 1960.
735 Donald McGavran, letter from Crystal Lake to Hamilton, La Paz, Bolivia, June 27, 1960.
736 Ibid.
737 Donald McGavran, letter from Berkeley, California to Keith Hamilton, Bolivia, Sept. 28, 1960.

My experience has been that as I live with a burning question, "What causes churches to grow (or stand still)" and roll up much evidence bearing on the subject. I receive flashes of insight—sometimes from interviewees, sometimes in the middle of the night . . . You always should look through what people say, thru the reasons alleged, to the real probable causes.[738]

Thus, because of the correspondence and the orientation given, Hamilton's time at ICG, in reality began in June 1960. For seven full months prior to his arrival on campus he was engaged in directed research. To have the privilege of a one-on-one relationship with McGavran was a rare and unique opportunity.

As of June 1960, McGavran's hope for the first session of ICG was that there would be three research fellows and a dozen students enrolled. Yet there is no evidence in his correspondence that he was discouraged or disappointed when only Hamilton was enrolled for the first semester. He had anticipated the difficulty for he wrote:

It is going to be difficult to get Research Fellows for the first session of the Institute, because they must be chosen, their research defined, their facts gathered on the field, before they leave their fields for the US this fall.[739]

McGavran and Hamilton assembled for the first sessions, the professor at one end of a long oak table and the student at the other.[740] The lectures given to Hamilton were his seminal ideas later enlarged and published as *Understanding Church Growth*. McGavran felt that during the six-month period with Hamilton he learned more than the student, especially as it related to an understanding of church growth in Latin America and in particular the seventy-two tribes living in the high Andes mountains.[741]

McGavran was pleased with Hamilton's work and in a letter to Tippett described the research as being: "quite impressive . . . It throws a flood of light on church growth in Peru, Ecuador and Bolivia and will be read around the world."[742] When the manuscript was ready, McGavran arranged for it to be published in Lucknow, India.

ALAN R. TIPPETT DISCOVERED

McGavran had always been a promoter of others. He had a way of sensing talent and ability. Men and women who owe a debt of gratitude to McGavran for the part he played in launching them into a significant ministry number into the hundreds. One person whom

---

738 Ibid.
739 Donald McGavran, letter from Crystal Lake to Ross Griffeth, Eugene, Oregon, June 24, 1960.
740 Works, "The Church Growth Movement to 1965," 192.
741 Donald McGavran, interview by Vern Middleton, May 12, 1988.
742 Donald McGavran, letter from Eugene, Oregon to Alan Tippett, Melbourne, July 29, 1961.

McGavran moved from a micro to a macro sphere of influence was Alan R. Tippett. His missionary career had been outstanding in the Fiji Islands and he authored numerous articles, yet he was virtually unknown outside of the South Pacific.

McGavran initiated correspondence with Tippett in November 1960. Tippett was deeply moved by the incident and recognized the timing as being of the Spirit. He promptly responded with a three-page letter in which he poured out his heart. Tippett described his life as being at a crossroads: "My term of service in Fiji is coming to a close. The factors responsible are things which I cannot control . . . I feel strongly led to direct myself towards the training of missionaries. I am . . . 49 years of age, and now looking for a new field of service."[743]

Throughout the letter Tippett detailed his experience, his research, and his convictions. Then he asked the following:

> Is there anything in your institution or its program which might help me on the way of my call, or where I could serve you in any capacity and engage in research at the same time? . . . I imagine you know well what it is like to stand at the cross-roads after many years in a mission field and wonder which road now has to be followed. I have written because clearly I find myself so whole-heartedly in support of your contentions for the future of the Christian mission.[744]

The two carried on extensive correspondence throughout all of 1961. McGavran was convinced that Tippett was a creative thinker and would make a powerful contribution to the Church Growth movement. He wrote Pickett:

> Alan Tippett is a rare missionary. He has not only put in twenty years at the front but has discernment. He not only wants a PhD but has the mind of a researcher. Such men are not common. When they turn up they should be conserved. The missionary movement needs men who, while deeply concerned about the evangelization of the world, are able to pierce the veil of common-place. Original thinkers are pearls of great price.[745]

Tippett's second letter to McGavran cast considerable light on the issue of "discipling" and "perfecting." He was not too anxious to commit himself to ICG if the only concern was to be on the discipling phase of church growth since the Fijian people were all nominal Christians. Tippett identified several aspects of the perfecting problem in the Fiji Islands:

---

743 Alan Tippett, letter from Nausori, Fiji to Donald McGavran, Eugene, Oregon, Dec. 27, 1960.
744 Ibid.
745 Donald McGavran, letter from Eugene, Oregon to Alan Pickett, Glendale, California, March 7, 1961.

A town Fijian who lapses, falls into materialism; a village Fijian lapses into animism
... The former is a new experience, the latter backsliding, which shows that traces
of the old religion may survive several generations ... Closely allied to animism
and its magical associations is the Nativistic Movement ... Its causes and character
leave much for research.[746]

By return mail McGavran sent application forms and promised to explore with the
University of Oregon the possibility that Tippett might complete a PhD in anthropology.
As for the thesis proposal related to perfecting, McGavran was somewhat cool. He replied:

I doubt whether it would be acceptable to say, "Here is an Island population
of 400,000 Fijians—all nominal Christians, whose growth in Christ is sorely
hampered by residual animism and nativism. Let us see how." In general the
Institute confines itself to studies in growth in membership, in "souls added
to the Lord." But of course, perfecting and discipling are always intertwined.[747]

Tippett's response concerning the possibility of PhD studies was positive but restrained:
"A PhD would help a lot. However I am at a crossroads and I'm looking for the will of God
more than a PhD. If the two are on the same road I shall be very pleased."[748]

Included with the letter was a proposition which focused on the "power encounter"
dimension of Tippett's thinking. Both McGavran and Tippett were interested in ways to
bring the migrant Indian population of Fiji to Christ. Tippett expressed, "This situation
calls for a direct attack of the dynamic of Christ Himself ... The Asiatic peasant in Fiji is
basically animistic or polydaemonistic ... My conviction then is that instead of trying to
promote Church Growth among the Indians from the institutional level ... more effective
effort might be made ... from the peasant level."[749]

McGavran wrote Tippett: "We would like you to get your PhD out of the venture.
We want to get men with a dynamic church growth point of view out into the teaching of
missions in the seminaries around the world—and that means men with PhDs. So while
our funds and our program at the institute are limited ... our ambitions extend somewhat
further."[750] Because of his belief in Tippett, McGavran arranged free housing for him and
negotiated admission for Tippett to the PhD program at the University of Oregon.

Tippett developed great skill in archival research. Enroute to the US for his studies, he
seized every opportunity to get into a library and sift the archives for some hidden gold.
He spent five days at the Mitchell Library in Sydney. He complained about the volumes

---

746 Alan Tippett, letter from Nausori, Fiji to Donald McGavran, Eugene, Oregon, Jan. 16, 1961.
747 Donald McGavran, letter from Eugene, Oregon, to Alan Tippett, Fiji, Jan. 22, 1961.
748 Alan Tippett, letter from Fiji to Donald McGavran, Feb. 4, 1961.
749 Ibid.
750 Donald McGavran, letter from Eugene,Oregon, to Alan Tippett, Fiji, March 7, 1961.

written on administrative matters and the lack of material relating to actual church growth. In Auckland, New Zealand, he studied the archives to ascertain the cause of church growth and its stoppage in the early missionary enterprise in that country. He also managed to work in several significant interviews. By the time he arrived in the US on December 26, 1961, he had, while enroute, worked out in tabular form "common points and variants of Polynesian and Melanesian religion."[751]

Tippett was appointed as teaching fellow in June 1962 and began to teach regularly in the Institute. In the summer of 1962, Tippett began taking McGavran's place at church growth seminars. He not only articulated church growth principles, but also brought fresh vigor and credibility to the movement through the application of his anthropological insights and his winsome Australian accent. Although Tippett was still classified as a student in 1963, McGavran insisted that he have a place on the agenda at the Iberville Conference of the WCC. Hence, Tippett became an invaluable member of the church growth team in spite of the protestations of Victor Hayward, the organizer.

Tippett was invited to collaborate in a study series planned by the WCC. His task was to focus on the Solomon Islands.[752] Thus when he completed his PhD in June 1964 he immediately departed to undertake the project. In the monthly circular of June 12, 1964 McGavran announced the following: "Rev. Alan R. Tippett for many years principal of the Methodist Seminary in Fiji and recently Teaching Fellow at the Institute of Church Growth, has just received his PhD. He will be away for some months doing a study for the WCC on the Solomon Islands Church. He will return to ICG in 1965 as full professor."[753]

In November of 1964 Tippett turned down an extraordinary offer in order to rejoin McGavran at ICG. He wrote McGavran:

> I received an invitation to be the first Principal (President) of the new Central Theological College of the Pacific with a free hand in planning and inauguration, with Anthropology and Church History as my teaching area . . . this came as a surprise . . . I thought you would be interested to know I had this offer. I wrote and told them I had committed myself otherwise. Had the offer come before I intimated to you that I would come back to the ICG it would have been difficult to explain my action in Australia. However, I feel quite convinced that it is of the Lord that I join you again.[754]

Although the future of the ICG from June 1964 to June 1965 was very tenuous, McGavran's understanding was that should the Institute survive, Tippett would definitely

---

751   Alan Tippett, letter aboard H. M. S. Orsova, mailed from Fiji to Donald McGavran, Eugene, Oregon, Dec. 12, 1961.

752   Victor Hayward, letter from London to Donald McGavran, Eugene, Oregon, June 13, 1962.

753   McGavran's monthly newsletter to All Executives, Mission Boards, June 12, 1964.

754   Alan Tippett, letter from Fouia Village, Tai Lagoon, Malaita, British Solomon Islands to Donald McGavran, Eugene, Oregon, Nov. 13, 1964.

be a faculty member. However the future of the Institute looked very bleak in the light of developments at Northwest because of the retirement of Griffeth. McGavran sent a strongly worded letter to Kenneth Johnston, chair of the Northwest Christian College Board, presenting the dilemma he was in. He stated:

> When Dr. Tippett arrives and we get 20 men enrolled here we are going to need the following minimum space in Northwest Christian College Library . . . It would be easy for me, at my age, with my home south of Eugene to retire on a rising tide of effectiveness . . . But I cannot bring myself to believe that . . . this is my duty. Besides, it would be grossly unfair to Dr. Tippett, who has refused an invitation to become principal of the full-fledged, ecumenical theological seminary in the South Pacific, because he had promised to come to Northwest Christian College's staff.[755]

In a letter to the American Consul in Melbourne, Griffeth stated that Tippett was "under contract to teach at the Institute of Church Growth."[756] However, even though the plans for Tippett's return were definite, ICG was at a crisis state in its relationship with NCC. Griffeth hoped to raise the necessary funds for salaries, but both he and McGavran knew that the task was herculean. It must be understood that Tippett's arrangements to return to Northwest were verbal. His year of research represented more than a sabbatical; it was in effect a break in relationships. However when McGavran was in negotiation with Hubbard over the ICG move to Fuller, Tippett was the number one item on the agenda. Hubbard agreed that he should be invited to become a faculty member and to commence his salary as of September 1, 1965.[757] Tippett ably served the School of World Mission until his retirement.

IBERVILLE MEETING AND THE INTERNATIONAL MISSIONARY COUNCIL

One of the most surprising dimensions of McGavran's ministry during the period from 1961 to 1965 was the extent of his involvement with the inner circle of the World Council of Churches. Men of such stature as Hayward, Newbigin, Stowe, and Max Warren read his books, articles, and letters with intense interest. They demonstrated Christian grace and statesman-like attitudes when they disagreed. Up until late 1964, the Institute of Church

---

755 Donald McGavran, letter to Rev. Kenneth Johnston, President, Board of Trustees of NCC, Portland, April 28, 1965.

756 Ross Griffeth, letter from Eugene, Oregon, to American Consul, Melbourne, Victoria, Australia, March 9, 1965.

757 McGavran Memo following conference with David Hubbard and Ross Griffeth regarding negotiations about the School of World Mission at Fuller Theological Seminary, May 29, 1965.

Growth had far more potential of becoming identified with the Conciliar Movement than the evangelical camp.

McGavran spent the morning of December 8, 1960 with Bishop Lesslie Newbigin at the Pacific School of Religion, in Berkeley, California. In the course of their conversation, Newbigin recommended that all the research manuscripts produced by ICG be sent to Victor Hayward. He also said that the IMC department of Research in Church Growth would list the ICG researches in their publications. One year after their encounter Newbigin wrote: "I can assure you that we on the IMC staff follow your writings carefully, and I think you will find our thinking is not a little influenced by it."[758]

McGavran maintained correspondence with leaders of the International Missionary Council, including Victor Hayward, secretary of the department of research. As early as 1960, discussions were going on "regarding church growth research on a world scale." Hayward expressed a desire for the newly appointed Commission on World Mission and Evangelism to pursue issues raised by McGavran and in fact assured McGavran that his ideas would be carefully considered for future work. The IMC had been engaged for some time in a series of research projects which were broadly church growth oriented. McGavran took exception to their breadth of focus. Hence in the same letter Hayward expressed a difference of opinion with McGavran's insistence that "numerical expansion is the heart of the subject. Yet Hayward gave McGavran the following commendations regarding the manuscript for "Church Growth in Jamaica."

> With the main line of the argument I find myself in whole hearted agreement . . . fresh and very helpful . . . deserves serious heed . . . very readable mss . . . relevant for the general strategy of missionary work in many other countries . . . In my capacity as Research Secretary I commend this book warmly.[759]

Hayward and his staff also took the view that since ICG under McGavran's leadership was doing an excellent job on quantitative growth that they should not duplicate efforts. He wrote:

> Our own series of "Younger Church Studies" has a close link with your particular concern, but as you recognize, we are concerned with Church Growth from every aspect . . . I think that our right policy will be to draw attention from time to time to the whole work of your institute, but to select for special notice and commendation those pieces of study which appear to us to be of outstanding value.[760]

---

758 Leslie Newbigin, letter from Edinburgh House, London to Donald McGavran at Eugene, Oregon, (obtained from WCC archives, Geneva), Jan. 20, 1961.

759 Victor Hayward, letter from the International Missionary Council (IMC), London to Donald McGavran, Bethany West Virginia, Feb. 8, 1960.

760 Victor Hayward, letter from IMC, London to Donald McGavran, Eugene, Oregon, Jan. 2, 1961.

As was McGavran's custom, after completing a manuscript he would distribute between twenty to thirty copies to mission executives and statesmen. He did this with *How Churches Grow*. The response from Hayward, Bishop Hollis, Canon Warren, and others was very favourable. The IMC even wanted to take chapter nineteen out of the book and publish it separately. Bishop Hollis wrote:

> I think he [McGavran] assumes that a foreign Mission Board can know what is good for an Asian or African country in a kind of paternalism which is obsolete. Yet it is essential that we all face the problem that vested interests have in a great measure immobilized the Missionary efforts of the Churches ... I'd very happily try to write something which might lead people to do the kind of thinking that he asks for and read his book first.[761]

After the more or less favourable comment, Hollis listed eight objections to the chapter:

1. It is written from the paternalistic point of view.
2. A distinction runs throughout the book between what used to be called the Mission field and the Churches of Europe and North America and this obscures the real issues.
3. "Winnable multitudes" belong to the mythology of missionary magazines.
4. "Large scale attempt at conversion" would provoke "violent opposition and governmental interference."
5. That the most effective witness can be given by living and working alongside of non-Christian fellow citizens rather than by aggressive evangelism.
6. That a picture of schools and hospitals run by Christians as the unrestricted concern of a purely Christian management is Dr. McGavran's idea of what obtains and is already out of date.
7. That Christian educators and doctors should not openly and unashamedly urge their patients, pupils, and others to accept Jesus Christ as Savior.
8. That teaching branch Sunday Schools, attending cottage prayer meetings, writing tracts commending Christ, preaching in public etc. are pious activities too narrow to be properly termed witness which should be understood as the "total Christ likeness of life."[762]

---

761 Bishop Michael Hollis, letter from Sheffield to Victor Hayward, London, (obtained from WCC archives, London), Oct. 25, 1961.

762 Bishop Micahel Hollis, letter from Sheffield to Victor Hayward, London, comments quoted by McGavran in his response of Jan. 24, 1962 in a letter to Hayward.

McGavran declared, "If I were before a magistrate, in all honesty I would simply plead 'not guilty to the whole lot.'"[763] Hayward found himself in the crossfire between Hollis and McGavran and cancelled the idea of printing chapter nineteen. However chapter nineteen of *How Churches Grow* was reprinted along with the comments made by Hollis. These were circulated by DWME to responsible people to gain their reaction.

In another letter Hayward talked about the upcoming conference planned to be held at Iberville, Quebec, which would provide a forum to debate church growth ideas with McGavran. He wrote, "What we have in mind is to bring together you and your colleagues on the one hand, and people like Bishop Hollis and us tough guys on CWME staff who agree with your main thesis . . . but have many serious reservations and difficulties about the kind of statements you make."[764]

Hollis also stated that he thought McGavran was moving into the right-wing theological camp. To which McGavran responded: "My consciousness is of writing from . . . a middle of the road theology, inclusive ecclesiology, and entirely dedicated to the main purpose of Christian Missions . . . it surprises me that what I write raises "many serious reservations and difficulties."[765]

Meanwhile, at the WCC Assembly in New Delhi in 1961, Hayward was able to raise the issue of church growth and expansion. The full Assembly voted positively on the motion that an exploratory consultation should be held, which "would make possible an exchange of findings and view of methodology between persons engaged on research into factors favoring or retarding church expansion, in terms of numerical growth."[766] When Hayward communicated this to McGavran he wrote, "We are thinking of a consultation of ten or a dozen people . . . Would you like to suggest two or three . . . names?"[767]

With this proposal in hand, McGavran took the concept to the missionary researchers of the ICG and requested their input as to the agenda items. They suggested the following topics to be treated at the conference:

1. Issues arising in rapidly growing churches.
2. Issues arising in slow growing churches in responsive populations.
3. Administrative, policy, and priority issues arising in many churches, illustrated pictorially.
4. Issues arising because of the vacuum in theological education in regard to church growth.
5. Describing what is at present being done throughout the world in research in factors favouring or retarding church expansion.

---

763 Donald McGavran, letter from Eugene, Oregon to Bishop Hollis, Sheffield, March 20,1962.
764 Victor Hayward, letter from London to Donald McGavran, Eugene, Oregon, Feb. 26, 1962.
765 Donald McGavran, letter from Eugene, Oregon to Victor Hayward, London, March 3, 1962.
766 A resolution proposed by the Research Committee of the IMC, and passed by the Assembly at New Delhi, Nov. 18–Dec. 6, 1961.
767 Victor Hayward, letter from London, England to Donald McGavran, Eugene, Oregon, Dec. 14, 1961.

6. Describing a broad-based methodology of church growth research . . . The consultation should see four modes of discovery, measurement and evaluation of church growth—statistical, historical, dynamic, and theological.
7. The issues in regard to the economics of church growth.
8. The biblical grounds for investigating the sheer physical expansion of churches . . . as a chief end of Christian mission.
9. How to pull church growth information out of denominational and geographical pockets? How to publish it?[768]

McGavran sent in an agenda of his own. It was as follows:

a. The case for research into church expansion.
b. What are the major problems in church growth.
c. Where should researches be carried out first.
d. Methodology of research in church growth.
e. How to secure men from all Branches of the churches of Christ who have prestige and position enough to communicate their findings to their fellows.
f. How to train 100 men . . . who in key seminaries . . . will teach the whole complex and enormously important subject of how God is increasing His Churches.
g. Publications and dissemination of resources.
h. Establishment of research and training centers.[769]

Of the two agendas Hayward preferred the latter. However these statements forced him to define the purpose of the projected consultation more carefully.

The purpose we have in mind is a more stimulating, difficult and exciting one than that indicated by the agenda you sent me. A conference like that could be arranged by you and your colleagues at any time! . . . We believe that if we could make a serious effort to hammer out an agreement together on the main relevant issues over which we disagree, it would be to our mutual benefit.[770]

Hollis also submitted a five-point agenda, a contrast to the other two.

1. The necessity of a complete evaluation, so far as it is possible, in terms both of individuals brought into the Christian church and of individuals and groups alienated by what seem to them to be unfair methods and the use

---

768 Donald McGavran, letter to Victor Hayward, London, Feb. 2, 1962.
769 Ibid.
770 Victor Hayward, letter from London to Donald McGavran, Eugene, Oregon, Feb. 26, 1962.

of pressure on immature minds . . . There have been some most unhappy relapses by people whose conversion was brought about by what they came to think unfair methods.

2. The way in which we can preserve the immeasurable importance of actually bringing men and women to be Christians and yet, in the world of Asia today, give to what is a real part of Christian service, educational, medical, social . . . without demanding any justification in terms of converts. We just must escape from the bait theory.

3. The importance of not holding on to Christian institutions when they are inescapably rendering less and less well equipped service to an ever smaller proportion of those dealt with . . .

4. The question of wholly or almost wholly unresponsive areas. Are we meant to use our efforts and resources where there is no result or should we switch them?

5. The whole problem of the degree to which work ought to be done by the church which can only be done if the church accepts large government funds. Many in S. India think that the enthusiasm for keeping on Christian schools and colleges has little to do with Christianity but much to do with prestige . . . and with opportunities for employment for Christians.[771]

Hayward further clarified the purpose of the consultation to McGavran saying it was "to iron out differences" and "to discover together a way of presenting your main thesis which would be more convincing, because evocative of fewer queries and reservations."[772] Then he described the desired outcome: "What we would like is to establish a common basis, so that we may on the one hand, give better support to your programmes, and on the other hand feed the findings of your studies into the consultations we are arranging . . . in various parts of the world designed . . . Joint Action for Mission.'"[773]

But McGavran believed the spirit of the conciliar leaders was increasingly pessimistic. He wrote: "It is this pessimism which basically leads today's theologians to cast Christian evangelism in the role of 'witness.' Crisis theology speaks out of . . . such profound defeat that the best it can do is make the Christian 'an obedient witness.' It cannot imagine him as proclaiming Christ and persuading men to become His disciples."[774]

In the same letter he described "crisis theology" as a product of recent European history. He identified the essence of this stance as "mission is obedient witness." He lamented the fact that this philosophy of mission even penetrated local churches, as reflected in the fact that at a mission conference he attended the theme was, "So send I you to labour unrewarded."

771 Bishop Michael Hollis, letter from Sheffield to Victor Hayward, London, Feb. 21, 1962.
772 Victor Hayward, London to Donald McGavran, Eugene, Oregon, April 9, 1962.
773 Ibid.
774 Donald McGavran, letter from Eugene, Oregon to Victor Hayward, London, April 12, 1962.

Then he packed a punch by declaring: "We are not sent to labour unrewarded but to find lost sheep and pack the banquet hall." This he announced is "harvest theology." He concluded the letter with a quote from the Bulletin of the Division of Studies of the WCC: "At such a point in our journey, we have to ask where the Lord of history is leading the Church."[775] He closed with this succinct sentence: "We have indeed."

The correspondence became more cordial, but Hayward still chided McGavran: "I fear your picture of 100,000,000 animist Africans who can be led to radiant Christian discipleship in the next thirty years is politically out of date."[776] Hayward revealed his own pessimistic stance; now we know McGavran's figures were conservative.

The same letter revealed some of the attitudes of the principal players in the World Council of Churches. George Vicedom was quoted as saying: "That the heart of McGavran's thesis was right and that a church cannot grow in quality if it does not grow in numbers, since it is the church's missionary outreach that takes it back to its source."[777] Dr. Hwang expressed that "a false dichotomy was unfortunately developing between spiritual growth and numerical expansion."[778] He was greatly stimulated by both McGavran and Karl Barth on this subject and felt the need for further study.

The conference was set for July 31 to August 2, 1963. Hayward sent out several background papers by McGavran and also instructed the participants to read in advance *Bridges of God* and *How Churches Grow*. Michael Hollis was appointed to bring the devotional sessions during the three days and E. H. Johnson was appointed as chairman.

In a last-minute letter to McGavran, Hayward asked him not to be on the defensive and not to put them on the defensive. He expressed that he wanted the participants to be free to follow the leading of the Holy Spirit. He desired that the major ideas would arise from the dynamics of the group interaction.[779]

The correspondence leading up to Iberville became increasingly friendly and there appeared to be a genuine interest in the principles of church growth in the Conciliar Movement. McGavran was greatly impressed to the point of asking Hayward if he could spend an afternoon together with him after the conference. McGavran proposed that they "discuss the promise, potential and problems of a center for the continuous study of church growth on an inter-church, inter-continental basis, in close cooperation with the World Council of Churches and yet separate enough for Evangelical Conservatives to attend."[780] On the same day McGavran sent a letter to Pickett arranging to meet him in New York so that they could spend a day together planning a mutual strategy for the conference. He also bared his soul regarding the future of the ICG.

---

775 Donald McGavran, "Theological Reflections," *Bulletin of the Division of Studies,* 7, no. 2: 8.
776 Victor Hayward, letter from London to Donald McGavran, Eugene, Oregon, Jan. 16, 1963.
777 Ibid.
778 Ibid.
779 Victor Hayward, letter from London to Donald McGavran, Eugene, Oregon, July 8, 1963.
780 Donald McGavran, letter from Eugene, Oregon to Victor Hayward, London, July 6, 1963.

The future after I retire is completely a question mark. I have a conviction that Christian Mission needs a center devoted exclusively to the study of church growth . . . but unless we get bigger money and much firmer foundations the work of these five or six years will lapse back into the fog.[781]

The participants in the Iberville conference included both churchmen and mission leaders. Four were professors of mission, four national leaders within their respective countries, and four, including McGavran, were representatives of the church growth point of view. They included Waskom Pickett, Alan Tippett, and Louis King H. B. Porter, a professor at General Theological Seminary, New York, who became an ally of McGavran's point of view in the early sessions of the conference. Three were staff of the DWME. Denominationally, there was a broad spectrum of representation and participants came from ten different countries of origin.

McGavran led two of the seven sessions on "The Methodology of Church Growth" and "The Application of Research to Church Growth." The outlines for these sessions are of historical significance, hence portions are reproduced here.

The Methodology of Church Growth

1. Recognize that church growth has a complex methodology varying with each population.
2. Recognize that church growth must be *sought diligently*. It does not come automatically.
3. Recognize that the general population is a mosaic made up of homogeneous units—each differently responsive.
4. Recognize that trained but unpaid lay leaders are essential for church growth.
5. Recognize and use the social structures as a vehicle for reconciling the whole man to God.
6. Recognize and use multi-individual decision as a normal desirable way to plant churches.[782]

He elaborated these points with material coming from the Research Fellows at ICG. Then he turned to the participants and asked each of them to elaborate from their experience how they obtained church growth. There is no record of the silence that followed. The second topic was the application of the research.

---

781 Donald McGavran, letter from Eugene, Oregon to Alan Pickett, Glendale, California, July 6, 1963.
782 Donald McGavran, "The Methodology of Church Growth," lecture outline, Iberville.

Application of Research to Church Growth

    a.   Limit ourselves strictly to research in church growth.

    b.   Consider questions basic to any progress of research in church growth.

          1.   What are some aspects of persuading men to become Christ's disciples and responsible members of His Church and multiplying churches on which we want light?

          2.   How can we get churches and missions to set apart men and money for research in church growth?

          3.   How can we get reliable research done?

          4.   How can research findings be disseminated across the churches?[783]

Hayward became the principal participant and vigorously attacked church growth concepts for the better part of two days. But as the sessions progressed his polemics moderated because he found McGavran's face-to-face discussion to be in sharp contrast to his vigorous writing style. The evening of the second day he retired and produced a twelve-point document. The essence of this document is reproduced here. McGavran used it for the next fifteen years as a promotional piece and distributed it widely in his personal correspondence.

1. The Church's Mandate

The Church of Jesus Christ has been commanded by her Lord to proclaim the gospel to men and women in every human situation. Her mandate is nothing less than the making of all nations His disciples . . . The Church must therefore seek to be ever growing in numbers, as well as in the grace and knowledge of her Lord and Savior . . . in pursuance of God's desire that all men should be saved . . .

2. Her Sin is Introversion

The vast increase of the world's population today outpaces the growth of the Christian Church. In spite of this tremendous challenge, we have to confess that churches are often introverted and missions frequently unfruitful . . . Such introversion has its roots in the egocentricity if the natural man, still unchanged into the likeness of Christ's selfless care for others. Its lack of expectancy not only betrays weakness of faith, it is also evidence of a profound misunderstanding of the measure of God's redemptive purpose. For the Church is called into being not merely as a saved community but as a saving community . . . Thus a church without a dynamic missionary purpose belies its own true nature.

---

783 Donald McGavran, "Application of Research to Church Growth" (lecture outline, Iberville).

3. A Call to Renewal

Only constant reformation and renewal through the power of God's Spirit, can save the churches from self-centered piety . . . Why are the questions raised by the absence of church growth so seldom squarely faced? We appeal for self examination, in a spirit of penitence and hope.

4. Now is the Acceptable Time

There are many indications that there will be abundant opportunities for winning men and women to faith in Christ in the years immediately ahead.

5. Study Each Situation

In surveying the world missionary situation generalities are of little help. Each population presents its own distinctive problems regarding church growth and solutions from one area must not be naively projected, without examination, into another. Analytical techniques can help immensely towards recognition and understanding of the facts.

6. God Gives the Increase

We fully recognize that it is God who "gives the increase." It is the Holy Spirit who converts men to Christ, not we. But not only are a planting and watering committed to us, so also is reaping in the times of harvest which God gives. Often, however, when there has been a movement of the Spirit, churches have been slow to perceive it and fearful to cooperate.

7. A Discerning Strategy

Emphasis upon care for the times and places of special opportunity for church growth does not imply the abandoning of unfruitful fields. It does imply a waiting and watching for such movements among people, and an obedient readiness to deploy, in a properly ecumenical spirit and strategy, the resources of personnel and funds required for true cooperation with the Spirit's work.

8. Expectancy Creates Expectancy

We have to confess that we have often failed in both expectancy and obedience. One reason for this is that, though churches which are not themselves dynamically engaged in evangelism may send missionaries to other lands, such missionaries are liable to reproduce the same contentment with state church life. It is truly missionary churches which are most likely to plant missionary churches . . . Every Christian needs to be trained for missionary service, each according to his gifts and opportunities.

9. The Crucial Question

Is the church growing, or not; and if not why not? . . . Numerical expansion and quality of Christian life are not alternatives but correlatives, inasmuch as each is vitally related with the other . . . It has been shown that the spontaneous expansion of a church quickens its own spiritual life . . . a church which is truly growing in grace thereby grows in concern for its missionary outreach.

10. Past Mistakes

Experience has demonstrated that many missionary methods used in the past are wrong and these continue to be repeated and defended because they are not honestly examined in the light of their results . . . Although teaching, healing, and other ways of meeting basic human needs have been an integral and vital part of witness to God's Kingdom, yet an over-emphasis upon institutions has often retarded rather than forwarded the missionary cause . . . Much of what is being undertaken by missions, with foreign resources, would be immeasurably more effective as a witness to the gospel if spontaneously undertaken, according to their own means, by members of the local church.

11. Discipling and Nurturing are Two Stages

In situations where whole communities have been ready to turn to Christ, the mistake has often been made of implying that qualifications other than repentance and faith are required . . . The New Testament shows that discipling, the winning of an understanding allegiance to Christ comes first, and that this must be followed by careful nurture in personal faith and in personal Christian life. To demand evidence of Christian growth before a convert is brought into the fellowship of the church is a denial of the meaning of the gospel . . . What is required is far greater emphasis upon post-baptismal training in which help in making immediate and sustained witness to Christ is extremely important.

12. A Need for Research

At our Consultation here, we have considered many illustrations of factors which favour or retard church growth . . . These have left us more than ever convinced of the need for scientific research into many different matters, some related to sociology, anthropology, and similar disciplines, others related to such administration and structures, all to the strategy of the Church's mission . . . We welcome the pioneering work of the Institute of Church Growth in Eugene, Oregon, and desire to see similar centers established in time in Asia, Africa, and Latin America. Reliable information concerning areas of special need and opportunity as regards church growth ought to be constantly collated and circulated. We urge earnest consideration of these matters by the WCC Division of World Mission and Evangelism, and by such bodies as the East Asia Christian Conference and the All Africa Conference of Churches. The object of this is that churches and mission boards in every part of the world may be stimulated to give to study of questions of church growth the importance which belongs to a subject so essential for fulfillment of the Church's mission in the world.[784]

POST-IBERVILLE DEVELOPMENTS

By September the Iberville statement was printed and thirty copies were dispatched to McGavran. Hayward reported that the DWME committee had reviewed the statement and that the response was favourable.[785]

McGavran requested permission to use it in one of his monthly circular letters. He wrote, "I think it would do the conservative brethren good to see that the World Council of churches does have a warm direct positive concern for church growth—and is not tied exclusively to the intricacies of continental theology."[786]

Permission was gladly granted and Hayward even dispatched 150 additional copies with the request that McGavran continue to send the books he published on church growth to his office in London.

McGavran's September newsletter betrayed his hopes for a new day for church growth in the conciliar circles. "Mr. Tippett, my colleague here at ICG and I attended the Consultation on Church Growth called by the Division of Studies of the World Council of Churches at Montreal this summer. The consultation met for two and a half days and drafted a positive statement on church growth commending it to the churches and discussing some of the main issues connected with it . . . It evidences a rising interest in church growth."[787]

One aspect of the Iberville statement which particularly pleased McGavran was the proposal that "various lands of the younger Churches start ICGs and train the men who will run them at the ICG in Eugene."[788]

The October circular letter from ICG to the Boards included the Iberville Statement along with an overall evaluation of the consultation. McGavran wrote enthusiastically: "ICG has never sent you a more important document than the enclosed. You will rejoice in it."[789] He described some of the topics considered at the meeting:

1. Hesitations some Christians feel in seeking church growth.
2. Amazing opportunities for expansion facing mission in so many places.
3. Lack of faith and expectation which keeps churches from multiplying.

---

784   The Iberville Statement entitled, "The Growth of the Church," drawn up by a special Consultation convened by the WCC Department of Missionary Studies, Iberville, Quebec, July 31–Aug. 2, 1963.

785   Victor Hayward, letter from Rochester, New York to Donald McGavran, Eugene, Oregon, Sept. 9, 1963.

786   Donald McGavran, letter from Eugene, Oregon to Victor Hayward, Aug. 29, 1963.

787   The ICG Board circular letter, dispatched to 150 Mission Board executives and directors, Sept. 5, 1963.

788   Donald McGavran, letter from Eugene, Oregon to Gordon Robinson, a prospective student for ICG, Oct. 21, 1963.

789   Donald McGavran, ICG circular letter to all Executives of Mission Boards, Nov. 13, 1963.

4. Theological and biblical underpinning of church growth.
5. Wrong priorities and methods which keep some churches introverted and small despite the winnability of many sections of mankind.
7. Other aspects of the growth of churches and Christianization of large populations.[790]

He recalled the events of Iberville. His description hardly sounded like the battleground he had anticipated before the consultation: "Give and take in session after session, where men from different Branches of Christ's Church were concentrating on His saving purpose, produced the remarkable consensus of opinion on church growth, expressed in the attached statement."[791]

While at Iberville, McGavran encountered an unexpected source of resistance. Miss Gwenyth Hubble who was the assistant editor of the *International Review of Missions* and had been principal of Carey Hall in Selly Oak, England, took strong exception to a article concerning training patterns for missionaries. Her response, although cordial, was sharp and critical. She stated, "If I were still principal . . . this article would have put my back up very badly." She then goes on to state, "It makes statements which show a lack of knowledge of the kind of job we were doing."[792] She then utilized the rest of the letter to describe the kind of training missionary candidates received where she had served, including a healthy exposure to McGavran's books and articles.

McGavran's response was surprisingly restrained. He did not back down but restated his position. "I am maintaining that the training of missionaries so largely omits the principles and practices of church growth that missionaries go abroad poorly equipped to help churches grow."[793] He said that Western seminaries train missionary candidates to be perfectors not disciplers. He pointed out that proof of his position is not to be found in the curriculum of a given seminary "but whether those trained recognize church growth, welcome it, know how to increase it, and play an active part in transforming the mindset of western and national Christians among whom they work."[794]

He stressed that the mere provision of a given course in a seminary is not enough. The key is the purpose for which the course is being taught. Then he summarized the main point of contention. "It is not important at all that they get my point of view, but highly important that they get a deeply Christian point of view on the Church becoming a saving Body as well as a saved Body."[795]

In Hubble's reply she stated that she agreed with his position for the most part and then went on to discuss the high profile church growth issues were being given at the DFM

---

790 Ibid.
791 Ibid.
792 Gwenyth Hubble, letter from New York, to Donald McGavran, Eugene, Oregon, Oct. 2, 1963.
793 Donald McGavran, letter from Eugene, Oregon to Gwenyth Hubble, New York, Oct. 25, 1963.
794 Ibid.
795 Ibid.

executive level and at the Mexico consultation in 1963. She even shared with her department McGavran's request that DWME sponsor a professor of missions to the ICG to:

a. Learn all we can teach about the church growth processes.
b. Conduct a thorough survey of what church growth education now exists in missionary training institutions.
c. Find out the extent to which graduates of various missionary training institutions do in fact carry with them a realistic church growth potency.
d. Suggest ways in which training in church growth can be made more effective in missionary training institutions.[796]

But the *IRM* did not print the Iberville statement. Instead it was printed in the *Ecumenical Chronicle*. This seemed to surprise Hayward and came as a great disappointment to McGavran. Hubble was an associate editor of the *IRM*, while Newbigin was the editor. The reason remains a mystery since the statement rightly belonged in the *IRM*.

THE IMPLEMENTATION OF RECOMMENDATIONS FROM IBERVILLE

One source of profound encouragement for McGavran during the months immediately following Iberville was David Stowe, the executive director of the Division of Overseas Ministries of the National Council of Churches. Shortly after Iberville, they began an extended period of correspondence.

On October 1, 1963 Stowe wrote asking if he could meet McGavran in New York. He also asked for information about research and publications of the ICG. Thirdly he asked about "important points to which to give attention in this Division."[797] McGavran utilized it as a means of presenting his central vision of getting church leaders and missionaries from around the world trained in church growth principles.[798] He also presented the need for cooperative research in growing churches and suggested DFM choose fifteen fields where significant growth is occurring and sponsor leaders for a year of study as research fellows at ICG. Finally, McGavran presented the idea that DFM might "profitably take steps to make the ICG permanent."[799] Stowe was not dismayed by McGavran's bold requests. He actually pursued possible arrangements where DFM could either assist or assume full "organic relation" with ICG.[800]

---

796 Ibid., 3.
797 David M. Stowe, letter from Division of Foreign Missions, National Council of Churches of Christ, US, New York to Donald McGavran, Eugene, Oregon, Oct. 1, 1963. National Council of Churches Archives, New York
798 Donald McGavran, letter from Eugene, Oregon to David M. Stowe, New York, Oct. 31, 1963.
799 Ibid.
800 David Stowe, letter from DMF Headquarters, New York to McGavran, Eugene, Oregon, National Council of Churches Archives, Jan. 4, 1964.

On November 4, 1963, Stowe convened a meeting of fourteen delegates to discuss the issue of Church Growth as a Guide for Mission Policy. The following points emerged:

1. Church growth can be looked at from the standpoint of a guide and criterion for mission policy . . . and as a problem in research as to facts of church growth and effective methods.
2. Church growth as basis for policy might be stated in its "purest" form as follows: God's Holy Spirit in sovereign freedom prepares certain places at certain times for maximum receptivity of the gospel . . . Our response should be to cooperate with the action of God by concentrating missionary resources at this point while the fruitfulness continues.
    [The paper records that considerable dissent arose at this point.]
3. It was agreed, however, that church growth ought to be one important factor in determining mission policy, and it probably should receive higher priority than in most cases it now does.

Again, considerable diversity of opinion arose with one suggestion that "missions ought to be helping churches become effectively missionary, not working directly for church growth."

1. It was agreed that research into church growth facts and methods has very useful effects.
2. A fundamental problem is that of basic evangelistic motivation and zeal. There is a general uncertainty about what precise difference it makes to become a baptized Christian and church member . . . and for some this takes the edge off motivation for specially evangelistic and church building activity.[801]

In the two remaining points of the seven-point outline, the committee discussed other church growth thinkers and programs besides that of McGavran's. Bishop Moshi of Tanganyika concluded with three illustrations from his experience.

Four specific recommendations were made by the committee:

1. DFM Area Officers should think through and present a recommendation concerning 3 or 4 countries which appear to have critical church growth significance.
2. Boards should designate personnel and funds for cooperative research projects in church growth in those areas.

---

801 Memorandum of Discussion for the Committee on the topic, "Church Growth as a Guide for Mission Policy," Nov. 4, 1963, National Council of Churches, New York.

3. Personnel involved in such projects should have training at the Institute of Church Growth.

4. The whole matter should be watched with care for 5–10 years as a crucial experiment, expected to produce data for mission policy making and for missionary training, methods, programs.[802]

During the ensuing months of 1964, church growth was center stage in Stowe's department of the National Council of Churches. As executive secretary of the DFM, he wrote and published a pamphlet entitled, "A New Look at an Old Subject." McGavran heartily endorsed his recommendations and urged the executives of mission boards to "implement his bold creative thinking."[803]

On June 21, 1964, McGavran met Stowe in New York. The meeting was literally a series of conferences with various departments and executives of DFM which lasted for several hours. Although the discussions were cordial, McGavran came away somewhat downcast because he hoped they would underwrite the Institute of Church Growth and relocate it near New York. He admitted that such a proposal was in their "thinking but probably not in time to effect McGavran's plans."[804] Three issues greatly concerned McGavran; one was his age (sixty-six), with retirement just around the corner. Another was the lack of financial backing for the ICG. By 1964 the budgetary needs had risen to sixteen thousand dollars per year and this was almost entirely underwritten by Northwest Christian College. He was distressed that the Institute was almost entirely funded from gifts from his denomination yet a majority of the students at the Institute were from others. The third issue was the pattern of training that was emerging—most of the men came to the Institute for one quarter and their research was very limited. McGavran envisaged a graduate school that would produce church growth specialists with PhDs who had been systematically developed and could teach church growth both from a theoretical and practical point of view.[805]

Meanwhile as the researches continued to pour forth from the ICG and circulated in one form or another, criticism continued to mount from conciliar circles. Accusations were made that the "findings won't stand up, are not thorough and reliable, are not sophisticated enough, and do not take account of anthropological and sociological realities."[806]

McGavran's response was not defensive. He admitted that where criticisms arose from vested interests he simply ignored them, but when accusations were legitimate he heeded them.

---

802 Ibid., 2.

803 Church Growth monthly newsletter from Eugene to all Executives, Mission Boards, June 12, 1964.

804 Donald McGavran, letter from New York to his mother, wife and sister (Helen, Mary, and Grace), Vancouver, Washington, June 21, 1964.

805 Donald McGavran, letter from Eugene to Stowe, DFM Headquarters, New York, July 10, 1964.

806 Donald McGavran, letter from Eugene to Stowe, DFM Headquarters, New York, July 15, 1964.

Exact figures are hard to get . . . Facing this difficulty, the safest thing to do is to say nothing . . . ICG instead ignores safety, starts with the data it can get . . . By extreme care and repeated checking it arrives at a true and meaningful picture.

We believe our techniques, worked out over the years, make our reports more accurate as regards church growth than anything else available. No place else has the experience and technique for separating the true from the false . . .

We go on to claim ICG studies have more anthropological insight harnessed to the growth of the Church than anything else published.[807]

McGavran concluded the letter saying that, "where criticisms arose because of the ICG's lack of emphasis on brotherhood, perfecting and justice and an excessive stress on church growth. To that charge we happily plead guilty. We are doing just that, and intend to continue."[808]

On August 24, 1964, Stowe prepared a draft statement which was presented to the DFM Executive Board in September of that same year. The paper took a positive attitude toward the Church Growth Movement and showed deep evangelistic concern only four short years before Uppsala. Some of the more salient points of the three-page draft were:

a. In planning overseas programs, considerations of church growth should play an important part. Allocation of funds and of missionaries should be decided with a view to the probable effect in helping the church to witness more effectively and winning more persons to discipleship.

b. Building a corps of persons skilled in analyzing church growth situations and in developing effective methods of promoting church growth is a priority in contemporary mission these persons should be available for service as evangelistic missionaries, as teachers and trainers of other church leaders, as staff for mission agencies and in other capacities . . . We recommend that DFM member agencies develop a systematic procedure whereby each year some of their most capable missionaries, staff members or leaders in partner churches should be encouraged to enroll for one or two semesters of study at the Institute of Church Growth.

c. The Evangelism Committee of the Division of Overseas Ministries should carry the responsibility for cooperative consultation, promotion, and supervision of such a program of developing church growth specialists.[809]

---

807 Ibid.
808 Ibid.
809 David M. Stowe, draft presentation to the DFM Executive Board. Prepared Aug. 24, 1964 and presented for discussion, National Council of Churches archives, Sept. 25, 1964.

McGavran was encouraged and delighted by the above statement. As a result he wrote President Griffeth suggesting that Stowe give the fall lectures on church growth in 1965.[810] Of course events soon arose to change the circumstances. The Institute of Church Growth was transferred to Fuller Theological Seminary in the summer of 1965. Shortly after McGavran's arrival on that campus he raised the issue of Stowe addressing the School of World Mission in fall of 1967. The response from the faculty was generally negative. The thought of having a World Council of Churches man on Fuller campus at that juncture in history was unthinkable. However McGavran pressed his demands. In the end, Stowe gave the fall 1967 church growth lecture series entitled, "Ecumenicity and Evangelism," published in 1970 by Eerdmans under that same title.[811]

After Iberville, McGavran felt at liberty to engage in battle with the leadership of the Division of World Mission and Evangelism of the WCC. He wrote to W. A. Visser't Hooft concerning a statement made in his book *No Other Name*. He understood Visser't Hooft to suggest the church has completed her responsibility with proclamation: "The Church's very calling is to proclaim the Gospel to the ends of the earth. It cannot make any restrictions in this respect . . . All must hear the Gospel. A Christianity which should think of itself as one of many diverse contributions to the religious life of mankind is a Christianity that has lost its foundation in the New Testament."[812]

McGavran complained because he understood the implication to be that the number of those who believe as a result of the proclamation is immaterial. Then he gave the essence of the church growth position: "We at the Institute of Church Growth deny that the Christian's duty is complete in proclamation. We affirm that the very purpose of proclamation its expectation and intention, is that men believe, are baptised and become responsible members of Christ's Church."[813]

On January 21, 1964 Victor Hayward informed McGavran of the intention of the Division to implement one of the proposals made at Iberville: "At a DWME staff meeting yesterday, we decided that, at our annual staff conference next May, we should take up the question of implementing our intention to follow our little Iberville conference with some regional consultations designed for practical action."[814]

A few months later Hayward wrote that plans were underway for a Consultation on Church Growth in Western Africa.[815] Immediately McGavran drafted a letter with several strong suggestions for the consultation. First he drew attention to the researches already carried on at the ICG on western Africa by Grimley, Robinson, Johnson, and Wold.

---

810 Donald McGavran note to Griffeth, interdepartmental communications, Northwest Christian College, Oct. 10, 1964.

811 David M. Stowe, Ecumenicity and Evangelism (Grand Rapids: Eerdmans, 1970).

812 W. A. Visser 't Hooft, *No Other Name* (Philadelphia: The Westminster Press, 1963).

813 Donald McGavran, letter from Eugene to W. A. Visser't Hooft, at World Council of Churches, Geneva, Switzerland, Oct. 5, 1964.

814 Victor Hayward, letter from Geneva, Switzerland to Donald McGavran, Eugene, Oregon, Jan. 21, 1964.

815 Victor Hayward, letter from Geneva, Switzerland to Donald McGavran, Eugene, Oregon, April 17, 1964.

He recommended that all the delegates read those manuscripts as a firm basis for facts about the situation.[816] Second, he warned about the confusion that results when various kinds of reports are "mixed together in a glorious hash and served out in liberal portions, as descriptive of the Church in Africa."[817] Finally he proposed that subcommittees be formed, one to address small, static, introverted churches where large growth occurred years ago, another to explore those churches where growth is going on, still another to focus on those situations where there is little mission money but much growth, and another to concentrate on those situations where there is much mission money but few converts.

The greatest controversy McGavran had with conciliar leadership during this period was that with Johannes Hoekendijk. The article which sparked the argument, was "The Call to Evangelism" which Hoekendijk first published in the April 1950 issue of the *IRM*. He said:

> To put it bluntly: the call to evangelism is often little else than a call to restore "Christendom," the Corpus Christianum, as a solid, well-integrated complex, directed and dominated by the church. And the sense of urgency is often nothing but a nervous feeling of insecurity, with the established endangered; a flurried activity to save the remnants of a time now irrevocably past . . . In fact, the word "evangelize" often means a Biblical camouflage of what should rightly be called the reconquest of ecclesiastical influence. Hence this undue respect for statistics and this insatiable ecclesiastical hunger for ever more areas of life.[818]

McGavran had his students and research fellows interact with the material and then wrote the article, "Essential Evangelism—An Open Letter to Dr. Hoekendijk" which Hayward published as number two in the third series of Occasional Papers. Responses to McGavran's article were three years in process. In July of 1968 the *IRM* devoted the entire issue to church growth and included a reprinting of the entire text of the Iberville statement. Just two months before McGavran challenged the WCC in the *Church Growth Bulletin*, "Will Uppsala Betray The Two Billion?"[819] He provided an assessment of the situation in the epilogue of *The Conciliar-Evangelical Debate*:

> All told a remarkable concentration of fire was directed at the 1965 article which advocated church growth as the correct strategy of missions. The bombardment was timed to come out in the July issue of the *International Review of Missions*

---

816   John B. Grimley and Gordon E. Robinson, *Church Growth in Central and Southern Nigeria* (Grand Rapids: Eerdmans, 1966). See also Johnson, "Church Growth in the Central Belt of Nigeria," MS and Joseph Conrad Wold, *God's Impatience In Liberia* (Grand Rapids: Eerdmans, 1968).

817   Donald McGavran, letter from Eugene to Hayward, Geneva, (obtained from USCWM archives), Aug. 19, 1964.

818   Johannes C. Hoekendijk, "The Call to Evangelism," *International Review of Missions* 39 (April 1950): 162–175. See also Johannes Christiaan Hoekendijk, *The Church Inside Out* (Louisville, KY: Westminster Press), 1966.

819   Donald McGavran, "Special Uppsala Issue," *Church Growth Bulletin* 4, no. 5 (May 1968).

just before the Fourth Assembly and to warn any who might be tempted at Uppsala to plead for the Great Commission, eternal salvation and reconciling men to God or classical missions. They too, would be demolished. What Geneva advocated was the new shape of mission. Discipling the nations was anachronistic, triumphalistic, and unsuited to the modern world. Humanization was the goal ... The plan of action was clear. The World Council of Churches would use its great influence to change mission from conversion to social action, from discipling the nations to championing the oppressed, from persuading men to believe on Christ to persuading them to be more brotherly, whatever they believed.[820]

The arena in which the battle between the church growth point of view and that of the World Council of Churches played out was in two journals. The *Church Growth Bulletin* and to some extent the *International Review of Missions* carried the articles, open letters, and replies. The issues of Universalism, the definition of mission, the meaning of conversion, and the primacy of the church became so polarized that it produced a parting of the ways for the conciliar and Church Growth movements shortly before Uppsala. Between September 1964 and May 1968, the divergence of opinion was heightened as McGavran used the organ of the *Church Growth Bulletin* to publish statements received in personal correspondence from leaders of the Conciliar Movement. Hayward complained that some articles directed at him were printed in the *Bulletin* without his first having received a copy.[821] Several books have since been published which chronicle the development of the debate.[822]

CONSERVATIVE EVANGELICALS RALLY TO CHURCH GROWTH

Conservative evangelicals became increasingly influential in the life and thinking of McGavran between 1962 and 1965. While McGavran had been very much a part of the Conciliar Movement, his speaking engagements and involvements were steadily increasing among the EFMA-IFMA circle of missions. Several conservative evangelical leaders of denominational and interdenominational missions played a major role in this reorientation. These included Cal Guy of Southwestern Baptist Theological Seminary, Edwin E. Jacques of the Conservative Baptist Foreign Mission Society, Louis L. King of the Christian Missionary Alliance, Kenneth Strachan of the Latin American Mission, Melvin

820 Donald McGavran, Epilogue in *The Conciliar-Evangelical Debate: The Crucial Issues* 1964–1976 (Pasadena: William Carey Library, 1977). 389.

821 Hayward, letter from Geneva to Donald McGavran, Eugene, Oregon, June 17, 1965.

822 See the following books on the subject: Donald McGavran, ed., *The Eye of the Storm* (Waco: Word Books, 1972), Arthur Glasser and Donald McGavran, *Contemporary Theologies of Mission* (Grand Rapids: Baker Book House, 1983), and McGavran, *The Conciliar-Evangelical Debate*.

Hodges of the Assemblies of God and Norman L. Cummings of the Overseas Crusades who supported McGavran during those formative years of the Institute of Church Growth.

The first contact of these leaders came through McGavran's writings. Shortly after *How Churches Grow* was published, a review written by Cal Guy appeared in the October 1960 issue of the *Southwestern Journal of Theology*. It was most positive. McGavran's response was: "You have been most generous. I am a bit overwhelmed . . . I hesitate to think that I have wrought as well as you believe . . . At any rate the review is heart warming to me . . . You lift my hands. You bring courage to my heart."[823]

Immediately McGavran began to include many conservative evangelical mission executives in his monthly mailings. He requested names of likely missionary candidates who would profit from a semester or two at the ICG. Lists of such names were provided and several mission executives arranged for their missionaries to study at the ICG. Edwin Jacques gave a list of thirteen Conservative Baptist missionaries who would be on furlough in the near future.[824] Louis King assured McGavran that in the school year of 1962–63 the CMA would send five key men, most of them were field secretaries.[825] This was gratifying as a high percentage of those recommended by their mission executives studied at the ICG or the School of World Mission at Fuller Theological Seminary in the years that followed.

One of the most significant events which raised McGavran's image before the leadership of conservative evangelicals came in September 1962. He was invited to address the EFMA Mission Executives Retreat at Winona Lake. Edward Jacques wrote a letter of appreciation shortly after the event:

> I would find it difficult to express adequately my appreciation for the series of lectures presented on Church Growth. It was rather remarkable that although this is the heart of our mission enterprise, we seem to have developed peripheral matters so much more thoroughly than this. Several of us are following with keen interest the developing plans for having you address a hundred or more missionaries of several of our societies this coming June or September.[826]

Although the evangelical leaders were appreciative of McGavran's principles of church growth, they were disturbed by his terminology and ecumenical vocabulary. Because of this a few leaders even questioned his conversion experience. At that point, men like Jacques, King, and Cummings drew alongside of McGavran and encouraged him to express his

---

823 Donald McGavran, letter from Eugene to Cal Guy, Southwestern Baptist Theological Seminary, Fort Worth Texas, Jan. 16, 1962.

824 Edwin E. Jacques, foreign secretary, letter from Conservative Baptist Foreign Mission Society, Wheaton, Illinois to McGavran, Eugene, Oregon, March 12, 1962.

825 Louis King, letter from Christian and Missionary Alliance, New York to Donald McGavran, Eugene, Oregon, March 15, 1962.

826 Edwin Jacques, letter from Conservative Baptist Foreign Mission Society, Wheaton to McGavran, Eugene, Oregon, Oct. 5, 1962.

ideas with a vocabulary more consistent with conservative evangelical thinking. In response McGavran drafted a statement to all conservative mission boards, "I believe I am an evangelical; but it is true that I have graduated from Yale and Union and I cooperate with 'liberals.' Yet we have a message . . . particularly valuable to conservative and evangelical Christians."[827]

For the most part, evangelical leaders of US-based mission societies were positively stimulated by church growth thinking. Several executives sent copies of the pamphlet, "How to Do a Survey of Church Growth." Jacques of the Conservative Baptist Foreign Mission Board wrote, "I shall encourage the field chairman, the chairman of the evangelism committee and two other most gifted to begin an analysis of their fields."[828] Louis King reported in September 1962 that he sent the pamphlets to each field chairman with the request that they each "prepare a properly documented study of church growth for his field and each district within the field."[829] Upon his visit to West Africa in January and February of 1963 the researches in church growth were the center of discussion. He evaluated the process as "the most significant and important business of the trip or of any trip I have taken."[830] He summarized the findings with the following comments:

We discovered a noticeable drop in baptisms when:

1. Missionaries were changed too often.
2. Policy changes were effected (i.e., subsidy withdrawn).
3. Trade language used instead of maternal language.
4. Energetic evangelistic effort discontinued.
5. Follow-up work inadequate.[831]

By 1963 McGavran was regularly scheduled to speak at seminars, mission conferences, and mission executive retreats in evangelical circles. This greatly increased his travel time and workload. Yet he felt it was worth the extra stress when the response was so positive. For example, he gave six two-hour lectures to a gathering of CMA missionaries in Phoenix, Arizona, in May 1963, then Louis King announced: "CMA was going to follow church growth principles and attempt to treble the numbers of their members and churches overseas in the next decade . . . I felt that here was a missionary society which was really doing the job of discipling the nations."[832]

---

827 McGavran memo drafted for Conservative Evangelical Missionary Leadership, circulated Sept. 1962.

828 Edwin Jacques, letter from Conservative Baptist Foreign Mission Society, Wheaton to McGavran, Eugene, Oregon, Sept. 16, 1963.

829 Louis L. King, Foreign Secretary, letter from The Christian and Missionary Alliance, New York to McGavran, Eugene, Oregon, Aug. 27, 1963.

830 Ibid.

831 Ibid.

832 Donald McGavran, personal memo, May 17, 1963.

Because of McGavran's unique situation of acceptance in both the evangelical and conciliar camps, he attempted to bridge their differences by getting evangelicals involved in WCC meetings. When intolerance was displayed from either section McGavran was quick to plead for tolerance and Christian grace.[833] On May 17, 1963, McGavran wrote to Hayward strongly recommending that Louis King be invited to attend the Iberville consultation. He presented King as "a Conservative Evangelical . . . but . . . not narrow or antagonistic, and he does represent a friendly section"[834] of the evangelical camp. As a result King attended that meeting.

Other church growth seminars for evangelicals in 1963 included a two-day session with the Assemblies of God missionaries and a Winona Lake seminar sponsored by the Evangelical Fellowship of Foreign Missions, an umbrella agency facilitating cooperation between conservative missions.[835] As McGavran began to feel more at home among the evangelicals, he began pressing for their support. He suggested to the EFMA leadership that evangelical mission boards make token grants of $500–$1,000 per year to ICG. He also proposed a five-year program of research and teaching which he envisaged would accomplish the following:

a. Focus attention on church growth.
b. Create a conscience on church growth.
c. Undertake researches in church growth to uncover facts.
d. Assemble the facts concerning responsiveness of populations essential to fruitful missionary administration.
e. Teach the principles and practices of church growth to many churchmen— nationals and missionaries.[836]

An evangelical leader who played a major role in McGavran's life from 1964 to 1968 was Norman Cummings, home director of the fledgling interdenominational mission, Overseas Crusades. In November 1963, Cummings and Edward Murphy spent three weeks with McGavran and then urged other mission leaders to do the same. Unlike most other evangelical agencies, he also encouraged his mission to stand behind the ICG financially raising support for full-time secretarial help. McGavran thanked God for this provision and rejoiced that "the ball and chain" of time restraints were struck from his feet.[837]

Cummings went further in his desire to publicize church growth concepts. In his June 12, 1964 circular letter McGavran announced: "Rev. Norman L. Cummings . . . President

---

833 Donald McGavran, letter from Eugene to George Beazley, leader from the Christian Church who took umbrage with Carl McIntyre, May 25, 1963.

834 Donald McGavran, letter from Eugene to Hayward, London, May 17, 1963.

835 Donald McGavran, interdepartmental memo, NCCE to Griffeth, May 25, 1963.

836 Donald McGavran, letter from Eugene to Clyde Taylor, Wayne Coggins, Brushwyler, Byron Lamson and Louis King, leaders of EFMA, Sept. 16, 1963.

837 Donald McGavran, letter of thanks to Norman L. Cummings, Palo Alto, California, April 6, 1964.

of EFMA has generously offered to publish for us a bi-monthly *Church Growth Bulletin*, a clearing house for the entire missionary enterprise. The first issue will be September 1964."[838]

Overseas Crusades continued to provide this service to the worldwide missionary enterprise through 1986. McGavran expressed his appreciation:

> As I think of this material in the effective format which you have worked out, and the beautiful printing job which has been done, going out to over 1,200 addresses of the most prominent leaders in the missionary movement, I can only thank God and believe that it will be used by Him to the extension of His Church and the carrying out of His purposes.[839]

Throughout 1964, McGavran was concerned about the future of the ICG. With his usual thoroughness he left no stone unturned as to possible future sources of support. Cummings discussed with him the possibility of the ICG and Overseas Crusades merging. Yet nothing came of it.

The benefits of the Cummings-McGavran relationship flowed in two directions. Several outstanding missionaries from Overseas Crusades studied either at the ICG or later at the School of World Mission at Fuller Theological Seminary. These included: James Montgomery, Edward Murphy, Larry Keyes, Clyde Cook, and many others from Overseas Crusades. Cummings took the church growth perspective and made it the raison d'être for that mission.

Cummings also played a vital role in the move of the ICG to Fuller Theological Seminary in 1965. He was appointed to the Fuller Steering Committee for the development of a School of World Missions. The move was not without its difficulties, one of which was caused by Fuller's newly established position on the inspiration of Scripture where the school chose to use the term "infallible" while other evangelicals insisted upon the term "inerrant" in describing it. Some conservative evangelical mission leaders were concerned about sending their missionaries for training there. Cummings, president of EFMA, and several mission executives sought his counsel. Cummings went to David Hubbard, president of Fuller, who sought to allay their fears by attending the annual conference of the National Association of Evangelicals, where he addressed the situation. After that some mission executives of EFMA/IFMA were willing to send their missionaries to the School of World Mission.[840]

Cummings was the key instrument in establishing the annual church growth seminars on the West Coast. In 1966 they were held on the Fuller campus. However, Cummings had close connections with Clyde Cook of Talbot Seminary at Biola and it was felt that they

---

838 Donald McGavran, monthly circular letter to mission executives, June 12, 1964.

839 Donald McGavran, letter from Eugene to Norman L. Cummings, Overseas Crusades, Palo Alto, California, Sept. 2, 1964.

840 Donald McGavran, interview by Norman L. Cummings, Richland, Washington, Aug. 4, 1988.

would provide a more representative environment for the evangelical community. Like the Winona Lake church growth seminar, Biola also did much to acquaint the evangelical community with McGavran.

Although the conservative evangelical community rallied around McGavran and his Church Growth movement, it was slow to support the cause financially, apart from the generous help from Overseas Crusades. Many EFMA/IFMA boards sent their missionaries to ICG for training, but rare was the day when a check of appreciation accompanied these trainees. The missions related to the Conciliar Movement, even though resistant to his ideas were far more willing to underwrite expenses incurred for seminars than were the evangelicals. Thus in the period from 1960–65, McGavran's ministry to the EFMA-related missions was often at considerable expense to himself. If he had a seminar for the conciliar branch he often used the opportunity to squeeze in another for the evangelical segment in a nearby location to minimize travel costs.

SUMMER RESEARCH AND CHURCH GROWTH LECTURES

Every summer throughout the 1961–65 period of McGavran's life was filled with intense activity. Church growth seminars became increasingly popular. The summer of 1961 included such speaking engagements as a seminar at St. Olaf's College with the American Lutherans, his annual lectures at Crystal Lake for the College of Missions, a stimulating four-day session at the Summer Institute of Linguistics at the University of Oklahoma, and most of September at the Spanish Language School in Costa Rica.

In the summer of 1962 McGavran spent the better part of six weeks in a survey of select church areas in Mexico. This research by McGavran, John Huegel, and Jack Taylor resulted in the *Church Growth in Mexico*, published by Eerdmans. As already mentioned, he spoke at the annual EFMA conference at Winona Lake in September.

McGavran's itinerary for May–September 1963 included the following:

1. May 13–14: He spoke to Annual Convention of the Christian Missionary Alliance which was held at Phoenix, Arizona. He spoke for twelve hours.
2. June 26–27: He spoke to the annual meeting of the Assemblies of God held at Springfield, Missouri.
3. June 29–30: He taught his regular eight addresses at Crystal Lake to the College of Missions, a seminar sponsored by UCMS.
4. July 13–22: He undertook a survey operation in connection with the Marine Medical Mission, now known as North America Indian Mission. He was flown into remote Indian settlements along the British Columbia Coast and even into Alaska.

5. July 31–August 3: He was totally involved in the Iberville meeting in Montreal Canada.
6. September 9–13: He led the Church Growth Seminar sponsored by the EFMA. McGavran considered this to be his heaviest assignment.

The summer of 1964 was interspersed with seminars, but the students and research fellows at ICG occupied most of McGavran's time. The time-consuming negotiations with Fuller Theological Seminary did not deter McGavran from church growth seminars in 1965. However the most significant summer activity was his time in Latin America and in particular Brazil.

THE CHURCH GROWTH LECTURE SERIES

From the beginning of the ICG McGavran thought big. Even before he had a single student for the Institute, he was planning as though it were a graduate school of fifty students. In late April 1960 he wrote to Bishop Pickett and inquired if he would be available for a lectureship on Church Growth.[841] It was both fitting and providential that the man who sparked the elementary stages of church growth thinking in McGavran should launch the lecture series. McGavran's friendship with Pickett down through the years was deep and meaningful. Commenting on the choice of Pickett for the series he said, "We could get no one better than Pickett for our first man."[842]

McGavran's goal for the lecture series was to have much more than a mere series of addresses. For that reason he wrote to Griffeth, instructing him that from the budget monies designated for research fellowships, one third was to be set aside for honorarium and publication costs for the lecture series. At the same time he discussed the date and confirmed Griffeth's idea of October 1961 for the series.[843] As early as October 1, 1960 he stated his determination to make available to the missionary enterprise a series of publications on church growth. He saw these as a combination of probing practical studies on various lands complemented by the theoretical aspect arising from the annual lectures.[844]

Intensive advertising in Eugene and throughout Oregon preceded Pickett's lecture series. The organization behind the scenes was superb. The interest of Christians in the city of Eugene was deeply aroused. Through an interview with McGavran, the local newspaper ran a feature story on Pickett with the following description:

---

841 Bishop J. Waskom Pickett, letter from Boston to McGavran, Bethany, West Virginia, May 9, 1960.

842 Donald McGavran, letter from UCMS Headquarters, Indianapolis to Griffeth, Eugene, Oregon, June 4, 1960.

843 Donald McGavran, letter to Griffeth, Eugene, Oregon, June 25, 1960.

844 Donald McGavran, letters to Pickett: May 5, 1961, June 17, 1961, Aug. 14, 1961, Aug. 15, 1961, Aug. 24, 1961.

Bishop Jarrel Waskom Pickett has some strong and interesting convictions regarding the growth of churches . . . During the Bishop's forty-six years in India, he served as pastor, district superintendent, editor, publisher, secretary of regional and national Christian councils, and bishop. For over twenty years, he was president of the council on Medical Work of the Methodist Church in Southern Asia, and was also organizer and first president of the United Christian Mission to Nepal . . . The Bishop conferred often with Mahatma Gandhi and was frequently consulted during the preparation of India's present constitution.[845]

McGavran assumed responsibility for editing the manuscript and arranging for a publisher. In his letter of January 27, 1962 in which he affectionately addressed Pickett as "Guruji," he described his strategy for getting Abingdon Press to accept the manuscript.[846] He also arranged for D. T. Niles of Ceylon to write the foreword for the book. This Niles did despite serious reservations for Pickett's concept of fighting communism with Christianity.[847]

Due to a misunderstanding, the lectures were published not only in the United States, but also in India. The Church Growth Lecture series for 1962 was a four-way conversation with Melvin Hodges of the Assemblies of God, Cal Guy of Southwestern Baptist Seminary, Eugene Nida of the Bible Society, and McGavran.

As was McGavran's custom, he edited the chapter submissions of the others. Nida was offended by McGavran's red ink policy of revision and responded with a three-page letter on September 9, 1962. This was followed up by Nida defending his original manuscript by sending the material to colleagues and experts for their advice. Differences were aggravated by a telephone conversation on September 28. On October 2, Nida wrote:

I am quite certain that my contribution would not be what you want. Though, of course, we are both interested in the same goals, your recent letter to me has confirmed some of my earlier misgivings (as a result of rereading some of your books), namely that we are simply not on the same "wave length." This would mean that my contribution would not do justice to what you are aiming to do, and I would not want to embarrass you in the least.[848]

This situation with Nida came as a serious setback to McGavran who had just returned from an outstanding church growth seminar at Winona Lake with the EFMA missionaries and executives. The evangelical camp was so excited about church growth principles that forty mission executives determined to make a pilgrimage to Eugene to take in the Four Way Conversation. Now Nida was all but scuttling the lecture series.

845 Donald McGavran, interview by *Eugene Register Guard* (newspaper), Oct. 27, 1961.
846 Donald McGavran, letter to Pickett, Jan. 27, 1962.
847 Ibid.
848 Eugene Nida, letter to McGavran, (obtained from USCWM Archives), Oct. 2, 1962.

McGavran swung into action, using telephone, telegram, and mail to convince Nida to change his mind. Meanwhile Nida had cancelled his plane reservations to Eugene and was in Mexico attending a conference. On October 10, Nida sent a telegram from Mexico confirming his decision not to attend the Four Way Conversation. Undaunted, McGavran sent a letter to Nida's home address with a plane ticket enclosed. Nida arrived in Eugene as the lectures were getting underway.[849]

Unlike the Pickett lecture series, the Four Way Conversation met for the most part in the upper floor of the library stack around the oak table with forty or so mission executives crowded into a rather limited space. This setting was chosen because of the nature of the series and the desire to have input from the mission executives. The lectures went off well, Nida notwithstanding. A week after the lectures were over McGavran wrote to Ralph Palmer:

> The Four Way Conversation on crucial issues in church growth was a great success. Getting Nida the anthropologist, Guy the theoretician, Hodges the mission executive who has more churches in his baliwick than any other executive in the world and McGavran who keeps insisting that promise be checked against actual churches, against performance on to one platform and holding them there for 24 hours was quite an achievement. The book will be a real contribution to missiology.[850]

The book *Church Growth and Christian Mission*, maintained a surprisingly cohesive theme. McGavran's comments both in the introduction and conclusion reflect much of the tension and duress he was experiencing through his correspondence and interaction with the Conciliar Movement. The concluding chapter took an interesting twist. McGavran paid special tribute to Nida's contribution and insights. Their differences were obviously overcome.

For further church growth lectureships, McGavran attempted to get John V. Taylor from Africa, but was unsuccessful. Dr. Harold Lindsell was invited to give the fall lectures in 1965. These were given two months after the opening of the School of World Mission at Fuller. Also, as mentioned earlier, David Stowe gave the 1967 lecture series after considerable debate from the Fuller faculty as to the implications of having a man involved in the Conciliar Movement on their campus.

RESEARCH FELLOWS, CLASSES, AND CURRICULUM

There was a direct relationship between student recruitment to the ICG and the Conciliar-Evangelical debate. On the surface the leadership of mainline denominational missions expressed a spirit of tolerance for McGavran's position, yet in practise they stood against

---

849 Works, "The Church Growth Movement to 1965: An Historical Perspective," 249–250.
850 Donald McGavran, letter to Ralph Palmer, Indianapolis, Oct. 22, 1962.

him. For example, Floyd Honey, secretary for the Board of World Mission of the United Church of Canada wrote:

> We have some concern here about the possible dangers of too narrow an emphasis on "church growth" in the statistical sense and a possible excessive downgrading of the service aspects of the mission program. We certainly agree that evangelism is basic, and that we must be very careful about being diverted from the basic objective. At the same time we are not sure that every Christian program can be fairly evaluated in terms of its direct contribution to the numerical growth of the church. It is for this reason that we have some hesitation in encouraging our missionary staff to undertake a study along the lines outlined. [851]

McGavran sent a letter of appreciation for the above statement and requested permission to utilize the quote in the Four Way Conversation sessions in October of 1962. He wrote, "Your letter phrases very well a rather common hesitation on the part of a good many leaders of Christian Mission in regard to church growth."[852]

Another indication of the growing polarity between the leadership of the WCC and McGavran is seen in a letter written to Roswell P. Barnes, a fundraiser for the agency. He sent a WCC brochure and a letter to McGavran requesting support. In response McGavran identified himself, his church, and his mission society as all being supporters of the WCC. Then he hastened to the heart of the matter:

> I am dismayed at the fact that in your letter there is no mention at all of the chief task of the World Council of Churches—discipling the nations. Rather the resurgent non-Christian religions are given a play. And when I turn to the pamphlet, the task of the Division of World Mission and Evangelism is given as "integrating the ongoing task of the former IMC with the program of the WCC"— no word of the billion plus living without Christ. It is this wholly a- mission stance, . . . its de-emphasis of the mission of the churches of Christ among all tribes, and tongues and peoples and nations which subjects us your friends to considerable embarrassment.[853]

Apart from the financial support from the UCMS for two years, McGavran received little encouragement from the mission under which he had served for thirty-eight years. Repeatedly he tried to identify the source of their resistance to the Institute of Church Growth. On March 2, 1961, as a result of rereading the Puerto Rican report he had prepared

---

851   T. E. Floyd Honey, Secretary of the Board of World Mission, letter from United Church of Canada, Toronto to McGavran, Victoria College archives, Toronto University, Eugene, Oregon, July 12, 1962.

852   Donald McGavran, letter to Floyd Honey in response to his July 12, 1962 letter, August 24, 1962.

853   Donald McGavran, letter to Roswell P. Barnes, New York, Oct. 12, 1962.

in 1956, he wrote: "Now six years after this report we are still sending out missionaries with eyes blinded to the available insights concerning church growth."[854] Then McGavran dealt with a wrong assumption held by most mission boards in the US, "that if a man gets the best seminary training possible here . . . and gets specialized missionary orientation, he will get as much church growth as it is possible to get."[855] Then he made a critique of seminary training in the US as far as mission field preparation was concerned:

a.   It does not fit him emotionally, theologically, or methodologically to carry out the great commission in highly particular populations of other lands.

b.   Missionary orientation is good, it fits a man to understand the organizational set up, national tenderness, and linguistic and anthropological facts. But it does not harness this knowledge to the discipling of men.

c.   Working faithfully in the younger Church is good . . . But in most cases the younger Church is not growing healthily and the missionary learns a pattern which is not working and will not work.[856]

McGavran recognized that the image of Northwest Christian College to people in the eastern part of the US was that of a small nonaccredited college. For this reason, he expressed, "It might be hard for UCMS missionaries to find it attractive to come to the ICG for graduate studies in church growth."[857]

Even though he now had no official status with UCMS, he continued to send reports of his research and the insights arising from his travels. He often used these opportunities to highlight the growing interest in the ICG from other boards, but even this would not provoke UCMS to jealousy.[858]

His persistent presentation of the unique training available to missionaries at ICG began to have its effect. Virgil Sly wrote defensively of the UCMS position: "We have not been able to contribute students. This has not been any desire on our part to bypass the Institute. However, Don, I feel, has taken this as a reaction of lack of interest. I have no evidence other than that the Institute is doing a good job. Don has felt that we should turn a whole section of the Foreign Division's work over to the type of training he is able to provide . . . but we cannot."[859]

What seemed a reasonable policy to UCMS and other conciliar boards as far as their involvement with ICG, stood in stark contrast to the kind of interest the Church Growth Movement was stirring in other circles.

---

854   Donald McGavran, letter to Virgil Sly, UCMS, Indianapolis, March 2, 1961.

855   Ibid.

856   Ibid.

857   Donald McGavran, letter to Ralph Palmer, Indianapolis, (obtained from USCWM Archives), Jan. 10, 1963.

858   Donald McGavran, letter to Virgil Sly, Indianapolis, (obtained from USCWM Archives), Oct. 22, 1961.

859   Virgil Sly, letter to Russel A. Dietch, (obtained from NV), Nov. 19, 1963.

Between January 1961 and June of 1965, a total of sixty-one research fellows and furloughing missionaries journeyed to Eugene, Oregon to glean church growth insights from McGavran. The denominational origins of these students are roughly categorized as one third from conciliar denominations, one third from EFMA/IFMA-related missions, and one-third from Christian churches and Churches of Christ.

The latter source of students largely came as a direct result of the influence the Institute was having on the undergraduate students at NCC. Clarification needs to be made as to the one- third students coming from conciliar churches. In a letter to Vincent Brushwyler, the general director of CBFMS, McGavran wrote:

> The ICG is inclusivist, but exclusively around persuading men to become disciples of the second Person of the Trinity. We appeal to only those in the DFM branch of missions who are heart and soul for discipling the nations. We are violently criticized by the others. We buttress the evangelical elements in the so called liberal wing of the Church . . . ICG drives a wedge between the evangelicals and the universalists in the DFM section of the Church.[860]

An unusually high percentage of those early students of the Church Growth Movement have gone on to make specialized contributions to missiology. This was due in part to the maturity and quality of the people who invested a few months of their lives in order that they might become more effective in discipling the nations. Another factor that provided such a high success ratio was the intense personal interaction with McGavran. The interaction of fellow missionaries sharing their blessings and frustrations from many diverse areas of the world also stimulated a high level of research quality and an environment for the pursuit of excellence. The case study method became a highly successful tool and McGavran insisted that they be comparative.

> For a real study we must see how other denominations, other missions have managed similar opportunities. The men contribute to each other. Part of the value here lies in seeing missions through each other people's eyes—or rather seeing the growth of the Church through the records of other denominations.[861]

As various researchers were published, McGavran received many recommendations. For example, Latourette expressed that Scherer's "Wildfire Church Growth" in Korea was worthy of a doctoral degree at any university.

The size of the classes ranged from one to a high of fifteen. The core courses offered were as follows:

---

860 Works, "The Church Growth Movement to 1965: An Historical Perspective," 196.
861 Donald McGavran, letter to R. J. G. Brushwyler, General Secretary of the Conservative Baptist Foreign Mission Society, Wheaton, (obtained from USCWM Archives), Aug. 7, 1964.

- Principles and Procedures in Church Growth (3 hours)
- Case Studies in Church Growth (3 hours)
- Animism and Church Growth (2 hours)
- The Meaning of Anthropology for Church Growth (2 hours)
- Theology and Church Growth (2 hours)
- Seminar on Missions (3 hours)
- Reading and Conference (3 hours).[862]

The research fellows were responsible for presenting seminars (case studies) of their materials. This helped to take some of the teaching load from McGavran. He took an intense interest in their research and in the details of each of their respective fields of service. He ordered interlibrary loan books from the top mission libraries in the US in order to provide the best tools for research.

Alan R. Tippett's appointment as teaching fellow in the spring of 1962 was a great asset. His materials, although from a perspective different from that of McGavran, reinforced strongly the church growth point of view. As a student, Tippett resisted vigorously against McGavran's attempts to red ink his manuscript. Yet their relationship was one of mutual admiration. McGavran wrote to the editor of an Australian journal:

> Tippett has written a definitive account of the way in which three quarters of the 4,000,000 people in the islands of the South Pacific have in the last hundred years become Christian . . . For the first time, under one heading, we shall have a scientific account of the dynamics of the spread of Christianity through the labors of the missionary societies of the Congregational, Anglican, Methodist, Lutheran and other Churches.[863]

He went on to describe the man whom he respected so greatly:

> As a trained historian, archivist, anthropologist and missionary, he demands supporting data for every claim. He knows the South Pacific from Tahiti to Sumatra . . . because he probes situations, digs out facts, and goes to all lengths to verify a single point. He knows where to find the facts in missionary records, archival and other collections . . . He has an uncanny knack of producing facts.[864]

---

862 Donald McGavran, letter to Linwood Barney, Professor at Nyack Mission College, Nyack, New York, (obtained from USCWM Archives), March 15, 1963.

863 Donald McGavran, letter to E. G. Lechte, editor of the Spectator, Melbourne, Australia, (obtained from USCWM Archives), Sept. 18, 1962.

864 Ibid.

BOOKS PUBLISHED BY THE INSTITUTE OF CHURCH GROWTH

Facts were gathered, historical and social issues were evaluated, church growth was measured, and manuscripts describing concrete situations were written. The Institute was the scene of unprecedented research activity. Semester after semester manuscripts were produced by the research fellows. These McGavran was determined to publish.

Initially all the church growth books were printed in India through the Lucknow Publishing House. Costs were very reasonable but the quality was less than desirable. McGavran exerted a great deal of energy seeking other publishers.

An interdepartmental memo was sent to Griffeth on March 5, 1963 detailing the status of various books and manuscripts. They were:

1. *Church Growth in the High Andes* by Keith Hamilton, printed at Lucknow Publishing House (LPH).
2. *Church Growth in West New Guinea* by James Sunda, LPH.
3. *Church Growth and Group Conversion* by Pickett, Warnshius, and McGavran, LPH.
4. *Church Growth in Jamaica* by Donald McGavran, LPH.
5. *God's Messengers to Mexico's Masses* by Jack Taylor. Five hundred copies have been printed by Baptist Spanish Publishing House, El Paso.
6. *History of Protestantism in Costa Rica* by Wilton Nelson, LPH.
7. *Church Growth in Mexico* by Donald McGavran. MS is likely to be taken by Eerdman's Press.
8. *Dynamics of Church Growth in the South Pacific* by Alan Tippett. This MS has been written in its first draft.
9. *Church Growth in Korea* by Roy Shearer.
10. *Church Growth in Southern Nigeria* by Gordon Robinson.
11. *Church Growth in Northern Nigeria* by John S. Grimley are research fellowships. Each will be printed in India.
12. *Church Growth in Brazil* by William Read.[865]

INSTITUTE OF CHURCH GROWTH FINDS A HOME AT FULLER SEMINARY

The future of the Institute of Church Growth increasingly concerned McGavran as the end of his tenure at Northwest Christian College drew near. This tenuous situation was exacerbated by the retirement of President Griffeth who single-handedly had given the

---

865 Donald McGavran, NCCE interdepartmental memo to Griffeth, (obtained from USCWM Archives), March 5, 1963.

institute a home and had underwritten it financially. McGavran envisaged a legally separate Institution, with its own board of trustees, and own campus. He also wrestled with the temptation of dropping the priority of administration and teaching and the shift to fund-raising. Potential alternative sites were explored with regularity. Latourette was asked if he might explore the possibility of talks with Princeton leadership regarding a move of the Institute to that location. David Stowe was pressed to consider providing a site through DFM somewhere near New York and the National Council of Churches Center there. Talks with executives of the EFMA/IFMA resulted in a consideration of a location in the Midwest, possibly Wheaton. Considerable energy was spent exploring ways by which the ICG could remain in Eugene. Efforts were made to create an independent board of governors for the Institute with men like Latourette and Mark Hatfield as members.

McGavran's correspondence indicated his growing concern regarding the future of the Institute if he were out of the picture. His misgivings continued to mount as a result of the absence of regular support from sources other than NCCE and Overseas Crusades. His brother Edward McGavran who had been an innovator in the whole area of public health and preventative medicine wrote:

> I am as certain as you that what I have been trying to give to the Health Field is as important as what you are trying to give to the Mission Field. I, too, was surprised and pleased by the apparent acceptance in high and low places of my concept. But the difference between acceptance and implementation is vast and slow, and at times I fear prostitution and perversion worse than frank opposition ... But I rationalize by observing that the importance and greatness of the concept is measured by the length of years it takes to be accepted and practiced ... Why, then, Brother Mine, does it trouble our hearts? This is the price we pay for being 50 years ahead of our time. We come from a long line of those who have suffered similarly.[866]

In 1964, Fuller Theological Seminary was not a remote consideration as far as McGavran was concerned. After his visit to Eugene, President David Hubbard had described the ICG as "a uniquely creative venture."[867] Hubbard and Griffeth developed a fraternal relationship throughout 1963–64, but the only contact between McGavran and Hubbard took place on a tour of the NCCE campus in March of 1964. It was during that visit that Hubbard and C. Davis Weyerhauser sat in on McGavran's classes gathered around the oak table in the library stacks. The only other significant contact McGavran had with Fuller prior to 1965 was through John G. Finch who had shared with him the memorandum regarding the proposed Graduate School of Christian Psychology. Finch had been an acquaintance

---

866 Edward McGavran, younger brother to Donald, letter from the Ford Foundation, New Delhi, India to McGavran, Eugene, Oregon, (obtained from USCWM Archives), Jan. 1, 1964.

867 David Hubbard, letter from Pasadena to R. Griffeth, Eugene, Oregon, (obtained from USCWM Archives), April 22, 1964.

of McGavran's in India. McGavran was certain that if Griffeth cultivated Finch, the School of Psychology could be redirected to NCCE.[868] There is no record of this idea ever getting past the dream stage.

Carlton Booth sheds some light on how the steering committee focused on McGavran as its choice to be the founding dean of the School of World Mission at Fuller Seminary. He was asked to go to the InterVarsity Fellowship's Mission Conference at Urbana, Illinois in 1964 to confer with missionary leaders. "I invited twelve of these men to a dinner and as we talked it seemed the conversation centered on one person. I returned to Pasadena and reported that the consensus of the mission leaders at Urbana was Donald McGavran . . . was the man we should contact. He was a stranger to most of us."[869]

Daniel Fuller wrote McGavran in January 1965 describing the proposed School of World Evangelism. His statements reflected the convictions of the search committee made up of Kenneth Strachan, J. Christy Wilson, Clarence S. Roddy, Carlton Booth, and William LaSor. His opening paragraph is almost a reflection of McGavran's church growth principles:

> Fuller Seminary is now working to found a School of World Evangelism. We are impressed by the great need for such a school as the Christian church faces a variety of complex tasks in attempting to carry out the Great Commission . . . We are also impressed by the fact that there is no evangelical program of study leading to a degree on a post graduate level which concentrates exclusively on matters directly related to world-wide evangelization. Furthermore, we recognize that there is a need for a school to serve as a center for grappling with the issues that confront Christians as they seek to establish churches throughout the world. Here research into these problems can be pursued and the results made available not only to the students but also to the Church at large.[870]

Daniel Fuller concluded the letter by requesting McGavran to come to Pasadena on February 18–20 of 1965 to share his insights with the committee and speak to the student body. There Hubbard requested him to draft a plan for the Graduate School of World Missions. He did so on the premise "that the heart of the missionary enterprise is proclaiming Jesus Christ and persuading men to become His disciples and responsible members of His Church."[871]

The four pages, "The Purpose, Objectives, Curriculum and Staff," for the proposed Graduate School of World Mission and Evangelism was the result. He set forth some criteria which determine the nature of courses in the School even to this day.

---

868 Donald McGavran, letter to Ross Griffeth, (obtained from USCWM Archives), March 14, 1962.

869 Carlton Booth, *On the Mountain Top* (Tyndale House, 1984), 156–57.

870 Daniel P. Fuller, letter from Pasadena to McGavran, Eugene, Oregon, (obtained from USCWM Archives), Jan. 25, 1965.

871 Donald McGavran, letter from Eugene to David Hubbard, President Fuller Seminary, Pasadena, (obtained from USCWM Archives), Feb. 26, 1965.

Mission history will not be taught primarily as a record of what missions and missionaries have done, but as a record of what church multiplication has taken place, with ample attention to the reasons which operated for and against the growth of each specific Church . . .

Theology of Mission will not be taught as some denominational system . . . which gives the only true answers whether churches in Africasia multiply or not; but will be taught as that Biblical system of truth which in Afercasia God has blessed to the propagation of the Gospel. Mission methodology will be commended not on a priori but on pragmatic grounds. The best methods, if they do not work, will not be taught . . .

Holding steadily to the essential purpose of Christian mission does not imply concentration on a narrowly conceived, stereotyped, North American evangelism . . . The establishment of growing Churches in every tribe and tongue and nation is a multi-sided operation. Education, medicine, agriculture, development of national leadership, and the like are legitimate parts of mission, but the obvious present danger is that essential mission gets lost in these legitimate parts . . . The cure is to proportion training in mission so that the parts further the central purpose rather than frustrate it. The phrase "church growth" is deliberately adopted as a term which while including . . . service and the like, steadily emphasizes the chief goal.

Holding steadily to the essential purpose means (1) that this Graduate School will take its stand squarely on the assumption that the salvation of men through faith in Jesus Christ is the chief purpose of Christian mission. (2) That the many good things done by mission today will not be permitted to obscure and hinder the supreme aim . . . (3) That conventional academic disciplines hallowed by use in older seminaries, will not be followed slavishly. Indeed they will be followed only to the extent that they provedly contribute to propagating the faith . . . in the world of today and tomorrow.[872]

Two weeks later McGavran wrote to Hubbard as though he had already been unofficially approached about moving the ICG to Fuller. He discussed the assets of keeping the Institute at the NCC, including the location across the street from a major university and the ability to address both the conciliar and evangelical camps. However he recognized the remoteness of Eugene. Yet he was fearful that identity with Fuller would cut him off from

---

872 Donald McGavran, draft of "Purpose, Objectives, Curriculum and Staff" for the Graduate School of World Mission and Evangelism, presented to Hubbard, (obtained from USCWM Archives), Feb. 26, 1965.

further ministry to his denomination and other conciliar groups.[873] He concluded his letter with the following:

> Evangelical mission needs a research and teaching center devoted entirely to church growth, a clearing house for the $60,000,000-per-annum missionary enterprise whose theology so emphasizes church growth and whose missions are, for the most part, so effectively diverted from it.[874]

Hubbard visited McGavran on April 5 and discussed issues related to the ICG and a possible move to Fuller.[875]

Daniel Fuller wrote a letter on April 22, 1965 which stated, "At its last meeting our faculty voted unanimously to extend to you an invitation to be the Dean of the School of World Mission and Professor of Missions."[876] The appointment was subject to a faculty interview with McGavran. Two days before the faculty vote, Carlton Booth wrote to Arthur F. Glasser requesting his opinion on the suitability of McGavran as dean of the new school.[877] Glasser's response is of historic significance:

1. Dr. McGavran is obviously an extremely competent man in this field. His formal training balances his practical experience . . .
2. Dr. McGavran is an enthusiast, a "vibration" in the best sense of the word. He can convey a glow. He has the thrust in his personality that would qualify him as a LEADER.
3. Dr. McGavran is recognized as the most seminal thinker in the business of church growth, world evangelism missionary methodology etc . . . He would be bound to draw top level missionaries to do furlough studies under his direction . . .
4. . . . located in Eugene, Oregon—off the beaten path—he was not realizing his fullest potential . . . By inviting him to Fuller we would be helping him: he would be grateful and would give us the right sort of loyalty.[878]

---

873 Donald McGavran, letter from Eugene to David Hubbard, Pasadena, California, (obtained from USCWM Archives), March 15, 1965.

874 Ibid.

875 David Hubbard, letter from Pasadena, to Donald McGavran, Eugene, Oregon, (obtained from USCWM Archives), March 31, 1965.

876 Daniel P. Fuller, Academic Dean, Fuller Seminary, Pasadena to Donald McGavran, Eugene, Oregon, (obtained from USCWM Archives), April 22, 1965.

877 F. Carlton Booth, chairman of the Fuller missions committee (search committee), letter from Pasadena to Arthur Glasser, home director, Overseas Missionary Fellowship, Philadelphia, (obtained from USCWM Archives), April 20, 1965.

878 Arthur Glasser, letter from Belfast, Ireland to Carlton Booth, Pasadena, (obtained from USCWM Archives), May 3, 1965.

McGavran did not immediately accept the offer from Fuller because he felt an obligation to give the trustees and the leadership of NCCE every opportunity to keep the ICG at Eugene. He wrote: "If it is their purpose to continue the Institute as a permanent part of the College, I could not accept any invitation to another school."[879]

After writing this McGavran wrote to Alan Tippett: "If NCCE says, we cannot match that salary, but we will build ICG into the NCCE set up in a clear cut definite way, will give you sufficient room for an ICG of up to twenty men, then I propose to stay on here and so inform Fuller. Are you agreed?"[880]

After these letters McGavran wrote to Kenneth Johnston, president of the Board of Trustees of NCCE. He challenged him and his board to give a definitive statement as to ICG's future within the college. He revealed to them the Fuller offer and then expressed that it grieved him that NCC has "done the plowing, weeding, and irrigating and someone else to reap the harvest."[881] He requested that the board of trustees guarantee ICG a $26,000 annual budget and adequate office and classroom space. He summarized the success of the ICG:

Four years' work . . . has begun to pay off. *The Church Growth Bulletin* goes to over 1,500 leaders of Christian mission in more than 20 countries. Researches in church growth are beginning to roll off the presses . . . The lectures on church growth given in the fall of 1962 . . are awarded a major review in *Christianity Today* . . . Northwest Christian College is known far and wide. Its professors of church growth are invited to conduct seminars and workshops on church growth for Lutherans, Baptists, Presbyterians, Alliance, Evangelical Foreign Missions Association, Assemblies of God, etc . . . It has become common place for boards to send missionaries here . . . This courageous venture of Northwest Christian College is beginning to blossom.[882]

While waiting for the trustees to respond, McGavran continued to work out details with Fuller Seminary. He wanted to insure the continuity of the ICG as he had developed it and obtain specific guarantees regarding research fellowships, teaching fellowships, a full-time secretary, the number of teachers, development and promotion, and Tippett's travel and status.[883] He also obtained assurance that the name "Institute of Church Growth" would be included along with the new title, School of World Mission. Details had to be worked out for the Latin American Church Growth Research Team which had been

---

879 Donald McGavran, letter from Eugene to D. Fuller, Pasadena, (obtained from USCWM Archives), April 28, 1965.

880 Donald McGavran, letter from Eugene to Alan Tippett, Melbourne, Australia, (obtained from USCWM Archives), April 28, 1965.

881 Donald McGavran, letter from Eugene to Kenneth Johnston, President, Board of Trustees, Northwest Christian College, Kern Park Christian Church, Portland, (obtained from USCWM Archives), April 28, 1965.

882 Ibid.

883 Daniel P. Fuller, letter from Pasadena to McGavran, Eugene, Oregon, (obtained from USCWM Archives), May 5, 1965.

funded by the Lilly Foundation. Fuller also agreed to purchase from NCCE select books in anthropology and sociology.[884]

The trustees of NCCE assured the maintenance of ICG only until June 1966. This was totally unsatisfactory for McGavran. On the other hand, the chief attraction offered by a move to Fuller was the potential for the perpetuation of ICG, yet this was not stated in any of the contracts negotiated. McGavran requested that such be included.[885]

On May 29, 1965 Hubbard, Griffeth, and McGavran met on the Fuller campus and eleven final issues were hammered out and these included: a budget to bring Tippett, the time table for the move was set for September 15 or before, moving budget for Tippett's confirmation of Lindsell as speaker for the fall church growth lecture series, details on publications, promotion and advertisement, details and policy on the functioning of the SWM student body on Fuller campus, assurance of potential funds for bringing David Barrett to Fuller as a special research fellow, and transfer of credit from ICG for those students who studied in Eugene.[886]

On May 30 McGavran accepted the position and met with the Fuller faculty and Board of Trustees. Their response to him was ably summarized by Carlton Booth:

> The presentation you made . . . yesterday afternoon completely won the hearts of all the men. The vision you have of the School of Mission and the Institute of Church growth is something which we all share . . . This is why your leadership is going to mean so much to us in launching this School in a way which will commend it, we believe, to the whole Church of Christ.[887] McGavran's response to the proceedings was very positive. He wrote, "I came away from meeting the faculty and trustees at Fuller more confident than ever that the hand of God was in this."[888]

Many further details had to be hammered out before McGavran's scheduled departure for Brazil. Details for the content and timing of the official announcement were coordinated. Speakers for the church growth lectureship series for 1965–66 were worked out. The transfer of the Lilly Foundation grant had to be arranged. Letterheads and cards were developed for the School of Mission. Some discussion went on regarding whether it should be called "Graduate School of World Mission" and whether the title should include "Institute of Church Growth." It is worthy to note that the choice of "School of World Mission" arose

---

884 Donald McGavran, letter from Eugene to Dan Fuller, Pasadena, (obtained from USCWM Archives), May 7, 1965.

885 Donald McGavran, letter from Eugene to Dan Fuller and Hubbard, Pasadena, May 17, 1965.

886 Minutes of the three-way negotiation session between Hubbard, Griffeth, and McGavran, held on the Fuller Theological Seminary Campus, (obtained from USCWM Archives), May 30, 1965.

887 F. Carlton Booth, Chairman of the Missions Committee, letter from Fuller Seminary, Pasadena to McGavran, Eugene, Oregon, June 1, 1965.

888 Donald McGavran, letter from Eugene to F. Carlton Booth, Pasadena, (obtained from USCWM Archives), June 3, 1965.

because of a philosophic issue that "there is unity to the mission of the Church which has aspects of mission at home and overseas, and that there is far less contrast between these two phases than there has been in the past."[889]

Several letters and telephone conversations were exchanged over the issue of maintaining the esprit de corps which had been developed at the ICG in Eugene. Daniel Fuller assured McGavran that such would be preserved. He expressed, "Your enthusiasm is contagious. I believe, therefore, that given freedom, you will be able to perpetuate this esprit de corps."[890]

Even in these initial weeks after his appointment, McGavran stressed that he wanted to have a ThD program in place within a year or two. Fuller agreed but set the date for 1967. Meanwhile Arthur Glasser in correspondence with Booth expressed his preference for MA and PhD degrees.[891]

Hubbard suggested that McGavran consider Ralph Winter as the next faculty addition. On McGavran's swing through Latin America in July and August 1965 he kept hearing positive comments about Winter and assessed him as "the kind of missionary who is able to excite good comment in his fellow missionaries, and I am interested in him."[892] McGavran also perceived that the missionaries in Latin America would be more likely to be interested in SWM at Fuller than those heading for Asia or Africa hence he determined that the next faculty member had to be "a top-flight man who is an expert and authority on Latin America and who talks their language and has met their problems and knows his way around."[893]

Both Griffeth and Hubbard were engaged in bureaucratic delays over Tippett's entry into the US. Finally Hubbard appealed to Billy Graham and the National Association of Evangelicals to use their influence. After a phone call from Billy Graham to the White House, Tippett's entry was assured within days.[894]

The move of the ICG to Fuller ended one of the most creative periods in McGavran's life. The Eugene years were a period of growing acceptance of church growth principles by many and the development of theological barriers to McGavran's ideas by others. These were also days when the missionaries who gathered around the oak table at NCCE, literally became disciples of McGavran. Those privileged to be a part of those early days in the Church Growth Movement created an esprit de corps which still continues in the School of World Mission.

889 R. Donald Weber, director of Public Relations and Development, letter from Fuller Seminary, Pasadena to McGavran, (obtained from USCWM Archives), June 15, 1965.

890 Dan Fuller, letter from Pasadena to McGavran, Eugene, Oregon, (obtained from USCWM Archives), June 22, 1965.

891 A. Glasser, letter from OMF Office, Philadelphia to F. C. Booth, Pasadena, (obtained from USCWM Archives), July 28, 1965.

892 Donald McGavran, letter from Mexico City to David Hubbard, Pasadena, (obtained from USCWM Archives), July 19, 1965.

893 Ibid.

894 David Hubbard, letters to Donald McGavran (on Latin American Tour), July 30, 1965, Caminas, São Paulo Brazil, Aug. 20, 1965, Pastor's and Missionaries Conference, Brasilia, Aug. 24, 1965.

With the move to Fuller Theological Seminary the Church Growth Movement moved into a new phase—that of implementation. Although there was risk that the ICG was in danger of being swallowed by the theological school in the seminary, both McGavran and Tippett set working parameters which prevented it, but not without struggles. However, those details are beyond the scope of this work.

CHAPTER EIGHT

THEOLOGICAL DEVELOPMENTS IN THE LIFE OF DONALD McGAVRAN

Donald McGavran was a pragmatist due to the disciplines of sociology and historical anthropology. However, he was also a great student of the word of God and had developed a regular discipline of memorizing vast portions of the Bible from his early years, being homeschooled by his mother in the context of India.

McGavran, although very pragmatic in discovering all the ways man can become more effective in the service of the Lord, combined that dimension with one of profound dependence upon God through prayer. In his recommendations for the West Utkal field in Orissa in 1956, he wrote:

> This is the time for great expectations and great prayer. It is no accident that numerous groups are ready to accept the Savior. It is the Lord's doing. He will provide the means to shepherd these seekers. He will be a shield and buckler to those who labour.

I collected one hundred or so prayers of Donald McGavran. These were prayed before classes, seminars, and in numerous other settings. They are more than a devotional expression of McGavran's spiritual conversation with God. They declare his theological convictions. They reveal his regular practise of memorizing large portions of Scripture. True to form as a member of the Disciples of Christ, McGavran believed the entire New Testament was the theological statement for the church.

In this final chapter, I have selectively taken a few of the prayers prayed from 1954–70 as representative of McGavran's theological roots. I have not utilized the prayers prayed during the period 1970–90. Many of the prayers in these later years were based or revised from his earlier prayers. These will be published at another time, in another volume.

McGavran's prayers have not been changed in any way. When he prayed he lapsed back into English forms of expression that were used in church life and conversational prayer in the pre-1960 era. Therefore "thy," "thee," "thou," "thine," "hast," and English spellings are retained as McGavran prayed them.

McGavran praying.

SECTION I

On February 12, 1958, McGavran prepared and prayed the following prayer at Butler before one of his classes. The class title was based on the early appellation of his manuscript *How Churches Grow,* which at that time was "The Church in a Ripening World." His extensive travel and surveys conducted in 1954–57 had reinforced his biblical conviction that the conciliar churches were very wrong in their pessimistic view of the future of world missions. Liberal influences in the World Council of Churches were prophesying retrenchment and the age of the "post-Christian era." For graduate seminary students accustomed to the prevailing theological mood, McGavran's prayers would have come with a freshness of conviction and an expression of a heart in fellowship with God. The first prayer considered here beseeches God as sovereign to reveal to finite man something of God's cosmic plan for the redemption of the myriad tribes and tongues where the gospel had not been declared and the church had not been planted. Obviously this prayer arose from McGavran's understanding of the Great Commission and passages such as Revelation 5:12 and Daniel 7:13–14.

Almighty God to whom all things are possible, break through the barriers of our small customary thinking and show us thy power. Pull aside the veil of our limited human concern and let us see Thy plan for the redemption of all men everywhere. Increase our faith that it is the desire of Thy heart that all tribes and nations be discipled and know the blessing of Thy Word and Thy Church. In Jesus' Name we ask, Amen.

The second prayer under consideration was given February 19, 1958. Once again, McGavran addresses God as sovereign ruler of history. He praises God for the way God mysteriously prepares the hearts of peoples, tribes, and nations to be receptive to God's leading. McGavran saw the missionary as God's specially prepared servant, who under orders from his Commander-in-Chief must be obedient, totally dedicated to his Master, and heedless of personal hardship. This prayer was no mere mouthing of platitudes for McGavran knew the cost of personal discipleship. He had every reason to be concerned for the generation of young aspiring ministers who sat before him. Due to theological dilution and clerical professionalism, many who attended his classes lacked the compassion and concern of a spiritual servant.

Almighty God, by Thy mysterious movements in history, tribes and peoples and tongues and nations become responsive to Thy Word. Then, to them Thou dost send Thy servants, as Thou didst send Moses to the Hebrews of old, to lead them out of bondage to the land flowing with milk and honey. Grant, O Lord our God, that when Thou dost call us we may obey. Deliver us from any softness or selfishness, and seeking for comfort or security. Make us good soldiers of the cross, anxious to be used by Thee to the discipling of the nations, the extension of Thy churches, and the coming of Thy kingdom. This we ask in Jesus' name, Amen.

On September 27, 1957 at Phillips University he delivered his fourth lecture, which was entitled, "Why Are the Opportunities for Growth Passed Up?" As McGavran prayed before the class he paraphrased John 10:1–18. It is readily evident that this expression came forth from a shepherd's heart. When this concept is applied to the wider dimensions of McGavran's church growth ideas we discover one of the foundational theological factors behind the movement.

Look mercifully, O God, upon the multitudes that are as sheep without a shepherd. Have compassion on them as they wander unfed and uncared for, from one ignorance to another. Deliver them from false shepherds and hirelings who seek to fill them with what is not food and quench their thirst with what is not water. Raise up for them true shepherds who will lead them in green pastures beside still waters and will protect them from the onslaughts of wolves and enemies. Grant that they may find the Door of the Sheepfold and go in and out and find abundant pasture for their souls. This we ask in Jesus' name, Amen.

On April 29, 1958, the lecture topic was "The Cultural Overhang." Before delivering his insights McGavran prayed the following which was in reality the outpouring of his heart by weaving together portions of several New Testament benedictions, such as Romans 16:8, Jude 24, and Ephesians 3:20–21, which he had committed to memory. Here it becomes readily evident that church growth theory arises out of the intense theological conviction that God is absolute ruler of this universe and that God will prevail and conquer all of his enemies. The believer has every reason to be optimistic when motivated by such a vision. Hence this prayer of McGavran's is not an expression of "North American triumphalism," but arises from biblical realism.

Even in those early years when church growth concepts were in their germinal state, McGavran saw culture as God-given dimensions of every tribal heritage. His prayer expressed desire that every culture on earth would regain the ability to use their unique resources to the praise of God's glory and which would result in the united fellowship of mankind. McGavran maintained a vision of the New Jerusalem of Revelation 21 which motivated him to new exploits for Christ.

Thine O Lord, is the greatness, and the power, and the glory and the victory, and the majesty, for all that is in the heaven and the earth is thine. Thine is the kingdom, O Lord, and Thou art exalted as head above all. Let all thy creatures serve Thee. From the rising to the setting of the sun and from pole to pole, let all Thy children of whatever race or color or standard of living, confess the Name that is above every Name and be counted in the great company of the redeemed. Let every language find new depths of devotion and holiness and fulfill the purpose for which thou didst create it. In Thy service let every tribe and kindred and nation find new resources for abundant joyful life. Bring about unity among mankind O God our Father. Reconcile the diversities of mankind because of their new standing in Christ Jesus our Lord. And bring speedily the day when the New Jerusalem shall descend, and Thou shalt dwell with men and wipe away every tear from their eyes and death shall be no more. This we ask in Jesus' name, Amen.

Among McGavran's lecture notes several little prayers on unattached slips of paper were inserted. Because there was no lesson plan it was impossible to determine the exact theme of the discourse that followed. However, the following prayer reflects several New Testament certainties which McGavran considered to be "theological bedrock" for the Church Growth movement. First, in a very descriptive manner he related two truths, that just as our Creator God attends to the mysteries of the seasons, so also God as Redeemer of mankind sovereignly prepares the soil of national hearts of tribes and peoples for the presentation of the gospel.

A second aspect of the prayer was for the men in his class, as well as all missionaries and ministers of America who through the cultural conditioning of North America, only see the individualistic dimensions of salvation and fail to perceive the way God deals corporately with tribes, castes, and clans. In this prayer he was expressing the theological basis for Christward people movements and the way missionaries are invited as servants to become shepherds over God-given flocks, so that the wandering sheep may all be brought into the safety of the fold.

In the wonderfully calculated operations of nature, with sunshine and shadow, dusty dryness and muddy fields, the killing cold of winter and the quickening of springtime, the tremendous mystery of casting seed into the ground and the hundredfold return, we see O Lord of Harvest, Thy concern for the welfare of mankind. Touch our matter of fact eyes that we may also see and understand the processes by which Thou dost ripen communities and tongues and nations, till white to harvest, they can be led to walk in the Way, to cleave to the Truth, and to accept the Life which is Jesus Christ, Thy Son our Savior, without whom none comes to Thee. Then Lord thrust us out, full of Thine own concern and power, that not a single soul may be left outside Thy House, to the raven, the wolf, and the worm; but that all may be brought with joy into the abundant life and bliss of Thy presence. Grant this O Lord, for Jesus Christ's sake, Amen.

Throughout 1958, McGavran was in correspondence with several field secretaries of missions working in Africa. He was exercised over the fact that he sensed God was preparing the continent of Africa, south of the Sahara, for the most vital Christward movement in world history. Yet, from mission leader after mission leader, the day of opportunity did not seem as important as the task of "perfecting" new believers. Hence a preponderance of missionary activity and finance was being channeled into "teaching all things" while the command to "disciple all nations" languished in neglect. McGavran's concern over this imbalance between discipling and perfecting was the theme of his lecture on Tuesday, November 26, 1958 at the theological graduate school of Drake University. Before the lecture and discussion period, McGavran earnestly prayed the following:

Gracious God Thou hast made us in Thine own image and our Savior commands us to be perfect even as Thou, our heavenly Father, art perfect. Grant that our

worship offered in reverence and awe may be acceptable to Thee and that as we are
bowed here in Thy presence the mind of Christ may be increased in each one of us.
As we pray for ourselves O Lord, we remember the hundreds of millions who live in
terror of evil spirits, and have no Savior. O kindle in our hearts and in the hearts of
Christians everywhere, the compassion of Christ, that, constrained by love, we may
present the Gospel so widely and truly that all men in every land may accept Him as
Lord and Savior Whom to know is life abundant and eternal. In Jesus' name we ask.

The next prayer reflects the creative tension that existed in McGavran's mind between discipling and perfecting. It also demonstrates his understanding of perfection in Jesus Christ. His phrasing contained many direct quotations from Scripture. He understood perfecting simply to be the process by which the believer becomes so fully attuned to Christ that he reflects Christ's very mind and spirit. In some theological circles this is described as sanctification.

While McGavran longed for and prayerfully desired being perfect, whole, mature, and complete in Christ, he also prayed that the believer would never become so totally preoccupied with that aspect of spirituality that he would fail to be obedient to Christ in declaring deliverance in and through the name of Jesus to those yet under the bondage of sin, fear, and the demonic.

Gracious God Thou hast made us in thine own image and our Savior commands us
to be perfect even as Thou, our heavenly Father, art perfect. Grant that our worship
offered in reverence and awe may be acceptable to Thee and that as we are bowed
here in Thy presence the mind of Christ may be increased in each one of us. As
we pray for ourselves O Lord, we remember the hundreds of millions who live in
terror of evil spirits, and have no Savior. O kindle in our hearts and in the hearts of
Christians everywhere, the compassion of Christ, that, constrained by love, we may
present the Gospel so widely and truly that all men in every land may accept Him as
Lord and Savior Whom to know is life abundant and eternal. In Jesus' name we ask.

As McGavran was nearing the end of his time at Butler University, he gave a lecture on May 20, 1958, on the subject of "The Younger Churches." As he opened the class in prayer he rejoiced in the worldwide impact of Christ's Universal Church. He was thankful for the vast sacred task entrusted to her of carrying the Good News to the ends of the earth. He petitioned God to raise up from within her ranks a large army of men and women who would be driven by a burning passion to lead others into the presence of Christ and his fellowship.

We thank Thee Almighty God for the great profusion of missionary efforts of the Church today—that the Good News of Thy Son is proclaimed in all lands and in every language. We to whom Thou hast given so much rejoice in the opportunities of service before us. Look graciously O God upon Thy churches everywhere granting them a worthy part in thy vast and ceaseless labor for the salvation of mankind. Save us all from the crime of Cain, save us from refusing to be our brother's keeper. May all Christian churches and Christian seminaries burn with the concern of Christ, Thy Son, for the redemption of the world, O Lord we pray. Thrust out, O God, sons and daughters of the Church that they may reach into every part of the world and bring men there into new life in Christ. This we ask in Jesus' blessed name, Amen.

On January 7, 1958, while still at Phillips University, McGavran's prayer reflects the fact that it was the second day after the Christmas vacation break, hence the focus on safe travel, abundant blessings, and privileges that they had but recently experienced. In preparation for his final lecture—where he was to provide a summarization of the course, he reminded the students through his prayer of the rich learning resources at their disposal. Then he earnestly prayed that the eyes of his students would be opened to the spiritual needs of the millions in various lands who as yet have not partaken in the riches of Christ's heritage. Such prayers were not motivated by the "disease of numberitus," rather it is evident that McGavran was motivated by the words of our Lord Jesus Christ, to pray to the Lord of harvest to send forth laborers.

It is good to give thanks to you, O Lord our God. It is good to remember your mercies, your guidance, the safe journeys, the joys and blessings so abundantly granted us. We appreciate the privileges thou hast so generously bestowed upon us. We thank you for our colleges and seminaries, our great libraries, the vast accumulation of knowledge, the advance of science, the freedom of study, and wealth and leisure enough to take advantage of it. Save us from careless acceptance of all these blessings. Awake us to a lively consciousness both of our privilege and of the hundreds of millions of your children who lack these good things. Make us uncomfortable in their lack. Make us keen to bring them into the Way, the Truth, and the Life. Deepen our dedication to the spread of thy Church. Use us mightily in Thy service. These favors we ask through Jesus Christ your Son.

During the decade of the fifties, ecclesiology suffered at the hand of the mainline churches as a result of their church union quest, meanwhile evangelicals also lost the focus as a result of the rising influence of interdenominationalism. McGavran stepped into this vacuum with his church growth thinking. His priority of multiplying local churches as Christ's vehicle for the extension of his kingdom came as a fresh breeze to beleaguered missions. Church growth theology has always given a very high view to the local church. Indeed, the chief cornerstone of the movement has been the determination to once again place the local church center stage in mission strategy. It is this kind of thinking that is reflected in McGavran's prayer of February 5, 1958 at Butler University just before his lecture on the subject of "Church Growth Through Indigenous Methods."

We thank Thee O Lord our God for thy great Church spread abroad throughout the world, for Thy Household gathering to worship Thee in a thousand languages and millions of church buildings. We praise Thy name for its planting among all the families of mankind. Now as we direct our minds to the study of Thy church, help us to remember that it is Thy church and without it people perish. Guide our minds, illumine our hearts, steel our resolutions, and use us as Thou wilt that Thy churches may be multiplied bringing life to many. In Jesus' name we ask, Amen.

Such a prayer cannot be criticised without attacking the New Testament view of the local church. Take note that McGavran saw the church as the very expression of Christ himself. Here in the infancy of the Church Growth Movement McGavran stressed that the local church must be the goal and purpose behind all evangelism.

Just before departure from Phillips University on January 13, 1958, McGavran lectured on the topic of "National Leadership." His concept of the call of God upon those raised up for leadership was based on biblical models. His prayer also attests to the central responsibility of Christian leadership, that of building and extending the church. McGavran has always insisted that church growth is costly. This principle rings out with clarity as he beseeches God for great grace for those who toil in difficult places.

Almighty God, King of Kings and Leader of leaders, from of old you have called men to lead their people. You called Moses and Gideon, David and Isaiah. You created mighty leaders of Paul and Barnabas, Luther, Fox, and Campbell. Today from among the older and younger Churches, you are calling men to take your children out of many an Egypt into many a promised land. Grant those called great grace that they may work and not seek for rest, fight and not heed the wounds, labor and

ask for no reward save that of knowing that they build and extend your church.
Grant this, O God for Jesus Christ's sake.

On January 1, 1970 McGavran wrote in the preface to the 1970 revised edition of *Understanding Church Growth*: "It is at once a book on mission theology, mission theory and mission practise. These three do not exist in isolation, but as an integrated whole, theology influencing theory and practise, practise coloring theology and theory, and theory guiding practise and theology."[895]

From the above statement it is clear that McGavran's theology did not exist as some abstract concept but rather flowed out of his practise and theory. McGavran goes on to clarify further how his theology shapes his concepts of church growth. He states, "In its theological foundation the establishment of churches is pleasing to God." Then he summarizes his theology as follows:

> Church growth is basically a theological stance. God requires it. It looks to the Bible for direction as to what God wants done. It believes that Acts 4:12, John 14:6 . . . are true. It holds that belief in Jesus Christ, understood according to the Scriptures, is necessary for salvation. Church growth rises in unshakeable theological conviction.[896]

SECTION II

The prayers expressed in this section were given in McGavran's early years at Fuller Theological Seminary where he began the School of World Mission and the Institute of Church Growth.

Opening day (January 5, 1967):

Gracious and loving God. Thou dost brood over the nations of mankind, not desiring that any man should perish, and you are constantly sending ambassadors of Thy grace to tell men of the way of salvation, and to beseech them to repent of their sins and be reconciled. It is Thee, O Lord our God, Whom we worship here this morning. We bless and praise Thee for Jesus Christ Thy Son our Savior. Thou hast sent us abroad and gathered us again together in a most marvelous manner, according to that Fatherly Providence which is ever over us. Grant us this quarter quiet studious hearts, the sure knowledge that thou art pleased when we love Thee with all our

---

895 McGavran, *Understanding Church Growth*, x.
896 Ibid., 7.

minds, and an increasing understanding of the growth and development of Thy Church. Make us effective ambassadors of Thine. In Jesus' name we pray, Amen.

Prayer prayed before a People Movement Principles Lecture (winter of 1967):

Almighty God, Who dost brood over the nations of the earth, looking on each nation and each family of men with yearning love and tender affection, desiring not their destruction, but willing that all should come to faith and obedience, we invoke Thy blessing upon this gathering of Thy servants during this winter quarter of the new year Thou has bestowed upon us. Thou knowest Lord the dedication and commitment of each one here. Thou knowest our weaknesses and our strengths. We come seeking Thy face and committing our way again to Thee. We ask for a double portion of Thy Spirit, for wisdom to discern the way, for understanding of the hearts and motives, the structures and dynamics of the men to whom Thou has sent as missionaries of the Gospel.

Touch our minds, kindle our imaginations, deepen our faithfulness to our calling, lift our eyes to new truth, defend us against all assaults of the Evil One, particularly against slovenly thinking, cynicism, self-seeking, and all forms of sloth and the love of ease. Place the cross in our hearts and pour out Thy Holy Spirit on us. We ask in Jesus' blessed name.

Prayer given before a lecture on the "Cost of People Movements" (September 7, 1967):

Almighty God, our kind and loving Heavenly Father, Thou art the Father of all the families, clans, tribes, and castes of mankind. Thou dost love them all. Thou art the Creator and Author of all the different cultures of man and the grand Designer of the Mosaic of peoples. Thou O Christ hast purchased with Thy blood the peoples, tribes, and castes of the earth and dost not desire that any should perish. Give us wisdom then our Lord, to forget the mad individualism of our modern West and long that every family of men may come to know and love and obey Thee and find life!!

Prayed before a lecture on "Kinds of People Movements" (January 24, 1967):

Loving Lord, You have placed the solitary in families, ordered class and tribal worship, and sent your immediate disciples to the lost sheep of the house of Israel only. You have commanded husbands to love their wives, and wives to respect their husbands and children to obey their parents, and parents to enfold their children in an effective Christian upbringing. You gracious Lord, have created the families and clans and societies of mankind to nurture noble loyalties and reinforce good desires.

Grant then, Lord, to us your servants, gathered here this morning, a heightened sense of the sanctity of class and family life and a greater appreciation of the tremendous strength which comes to tribe and family in Christ. Grant that your churches may reinforce family life everywhere they multiply, becoming a means through which multitudes, within family and tribal organizations, may repent of their sins, and burn their idols, and find great joy and peace and family solidarity in You and Your household, the Church. Grant this we beseech Thee, for we pray thru Jesus Christ your Son and our Savior.

Prayer entitled "How is Your Call Progressing?" (January 31, 1967):

Almighty God, who of Thy good mercy hast appointed us to be ambassadors entreating men to be reconciled to Thee in the Church of Jesus Christ Thy Son, give us grace and wisdom so to win men to Thee and so to plant and multiply Thy churches that they may be truly Spirit-filled Christians and Spirit-filled churches—strong, self-reliant, holy, full of passion to spread the good news to their fellow men. Deliver, prevent, and restrain us, Almighty God, from adulterating the Gospel with Western accretions, or from requiring babes in Christ to eat solid meat. Grant that we may never minimize the offense of the cross; nor add to it offenses of our own persons or culture. In Christ's name we pray, Amen.

Prayer utilized on September 25, 1962 at the Institute of Church Growth in Eugene. McGavran repeated this prayer at the School of World Mission on September 27, 1966. This prayer is based upon the following Scripture passages: Deuteronomy 1:6–8, 19–21, 30–31; 4:7, 9–12; and 6:4–5.

McGavran's meditation:

Horeb: The mount of Revelation; organization in preparation. You have stayed long enough in preparatory pattern, organizational, organizers, splendid mission work, theological understandings of mission.

Canaan: The land now group and possess the land. Now group and multiply churches, disciple the nations, propagate the faith. This is what I called you out of Egypt to do.

The great and terrible wilderness, where you get lost and wander in circles, doing many good things, walking many a mile but getting no closer to Canaan. Planting very few churches, losing direction—deciding to settle in the desert.

Prayer: Almighty and everlasting God, gracious and loving Heavenly Father, in the midst of our pilgrimage, standing each one of us at his Horeb, we assemble at the beginning of this period of search and study, to acknowledge ourselves as Thy servants, Thy people; to listen to Thy voice and ask for Thy commands; to petition Thee for insight and imagination, for understanding and wisdom; to brush aside the petty concerns of life and fix our eyes only on Thee; to see Thy Church and the multitudes both within and without Her; to be purged of careless thinking and easy untested conclusions; to see the Truth in all things, and specially about the ways in which it pleases Thee to increase Thy churches.

Grant us, we beseech Thee, O Lord our God, Thy Holy Spirit, that our weakness may become strength, our discouragement may be transformed into determination, our limitations [Thou knowest them, Lord] may be transcended, and that the treasure we have in earthen vessels may be used to Thy honor and glory.

Guide us, O thou Great Jehovah, through the barren lands of sterile routine and unfruitful procedures, till we come to that good and large land, flowing with milk and honey, which it is Thy pleasure to give us. In Christ's name we pray, Amen.

Prayer (October 1, 1968):

Almighty God, at the beginning of this day we turn to Thee, praising Thee for Thy goodness to us, for calling us to Thy service, and giving us the privilege of a commission to bring the tribes and families of mankind to faith in Jesus Christ and obedience to Him. During these days of study grant us faithfulness in our work, intellectual honesty, clarity of vision, and Lord, knowledge of Thy will for the salvation of men.

A prayer prayed before the Principles and Procedures class (October 31, 1968):

O Lord our God, when at the first Pentecost you poured out your Holy Spirit on the common people of Jerusalem, and 3,000 were added to the church, it grew in one population and one culture and among the adherents of one religion. Today Sovereign Lord, maker of heaven and earth, when you pour out your Spirit among men, the Church grows in hundreds and thousands of cultures, sub-cultures, languages, and populations. It thrives among the adherents of many religions. Yet in all these populations, it is your church, it is the Body of Christ and the very Household of God. Help us to understand this mystery. Help us, your servants, to discern your hand in all the many manifestations of your Church. Help us to be good stewards of your grace, good channels of the water of life, that multitudes, as in the days of the Apostles, may be added to you our Lord and Savior. Amen.

A prayer given at the introduction to *Understanding Church Growth* and the message of *The Complex Faithfulness Which is Church Growth.*

O Lord our God, standing before the magnitude and complexity of Thy mission, and in the midst of the great argument and debate as to priorities, we seek Thy holy will. Reveal to us, we beseech Thee, what Thou dost desire in regard to the salvation of men's souls, the healing of their bodies, the education of their minds, and the reformation of society. Help us to base our actions, not on the accident of history, not on the decisions of our predecessors, not on outworn and outdated methods of mission, but on Thy revelation in the Bible and in Christ Jesus our Lord. Deliver us, Good Lord, from carelessly following the desires of our own hearts. Show us Thy way in which lies peace and joy and wholeness of body and spirit. Pour out Thy Holy Spirit on us, we pray, that we may be utterly Thine in all we do, say and think. In Jesus' name we pray, Amen.

A similar prayer prayed in the same context as the above (October 3, 1968):

Loving and gracious God, who of Thy great goodness hast opened a way of salvation to all who believe on Jesus Christ, Thy son our Savior, we praise Thee. That He took on Himself human form. That He bore our sins upon the cross making full propitiation for them, that He rose again from the dead, the first fruits of them that believe, and that He has taken His place at Thy right hand, there to make intercession for us, and for all men. We thank Thee Sovereign God that He is the only way, that there is no other name under heaven given among men whereby we may be saved [Acts 4:12]. And we pray that at this morning hour as we are gathered here together, we like our Master may look out upon the myriads of the unsaved with compassion, knowing that they are sheep without a Shepherd, knowing that we are sent to them to bring them home. This we ask through Jesus Christ our Lord, Amen.

McGavran was teaching chapter three of *Understanding Church Growth*: "Today's Task, Opportunity and Imperative in Missions" (October 15, 1967):

Almighty God, we confess that in the complex business of missions, when such a large variety of peoples and patterns of missionary action exist, we are often confused. We take our promotional addresses far too seriously. We are blinded by our own desires to put matters in a favorable light. We are not as careful in accounting for church growth as we should be. We are unfaithful stewards of Thy grace [though Lord, not intending it].

Forgive us, we beseech Thee, clarify our vision, give us great honesty and a great passion that thy sacrifice on the cross may be echoed in a more effective finding on our part. In Christ's Name we pray. Amen.

Chapter four of *Understanding Church Growth*: "Universal Fog Obscures Church Growth." (October 19, 1967). Here McGavran displays his total dependence upon the guiding Spirit of Christ. The overriding principle in this prayer is to know the mind of God—there is no flaunting of pragmatism in this prayer:

❦

O Thou Who Art the Way, the Truth, and Life, we bow humbly before Thee at the beginning of this class asking that Thou will indwell us, illuminate our minds, make us to love truth and to follow the Light which Thou dost impart. Deliver us from darkness and error, from wishful thinking, and easy rationalization. Give us grand honesty and clear sightedness as we deal with the sacred things Thou dost entrust to us. In Christ's name we pray, Amen.

❦

Chapter five of *Understanding Church Growth*: "Facts Needed to Discern Church Growth" (October 25, 1967):

❦

O Mind of God, Infinite Intellect who hast created the world out of nothing, who designed all the incredibly intricate patterns of life and properties of matter before they ever existed and which we now, in accordance with Thy will are beginning to discover, bless and fructify our minds, grant us keen intellects, speed our search for truth, O Lord our God, that we may be faithful servants of Thine and do the works Thou has sent us to do, Amen.

❦

Discussion on chapter five (November 5, 1968):

❦

O Lord our God, who hast again and again assured us that we shall render to Thee accounts of our stewardship, who hast said that to whom much is given, of him much is expected, whose revealed Word contains the parable of the talents and the last Judgment, help us as we press forward on Thy business to be willing to render accurate accounts of our stewardship at all times. Deliver us, Good Lord, from keeping our own financial accounts in great detail and accounting carelessly for Thy children committed to our care. Help us to rejoice in every forward surge of salvation, in the great increase of Thy Church which Thou art giving us to see. In Christ's name we pray.

❦

Dr. Ray Ortland was present for the lesson and discussion.

Chapter seven of *Understanding Church Growth*: "Sources to Search for Causes of Growth" (November 19, 1968):

Almighty God, whose heart yearns for the discipling of the multitudinous families of mankind—the tribes and tongues and peoples and nations—the urban masses and the myriad peasant hamlets and villages—we bow in prayer before you this morning asking that you teach us the secrets and the mysteries of how men become new creatures through faith in Jesus Christ our Lord. Touch our hearts, arouse our compassion Lord, open our eyes, that we may understand the complex ways in which your household grows and multiplies. In Christ's name we pray.

Two other prayers were attached to the same section. These may have been prayed in different classes in later years.

Almighty and most merciful God, we gather here as Thy redeemed. We have by Thy grace believed on the Lord Jesus Christ and been born anew and been sent out to reconcile men through proclamation of the blessed Gospel, and to disciple the nations. By Thy command, Sovereign Lord, we are therefore inevitably, necessarily, inescapably committed to and involved in the growth of Thy Church. Help us to understand its magnitude and urgency, its nature and its structures, its complexity as regards the societies of men and its utter simplicity as regards Thee Above all, Good Lord, give us compassionate hearts that we may see and feel how essential it is that men know Jesus Christ, whom to know is life abundant and eternal. And without whom millions starve, never eating of the Bread of Heaven, and suffer, not knowing the Comforter, and die, not knowing the resurrection and the Life. In Christ's name we pray.

Obviously the above prayer is an elaboration and development of McGavran's thought as it pressed upon him the need to carry the gospel to the ends of the earth.

The next prayer attached to the same section, emphasizes the sovereignty of God, his divine plan, and empowerment. McGavran was a pragmatist but also a biblical realist with regard to God's eternal purposes.

Gracious and loving God, our heavenly Father: We so easily work ahead in our own strength. We so readily forget your almighty power and Your constant presence. We think of the work as ours and so quickly the transient things of life pass and we see so dimly the things that are eternal. As we bow here in your presence, pour on our consciousness the sense of your wonderful nearness to us. You are our Father, we are your children. You are the Real: we are the unreal. You are the Master; we are the servants. If we are missionaries of the Gospel, it is only because you are the Gospel and ceaselessly search for lost men. Be reconciled with God.

And so Lord we praise You and adore You and submit ourselves to Your will and renew our vows of dedication and accept again the grace you extend to us, of which we are so unworthy, and stand in such great need. In Christ's name we pray, Amen.

The above prayer reflects the true balance in McGavran's life. Although there was a drivenness in his nature, there was also a deep dependence upon God for strength, guidance, and wisdom. In other words, the ideas McGavran wrote arose from his meditations and communion with the living God.

A footnote attached to the notes of *Understanding Church Growth* explains the need for a right focus.

By way of contrast, consider the following reason for non-growth in a nearby field in China advanced by a highly trained observer. "Our missionaries went back into China after World War II ended, but had only four years and those in most places were taken up with rebuilding the destroyed properties." The same people, the same environmental factors, exactly the same years—and no growth because attention was centered on rebuilding properties.

Study on "Helps and Hindrances to Understanding," chapter eight of *Understanding Church Growth* (November 25, 1968):

Expand our minds, O Lord, deliver us from narrow and hide-bound ideas. Help us to change what should be changed and to cleave to those things which are eternal. Help us outgrow our mistakes, adventure in new methods and means, and learn from our brethren, while at the same time we proclaim the unchanging Gospel and Thee our unchangeable Lord, Amen.

A second prayer in the same context, with a similar theme to the prayer above. Not sure of the year prayed.

Almighty God, how greatly we need wisdom to discern our duties and opportunities in spreading the Good News to every land. We thank Thee for Thy abundant grace and for the consciousness of thy nearness and love. Grant us greater insight than we have ever had into the mystery of Thy working in the Church and thru Thy servants to the redemption of men. Deliver us from cheap and superficial thinking. Keep us faithful to Thy commands and ready to render an account of our stewardship. In Christ's name we pray.

A third prayer connected with the materials in chapter eight but one year earlier (November 16, 1967):

We thank Thee Lord for Thy abundant goodness toward us, for the privilege of a commission to bring men and families and peoples to faith and obedience, for the forgiveness of our sins, the high privilege of Thy open Word before us, the riches of this library, the time to study, the excitement of understanding more and more of Thy ways with men, the enlargement of our thinking and our sympathies, the fellowship of so many of Thy servants from so many Branches of Thy Church. For all these, Good Lord, accept our gratitude and praise. Bless, we beseech our minds and our imaginations, deliver us from all lack of trust, increase in us faith in Thy Son our Savior, and grant that our day by day pilgrimage may be made walking in His footsteps. In His blessed name we pray.

Note McGavran's gratitude and praise for the trust given to God's Church in the Commission, for the gift of forgiveness for sins, for the wonder of God's Word, for the blessing of fellowship with diverse servants from so many different denominations, and for the pilgrimage to walk in Christ's steps.

A prayer attached to chapter nine of *Understanding Church Growth*: "Revival and Church Growth" (November 19, 1969):

Eternal God: who broods over all the earth, America, and India, Africa and the Philippines, Japan and Jamaica, the High Andes, and the swamps of Indonesia, it is in Your presence that we bow this morning, seeking Your face and Your blessing, seeing ourselves yet once again as Your servants, and You as our Lord and our Savior. Gracious God we have a special request this morning.

Each of us has come here from some narrow field. We know one small segment of mankind and one tiny portion of Your Body, the Church. Our experience has been so limited. We listen in amazement as others of our company tell of their labours and missions and churches. O Lord our God, we want to be faithful stewards in the specific populations to which You send us. Yet Lord deliver us from narrow parochialism. Help us to see your Gospel advancing throughout all the earth. Help us to see our problems in the larger perspective of Your global purposes. Show us Your Will through the vivid pictures of Your Work in so many places, which we read about and hear about from day to day. Keep us reaching for solutions to our insoluble problems. Illuminate us by your Holy Spirit so that we shall welcome the possibilities which keep flooding into our minds. May each week see an advance in our understanding of Your plans for the propagation of the Gospel and of Your will and power to bring those plans to pass.

Keep us from merely studying, merely listening, merely reading, and merely learning. Make each advance in understanding, Good Lord, an increase in dedication, a new offering of body and soul to Your Holy will and purpose. Make each turning of the page a sacramental apprehension of Your Spirit and Your Life. Be known to us this morning and every morning in an ever larger vision of the Gospel, and the Kingdom, and the Church, and the Resurrection, and the Life. In Christ's blessed name we pray.

This prayer reflects McGavran's passion and love for his Lord and Savior. McGavran is not expressing an overriding pragmatism, but rather an adoration and love for the Creator, King of the earth. McGavran's passion to be an obedient servant has an infectious atmosphere about it. He sees revival as those God-given events in human history when men are so filled with the powerful cleansing of the Holy Spirit that their every breath is filled with the sheer joy of servanthood.

A prayer uttered before teaching a lesson on revivals and their connections to mission and church growth (November 21, 1967):

Loving and gracious God, who answerest prayer and hast commanded us to pray without ceasing, and reminded us that he who seeks finds, we bow before Thee as we continue our study of revival. Deliver us, we beseech Thee, from prideful dependence

on ourselves. Help us to remember that our strength and our wisdom are in Thee. Let our studies make us more responsive to Thy every leading, and thus Lord revive us and fill us with divine Power and divine love. Only so Lord, can we be faithful servants or effective instruments of Thine. In Christ's name we pray.

The prayer above is a humble admission of our absolute dependence upon the Lord for our power and strength to proclaim the gospel and plant churches. McGavran pleads with the Lord to use the studies to make men and women responsive to Christ's leading and direction. He pleads for a great inner revival in the hearts of missionaries so that they can be faithful, effective instruments of the Lord's.

McGavran concludes the *Understanding Church Growth* story with eight factors where revivals have a bearing on church growth. "Missions Biblical Imperative, Historical Development Since 1800" (March 22, 1966):

Almighty and all wise God, our Father who art in Heaven, at the beginning of this quarter we turn to Thee in humility and praise. We thank Thee for this school and our opportunity to study and learn. We ask that Thou wilt lift our minds above petty provincialism and narrow self-interest, and let us see Thy world, Thy will for Thy peoples, and nations, and Thy Church at work carrying out your work everywhere. Activate our minds, stimulate our curiosity, guide our thoughts, preserve us from frittering away our precious minutes, make us earnest in our search for truth. This we ask in Jesus' name, Amen.

Prayer (May 24, 1966):

Lord God of Hosts, Who directs and marshals the Church and sends it out conquering and to conquer, we turn to Thee as we consider this morning the strategy of world mission. We would not devise our own strategy, to gratify our pride of cleverness, to advance our own petty interests; but we do wish to seek most assiduously, O Lord Our God, Thy will for Thy Mission, the strategy Thou dost command in these days, and for these churches and missions in which Thou dost send us out to work. Never was there greater need than today, O Lord. Never have there been more people to whom the Gospel must be preached, and whose lives, individual and corporate, must be redeemed if Thy will is to be done.

We thank Thee for all the evidences that Thy Church is awake and moving toward goals set by Thee. We rejoice in being called by Thee to labor in these exciting days. We do not ask for self-fulfillment O God. What happens to us is of little account. But we do ask that we carry out Thy designs, Thy policies, and Thy strategies, and lead Thy churches to fruitful action: that Thy liberating Gospel may be known to the ends of the earth, and thy will done among men on earth as it is heaven. In Christ's name we pray, Amen.

The thoughts for the above prayer are reflected in the Wheaton Declaration. Some issues discussed in the class that followed: It is important to know whether the population is receptive. Do we face closed doors? In most resistant nations or districts there are those that are responsive units. Sometimes a whole population turns responsive theological significance of responsiveness. Does it happen by accident? No! It is the finger of God.

Dated Outline for Core Course in Missions: M22, Winter Quarter, 1967:

The Biblical Base of Missions
Historical Development Since 1800
The Revolutionary World to Which God Sends Us to Evangelize
The Younger Churches
Theological Trends in Missions Today
The Ecumenical Movement and Missions
Strategy of Missions Tomorrow

In the foreward to the course Donald McGavran quotes his friend and fellow missionary Lesslie Newbegin in his lecture entitled, "The Mission and the Unity of the Church," given at Rhodes University, Grahamstown, Union of South Africa.

For a thousand years when Christendom was sealed off by Islam from effective contact with the rest of the world, and was contracting not expanding, it lived in almost total isolation from non-Christian cultures. In this situation the illusion that the age of missions is over became almost an integral part of Christianity. The perpetuation of the illusion is revealed in our normal church life, in the forms of congregations and parishes, in our conception of the ministry, and in the ordinary consciousness of churchmen.

Our theological curricula bear eloquent testimony to this illusion. Our church history is normally taught not as the story of triumphs of the gospel but as the story of internal quarrels of the church: our systems of dogmatics are not directed toward the non-Christian systems of thought but against rival statements of the Christian faith. The training of the ministry is not for a mission to the world but almost exclusively for the pastoral care of established Christian congregations.

Prayer (January 4, 1967):

Almighty and all-wise God, our Father Who art in Heaven; at the beginning of this quarter, we turn to Thee in humility and praise, thanking Thee for Church and worldwide mission Thou hast given to her. As we study this aspect of the Church, we pray that Thou wilt lift our minds above petty provincialism and narrow self-interest. Let us see Thy world, O Lord our God, and Thy will for its peoples and nations. Kindle our imaginations and our affections as we see Thy Church at work in all nations of mankind, bringing to them knowledge of Thy justice and truth and Thy plan for the salvation of mankind. Activate our minds, stimulate our curiosity, guide our thoughts, preserve us from frittering away our time, make us earnest in our search for truth, help us to see what the task to which Thou dost command us is. This we ask in Jesus' blessed name, Amen.

Attached to the above prayer are the following insights:

Rapid growth of the church must be seen again, as in Apostolic times, to be pleasing to God. He wants ripe fields reaped to the last sheaf. The Savior, not secular hunger for numbers—constrains obedient Christians to harvest. Non-growth, always ascribed to the difficulty of the field, must now be seen as often due to remediable causes—and ended.

Recommended reading, W. A. Visser't Hooft's *No Other Name*, Westminster Press, 1963. This book is a classical treatment of Christianity's struggle with syncretism. It bears the marks of Visser't Hooft's massive educated mind. The great figures of antiquity and the modern world march across its pages. The central issues of the day are presented with clarity. Hooft brings Radhakrishna, Toynbee, Goethe, Emerson, Rousseau, Whitman, Symaschus, Vivekananda, Jung, and Marcus Aurelias to the bar. He also meets their argument with what is now and ever shall be the essential Christian argument: that it pleased God to reveal himself once for all in Jesus of Nazareth and Hooft adds convincingly that the road of syncretism is in fact the road of skepticism. The first lesson focused on the extraordinary extent of missions today.

Section II of the course focused on the doctrinal foundation. McGavran listed eleven foundational doctrines for the cause of mission which he described as the pillars of the revealed religion of Jesus Christ.

1. Man made in the image of God.
2. The sinfulness, the fallen condition of natural man.
3. The inadequacy of Law—the impossibility of salvation by works.
4. The incarnation of the second person of the Trinity.
5. His atonement for sin sufficient, final, sole.
6. Justification by faith to all who believe regardless of race and condemnation of those who will not believe.
7. The indwelling and empowering of the Holy Spirit.
8. The church, the Body of Christ thru which He carries out His saving work of both persons and societies.
9. The command to reconcile men to Christ in the church and the command to disciple the nations.
10. God the Father, Almighty—no pantheism, no polytheism.
11. The return of Christ on the Day of Judgment.

McGavran recommended reading Johannes Blau's *The Missionary Nature of the Church*, for background to the above biblical base.

Prayer (March 23, 1966):

Eternal and All-wise God, in whose mind the intricate laws of nature existed before the worlds were created, to whom all our thoughts are open and from whom there is nothing hidden, we praise Thee for the Revelation of Thy Holy Will in the Bible. Grant that our study of Thy Word may not be rendered fruitless by the callousness or carelessness of our hearts; but that by it we may be roused to penitence, instructed in the way of life, and steeled to do and endure what shall please Thee, so that the Gospel may be proclaimed to all men and churches of Christ may spread abroad throughout the entire earth. In Christ's blessed name, Amen.

Prayer (January 10, 1967):

O thou Great Finder of the Lost, Who didst send Thine only begotten Son to share our lowly estate and die on the Cross that wayward, ignorant, and rebellious men might be found; grant, we beseech Thee, that the divine compassion of the Lost, manifested by our Lord Jesus Christ, may more and more characterize our own lives. We remember before Thee this day of unimaginable multitudes of Thy children who are now lost, have never heard Thy Word, do not know the name of Thy Son, for whom it is humanly impossible that they shall ever see the Bible or partake of the communion, make us keenly aware of the huge famine of Thy Word in which hundreds of millions starve. Fill our hearts, O Lord our God with such an acute sense of Thy presence, that these spiritually starving millions who we have never seen, become to us in truth, our brothers and sisters, our mothers and fathers, because they are Thy children. Help us to see them thru Thine eyes of Christ. Rebuke our selfishness, our provinciality, our nationalistic concern with our own richly served land, and send us as flaming ministers of Thy good news to multiply churches everywhere. We humbly ask in Jesus' name.

Attached to the prayer above was McGavran's article, "The God Who Finds and His Mission."

McGavran's prayer offered at Karn Griffen's Ordination at La Canada Presbyterian—in the first paragraph of this prayer McGavran prayed thoughts from 1 Peter 2:9–10.

Almighty and Everlasting God, in whom we live and move and have our being, to whose tender compassion we owe our safety in days past, all the comforts of this present life, and our hopes of that which is to come, we gather here this evening as a chosen race, a royal priesthood, a holy people, a part of your household, to worship you, to praise your Holy Name, to study your revealed Word, to ask forgiveness for our sins, and to submit ourselves wholly to your will and purposes for our lives. We do this both for ourselves and for our son and brother Karn Griffen whom we are met to ordain to the Christian ministry.

We give you thanks that You called us out of the world into the Church, that through the merits of Jesus Christ You have forgiven our sins and given us an inheritance beyond the ravages of time and the reach of Satan. We give you thanks for the hope to which you have called us . . . We praise your name for the vast resources of Your power open to all who trust in your Son, our Savior.

Pour out upon your Church, we beseech you, Your Holy Spirit that we may be freed from our fears and hesitations, and given courage to undertake those urgent tasks which lie all around us. Grant us O God such an honest and accurate knowledge of your Word that we may know what is right to do in regard to the innumerable decisions, great and small, which face us day after day. Grant us power to do the right and endurance in the cause of Christ that we may labor on as faithful servants till eventide when you call us home.

Note that large sections of this opening paragraph are interlaced with direct quotes from Scripture. Note the comprehensive view McGavran expresses concerning the activities of the church in worship. This prayer was also personal as it included the purpose for the assembly was to ordain Karn Griffen, McGavran's son-in-law.

The section below of McGavran's prayer is a biblical overview of the nature of salvation, the forgiveness of sins through the merits of Jesus our Lord, the eternal hope we have in Christ, and for the spiritual gifts of power given as gifts to God's servants (April 31, 1980).

Loving and merciful God we gather this week in the shadow of thy cross. Calvary is ever before us. We and your whole household throughout the world are living again the pain, and shame and agony of your Son, our Savior and realizing afresh the price that was paid for our salvation and the salvation of the myriad who have yet to believe. Grant us grace, as we study the theologies of mission, to realize that we are talking not about mere words. Grant us power to act, to do theology, to spread the good news of redemption to your lost children everywhere. In Christ's blessed name, we pray, Amen.

This prayer reflects the Easter season and McGavran's concern that we do theology arising out of the Calvary Event.

A prayer given in the Contemporary Theology of Mission Class which is a series of direct portions from Psalm 119 (April 19, 1980):

Forever, O Lord our God, Thy Word is firmly fixed in the heavens. Thy faithfulness endures to all generations. Thy Word is a lamp to my feet and a light to my path. I have sworn an oath and confirmed it, to observe Thy righteous ordinances. I am Thy servant: give me understanding that I may know thy testimonies. Thy testimonies are wonderful, therefore my soul keeps them. The unfolding of Thy words gives light and imparts understanding to the simple. Amen.

The prayer below stresses we are stewards of the gospel (April 11, 1979):

Again, O Lord our God, we gather to praise You, to rest our weakness on your strength, our uncertain opinions on Your sure Word. As we consider the contemporary theology of missions held by your servants who call themselves evangelicals, guide our minds into all truth. Indwell our spirits. Prepare us for the day when we shall render accounts to You our Savior and our God. In Christ's name we pray, Amen.

Cultural sensitivity, but no compromise with the Truth (March 14, 1974):

Almighty and everlasting God, Who for our sake and for the sake of all men, of all ethne became flesh and lived amongst us full of grace and truth, that we might know authoritatively what is your good and perfect will . . . help up to present your unchanging revealed truth in ways in which our children and our neighbors and the distant tribes of men can understand. Help us to make salvation in Jesus Christ real and vivid and meaningful to those to whom you send us. Grant that we ever consider this an important part of our work—to learn the language well . . . to listen to those we evangelize and to put ourselves in their places and to prepare a right mix of Christianity and culture. In Christ's Name we pray, Amen.

McGavran held to a high view of the Bible (January 1, 1974):

We thank You Lord, for the infinite variety of man's apprehension of goodness, truth and beauty. How greatly we are pleasured by them. How we revel in the literature, the music, the art, the stories, the architecture, the forms of government and the whole variegated panorama of life. When we consider the equally infinite errors, ugliness, cruelty, deception, and exploitation however, Lord we thank You, that You have made known Your Holy Will. You have not left us fatherless to play of speculation, appetite, error, and sin. You have given us a sure guide in Your Word and supremely in Your Son. Help us rightly to understand and courageously to follow and obey. Give us clearly to see the right and fearlessly to follow the Light. Thanking You for the Bible which is a lamp to our feet, we pray in the name of Him who is the Light of the world. Amen.

Believers are subject to God's leading (October 5, 1967):

The Mission, O Lord our God is Thine. It arose in Thy heart. Thou didst send the Savior and didst lay down the way of salvation for all men. Thy Son on the cross made atonement for the sins of men. Thou dost choose and send forth missionaries of the Good News. You do breathe upon peoples and churches arise. Give us, thy servants, we beseech thee, right knowledge and right doctrine, that the mission may be carried forward in accordance with thy will. Not what seems reasonable to us, O Lord, but what thou dost desire and what thou dost command and what thou dost empower us to do. We wait on thee, in these days and every day of our lives. Speak Lord, for we thy servants hear. In Jesus' blessed Name, AMEN. [P and P notes]

For McGavran even the academic world was a spiritual quest into the presence and purposes of God. He served a Sovereign God who is at work in the world. The stress of the above prayer is for the spiritual disciplines of life to be so ordered in each of his students and fellow faculty members that they would constantly be discovering where God is at work and join Him in the task of extending Christ's kingdom through the multiplication of churches. He understood the concept of "Missio Dei" long before it was coined.

(October 1, 1964) Almighty God, at the beginning of this day we turn to thee praising thee for thy goodness to us, for calling us to thy service and giving us the privilege of a commission to bring the tribes and families of mankind to faith in Jesus Christ and obedience to Him. During these days of study grant us faithfulness in our work, intellectual honesty, clarity of vision, and knowledge of Thy will for the salvation of men. Amen.

Concluding Thoughts on McGavran's Prayers

All of the above listed prayers flowed out of McGavran's heart and soul. All were prepared well in advance of their actual use. All were related to the lesson topic of the class that was to follow. All had an authenticity that prepared the hearts of his students and laid a theological base for the lesson to follow.

These prayers establish the fact that the lessons of church growth and missiology which McGavran taught came out of biblical convictions and a life of prayerful obedience to Christ.

CONCLUSION

The eight preceding chapters can give the impression that McGavran was planning, plotting, and preparing for the day when the Church Growth Institute would come into existence and the Church Growth Movement would flourish and have a worldwide impact. There are several strands in the period from 1954–65 that give this impression: his residence for several years in the vicinity of the Day Mission Library where he had opportunity to read widely regarding the expanding worldwide network of missions, during this same period he frequently attended conferences of the leaders of mission, the publication of *Bridges of God* and numerous articles on church growth, his rare opportunity to traverse Africa visiting Kenya, Uganda, Ruanda, Congo, Nigeria, Ghana in 1954, later he had opportunity to study church growth in Jamaica, Puerto Rico, Philippines, Thailand, and Taiwan, and for his growing volume of correspondence with Christian leaders around the world on a vast array of topics relating to the growth of Christ's kingdom.

What may appear as a series of supernatural events converging to produce the Church Growth movement did not appear that way to McGavran during the decade of quest. He perceived himself as a lone voice crying out in the wilderness with no one listening. His message to arouse the church to do more toward fulfilling her obligation to propagate the gospel seemed to fall on deaf ears. Many mission leaders dismissed McGavran's ideas as irrelevant. Victor Hayward reminded McGavran that the Lord was not pleased when David numbered the tribes of Israel. One former colleague from India denounced People Movements as of little significance compared to the old fashioned gathered colony approach of evangelism. Several mission societies in the late 1950s interpreted church growth thinking as a direct attack on their failure to be productive for the Lord.

McGavran frequently read the thirty-third chapter of Ezekiel and saw himself in the text as the "watchman." If the people of the land take a man from among them and make him their watchman, and if he sees a sword coming upon the land . . . and does not blow the trumpet . . . and the sword comes and takes anyone of them away . . . his blood will I require at the watchman's hand.

During this decade from 1954–65, McGavran saw his former friends and colleagues hardening themselves against church planting evangelism in favor of the spiritual drift of the Conciliar Missionary Movement. There was a deliberate attempt to rethink missions in terms of coexistence with the great religions. As a result of a growing focus on social action and a growing opposition to biblical principles within the World Council of Churches, McGavran found himself diametrically opposed to their position. The UCMS mission board under which McGavran served for thirty-five years was also showing signs of intolerance to McGavran's vision and passion for fostering people movements to Christ.

McGavran grew impatient with the role assigned him by UCMS as the peripatetic professor of mission. He and Mary moved from one side of the US to the other, taking up residence in various temporary housing situations for six months in any one location. In each college McGavran would teach ministerial candidates that "missions is wonderful." Aside from teaching in colleges, he gave missionary talks in churches seeking to advance the missionary cause. Such opportunities came during evenings, weekends, and vacation periods. But after a period of six years in this routine he grew restless and dissatisfied. He and Mary began searching for real estate. They tramped over properties in the Salem and Portland areas. One situation appealed to them—it was located in the hills west of Salem—it was an attractive ten acres, with walnut trees. The McGavrans fantasized retiring to such a property to tend their rose garden and the price was right, $12,000, which was a good buy even in 1959. He felt he had done his part as God's watchman—he had warned the churches of the coming sword—but they would not listen. He sensed it was time to stop being a nuisance—it was thoughts like these that came to him in his weaker moments and that weighed on his soul when he was overwhelmed by the failure and ineffectiveness of this period of time in his life.

Then McGavran struck up a relationship with Ross Kinsler who was president of the Northwest Christian College located next to the University of Oregon Campus in Eugene.

Ross had a kindred spirit with McGavran—he moved mountains to get the Church Growth Institute established on his campus. Mary and Don McGavran found a ranch southwest of Eugene and they, along with Don's sister Grace, were able to scrap up enough money for their dream estate of 250 acres. They named the place Fox Hollow.

It was home! This purchase became a gold mine for them as prices for property quickly arose. They sold the ranch sometime in the seventies and used the funds to endow the Chair of Church Growth at Fuller Seminary.

The McGavrans' move to Pasadena in 1965 to direct the newly founded School of World Mission and the Institute of Church Growth at Fuller Seminary had the hand of God written over it. The timing and the circumstances of McGavran being called to serve at Fuller Theological Seminary were beyond his wildest dreams . But now that dimension must remain for the second section of this story which should be published in the next few years.

APPENDIX A

McGAVRAN'S MISSIONARY ROOTS

In a biographical sketch of Donald McGavran, Fishburn described missions as the "natural expression of his [McGavran's] heritage."[897] Nineteen fifty-four was a centenary of the Anderson-McGavran families' missionary service. James Henry Anderson, Donald McGavran's grandfather, had sailed for India in 1854. The centennial celebrated the combined ministry of various family members totaling 362 years in India.

James Henry Anderson

Following the example of William Carey, James Henry Anderson and his wife, Agnes, set sail in 1854 from London for India via the Cape of Good Hope. Their journey lasted a total of six months, and during the trip they were becalmed for some time in the Indian Ocean. Drinking water on the vessel was exhausted, but God providentially supplied rain which spared their lives. The English Baptist Mission was centered in the state of Bengal, and so James Anderson began his missionary work in the town of Jessore. An article written as part of the Anderson-McGavran centenary described the scene which greeted this couple. "It was a day of sailing vessels, oxcarts, camel trains, hand looms with jungle unlimited, tigers, panthers, wolves and hyenas on the outskirts of every village."[898]

James Anderson served in a variety of posts, including two years as principal of Serampore College and Seminary, a school founded by William Carey. This is the only graduate theological school in India with a government charter.

Because of the close historical identity between the Christian churches of the US and the Baptist denomination in England, Anderson assisted the missionaries of the Christian church in getting established. As a result in the late 1880s, the Andersons were posted to Bhilaspur in Central India for several months. McGavran's grandfather was directly responsible for opening up this region for the Disciples of Christ and it was this area where the McGavrans served from 1936–54.

James and Agnes Anderson parented four sons and four daughters. Three of these children returned to India as missionaries and were later to play a major role in the life of Donald McGavran.[899]

---

897 Fishburn, *They Went to India*, 89.
898 Donald McGavran, "India Through a Century," *World Call* 36, no. 7 (July–Aug. 1954): 36–37.
899 Donald McGavran, interview by Vern Middleton, June 2, 1985.

Herbert Anderson

Herbert Anderson was the second son of James and Agnes. As a young man he returned to India to serve Jesus Christ and establish churches. Early in his missionary career he was appointed field secretary of the Baptist Mission and took up residence in Calcutta.

Herbert Anderson's reputation spread throughout India as a result of his part-time position as Secretary of the National Council of Churches, a post he assumed shortly after its formation on February 4, 1914. He served the Council for eight years and traveled widely. He was a major source of inspiration for the Evangelistic Forward Movement launched by Sherwood Eddy in 1916. During Anderson's tenure the missionaries and church leaders throughout India were galvanized into bold, aggressive evangelism.[900] More will be said about this movement in chapter three.

Poor health forced Herbert Anderson to retire from the post as secretary in 1922. A minute of the National Council of Churches reads, "Because of the thoroughness of his work and the ability, tact and courtesy with which he discharged the duties of his office, the Council has been firmly established."[901]

Due to Anderson's involvement in the Christian temperance movement in India he became friends with Raja Bhopal Achariya. Achariya later became governor general of India and invited Anderson to the Vice Regal Lodge in Delhi in 1946. Enroute to Delhi, Anderson visited the McGavran home in Takhatpur. Donald McGavran had just read a book entitled, *Religious Liberty*, which addressed the issue of freedom of religious expression and propagation. Anderson and McGavran felt the book was exactly what the framers of India's constitution needed to assist them in their task. Thus when Anderson was in Delhi, he diplomatically presented the book as a gift to Achariya who was a member of the task force for framing the constitution.

Forty years later, McGavran still wondered what significance that book played in the rather strong statement in the Indian Constitution guaranteeing freedom to preach, propagate, and practise one's faith.[902]

Isabelle Anderson

Isabelle, the sister of Herbert, strengthened the Anderson-McGavran missionary ties in 1886 by marrying George Walker Jackson, a missionary of the Disciples of Christ stationed at Bhilaspur in Central India. Among their first converts were Hira Lal and his bride-to-be, Sonarin. The Jacksons established a reputation for their combined gifts of music, evangelistic zeal, and fluency in Hindi. Tragically, George suffered a nervous breakdown, forcing them

---

900 Baago, *A History of the National Council of India*, 16–18.
901 Ibid., 16–18.
902 Donald McGavran, interview by Vern Middleton, June 2, 1985.

to return to England in 1891, the very year John McGavran arrived to begin his missionary career. However, their labors were not in vain. In 1936, the Jacksons' first convert played a major role in the ministry of Donald McGavran. Hira Lal became McGavran's Indian coworker. McGavran respected Hira Lal as a spiritual guru and regarded him as the key for the Satnami people movement for which he labored seventeen years.

Helen Anderson

Helen, a second sister of Herbert, after college in England, returned to Darjeeling where she taught the children of tea plantation owners and managers. She met her future husband John Grafton McGavran there while he was recovering from a life-threatening case of malignant malaria.

Shortly after his return to Bhilaspur, where he had been working, Helen departed with her parents for England. Because he rarely spoke to her it took several months for John to muster up enough courage to ask, "Miss Anderson, would you allow me to correspond with you?" Her negative response to this request delayed him several more months, before he dared to write again. This time her response was: "Well, what took you so long?"

Helen and John married in Bombay in 1895. They had a brief honeymoon in Poona, which was spent nursing John back to health since he had come down with another bout of malaria shortly after the wedding. Their honeymoon was also a time of cultural adjustment, especially for Helen. She was a prim and proper young English lady, and John was something of a rugged pioneer who had lived as a bachelor on the edges of India's jungles for four years.

Damoh at that time was in the grip of a devastating famine. John and Helen initially lived in a tent upon their arrival in Damoh in October 1895. Then they graduated to a grass hut, twelve by fifteen feet in size. Here their first child, Grace, was born in November 1896.[903]

Helen McGavran's depth of character, her undiluted love, and her great intellect were a tower of strength to her family. Fishburn described her contribution to the missionary cause as:

> She helped train Bible Women for service and worked with them in their homes.
> She taught in Sunday Schools, taught her own children and others, helped mother
> the orphanage boys, went on evangelistic trips with her husband. She helped new
> missionaries get a start in the language and an understanding of the customs.
> She did considerable writing of materials for use by the Indian Christians and
> prepared a book of the Christian hymns of India.[904]

---

903 Donald McGavran, interview by Vern Middleton, December 20, 1984.
904 Fishburn, *They Went to India*, 22.

Her genius is seen in the fact that she was the first to write music for Indian *bhajans* (an Indian musical). This talent was later inherited by her son Donald. This meant a thorough mastery of the Hindi language as well as skill with music quite unfamiliar to the Western ear. The above would be enough to keep any woman busy, but beyond that she mothered and raised four children: Grace, Donald, Edward, and Joyce. Her input into their lives produced profound dividends in each of her children.[905]

John Grafton McGavran

John McGavran came from Scotch-Irish ancestry. His forebears in Ireland fled that land after a bomb violently disrupted a prayer meeting in which several were killed. Possibly because of his roots, as well as his character, John McGavran became known as "Fighting Mac" to his classmates at Bethany College.[906]

John McGavran was born in West Virginia and raised in Colombiana County in northeastern Ohio. His grandparents were among the early converts and followers of Alexander Campbell, the founder of the Disciples of Christ movement.[907]

While at college John had plans to study medicine, but the missionary challenge led him to abandon these plans. He sailed for India in 1891, at the age of twenty-four. He took up work in Harda, a station that had been opened by pioneer Disciples missionaries, G. L. Wharton and Albert Norton in 1882.

> After his marriage to Helen Anderson, John McGavran pioneered the work at Damoh. The rationale for this was expressed in an interview with Donald McGavran. Eighteen ninety-five was the beginning of the great famine, which swept India, killing hundreds of thousands of people. The India Mission of the Disciples of Christ found that all its missionaries were starting little orphanages in their compounds. Knowing that something much better was required the mission decided to start a boy's orphanage at Damoh. Two hundred acres of land were secured from the government, with no buildings or well. John McGavran and his fellow missionary, Rambo, went there and lived in grass huts while building shelters for the orphans who poured in day by day.[908]

John McGavran possessed a sharp mind which he ably used as he presented the gospel. He would chide the Brahmans who debated with him, "You carefully avoid killing animals, but you kill when you drink water. Then he would proceed to put some drinking water between two slides and project it on a screen showing the people microbes and bacteria which populate each drop."

---

905 Baago, *A History of the National Council of India.*
906 Donald McGavran, "John Grafton McGavran."
907 Donald McGavran, interview by Vern Middleton, June 2, 1985.
908 Donald McGavran, interview by Vern Middleton, December 20, 1984.

John McGavran became professor of Indian Studies at the Disciples' College of Missions. The College was the direct outgrowth of the insights and inspiration John McGavran and other Disciple Mission leaders received while at the Edinburgh conference (1910). There they heard much about the importance of the training of missionaries. The Foreign Christian Missionary Society and the Christian Women's Board of Missions raised $400,000 and built a College of Missions, at which they would train the many missionaries they were sending out to the ten mission fields in which they were carrying out the Great Commission. They called John McGavran to be the professor of Indian subjects, to teach Hindi to the missionaries going to India.

SUMMARY OF HINDU BELIEFS: McGAVRAN'S SYSTEMATIZATION OF HINDU THEOLOGY

A. Beliefs about Deity

1. God—the Absolute—is conceived of in nonethical form, either pantheistically or monistically.

a. God is not limited by moral laws. God is beyond morality.

b. God is indifferent to men, neither loving nor hating, neither helping nor hindering them.

c. God is impersonal—attributes of personality cannot be ascribed to him.

d. God is responsible—the world is a creation of his sport, whim, or lila.

e. God is unknowable and remote.

2. God is to be known and worshipped in the forms in which one's ancestors have worshipped him—trees, animals, images, persons, incarnations, or the three great gods.

a. The lesser gods not only represent the Absolute, but are in themselves definite supernatural personalities to be worshipped and propiated.

b. Any form of worship is right if one's ancestors or one's caste have practised it. All religions, therefore, are equally true.

c. No one should change from the religion of his ancestors to another religion.

d. From among all gods each person should choose a patron deity especially appealing to him—the *isht devata*.

e. Many gods should be worshipped.

3. Much of life is affected by the wills or potencies of spirits.

a. Disease, harvests, accidents, success, and fruitfulness are largely influenced by the actions of various kinds of spirits.

b. Many natural phenomena, such as fields, mountains, animals, plants, rivers, and forests are the dwelling places of the field spirits, and mountain spirits; rivers and forests are themselves divine.

c. Cow killing is a very great sin.

B. Beliefs about the World

4. The material phenomenal world is illusory.
    a. The only real good is in the nonpersonal spiritual realm.
    b. Machinery does not provide any valid progress.
    c. Poverty and wealth are parts of illusion.
    d. Asceticism or the renunciation of the world is a most certain way to real progress.
5. The world is growing progressively worse towards dissolution.
    a. There are four stages in the world's existence of which this is the worst and last.
    b. Nothing man can do will change the inevitable downward trend.
    c. Life is essentially pain, suffering, sorrow, and evil.
6. The old is better than the new. (Not distinctively Hindu but thought to be true today among ninety percent of the population).
    a. The old customary way is the best way.
    b. Caste laws and regulations rule supreme.
    c. The Vedas contain all knowledge and all truth. Any modern discovery is a rediscovery. Ancient India knew all that we know today and more. Old India was a great deal better and wiser than the India of today. The tendency to idealize Ram Raj.
7. What is to be, will be, despite man's efforts to promote or hinder it.
    a. Conditions in this life are determined by fate.
    b. To attempt to change them is useless.
    c. Resignation to one's lot is a virtue.

C. Beliefs about Man

8. Men according to their natures are born into four castes: Brahman, Kshatriya, Vaishya, and Shudra.
    a. The caste of the physical body mirrors the spiritual development of the soul.
    b. Each caste has its own distinctive social functions or occupations, for righteousness.
    c. Outcastes are not Hindus.
    d. No man should change his caste.
    e. Man's first loyalty is to his caste, rather than to his city, profession, or village.
9. The individual is subordinate to the social group.
    a. Even a grown man should obey his father and grandfather in all matters.
    b. A man's ancestors continue as a genuine living part of his household and must be fed and worshipped at the festival of *Pitr Moksh* (ancestor redemption).
    c. Marriage should be arranged for the young man and young woman wholly by parents or other elders.

d. Right actions for the individual are those which the caste engages in or approves.

10. Women are inferior to men.

a. Birth as a woman indicates a low stage of spiritual development.

b. The ideal woman is an obedient, chaste, loyal, and devoted servant of her husband.

c. Women are less truthful, less intelligent, and more sinful than men.

d. Sons are to be desired more than daughters.

e. Nevertheless, motherhood is to be honored and is semi-divine. Mothers are to be reverenced as much as fathers.

11. The Brahman is a god and is to be revered as such.

a. All Brahmans are per se spiritually superior.

b. To help a Brahman is very meritorious, to hurt one is a heinous sin.

12. Morality is chiefly to abide by caste laws.

a. Different types of action are permitted and forbidden to different castes.

b. The caste virtues, which to fulfill is righteousness are:

i. For the **Brahman,** quietude, self-restraint, austerity, purity, uprightness, continence, knowledge, religion, and the like.

ii. For the **Kshatriya,** bravery, fighting the enemy, lordliness, generosity, etc.

iii. For the **Vaishya,** to engage in commerce, agriculture, to produce, to earn, etc.

iv. For the **Shudra,** to serve the upper castes, to obey his betters, and the like.

c. Different castes differ in degree and kind of morality possible to them.

d. In general, the good of the caste, not the good of mankind, determines what is right.

e. There is strict enforcement of caste moral code or of caste mores.

13. Each soul is reborn higher or lower in the scale of being for countless incarnations.

a. The soul—that which passes from one body to another—is not personality (will, memory, purposes, and organization of habits and values) but is the *atma*, a drop of God, a portion of the Absolute, colored by unexpiated karma.

b. It is possible for a soul to be reborn in animal, reptile, and vegetable as well as human forms.

c. Salvation occurs when through some means the atma imprisoned in a series of bodies achieves union or amalgamation with the Absolute—as a drop of water falling into the ocean—and thus escapes rebirth.

14. All events in the lives of men are predetermined by prior actions in former births.

a. A person's wealth, caste, fortune, health, and all other aspects of his life depend upon the quality and quantity of his acts in former births.

b. Suffering is the just, proper, and inevitable punishment for former sins.

15. Nonkilling is the most excellent duty (Ahimsa parmodharm).

a. Nonkilling means primarily, not killing any living thing and secondarily, kindness, humaneness, or harmlessness.

b. To take life is inherently a sin.

c. To take life is a supreme sin.

d. Meat eating is sinful, since it involves killing animals.

e. The degree of sinfulness in killing depends on the degree of excellence of the soul in the life taken.

D. Miscellaneous Beliefs

16. Manual labour is degrading.

17. Charms, amulets, magic, and the stars have undoubted potency.

18. Beliefs about sacred books.

APPENDIX C

BRIDGES OF GOD THESIS STATEMENT

To Family: Ed, Mary, Helen, Kip, Malcolm, Mither, and Grace.
November 15, 1951, McGavran in jungle for twenty-eight days.
I am writing a book on how peoples are Christianized. My thesis is this:

I. That the normal way in which peoples are Christianized is by group action. The individual acceptance of Jesus Christ as Lord and Savior, which is what the individualistic Western Church now believes is the only correct, orthodox, and meaningful way, is not the way in which peoples, societies, races, castes and clans turn to Christ. Peoples (as opposed to individuals) turn to Christ in group action, by consultation among themselves, by following some convinced leader, by religious migration, so to speak. After that, sanctification can proceed through individual conversion and meaningful dedication by individuals.

II. That Christian missions during the last century, depending on the one-by-one conversion pattern, have, in general, met with disappointing results. They have established a vast number of mission stations in each of which there is a small, static, non-growing church made up of the one-by-one converts. Then, the leaders of the mission station, frustrated by the small growth of the church, have turned to secondary goals such as removing illiteracy, aiding in educational advancement of the nation, improving the health of the nation, relieving human suffering, promoting international understanding, and the like. In this way they have rendered tremendous service and have helped far more than most people imagine to bring about a national rebirth among the Eastern nations.

III. But the day of their influence is rapidly coming to an end, with the intense nationalistic spirit in the East and the resolve of Eastern peoples to do their own education, their own medicine, their own social programs, and to clean their own houses.

IV. While the Mission Station Approach has been the typical approach of the last century, people movements, race movements, caste movements, and tribe movements to Christ have started all over the world. These have suffered from malnutrition as the missionary movement, enamoured by the institutional approach and indirect influence on non-Christian societies, gave most of its attention to the building up of institutions among the missions stations. But these group movements have survived in many cases despite malnutrition, and exist as the great field of missionary endeavour in the years ahead. Non-Christian nations will probably refuse much entry to missionaries, except where politically powerful Christian movements call missionaries to come and serve them. There will continue to be free entry . . . in the aid of an existing Christian movement, aiding it to be more Christian, more educated, more health, and more growing, the missions of the future will find their raison dêtre. It is an ambitious undertaking. If successful, it will point a new direction in foreign missions. However, it is sure to be attacked as narrow and unsound. I am having to write it very carefully.

APPENDIX D

McGAVRAN'S *UNITED CHURCH REVIEW* ARTICLES AND EDITORIALS

Articles

1936 "Revival in Sterile Areas," I and II
1938 "India's Oppressed Classes and Religion," 183–92

Editorials

1941 May, vol. 12, no. 5
"Christianity and War"— an evaluation of Christian attitudes and war
"Jai Yishu ji ki"—McGavran introduces himself as editor
"Stages in Church Growth"—church–mission issues
"The War on Leprosy"

1941 June, vol. 12, no. 6
"Chiang Kai Shek and Matsuoka"—two Christian leaders and Japanese aggression
"Christian Magazines and the War"—critique of pacifism
"Quo Vadis?"—staying at one's post in the face of war
"The Use of Christian Literature"—need for book promotion
"Under the Shadow of Death: The Gospel Witness"—new magazine
"Unoccupied Territory"—church growth

1941 July, vol. 12, no. 7
"Did You Know?"—current events
"Evangelism, Sanctification, and the Social Gospel"—critique of the social gospel
"Four Significant Agreements"—new directions of cooperation
"The Church Tomorrow"—church–mission issue
"The World Tomorrow"—evaluation of the Malvern Conference
"Where Was the Leadership?"—critique of social action ideas

1941 August, vol. 12, no. 8
"Courage"—war produces more Christ-likeness in believers
"Depressed Classes On the Move"—20,000 join the Sikhs
"Facing Tomorrow Intelligently"—church mission issues in the light of the advancing war
"Fifty Reasons"—evaluation of the rural churches
"German Christian Contribution"—positive comments on German theology and insights
"Getting Together"—church union
"Institutions and Evangelism"—danger of isolation and failure to evangelize
"Jai Pal Singh"—leader of Untouchables in Bihar
"Money for Defense"—Christian contributions
"Undreamed of Opportunity"—church growth opportunities

1941 September, vol. 12, no. 9
"And Marched"—church growth quote from Babar
"Christian Unity at Panama"—Episcopalians cooperate with Evangelicals
"Pacifist and Non-Pacifist Christians"
"Praying for Gandhi's Conversion"
"The Apostles Creed"—a defense
"The Basic Bible"
"The Christian Marriage Act"—mixed marriages suggested in act
"Union Evangelization"—cooperation for evangelization
"Yes, It Happened in India!"—assisting churches in construction
"Why Not a Thoroughly Indian Party?"—politics

1941 October, vol. 12, no. 10
"Caste and Christianity"—McGavran evaluates caste as evil
"Caste-Indians"—McGavran objects to Christians putting caste name down
"Hodgepodge"—current events
"The Authority of the National Christian Council"—less sovereignty more brotherhood

1941 November, vol. 12, no. 11
"Body or Spirit"— the evil of caste
"Final Qualification for Voting"—tithing and right to vote
"Seasonal Evangelism"—appeal for prayer
"The Fish Incarnation"—theology of God
"The Indian Christian Book Club"

1941 December, vol. 12, no. 12
"A Great Church"—church growth measurement

"Animal Sacrifice in Hinduism"—a regular occurrence

"Ceasar and God"—is it right to celebrate Gandhi's birthday?

"Church Gov. and Freedom"—Congregationalist polity

"Missions in War Time"—missions hardly imperialistic!

"Service as Bait"—question of social service

"The Irreducible Minimum of Belief"—Jesus is Lord

"The Peace and India"—concern for freedom of religion

"Things of Interest"—current events

1942 January, vol. 13, no. 1

"100 Lakhs of Christians"—ten million Christians in India

"A Church Standard"—church growth quality concern

"Dogma"—apologetic for dogma

"Here and There"—current events

"Praying for Church Union"

"The Church—A Problem or a Power"—concept of lift

"Today and Revelations"—a brief commentary from an Indian perspective

"Unity in Foreign Missions"

"World-Wide Communion"

1942 February, vol. 13, no. 2

"Ashrams"—a sub-Christian practise

"God's Conversation"—God's sovereignty even in times of war

"In the War"

"Mission Compounds"—small ashrams

"Mixed Marriages and the Marriage Act"

"Standing Committees on Church Union"

"The Indian Group of Nations"—India's makeup and independence

1942 March, vol. 13, no. 3

"Evangelism—Two Schools"—church growth people movement issue

"Fellowship of Christian Authors and Artists"

"Federation of Evangelical Churches in India"—church union among Lutherans

"Front Page News"—aid extended to Harijans

"Prayer and the War"

"Pre- and Post-Baptismal Instruction"

"The Bible Suppressed and Sought"

"Union Within the Family"—advocates churches of same polity form initial stage of union

1942 April, vol. 13, no. 4
"Basic English Bible"
"Be Fair to the Nazis"—do not confuse Nazis with Germans
"Carry On"—God's Concern for those embroiled in war
"Caste and Anti-Semitism"
"Christians Under Persecution"—preparation for persecution
"Front Page News"—church union
"Joint Ordination"—church union issue
"Neutrality and a Free India"—rebuke to Indians who want to be neutral about the war
"The World Council of Churches"—new members

1942 May, vol. 13, no. 5
"Hendrik Kraemer"—on biblical revelation
"India's Freedom"—Untouchables
"Redemption and Righteousness"—church growth quality
"Reinhold Niebuhr"—book review

1942 June, vol. 13, no. 6
"Clerical Costume in India"—indigenization
"Front Page News"—church union
"The Churches and the War"—US and Christian attitudes to war
"The Irenic Approach Tested"—apologetics—crown of Hinduism idea
"What is Truly Indigenous"—indigenaity
"Why Missionaries Stay"—missionaries held by the Japanese

1942 July, vol. 13, no. 7
"Co-operation of Major Faiths"—no place for syncretism
"High Mass in a Congregational Church"—church union
"Indian Christian Book Club"—caste issue
"Khicharee"—current events
"Laymen and the Church"—church growth lay leadership
"Missionary Advance Following the War"—prophetic insights
"Regeneration"—need for born-again Christians
"The Education of the Germans and the Japanese"—after the war
"What Constitutes the Bulwark"—quote from Lincoln

1942 August, vol. 13, no. 8
"Barth, Baillie and Ward"—on a Christian view of war
"Education and Salvation"—secularization of education must stop

"Evangelization a Mission Task?"—church growth and the local church
"Just Retribution"—war issues
"Muddy Thinking"—church–mission issue
"Presbyterianism and Episcopalianism"—church union

1942 September, vol. 13, no. 9
"God is our Refuge and Strength"—sobering trends
"Lack of Biblical Rootage"—problem of secularism
"Potpouri"—current events
"The Gospel of Barnabas"—Islamic issue
"The Will-o'-the-Wisp"—church–mission issue

1942 October, vol. 13, no. 10
"After Deducting"—fund raising
"Americans and the War"— reversal of pacifism
"I Was in Hell with Niemoeller"
"Missionaries: Quit India"—church–mission issue
"Pakistan and the World Federation"—Indian independence issue
"The Cutting Edge of the Apostles Creed"—commentary
"The Servant in the house"—McGavran's high regard for servants
"United Church Canvas"—cooperation church union

1942 November, vol. 13, no. 11
"Foreign Soldiers"—entertain in homes
"Minimum conditions for a Christian Way of Life"—famine
"Students and Politics Today"—Ralla Ram's advice
"The Church to Come"—church union
"The Conversion of the Church"—church must be rooted in doctrine

1942 December, vol. 13, no. 12
"Indigenous Christianity"
"Pastor Schneider"—denounces Nazis
"Potpouri"—current events
"The Great Split in Christendom"—humanism in the church
"The Post War World"—prophetic insights
"The Shot of the Month"—McGavran's uncle's action in Calcutta
"The West Exposed"—war issues
"Whose Priyashisha?"—syncretistic issue

1943 January, vol. 14, no. 1
"A Better Christian Than"—Christian is a redeemed man
"Christian Havildar Major Receives I.D.S.M."
"Conversion and Freedom"—freedom to propagate one's faith in new constitution
"Political Parallels"—church–mission issues
"Study Non-Christian Religions"—insight and attitudes to other faiths
"The Prophet of the Absolute"—book review on Kierkegaard
"Union Now"—church union
"Victory and Harvest"—Christianity and the war
"What Does Ambedkar Think?"—people movement

1943 February, vol. 14, no. 2
"A Common Sense View"—independence
"Akand Bharat"—Division of power after independence
"Christianity has the Answer"—its universality
"Churches Awake"—alert to church growth
"Deep Seated Suspicion"—England—independence and the war
"More Must Be Done"—churches in the vanguard
"Potpouri"—current events
"Self Government Within a Commonwealth"—India's prospect of dominion status
"The Future Bright"—battle of brotherhood

1943 March, vol. 14, no. 3 (missing)

1943 April, vol. 14, no. 4
"Free to Believe and Proclaim"—the church strong to withstand communism
"Freedom in Brotherhood"—Hindu–Moslem debate in India
"Food and Famine"—famine of Central India
"Justice in Germany and Japan"—war crimes
"Growth the Touchstone"—church growth issue
"Mr. Whittaker Goes to a Growing Church"
"Our Shield and Defender"—comments on the American army's lack of ethics in India

1943 May, vol. 14, no. 5
"Back of Beveridge"—a social concern issue
"Christians and India"—minority rights in independent India
"Drink and Frivolous Living"—issue of alcohol
"Holi"—a Hindu festival
"The Dead Old World"—optimism about post-war conditions

"The Stupidity of Bhajans"—indigenaity

1943 June, vol. 14, no. 6
"Religious Freedom Again"—Hindu domination in independent India
"Stopping the Flow of Illiterates"
"The End of the War"
"The Presbyterian Bridge"—church union issue
"The Rural Church"—rural–urban issues in churches

1943 July, vol. 14, no. 7
"A Very Debatable Matter"—church union and apostolic succession
"Christians and Post War Europe"—reconstruction
"Christian Colleges"
"The Federal Council at Cleveland"—WCC
"The Honest Stranger"—beggars

1943 August, vol. 14, no. 8
"Contact"—friendship evangelism
"Every Student back to the Village"
"Jericho 1943"—the advance of the war
"The Christian Way of Life"—Christian worldview

1943 September, vol. 14, no. 9
"After the War Jeeps"
"Co-operation With Growing churches"—church growth mobility
"Free India"—champion for the rights of Untouchables
"Is it Reproductive?"—indigenization
"The 20 million in Korea"—prophetic

1943 October, vol. 14, no. 10
"Dornakal Bulls Again"—church mission
"Fouling One's Own Nest"—quality of Christians
"Free—to Sacrifice or to Rule"—will freedom bring renewed zeal to evangelize?
"Madame Chiang and Caste"—race discrimination
"No Ordinary Possibility of Salvation"—indigenaity
"The Bread Front"—food production
"The War as God's Judgment"

1943 November, vol. 14, no. 11 (missing)

1943 December, vol. 14, no. 12
"An Open Letter to the International Missionary Council"
"Bricks in the Bridge of Brotherhood"—racism being conquered in US
"Building Burma"—assistance for Christians
"God Will Hold Responsible"—mobility for open doors
"India Enjoys Right Now"—Untouchables
"Let Your Light Shine"
"No Global Strategy"
"The Book of the Month"—indigenaity
"We Appreciate the Degree of Deference"
"We are Not to Blame"—need for research

1944 January–February, vol. 15, no. 1 and 2 (missing)

1944 March, vol. 15, no. 3
"A Number of Things"—current events
"Abraham in China"—mission church–mission issue
"Preaching the Good News"—priority of evangelism
"Presbyterians and Episcopal Unity Moves"
"The Backbone of India"—uniqueness of the rural community
"The Mass Movement" continues
"The Politics of Missionaries"—cooperative spirit

1944 April, vol. 15, no. 4
"Baptisms"
"Devolution"—church–mission issue
"New Guinea, New Britain, New Ireland"—scene of war battles
"No Defense of Conversion"—its value
"The Britasian Scheme"—Andamans to be settled by Anglo–Indians
"The Conversion Issue"—anticonversion activity
"Who Else in All the World"—Danish pastors defend Jews

1944 May–August, vol. 15, no. 5–8, (missing)

1944 September, vol. 15, no. 9
"Geographical Church Union"
"It Seeks Their Conversion"—a priority of Christians
"The Industrialization of India"
"The King's Business Requires Haste"—need for good vehicles for missionaries

1944 October, vol. 15, no. 10
"Christian Bridgeheads"
"Creative Christianity"—nominal Christianity in the Indian church
"How It Actually Works"—indigenization
"The Bridgehead Against Caste"—fighting racism
"The Church of Christ"—Bible must be central
"The Gospel of Industrialization"—need for a holistic approach
"The Japanese Church of Christ" —comment on name
"Unconditional Surrender"—dealing with Japan and Germany

1944 November and December, vol. 15, no. 11 and 12
"Conversion"—its importance
"The Church in Post-War India"—church growth, nominalism, and people movements
"Truly the Lord Hath Delivered"—evaluation of the war

1945 January–September, vol. 16, no. 1–9 (missing)

1945 October, vol. 16, no. 10
"Big and Good"—new school for the Punjab
"Christians and Emperor Worship"—Japanese situation
"The Brains of the Church"—the Christian college
"The Road to Serfdom"—evaluation of missionary deployment

1945 November, vol. 16, no. 11
"Airman's Missionary Fellowship"—prophetic insights
"Bombast or Dynamite"—independence issues
"Deadlock in the Indian Church"—an assessment of indigenization and spiritual growth
"In Hoc Sigma"—material progress and secularization

1945 December. vol. 16, no. 12 (missing)

1946 January–July, vol. 17, no. 1–7 (missing)

1946 August, vol. 17, no. 8
"Don't Shoot the Tiger"—evaluation of pacifism
"Foundations"—money and spiritual issues
"Jews and Christians"—fairness to Jews in the US
"Indian Music"—an evangelistic tool
"More Democracy"—Anglican influence in the NCC
"Prohibition"

"South Africa"—racial tensions
"The Adibasis"—tribal concerns
"The Church of Christ"—church union
"The Reconversion of All England"—church growth

1946 September, vol. 17, no. 9 (missing)

1946 October, vol. 17, no. 10
"A Trail Balloon"—government planned repression of Christians
"Conservative Scotland"—Bible translations
"Hitch the New God"—new thrust for literacy
"Make it Effective"—persecution of Christians
"No Hungry Christians"—funds for Christians too
"The Christian Underground"
"The New Fact of our Time"—church union

1946 November, vol. 17, no, 11 (missing)

1946 December, vol. 17, no. 12
"Efficient Language Study—language school proposal
"Mastery of Indian Languages"—high standards
"That Sinful South Africa"—irony on Untouchability
"The Wealthy Indian Church"—institutions
"Tiger's Milk"—in defense of the West

1947 January, vol. 18, no. 1
"Dear Mr. Nehru"—apology for the mission enterprise

1947 February, vol. 18, no. 2
"The Future of Woodstock"
"The Growing Church and the New India"

1947 March, vol. 18, no. 3
"Abundant Power"
"Honest Portrayal"
"The Growing Edge"
"The Last Word"—McGavran's farewell
"The Serpent's Coil"—missionaries remain apolitical
"Your Obedient Servant"—indigenization

OUTLINE: THE WORLDWIDE CHURCH GROWTH MOVEMENT TAKES SHAPE

1961–65

1. Introduction to this period in McGavran's life.
    a. Change of focus
    b. Evangelical, interdenominational influences
    c. Retirement versus realization
    d. Cutting ties with the denomination
2. Factors leading to the final location for the Institute of Church Growth.
    a. Legacy and funding
    b. Evangelical milieu
    c. Ross Griffeth, a kindred spirit
    d. Proximity of graduate school of anthropology
3. McGavran's promotional blitz through correspondence.
4. Slow beginnings: Keith Hamilton's unique opportunity.
5. Alan R. Tippett: discovered and developed.
6. Iberville and McGavran's impact on the Conciliary Movement.
7. The Evangelical wing gravitates to church growth ideas.
    a. Louis King
    b. Edwin Jacques
    c. EFMA
    d. Norm Cummings
    e. Wycliffe Translators
    f. Winona Lake Seminar
    g. Pentecostals
8. The church growth lecture series.
9. The research fellows, the classes, and the curriculum.
10 Unexpected overtures from Fuller Theological Seminary and shaky relationships with NCC.
11. Research and church growth lectures filled the summer months.
    1961—West Coast Indian Survey, Costa Rica, Guatemala

1962—Mexico research

1963–65—research

12. In the providence of God, McGavran and the ICG invited to move to Fuller Theological Seminary during the summer of 1965.

APPENDIX F

INTERNATIONALIZATION OF CHURCH GROWTH PRINCIPLES BY McGAVRAN

BOOKS

1955a   *Bridges of God*, London: World Dominion Press.

1955b   *Formosan Church Growth*, unpublished MS.

1956a   *Church Growth and Group Conversion*, (3rd ed.), Lucknow: Lucknow Publishing Co.

1956b   *Church Growth in West Utkal*, Indianapolis: Division of World Mission.

1956c   *The Work and the Church in the Kond Hills*, Report of Survey.

1956d   *A Study of the Life and Growth of the Church of the Disciples of Christ in Puerto Rico in View of the Strategy of World Missions*, Adopted by the United Christian Missionary Society. Indianapolis: United Christian Missionary Society.

1958   *Multiplying Churches in the Philippines*, Manila: United Church of Christ.

1959   *How Churches Grow*, London: World Dominion Press.

1962   *Church Growth in Jamaica*, Lucknow U.P. India: Lucknow Publishing Co.

ARTICLES

Articles Published in the *Christian Evangelist* (1954–60)

1955   "Preaching Missions in a Whirlwind," 111, Nov., 5–7.

1957   "Among the Golden Grain," 113, Jan., 10 and 20.

1960   "Of Churches, Sects and Denominations," 118, Feb. 8, 9, 20.

Article Published in the *Ecumenical Studies Series*

1958   "Have We Lost Our Way in Missions?"

Article Published in *Encounter*

1958   "The Independent Church in the Philippines," 19, no. 3.

Articles Published in *International Review of Missions* (1954–60)

1955   "New Methods for a New Age of Missions," 62, 394–403.

1959   "After the First Flush of Success," 68, 265–75.

Articles Published in *World Call* (1954–60)

1954a   "India Through a Century," 36, July–Aug., 16–17.

1954b   "A Continent is Being Discipled," 36, Dec., 20–21.

1955a   "I Visited Congo's Discipleland," 37, Jan., 18–21.

1955b   "Disciples Cooperate in India," 36, April, 11.

Article Published in *World Dominion* (1954–60)

1955   "Satan and Missions," March and April.

Articles Published in the *Christian Herald*

1951   "An International Institute of Scientific Missionary Research," Oslo: Egede-Instituttet Trimingham, Spencer J.

1955   "Discipling Africa in this generation." Paper #a744. Myklebust, Olav Guttorm.

LECTURES

1959   "What Shall the Christian Say of Other Faiths?" lecture given to the Division of Foreign Missions Africa Committee, NCC, New York.

1960   "Theology of Evangelism, Critique of an Ecumenical Document," lecture given at Bethany College, West Virginia.

SELECT CONTEMPORARY BOOKS WHICH EXPAND, CRITIQUE, AND POPULARIZE McGAVRAN'S IDEAS

Costas, Orlando E.

1974   *The Church and Its Mission*, Wheaton: Tyndale House Publishers.
Chapter five: The Imperative of Church Growth
Chapter six: The Church Growth Movement
Chapter seven: An Appraisal of Church Growth Theory

Gibbs, Eddie

1979   *Understanding Church Growth and Decline*, Grand Rapids: Eerdmans.
Chapter twelve: Church Growth Research: The Paradigm and Its Application

1981   *I Believe In Church Growth*, Hodge, Dean R., and David A. Roozen (eds.), Grand Rapids: Eerdmans.

Shenk, Wilbert R. (ed.)

1983   *Exploring Church Growth*, Grand Rapids: Eerdmans.
         Chapter seven: Looking for a Method: Backgrounds and Suggestions
         Chapter thirteen: Missions and the Renewal of the Church
         Chapter nineteen: The Holy Spirit and Church Growth
         Chapter twenty: Strategy for Mission in the New Testament
         Chapter twenty-two: The Unity of the Church and the Homogeneous Unit Principle

Trimingham, Spencer J.

1952   *The Christian Church and Islam in West Africa*, London: SCM Press.

Van Engen, Charles

1981   *The Growth of the True Church*, Amsterdam: Rodopi.
         Chapter six: The True Church in Church Growth Theory
         Chapter seven: The True Church and the Growth Idea
         Chapter eight: The True Church and the Theology of Harvest

Wagner, C. Peter

1980   Review and Expositor, "Evangelism and Church Growth," 77, no. 4., fall.
1986   *Church Growth: State of the Art*, Wheaton: Tyndale House.
         Parts five and six.

GLOSSARY

AHIMSA—nonviolence of any living creature to the Hindu

AWASHYAK MASIHI GYAN—essentials of Christian knowledge

AYAH—an Indian lady who assists in the home

BHAGAWA—a religious narration

BHAJANS—Indian music

CHUNGIA CHAMARS—leather workers who use smoke

DABI HUI JATIYAN—suppressed castes

DALA—the oppressed

DALITS—preferred word in India to refer to the oppressed

GURU-CHELA—master-student

HARI KITAB—meaning "green book." A Hindi language book

KANSAMA—cook

KHADDAR—homespun cotton

MALGUZAR—village headman

MANKU GHAT MELA—an annual four-day camp meeting with a focus on spiritual renewal

MATAJI—mother

MUNGELI SHAETRA KI PRACHARAKON KI PUSTAK—a book written by McGavran for the local Mungeli-area preachers

PANDITS—scholars

PITR MOKSH—ancestor redemption or ancestor worship

PREM SABHA—a spiritual love gathering

PYARA HINDUSTAN—beloved India

RAS LILA—sinful past

SAHIB—honorific term, mainly for white men; now also used for people of note within the community

SAMOLANA—silver scroll

SAT NAM—True Name (the person)

SATNAMI—people group, which means the true name

SHUDDI—meaning purification

SWARAJ—independence of India from colonial rulers

BIBLIOGRAPHY

Azariah, V. S. "The Caste Movement in South India." *International Review of Missions* 21, no. 4 (Oct. 1932): 457–467.

———. "Living Forces behind Mass Movements." *International Review of Missions* 18, no. 4 (October 1929), 509–517.

Bandy, C. H. "The Building of the Church Among Village Communities." *International Review of Missions* 8, no. 2 (April 1919): 193–204.

Beazley, George, ed. *The Christian Church* (Disciples of Christ): *An Interpretive Examination in the Cultural Context.* St. Louis: Bethany Press, 1973.

Booth, Carlton. *On the Mountain Top.* Carol Stream: Tyndale House, 1984.

Butterfield, Kenyen L. *The Christian Mission in Rural India.* New York: International Missions Council, 1930.

Cave, Sydney. "A Typical Mass Movement Church—1806–1918," *International Review of Missions* 7, no. 4 (Oct. 1918): 470–480.

Christian Council, "Mid-India." *Mass Movement Newsletter* (Nov. 1937).

Cronier, Vincent. *A Pearl to India*: *The Life of Roberto do Nobih.* New York: E. P. Dutton & Co., 1959.

"Donald McGavran and Gandhi." *Missiology: An International Review* 8, no. 2 (April 1985).

Duff, Alexander. "Our Earliest Protestant Mission to India." (May 1844).

Fishburn, A. L. *They Went to India*: *Biographies of Missionaries of the Disciples of Christ.* Indianapolis: Missionary Education Department, 1946.

Forrester, Duncan B. *Caste and Christianity*: *Attitudes and Policies on Caste of Anglo-Saxon Protestant Missions in India.* London: Curzon Press, 1980.

Gandhi, Mohandas Karamchand. *Christian Missions: Their Place in India.* Ahmedabad: Navajivan Press, 1941.

———. *Madras Guardian.* (June 1928).

Ghose, S. R. "Lecture Notes on the Life of Gandhi." Lecture presented 1947.

Gottschalk, Louis, Clyde Kluckhohn, and Robert Cooley Angell, eds. *The Use of Personal Documents in History, Anthropology, and Sociology.* Brooklyn: Social Science Research Council, 1945.

Gresham, Perry E. "Response to Lund." *World Call* (1952).

Grimley, John B. and Gordon E. Robinson. *Church Growth in Central and Southern Nigeria.* Grand Rapids: Eerdmans, 1966.

Hewat, Elizabeth G. K. *Christ and Western India.* Surat: Mission Press, 1950.

Hiebert, Paul. *Konduru.* Minneapolis: University of Minnesota Press, 1974.

Hodge, J. Z. "Evangelism in India." *International Review of Missions* 24, no. 4 (October 1935): 498–501.

——. *Salute to India*. London: SCM Press, 1944.

Hoekendijk, Johannes C. "The Call to Evangelism." *International Review of Missions* 39 (April 1950): 162–175.

Houghton, Graham. "Caste and the Protestant Church." *Transformation* 2, no. 2 (April–June 1985): 32–33.

Kaj, Baago. *A History of the National Council of India: 1914–1964*. Nagpur, India: The National Christian Council, 1965.

Keer, D. *Dr. Ambedkar's Life and Mission*. Bombay: Popular Prakashan, 1962.

Kraemer, Heinrik. *World Cultures and World Religions*. Philadelphia: The Westminster Press, 1960.

Marriot, *Sir John A. R. The English in India: A Problem of Politics*. Oxford: Clarendon Press, 1932.

Mayhew, Arthur Innes. *The Education of India: A Study of British Educational Policy in India, 1835–1920, and its Bearing on National Life and Problems in India Today*. London: Faber and Gwyer, 1928.

McGavran, Donald A. "A Christian Looks at Japan." *Christian Evangelist* (March 23, 1949).

——. "A Day's Fighting." *World Call* 7 (June 1925): 43.

——. "An Open Letter." *United Church Review* 14, no.12 (Dec. 1943): 192.

——. *Awashyak Masihi Gyan*. Jabalpur: Mission Press, 1937.

——. "Book Review of Christian Message in a Non-Christian World." *Sahayak Patrika* (July 27, 1938): 240.

——. "Character Building En Masse." *World Call* 13 (March 1931): 28.

——. "Christianity in India's Life." *World Call* 22 (1940).

——. *Church Growth in West Utke*. 1956.

——. "Deadlock in the Indian Church." *United Church Review* 16, no.11 (Nov. 1945): 127.

——. "Disciples and the World Mission." Lecture to the Commission on Theology of Missions, USCWM, April 4–5, 1960.

——. "Disciples Cooperate in India." *World Call* 36 (April 1955): 11.

——. *Education and the Beliefs of Popular Hinduism*. Jabalpur: Mission Press, 1935.

——. "Evangelism and Basic Missionary Policy." *Christian Evangelist* (Oct. 10, 1940).

——. "Evangelism in Central India." *World Call* (Feb. 1942): 11.

——. "The Evangelization of Teri-Garhwal." *Indian Witness* (1936): 12.

——. *Founders of the Indian Church*. Jabalpur: Mission Press, 1937.

——. "Gandhi in the Central Provinces." *Sahayak Patrika* (Dec. 1933): 2.

——. "Growth the Touchstone." *United Church Review* 14, no. 4 (April 1943): 63.

——. "Have We Lost Our Way in Missions?" *Christian Herald* (March 1958): 2.

———. *How Churches Grow*. New York: Friendship Press, 1959.

———. *How to Teach Religion in Mission Schools: A Brief Manual of Method*. Jabalpur, India: Missions Press, 1928.

———. "I Visited Congo's Land." *World Call* 37 (Jan. 21, 1955).

———. *India News Letter* 2, no. 5 (Jan. 1933): 23.

———. *India News Letter* 7, no. 3 (1929): 14.

———. "In India." *World Call* 14 (June 1932).

———. "India's Oppressed Classes and Religion." *United Church Review* (1938): 184.

———. "India Through a Century." *World Call* 36, no. 7 (July–August 1954): 36–37.

———. *International Review of Missions* 25 (1936): 116–129.

———. "John Grafton McGavran, Scholar, Crusader and Saint: An Appreciation by His Son." *World Call* 13 (March 1931).

———. "Managing Day Schools More Evangelically." Lecture presented at a conference for missionaries, Landour Mussoorie, India, 1938.

———. Mass Movement Committee Report (April 1936): 2.

———. Mass Movement Opportunities in Bengal. Calcutta: Navana Printing Works, 1936.

———. "Mastery of Indian Languages." *United Church Review* 17, no. 12 (Dec. 1946): 176–80.

———. "Missionaries and Indigenous Standards of Living." *International Review of Missions* 22 (January 1933): 33–49.

———. Orissa Report: West Utkal (1956).

———. "Paternalism and the Strong Hearts." *Sahayak Patrika* 8 (Nov. 11, 1936): 7.

———. Philippine Report (1956): 9, 518.

———. "Preaching the Word in India." *World Call* (Sept. 1947): 16.

———. "Revival in Sterile Areas." *United Church Review* (Sept.–Oct.1936): 2.

———. "Rising Tide of Evangelism." *Sahayak Patrika* (Nov. 28, 1984).

———. "Sending the Church to School." *World Call* 7 (Feb. 1925): 21–24.

———. "Sown Fields." *World Call* 7 (Sept. 1925): 55.

———. "Special Uppsala Issue." *Church Growth Bulletin* 4, no. 5 (May 1968).

———. "The Battle for Brotherhood in India Today." *World Dominion* (July 1938): 261.

———. *The Conciliar-Evangelical Debate: The Crucial Documents, 1964–1976*. Pasadena: William Carey Library, 1977.

———. "The Economic Liabilities of Village Christians." *National Council of Churches Review* 73, no. 4 (April 1953): 177.

———. *The Eye of the Storm*.Waco: Word Books, 1972.

———. "The Growing Edge," *United Church Review* 18, no. 3 (March 1947): 241.

———. "The Implementation of the Strategy for the India Mission." Lecture presented in Indianapolis, Feb. 2–4, 1960.

———. "The Independent Church in the Philippines." *Encounter* 19, no. 3 (1958): 300.

———. "The Poets meet in Harda." *World Call* 7 (Dec. 1925): 61.

———. "Theological Reflections." *Bulletin of the Division of Studies* 7, no. 2: 8.

———. "Training Teachers for a New Christian Movement." *World Call* (Feb. 1942): 42.

———. "Two Schools of Evangelism." *United Church Review* 13, no. 3 (March 1942): 70.

———. *United Church Review* 12, no. 5 (May 1941): 16, 18.

———. *United Church Review* 12, no. 6 (June 1941): 140.

———. *United Church Review* 12, no. 12 (Dec. 1941): 311, 313.

———. *United Church Review* 13, no. 1 (Jan. 1942): 14.

———. *United Church Review* 13, no. 3 (Feb. 1942).

———. *United Church Review* 14, no. 7: 103.

———. *Understanding Church Growth*. Grand Rapids: Eerdmans, 1972.

———. Review of *Christ's Way to India's Heart* by Pickett, J. Waskom. *International Review of Missions* (June 1938), 2.

McGavran, Donald A. and Burton L. Goddard, eds. *The Encyclopedia of Modern Christian Missions*. Camden, NJ.: Thomas Nelson & Sons, 1967.

Middleton, Vern J. "Breaking Cast Barriers in India." *International Journal of Frontier Missions* 1, no. 4 (1984).

Moore, Clark D. and David Eldredge eds., *India, Yesterday and Today*. New York: Bastam Books, 1970.

Neil, Stephen. *Colonialism and Christian Missionaries*. New York: McGraw Hill, 1966.

Newbigin, Lesslie. *The Household of God*. New York: Friendship Press, 1953.

Perrill, Fred M. *Dr. Ambedkar and the Christian Message*. Lucknow: Lucknow Publishing House, 1971.

Pickett, J. Waskom. "Book Review of Christian Mass Movement in India." *World Call* (June 1935): 29.

———. *Christian Mass Movement in India*. Lucknow: Lucknow Press, 1933.

———. "The Bhil Mass Movement." Jabalpur: Mission Press, 1937.

Pickett, J. Waskom, G. H. Singh, and Donald A. McGavran. *Christian Mission in Mid-India*. Lucknow: Lucknow Press, 1936.

Richter, Julius. *A History of Missions in India*. Edinburgh and London: Oliphant, Anderson and Ferrier, 1908.

Rizvi, S. A. A. *The Wonder that Was India*, Part II. (New Delhi: Rupa, 1987).

Schoonhove, Evert Jansen. "Tambovram." *International Review of Missions* 67, no. 267 (July 1978): 311.

Sharpe, Eric. *Not to Destroy but to Fulfill: The Contribution of J. N. Farquhar to Protestant Missionary Thought in India Before 1914*. Lund: Gleerup, 1965.

Smith, Cadwell. *Hindi* (Printed in different presses, Etawah U.P., 1951).

Smith, Donald Eugene. *India as a Secular State*. Princeton: Princeton University Press, 1963.

Smith, Vincent A. *The Oxford History of India*. Delhi: Oxford University Press, 1981.

Smith, William Roy. *Nationalism and Reform in India*. New Haven: Yale University Press,1938.

Stowe, David M. *Ecumenicity and Evangelism*. Grand Rapids: Eerdmans, 1970.

"Survey-India" (an editorial). *International Review of Missions* 26 (1937): 33.

Thangassamy, D. A. *The Theology of Chenchiah*. Bangalore: Christian Institute for the Study of Religion and Society, 1966.

"The Gathering of the Peoples." The Bible Society of Scotland (1937).

Verkuyl, Johannes. *Break Down the Wall*. Leis B. Smedes, trans. Grand Rapids: Eerdmans, 1973.

Verrier, Elwin. *Religious and Cultural Aspects of Khadi*. Sarvodaya Prachuralaya, 1964.

Vink, Harold. "Thesis on Polygamy." (March 27, 1954), submitted to Kennedy School of Missions.

Wilkinson, T. S. and M. M. Thomas, C. L. S. *Ambedkar and the Neo-Buddhist Movement*. Madras: CLS, 1972.

William, Paton. *Alexander Duff: Pioneer of Missionary Education*. New York: George Doran Co., 1922.

Wodarz, Donald M. *Church Growth: The Missiology of Donald Anderson McGavran*. Gregorian University, Rome, 1979.

Wold, Joseph Conrad. *God's Impatience in Liberia*. Grand Rapids: Eerdmans, 1968.

INDEX